Personal Idealism
and
Strong's Theology

Personal Idealism
and
Strong's Theology

by

CARL F. H. HENRY

Professor of Theology and Christian Philosophy,
Fuller Theological Seminary

WIPF & STOCK · Eugene, Oregon

Wipf and Stock Publishers
199 W 8th Ave, Suite 3
Eugene, OR 97401

Personal Idealism and Strong's Theology
By Henry, Carl F. H.
Softcover ISBN-13: 978-1-6667-4420-0
Hardcover ISBN-13: 978-1-6667-4421-7
eBook ISBN-13: 978-1-6667-4422-4
Publication date 4/1/2022
Previously published by Van Kampen Press, 1951

This edition is a scanned facsimile of the original edition published in 1951.

PREFACE

Theology and philosophy of religion have ranged themselves again on opposite sides for vigorous warfare in the mid-twentieth century.

Graduate studies involved my concentration on both of these spheres, under scholars who stood on the two sides. Among my teachers who championed the cause of theology I numbered Prof. W. Harry Jellema, Prof. Gordon H. Clark, Prof. William Emmett Powers, and the late Prof. Henry C. Thiessen, all of whom especially stimulated me. Among those who cast their weight for the cause of philosophy of religion were forceful exponents like Prof. Edgar Sheffield Brightman and Prof. Peter A. Bertocci, of the school of Boston Personalism.

One of the leading Baptist theologians in American circles, Augustus H. Strong, had sought at the turn of the century to mediate between the two spheres, by an appeal to the idealistic tradition as well as to the Christian revelation. For a number of years, as divinity professor on the faculty of Northern Baptist Theological Seminary, it was my privilege to teach young seminarians—many hundred of them in the space of those years—systematic theology, using Dr. Strong's text.

The necessity for writing a dissertation in connection with doctoral studies at Boston University, where the philosophy department has served as a center of personalistic idealism, quite naturally suggested that this work on Strong's theology would serve both my own interests, and those of many contemporaries interested either directly or marginally in Strong's views. The dissertation on "The Influence of Personalistic Idealism on the Theology of A. H. Strong," was submitted in partial fulfilment of the requirements for the doctor of philosophy degree. The reading committee included Professor Brightman, Professor Albert C. Knudson, and Professor L. Harold DeWolf, whose valuable exchange of thought and helpful suggestions are recalled in the pleasant opportunity of writing thise preface as the work is made available to a larger circle.

The proof-reading of this volume was done by my faculty colleague, Dr. Arnold D. Ehlert, librarian at Fuller Theological Seminary, to whom I express my appreciation.

              Carl F. H. Henry

Fuller Theological Seminary.

COMMENDATION

Dr. Edgar S. Brightman, Boston University Graduate School: "The manuscript of Professor Carl F. H. Henry on 'The Influence of Personalistic Idealism on the Theology of Augustus H. Strong' is both scholarly and fascinating in its interest. It is the only thorough study ever made of the development of Strong's thought and of the interplay of his interpretation of revealed truth with the contributions of personalism. The book is not only an important and thorough contribution to the history of American theology, but it is also a wrestle with the relations between conservative theology and philosophy that rests on ordinary experience and reason. Professor Henry's work is objective and stimulating at once. It is worth the careful attention of any reader regardless of his point of view."

Dr. John Henry Strong, son of the distinguished Baptist theologian: "I have been impressed with the thoroughness with which Dr. Henry has dealt with Father's thought and the faithfulness with which he has represented him."

CONTENTS

I. INTRODUCTION 11
   1. The Nature of the Problem 11
   2. The Importance of the Study 11
   3. The Sources Aiding Research 12
   4. The Method of the Project 15

II. THE EARLIER THEOLOGY OF AUGUSTUS HOPKINS STRONG 16
   1. The Heritage of a Christian Home 16
   2. The Conversion and Accompanying Struggle 17
   3. The Formal Theological Studies 18
      i. The Arminian Antecedents 18
      ii. The Calvinistic Formulation 19
      iii. The Theology of Strong's Teacher 20
         (1). Theology 22
         (2). Anthropology 30
         (3). Soteriology 34
         (4). Eschatology 46
   4. Strong's 1867 and 1868 Addresses 47
      i. Address on "Science and Religion" 48
      ii. Address on "Philosophy and Religion" 49
   5. The Initial Theology Taught by Strong 51
      i. The 1876 Lectures 52
         (1). Prolegomena 52
         (2). The Existence of God 52
         (3). The Scriptures a Revelation from God .. 54
         (4). The Nature, Decrees and Works of God . 55
         (5). Anthropology 58
         (6). Soteriology 59
         (7). Ecclesiology 63
         (8). Eschatology 63
      ii. Addresses and Essays Between 1876 and 1884 ... 65
         (1). Sermon on "The Holiness of God" 65
         (2). Address on "The Philosophy of Evolution" 65
         (3). Essay on "The Christian Miracles" 66
         (4). Article on "The Believer's Union with Christ" 68
         (5). Article on "The Will in Theology" 69
         (6). Sermon on "The Baptism of Jesus" 69
         (7). Essay on "The Method of Inspiration" . 70
         (8). Essay on "Modified Calvinism" 70
         (9). Sermon on "The Two Natures of Christ" 72
      iii. The 1882-1885 Lectures 73
         (1). Supplementation in the Traditional Direction 73
         (2). Tendencies in the Liberal Direction .. 77
         (3). Glances in the Idealist Direction 78
      iv. The 1886 Lectures 79
         (1). The Intuitive Knowledge of God 80
         (2). The Classification of Divine Attributes 81

		(3). The Statement of Divine Decrees 82
		(4). The Subject of Race-Sin and Race-Responsibility .. 83
		(5). The Debate over Ability or Inability 83
		(6). The Ethical Theory of the Atonement 84
		(7). The Final State of the Wicked 84

    v. The 1888 Volume, *Philosophy and Religion* 85
       (1). Sermon on "The Necessity of the Atonement" 85
       (2). Essay on "The New Theology" 86
       (3). Essay on "Modern Idealism" 89
   vi. The 1889 Lectures 93
  vii. The 1890 Lectures 93
 viii. The 1892 Lectures 93

III. THE LATER INTERACTION WITH PERSONALISTIC IDEALISM 95
   1. The 1894-1895 *Examiner* Articles 102
     i. "Christ in Creation" 102
     ii. "Ethical Monism" 106
     iii. "Ethical Monism Once More" 114
   2. Address to the 1895 Graduating Class 123
   3. The 1896 Lectures 124
   4. The 1896 Essay on Robinson's Theology 129
   5. The 1899 Volume on *Christ in Creation and Ethical Monism* .. 131
     i. Address on "Modern Tendencies in Theological Thought" 131
     ii. Address on "The Fall and the Redemption of Man in the Light of Evolution" 133
     iii. Address on "Fifty Years of Theology" 135
     iv. Essay on "The Authority of Scripture" 138
     v. Essay on "God's Self-Limitations" 140
   6. The 1901 Class Notes in Theology 142
   7. The 1907 Final Theology Revision 143
     i. Religious Epistemology 149
     ii. The Nature and Decrees of God 156
     iii. The Works of God 159
     iv. Anthropology 165
     v. Soteriology 172
     vi. Ecclesiology 184
     vii. Eschatology 184
   8. The 1922 Primer, *What Shall I Believe?* 185

IV. THE EVALUATION OF STRONG'S FINAL POSITION 193
   1. Dissatisfactions from the Side of Evangelicalism 194
   2. Dissatisfactions from the Side of Liberalism 196
   3. Dissatisfactions over Basic Assumptions 197
   4. Dissatisfactions with Specific Doctrines 203
     i. The Nature of God 205
     ii. The Works of God 208
     iii. Anthropology 216
     iv. Christology 220
     v. Soteriology 225
     vi. Eschatology 226

V. CONCLUSIONS 228
   BIBLIOGRAPHY 230

Chapter I

INTRODUCTION

The purpose of this dissertation is to examine the influence of the philosophy of personalistic idealism upon the theology of Augustus Hopkins Strong (1836-1921).

I. THE NATURE OF THE PROBLEM

More specifically, the study will inquire into the factors which encouraged Dr. Strong's appropriation of philosophical premises issuing from personalistic idealists; will seek to fix the precise extent to which he modified his earlier theology in view of such influences; and will evaluate the satisfactoriness of the theological position at which he finally arrived.

II. THE IMPORTANCE OF THE STUDY

The appropriateness of such an inquiry is evident from several factors. The Baptists are, numerically, the strongest non-Catholic religious body in the United States, and, among Northern Baptists, no theological treatise has been more influential than Strong's *Systematic Theology*.[1] But denominational considerations aside, there remains the still broader question whether personalistic idealism, in the specific turn which Strong gave to it, furnishes a satisfactory metaphysics for the Christian interpretation of reality.[2] "Ethical monism"—as Strong preferred to designate his view—will be seen to involve the whole gamut of theological structure, from the initial problem of religious knowledge, to the setting forth of the inner content of the successive doctrines of Christian faith. The principles here involved bring to the forefront the question of the ultimate relationship of philosophy and theology.

The proposed study, therefore, concerns much more than the self-consistency of the theological system of a prominent American theologian. It inquires beyond this into a framework which that theologian viewed as the resolution of the doctrinal tensions within contemporary Protestantism, and which he felt to enrich the cardinal convictions of the historic Christian faith. In the personalistic view, as formulated by Strong, he detected

---

[1] Strong has been ranked with William Newton Clarke, Alvah Hovey and George W. Northrop as one of the four most influential Baptist theological teachers of his period (Malone [ed.], DOAB, XVIII, 142).

[2] Knudson has pointed out that statements of the Christian view have been attempted within the general framework of Platonism, Aristotelianism, Hegelianism, and now Personalistic Idealism (POP, 254). Strong's view is, of course, but one possible formulation of personalistic metaphysics, but it is with this specific statement that this dissertation is concerned.

a mighty movement of the Spirit of God . . . preparing the way for the reconciliation of diverse creeds and parties by disclosing their hidden ground of unity.[3]

He expressed the conviction that ethical monism is Biblically supported,[4] and speculated that its late acknowledgment is to be accounted for because, in the divine instruction of the race, preparatory doctrines needed first to be taught as a safeguard against misinterpretation of the monistic view upon its appearance.[5]

Did ethical monism prove, in fact, to placate both the evangelical and liberal camps within Protestantism, and if not, why not? Did it, in fact, make good its promise of an enrichment of the Christian view? Did it afford a coherent framework for the doctrinal structure of the Biblical outlook? Such are the important issues which overarch the research effort confronting us. These questions look beyond a subject which itself holds no little historical interest—the influence of a contemporary philosophical view upon a Biblical theologian of prominence—to the deeper concern of an adequate Christian metaphysics.[6]

III. THE SOURCES AIDING RESEARCH

A preliminary explanation concerning the implication of the title of the dissertation may clarify the research limitation imposed by it. The designation of "personalistic idealism" is applied with some reserve, but, it will appear, nonetheless justifiably. The reserve grows out of the circumstance that at the specific time of Strong's idealistic affinities, personalism or personalistic idealism was not a common designation, and Strong himself assigned the phrase "ethical monism" to his view. But in our day the words "personalistic idealism" serve to identify one's position almost at once as involving a spiritual view of reality, whereby all existence is regarded as of the nature of conscious experience, and an insistence that individual selves are not parts of God, as attested by man's freedom and his moral failure. Since this combination of "metaphysical monism" and "psychological dualism"—to use Strong's characterization—is represented today by the personalistic idealists, and since it was espoused influentially in Strong's day by Borden P. Bowne, who applied the term "personalism"

---

[3] CCEM, 22 (all references in this dissertation are to the writings of Augustus Hopkins Strong, unless otherwise indicated). The complete statement is: "This universal tendency toward monism, is it a wave of unbelief set agoing by an evil intelligence in order to overwhelm and swamp the religion of Christ? Or is it a mighty movement of the Spirit of God, giving to thoughtful men, all unconsciously to themselves, a deeper understanding of truth and preparing the way for the reconciliation of diverse creeds and parties by disclosing their hidden ground of unity? I confess that I have come to believe the latter alternative to be possibly, and even probably, the correct one, and I am inclined to welcome the new philosophy as a most valuable helper in interpreting the word and the works of God."

[4] CCEM, 47.

[5] CCEM, 50.

[6] CCEM, 22: "Monism is, without much doubt, the philosophy of the future, and the only question would seem to be whether it shall be an ethical and Christian, or a non-ethical and anti-Christian monism . . . Let us tentatively accept the monistic principle and give to it a Christian interpretation. Let us not be found fighting against God."

to his system in 1905,[7] the designation "personalistic idealism" is employed in the interest of clarity from a contemporary perspective.

The writer has found no earlier effort to trace the change in Strong's theology which followed upon his acceptance of "the combination of psychological dualism and metaphysical monism,"[8] nor to evaluate the self-consistency of the final theology to which it led the Baptist theologian.

Nevertheless, there exist aids to research which have eliminated many of the difficulties which might ordinarily confront an inquiry of this nature.

The paucity of secondary sources has its compensation in the fact that Strong was himself a rather prolific writer. This, indeed, might prove a barrier to effective study, were the material such that it indicated a constant modification of viewpoint, with no relief for theological fluidity. But the fact is that Strong's writings appeared at such intervals,[9] that the materials for our study have been given us in a rather useful form,[10] whatever effort may be required for adequate interpretation and synthesis.

Strong's initial *Lectures on Theology*, which appeared in 1876 and constituted his first systematic effort, reflect the early theology, essentially fundamentalist in its insistences, to which he adhered at that time. During the ten years of its class use, students employed interleaved copies, in which lecture comments not contained in the printed pages were inserted. At the termination of that decade Strong's *Systematic Theology* appeared in 1886, with revisions in 1889, 1890, 1892 and 1896. Then came the essays on ethical monism, appearing first in theological journals in 1894 and later included, in 1899, in *Christ in Creation and Ethical Monism*, which most nearly approximated a well-rounded statement of the newer view. On top of this came, in 1907, the final revision of *Systematic Theology*,[11] in the light of the personalistic approach, which revision afforded at the same time the more or less standard conservative textbook in theology among Northern Baptists. If not on every page, at least in the treatment of almost every major doctrine, Strong disclosed in this work the implications of his ethical monism. The essentials of that position he emphasized again in his valedictory primer, *What Shall I Believe?* which appeared in 1922, the year after his death.[12]

---

[7] McConnell, BPB, 131. McConnell considers the reasons for the slow acceptance of the term "personalism" (BPB, 133).

[8] CCEM, 56. By "metaphysical monism" Strong asserted, as we shall see, that all reality is the externalization of the divine thought by an act of will, and is spiritual; by "psychological dualism" he affirmed that human persons are not parts of God, but are possessed of a relative independence, although divinely created. Whether the two positions were satisfactorily and consistently maintained remains for later consideration.

[9] See bibliography under A. H. Strong.

[10] Even a special typography to distinguish the main points of Strong's view, the comments, the illustrations and proof texts are used in several works.

[11] Referred to hereafter as ST (1907), to distinguish it from prior editions. This revision was published in one and three volume editions. The third volume, however, did not appear until 1909. By 1948, 20,000 copies of the one-volume, and 8,000 copies of the three-volume edition had been printed.

[12] In the administrative files at Northern Baptist Theological Seminary the author also located the manuscript of the 1921 Wilkinson Lectures delivered there. This was one of the last lecture series given by Strong previous to his death on November 29 of that year.

The writer has had a long-standing familiarity with some of these sources, especially with Strong's theological *magnum opus,* by virtue of former service as professor of systematic theology in Northern Baptist Theological Seminary, where that work has been for many years, as in some other conservative Baptist seminaries, the standard theology text. This has afforded an opportunity to evaluate Strong's final systematization in a careful manner on numerous occasions, so that the convictions recorded here have impressed themselves in some degree across the years.

Leaving aside the primary sources for this study, it may be remarked that while no lengthy and thorough study of the influence of personalistic idealism on Strong's theology is available, secondary sources of some importance do exist. Such materials are to be found in the theological journals, where in the reviews of Strong's books and in the replies to his essays, contemporary thinkers in the areas of theology and philosophy of religion voiced their sentiments pro and con. These reviews have been examined, and references to them will be made in appropriate places in the text.

The shelves and files of libraries crucial for this particular project have been examined also, especially that at Colgate Rochester Divinity School, the parent institution which Strong served from 1872 to 1912 as president and professor of theology. Further research was pursued at Widener Library of Harvard University, at Andover-Harvard Library of Harvard Divinity School, at Union Theological Seminary in New York City, and at Hoose Library of Philosophy of University of Southern California. The old files of *The Examiner* and *The Watchman* were perused in the New York City offices of the national Northern Baptist magazine, *The Watchman-Examiner*.

In addition, the writer has corresponded periodically with Dr. John Henry Strong, a son of the theologian upon whom the study focuses and a retired Baptist pastor now residing in LaCanada, California. This correspondence yielded both suggestion and counsel, and was followed by personal interview.

Thus the difficulties which confront a comprehensive research project of this nature are mitigated to some extent by the availability of peculiarly helpful research aids. But the task of unravelling complex philosophical influences has remained. Ideological changes frequently accrue as a result of interacting and parallel motivations, and here the personal unavailability of the theologian whom we study precludes a direct interrogation. But substantial inferences can be made, and sometimes indubitable guides have been found. One example concerns the relationship of Strong's acceptance of theistic evolution to his espousal of ethical monism. The sources leave no doubt that evolutionism preceded monism in Strong's convictions, and he later affirmed that the acceptance of ethical monism was encouraged by considerations other "than for the sake of its Christian explanation of evolution."[13] The factors contributory to theological change are not always as few nor as unrelated as men are tempted to portray them. But the difficult task of discerning theological elements which owe their encouragement to personalistic idealism, from the non-personalistic mo-

---

[13]CCEM, 78.

tivations in the theological world of Strong's day, gains assistance from the fact that Strong was a prolific writer, that he constantly revised these writings in a form which reflects the changes, and that his later writings contain full quotations from Lotze, Ladd, Bowne and others[14] at points of ideological affinity and disagreement, that his studies of the theology of the great poets interact especially with the problem of pantheism and its avoidance, and that Strong has left us, in the course of his writings, a considerable heritage of autobiographical materials.[15]

IV. THE METHOD OF THE PROJECT

Fortunately, a chronological approach to Strong's convictions affords an ideal opportunity for ideological contrasts also. There is, as we shall see, the earliest period, which reflects beliefs uncompromisingly fundamentalist; there is a middle period, when under the pressure of the modern philosophy of science he supported an evolutionary view, coupling this with theism in its traditional form; there is the later period, when the affirmation of an intensified divine immanence issued in his ethical monism.

The method of this study, then, will be at once chronological and ideological. We shall inquire first into Strong's early, middle, and late convictions, seeking to indicate the basic reasons for modification, with a view to establishing in clear manner the precise influence of personalistic idealism upon his theology, and also of weighing the satisfactoriness of the outlook for which Strong finally declared.

---

[14]Doubtless a partial motivation for this was the desire to reply effectively to critics of a monistic position. Strong wrote: "From much recent writing it might be inferred that the combination of psychological dualism and metaphysical monism is a novel and absurd speculation. Those who occupy themselves in this criticism would do well to study Lotze and Ladd and Upton. Ladd at New Haven . . . and Upton at Manchester . . . are both following the German Lotze, the leader of the higher thought of our time" (CCEM, 56).

[15]OHCT is prefaced by two autobiographical addresses delivered in 1913, when Strong had completed his fortieth year as president and professor of systematic theology at Rochester Theological Seminary.

CHAPTER II

THE EARLIER THEOLOGY OF AUGUSTUS HOPKINS STRONG

By the earlier theology of Augustus Hopkins Strong, into which this chapter will inquire, we intend the period prior to 1894 when Strong first espoused ethical monism. It is the ideological rather than the chronological factor, therefore, which affords the principle of division, setting in clearer relief the two periods in which Strong's writings reflect first the traditional stress on divine immanence as found in evangelical theology (1876-1894), and then the greater stress on divine immanence which characterizes idealistic thought (1894-1922).

This early period, prior to the clear impact of personalistic idealism upon his theology, may be considered conveniently by attention to Strong's theological heritage as a youth, his early conversion experience, his divinity studies preparatory to the ministry, and then his initial years as a teacher of theology. The purpose of this study requires not so much an abundance of detail, as an alertness to such influences which will anticipate the modification of Strong's views, for subsequent comparison and contrast with the specific tenets of personalistic idealism.

I. THE HERITAGE OF A CHRISTIAN HOME

In his autobiographical addresses, Strong relates for us the circumstances of his birth (August 3, 1836) and upbringing in a Christian home.[1] His father had been converted during the great Rochester campaigns of the evangelist Charles G. Finney.[2] The oldest religious experience in Strong's memory was the occasion when, at the tender age of six, he knelt with his mother in a dimly lighted closet as she tried to teach him to pray.[3] Again, he never quite forgot a snow-storm experience at the age of ten, when his father led him through the deep snow-drifts and impressed him, on a Sunday when very few worshippers managed to get to church, with the importance of faithful attendance.[4] At twelve years, on New Year's eve, he experienced intense sense of guilt and fear of judgment, and resolved to begin a Christian life, but the festivities of the following day, he writes, "banished the resolutions from my mind, and I had no conviction of sin for quite a number of years afterward."[5] His intellectual awakening he records as having occurred at fourteen, when Latin classics began to intrigue him, and then other literary masterpieces. But apparently no significant spiritual crisis followed until his college days at Yale, where in 1857 he was to receive the A. B. degree as a Phi Beta Kappa graduate.

---

[1] OHCT, 5.   [2] OHCT, 12.   [3] OHCT, 5.
[4] OHCT, 5, 6; "We had a prayer meeting, *quorum magnaque pars fui,* and never since that time have I been able to be quite comfortable away from church on a Sunday morning."
[5] OHCT, 6.

II. THE CONVERSION AND ACCOMPANYING STRUGGLE

The early college days were, on Strong's own estimate, neither academically nor spiritually promising.[6] To what extent the collegiate studies permanently shaped his metaphysical outlook can hardly be determined from materials available to us, although it is known, of course, that in those days Dr. Noah Porter, who defended conservative Christianity and realism, was Clark Professor of Metaphysics and Moral Philosophy in Yale College.[7]

But in Strong's junior year, one March afternoon in front of the chapel just as the college bell rang for evening prayer, Wilder Smith, a student who for two-and-a-half years had sat next to Strong in recitation room, placed a hand upon his shoulder and said intently: "O Strong, I wish you were a Christian."[8] Strong could not escape those words. During the spring vacation his young lady cousin, then visiting at the home of his parents, invited him to hear Finney, under whom his father had been converted, and whom he had himself heard once in Oberlin. That night, in response to the pulpit invitation, Strong determined upon a Christian life.[9] But he remained spiritually restless, despite Bible-reading, personal prayer, and prayer-meeting attendance, all of which failed to yield the peace of soul for which he yearned.

Three weeks of spiritual struggle ensued. Though he consecrated his life by prayer, gave up wrong associations and habits, read his Bible, and even witnessed to and prayed with unconverted students, he lacked assurance to such an extent that, attending a college prayer meeting, he stated publicly: "My friends, I am not a Christian; I do not pretend anything of the sort, but I want to be; can you do anything to help me?"[10]

---

[6]OHCT, 10: "Concluding that devotion to scholarship was not the thing for me, I fell into irregular habits and associations; and, if I had religious thoughts and ideas at all at the beginning of my college course, I lost them very speedily after that course began. In my ungodly and half-dissipated course I was a model of merely selfish and worldly ambition. I was never intoxicated in my life, but I was on the verge of evil; I knew that if I went very much farther I would be damned; and yet, until just before the spring vacation in my junior year, no single man in my class and no single man in college ever said one word to me about the subject of religion."

[7]One of Dr. Strong's two sons, Dr. John Henry Strong, comments: "That Father, brought up at Yale on Porter's *The Human Intellect*, was deeply influenced by Lotze and Bowne, I well remember; but he gave us in class the results rather than his mental processes" (Letter to the writer, June 19, 1948). Porter's well-known volume first appeared in 1868, but he had doubtless emphasized its essential content for many years, having held the Clark professorship from 1846. Regarding Porter, we learn that "he had little aptitude for teaching, though some of his later graduate students professed much indebtedness to him. The undergraduate respected and liked him, but he awakened in them little interest in his subject" (Malone [ed.], DOAB, XV, 98).

[8]OHCT, 11. Strong narrates that years later, when he spoke to Smith about the incident, the latter could not recall it. "But that one word never left me until I gave my heart to God."

[9]OHCT, 12: "I do not remember what the sermon was, but I do remember that great, stalwart man standing up at the close of the service, with his eyes fixed apparently upon me, and saying: 'If there is anyone in this congregation who thinks he ought to begin to serve God, let him rise out of his place and go down the aisle into the basement. There will be some ministers there who will talk with him on the subject of religion.' It was like a thunderbolt to me. I did not expect anything like that. But I somehow felt that my hour had come." Downstairs, Strong told

But, while some of the students rallied to encourage him, it was not until Strong read by lamplight the words, "Wherefore come ye out from among them, and be ye separate, and touch not the unclean thing, and I will be a Father to you, and ye shall be my sons and daughters, saith the Lord Almighty,"[11] that he felt a real tie between him and God. Strong appears to regard this as his conversion night.[12]

III. THE FORMAL THEOLOGICAL STUDIES

Before proceeding to subsequent spiritual experiences which Strong recounts and interprets for us, it may be well to remember that these come to us not from any diary of those early years, but rather as the recollections of a mature theologian.[13] It is impossible to be certain, therefore, of the various factors at work in the selection and rejection of particular experiences. Yet the narration of these inner experiences, in the absence of a diary, can hardly be better authenticated than by the subject's autobiographical memoirs of a later date.

In relating his earlier religious activities, Strong affirmed that from those experiences he derived certain "lessons in theology" and that the experiences themselves are related for the specific purpose of showing "how my views of evangelical doctrine have been necessarily determined by the circumstances of my individual history."[14]

Thus, we are told that the weeks of disturbing spiritual struggle which elapsed between his attendance at the Finney meeting and the final assurance of conversion, taught him his initial lesson in theology, that of *the depth and enormity of sin*.[15]

1. The Arminian Antecedents

The recurrence of old habits, and his inability to cope with them in his own strength, declared Strong, led him on to a second theological lesson, *man's need of God's regenerating grace*.

Thus far he had come, he remarked, prior to the commencement of formal divinity training, and, he added,

please notice that my experience was thus far a purely Arminian experience. I had yet to learn the truth in Calvinism. In my conversion, so far as I can remember, I had no doubt of the Holy Spirit or of Christ. I had no idea that God was working in me to will and to do; I was only bent on working out my own salvation. There was no reliance on Christ's atonement; I was trusting in my own power to begin and to continue the service of God . . . As he had taught me the greatness of my sin, so he next taught me that salvation is of the Lord.[16]

the pastor of the church that he would "now begin to serve God . . . looking to God for light" (OHCT, 13).
[10] OHCT, 16.
[11] II Corinthians 6:17.
[12] OHCT, 17.
[13] The two introductory autobiographical essays in OHCT were delivered in 1913, when Strong had completed forty years as president and professor of Biblical theology at Rochester Theological Seminary.
[14] OHCT, 4.
[15] OHCT, 14-15: "It was my first lesson in theology, and it prepared me to accept from my own experience, as I afterward did, Doctor Shedd's statement that 'sin is a nature and that nature is guilt.' " The importance of this deep conviction of the seriousness of sin will be seen in Strong's subsequent protest against pantheism as precluding such an insistence.
[16] OHCT, 18-19. Strong did not here intend to suggest that "thought of the Holy

Strong's Theology

The pre-seminary spiritual experiences, then, took place in a predominantly Arminian context; the stirring ministry and mood of Charles G. Finney stood in the background of Strong's Christian heritage, both through his father's conversion and his own. But, having yielded his life for Christian service, graduation from Yale in 1857 meant the beginning of divinity studies at Rochester Theological Seminary, where he was to graduate two years later.[17]

2. The Calvinistic Formulation

The experientially-grounded lessons in theology, which Strong later recounted in their chronological unfolding in his long life, came now to interact with divinity studies. In those days, Ezekiel G. Robinson, whose main emphasis was Calvinistic, was professor of Biblical theology and there is every indication that the transition from Arminianism to Calvinism in Strong's thinking came about, or at least was well underway, in seminary days.

Strong's third lesson in theology he dated to his seminary years, when he led a young woman to Christ after speaking at the little mission church which he pastored, on the fifty-third chapter of Isaiah. She found such assurance, upon trust in the substitutionary death of Christ, that Strong learned from the experience, he reported, a third lesson in Christian doctrine: *that only the objective atonement of Jesus Christ, only Christ's sufferings upon the cross, can furnish the ground of our acceptance with God.*[18]

When Strong completed his seminary course in 1859, he intended to go abroad as a foreign missionary, but a hemorrhage of the lungs prompted physicians to press him to spend two years in the open air and travel. So Strong made an extended tour to Europe and Palestine, visited in Germany and studied the language, and gathered a library of German books.[19] Falling in with the current of pleasure-lovers, he almost lost the

---

Spirit or of Christ" are exclusively Calvinistic possessions but that, so far, his thoughts centered in the human rather than divine elements in his conversion. At the end of his life Strong recalled: "If ever there was a purely Arminian or Pelagian conversion, mine was such an one . . . Except for the fact that I had a sort of traditional and theoretical belief . . . in the background of my consciousness, my conversion might have been a purely Unitarian or agnostic reliance upon the love and truth of God. This fact makes me tolerant of Unitarian Christianity, although I now recognize it as an infantile faith" (WSIB, 86, 88).

[17]"I knew, from the very moment of my conversion, that I must serve God in the ministry. So I went to Rochester" (OHCT, 19). Elsewhere he stated that the magnificent pulpit ability, exact statement and love of truth of Rochester's president, Dr. Ezekiel G. Robinson, drew him there for study (Art. [1896], 163). With an experiential reference, Strong also added that he "had another source of instruction . . . in a little mission congregation in the neighborhood of Rochester" (OHCT, 19).

[18]OHCT, 21.

[19]Nothing indicates that Strong pursued formal studies in Germany, but his frequent quotation from German scholars disclosed a familiarity with their writings. His letters appeared in the *Rochester Democrat* published by his father. They commented on the university lectures in Berlin as about to begin, 347 courses of them; on the drunkenness and profanity of German students, and on the spectacles they wore; and on the ability of Tholuck, Julius Müller and Roediger at Halle—"the three of them alone would make a great Faculty." He mentioned also the unconvincingness of German preaching: "The last generation that numbered a Schleiermacher, a Neander, and an Olshausen . . . began a great progress in German religious thinking, but even this progress will be obliterated unless there is a higher

desire for Christian service.[20] But behind him, as a living memory, were his theological studies at Rochester, and behind that the conversion experience which steadied him.

3. The Theology of Strong's Teacher

E. G. Robinson served Rochester Theological Seminary as professor of Biblical theology from 1853 to 1872, and as president from 1860 to 1872. When Strong sat in Robinson's classes in 1858 and 1859, it is hardly likely that anyone imagined that the young scholar would, in 1872, when Robinson was to become president of Brown University, succeed his teacher in both positions, becoming from 1872 to 1912 president and professor of Biblical theology at Rochester.

It was from Robinson that Strong first learned theology as a discipline. Yet in his autobiographical notes, Strong made hardly a mention of his studies with Robinson.[21] That those essays have a strong theological concern does not minimize the circumstance. But several disclosures bearing on Strong's major theological relations to Robinson are afforded in an appreciative chapter titled "Dr. Robinson as a Theologian" which Strong contributed to the memorial volume *Ezekiel Gilman Robinson: An Autobiography, With a Supplement by H. L. Wayland and Critical Estimates* shortly after Robinson's death in 1894. There Strong recorded that it was in Robinson's classroom, under his searching questions and discussions, that he experienced his "intellectual awakening."[22] More than this, he declared that "to my teacher and predecessor I owe more than I owe to any one else outside of my own family circle."[23] Yet he noted that

> of dogmatic instruction in theology in 1857-59 there was little. His brief dictations constituted not so much a system as a series of suggestions to stimulate inquiry. Our teacher appeared to be feeling his way along, and his great anxiety seemed to be that each of his pupils should feel his own way. Nothing vexed him more than a lazy repetition of traditional formulas . . . He dictated . . . cautious statements of the dominant orthodoxy, with its more mechanical features greatly softened down, and with the accompanying suggestion of new points of view which logically imply another and a better faith.[24]

Robinson's lack of finality[25] and of system, then, was one factor.[26] But there was another, which will take on special significance when, at a later point,

---

power to carry it forward. Tholuck says that there are no young men to fill the place of the orthodox theologians who are just gone."
[20]OHCT, 22.
[21]"A certain sternness and a rigorous attitude in the matter of discipline is said to have cost Robinson the affection of students, who thought him lacking in patience and tact and brusque in manner" (Malone [ed.], DOAB, XVI, 43).
[22]Art. (1896), 163.
[23]Art. (1896), 163.
[24]Art. (1896), 164-165.
[25]Strong elucidated that Robinson represented the tendencies of Brown and Newton, rather than of Hamilton, from which Robinson's predecessor Dr. Maginnis (who took the viewpoint of the Princeton school) had come. None of Robinson's teachers had been strongly conservative, but neither Andover nor New Haven had won him for the new theology. Yet Robinson resisted both what seemed to him to be the arbitrariness and externalism of the Princeton theology of the covenants and the subjectivism of the non-conservative views.
[26]Robinson was beginning his fifth year as professor of Biblical theology at Rochester when Strong entered in 1857. From 1868 to 1872 Robinson served also as president, and then Brown called him to its presidency. Strong remarked that Robinson had

Strong's early teaching is appraised theologically. For Strong explained that, in order not to stifle the creative urge on his own part, he did not lean heavily upon Robinson's writings and, in fact, avoided them, when he was called as Robinson's successor in 1872. These circumstances might indicate that Robinson was not tremendously influential in shaping Strong's theological outlook.

And yet, Strong himself precluded a hasty dismissal of Robinson's influence upon him. For when, a few months before Robinson's death in 1894, Strong first carefully scrutinized Robinson's *Christian Theology*, his impression, he tells us, was twofold: first, the general weight and correctness of Robinson's theological teaching; second, the realization of the extent of his personal debt, of which he was quite unaware, to Robinson's instruction. Strong acknowledged:

> I am humbled to find how much of my own thinking that I thought original has been an unconscious reproduction of his own. . . . And the ruling idea of his system—that stands out as the ruling idea of mine; I did not realize until now that I owed it almost wholly to him.[27]

Under those circumstances it seems obligatory to work through Robinson's *Christian Theology* for elements of significant similarity and difference, aware that Robinson's earlier teaching was less systematic, and that fifteen years intervened between Strong's studies and the public appearance of *Christian Theology*, the bulk of which was revised and printed during Robinson's last year of instruction at Rochester.[28] In the various editions of his later writings, Strong quoted liberally from Robinson's volume.[29]

Robinson's theology was quite substantially on the evangelical side, and it will be necessary, for purposes of this study, only to indicate those high points which afford interesting comparison and contrast with Strong's position. It does not follow, of course, that in cases of agreement between the two theologians, Robinson must always be made the occasion, as Strong's teacher, of the latter's beliefs, although the circumstances in that case surely afforded Strong encouragement, as he himself acknowledged, in the views which he held.

Robinson's very inaugural address, titled "Experimental Theology,"[30] was studded with an emphasis on the significance of Christian experience

---

neither time nor strength, under such circumstances, to mature with and to publish his theological system. "He was not a ready writer, and systematizing with him, was a slow work. . . . But before his teaching at Rochester ended, his views had to a considerable extent crystallized, and he had proceeded a long way in the elaboration of his 'Christian Theology' " (Art. [1896], 167).

[27] Art. (1896), 168.

[28] The preface of the 1894 edition of CT (as Robinson's volume will be referred to hereafter), which comprised considerably less than four hundred copies, notes that "with the exception of pages 81-96, pp. 161-176 and pp. 305-320 which are reprinted almost without change, the first 320 pages are the identical sheets which were printed in 1872." In 1872, Strong recalled, 320 pages of the work were printed, but Robinson stopped with the subject of regeneration, and his new duties at Brown never permitted him to finish the desired revisions, although the additional notes were later included (Art. [1896], 167).

[29] Since these references cover leading theological motifs, we are not left overly much to inference in tracing the connections.

[30] CT, 355-367. Robinson stressed in this adddress the need "of earnest regard to that experimental knowledge of the doctrines of Christianity, which, if Christianity is to be of any practical avail to us, must always be found in the heart of the believer"

as well as of doctrine which is often reflected in Strong's outlook. Not only with regard to Robinson's traditional doctrinal affirmations, and in modifications of these, but also in the final appeal to ethical monism, Strong contended that he had found anticipations in his teacher's theological views.

(1) Theology

Robinson defined theology as "the science which treats of God."[31] But Christianity is "distinctively a Revealed Religion," and "its one direct and controlling source, to which the decisive appeal must always be made, is the Sacred Scriptures."[32] Yet "the Church and the Scriptures are authorities which can never be justly or safely divided,"[33] contrary to both Romanists and ultra-Protestants.

His theory of inspiration was broad.[34] The inspiration of the Scriptures is not invalidated by "any of the literary, logical, scientific or historical defects which modern criticism have made apparent."[35] The claim that the Bible has errors in cosmogony and cosmology is "founded in an attempt to interpret the orientalisms of Genesis according to the exact and scientific rules of the occidental mind" and the contention that there are statistical errors forgets that "in rude ages and among semi-civilized peoples, like those of the early periods of the Jewish history, exaggerations and employment of round numbers always prevail."[36] The imprecatory psalms are not to be judged in the light of fuller Christian revelation, but were the necessary vehicle in those times for the divine ideas.[37]

Mankind possesses a natural knowledge of God and of his will which "so far as it is positive and indubitable, cannot but be authoritative."[38] Natural theology, however, should not serve as the basis of revealed theology; nor, on the other hand, should it be disregarded.[39] These are

---

(CT, 356). Christian doctrine was not reasoned out, but was divinely revealed; yet the prophets and apostles *felt* out (i.e., made their own by experience) the revealed truth (CT, 357). "A man's real creed will always be just what he has experienced, and no more" (CT, 358). Yet Robinson added carefully that experience has no authority of its own; the Bible does, whereas the authority of experience is derivative (CT, 360).

[31]Robinson, CT, 1. Christian theology is most specific: "The Christian theologian . . . is strictly concerned with the principles and doctrines . . . of the Christian religion alone, or with the convictions embosomed in the Christian consciousness, resolved into formulas in the creeds of the church, and referable to a formal Revelation, which has been authenticated as authoritative and divine" (CT, 2).

[32]CT, 3. Robinson affirmed that theology—not revelation—is progressive, contrary to the rationalists (CT, 4, footnote).

[33]CT, 6: "Without the Scriptures . . . the Church has no accredited or infallible guide for herself, or authority for her teachings; and without the Church, the Scriptures have no visible, trustworthy expounder of their meaning."

[34]It is noteworthy that Robinson wrote of defects, not errors, and then proceeded to justify these. But Strong later pointed out that while higher criticism was not rife in Robinson's day, "the principle and spirit of it, so far as it is theistic and reverent, are Dr. Robinson's own, and his whole conception of inspiration is surprisingly like that which has of late become so current" (Art. [1896], 171). Robinson, he added, discarded all theories of the method of inspiration, holding that the whole church was inspired, not the writers alone. As against the prevailing proof-text theology, Robinson found inspiration in the Bible as a whole, rather than in its separate parts; the organic unity with its analogy of faith was important, and hence errors in historical and scientific detail were not viewed as destructive (Art. [1896], 172).

[35]CT, 42.   [36]CT, 44.   [37]CT, 45.   [38]CT, 3.   [39]CT, 8.

two sources of truth, but the Bible interprets, supplements and completes the prior revelation of nature.[40]

The Bible is viewed as a corrective for both philosophy and science. We must guard "lest our Theology should anywhere substitute the suggestions of our Philosophy for the plain declarations of Scripture."[41] True theology and true science must harmonize, but before accommodating Scripture to the demands of science "we must first justly demand that the claims of the science be established beyond dispute."[42]

The Scriptures disclose modes of existence and personal relations "for the judging of which finite minds have no experiential criteria, and for even the understanding of which they have no correlative knowledge whence the omniscient Spirit in his revelation could draw metaphorical or typical forms of thought"[43]—as, for example, the doctrines of the Trinity and of the two natures of Christ. Yet the Scriptures are often silent, due perhaps to our incapacity to understand. Yet "there are certain questions about which we are instinctively disposed to be inquisitive, and to which, so far as we know, the answer might have been intelligible."[44] As specific examples, Robinson cited the questions of God's relation to the material universe, the origin of sin, and the relation of departed and living spirits.[45]

The natural arguments for God were proclaimed inadequate. Robinson was one of the first American theologians to criticize the theistic proofs in Kantian fashion.[46] The weakness of the cosmological argument is "its inability to show beyond a doubt, that the Cosmos is not an endless self-contained succession of phenomena, an infinite series of causes and effects."[47] The design argument proclaims the existence of a supreme Mind.[48] The ontological argument does not escape a *petitio principii*, as also the historical argument.[49] The moral argument, Robinson implied, has value, yet he did not carefully evaluate it. But the inadequacy of natural theology was clearly affirmed:

But of all the arguments that can be adduced in proof of the existence of God, no one can be said to be a demonstration, nor can all combined suffice to convince a determined atheist. The evidence of the divine existence is not so much logical as moral; it is adjusted rather to the "eye of the soul" than to the "logical faculty"; if that eye be darkened God is not seen in any evidence he may give of his being. The validity of the evidence is not so much to be tested by syllogisms as by analysis of the moral consciousness.

---

[40] CT, 9. [41] CT, 14.
[42] CT, 15. Note, however, the following: "But a help which so far proves a master as to compel the discontinuance of interpretations that have existed for centuries, and to put meanings into the words of the Bible not before thought of, must be regarded, however ancillary its positions, as having some kind of authority and some kind of right to speak in its own name" (CT, 3, footnote).
[43] CT, 21.
[44] CT, 22.
[45] Curiously, Strong's final theology concentrated specially on the first of these problems. Robinson had suggested that, in view of Biblical silence, "the prudent theologian will be cautious of conjectures and theories" (CT, 22).
[46] Strong (Art. [1896], 169). The Kantian critique may have been applied, more consistently than in CT, at a later date; cf. footnote 50 below.
[47] CT, 49. Strong pointed out that while Robinson did not refer to "immanent finality" he avoided a "carpenter phraseology" in the interest of an organic, rather than a mechanical, view of God's relations to the world (Art. [1896], 179).
[48] CT, 53.
[49] CT, 55.

If it be asked, what then is the value of these formal proofs, we answer, all depends on the use to be made of them. To one who already believes in the existence of God, they have value as corroborative evidence and corrective knowledge; to honest enquirers, though insufficient to convince when taken simply, yet unitedly they are well nigh irresistible; but in the conflict with theoretical atheism they cannot be regarded as decisive.[50]

It is apparent however—from such statements as that the theistic proofs are "well nigh irresistible" to honest inquirers—that Robinson did not work out critically the relationship of general to special revelation in his system, despite his introductory emphasis on the prior significance of Biblical revelation for Christian theology. Hardly was the treatment of natural theology concluded, moreover, than he remarked, in treating of the origin of our conceptions of God, that it is to the sacred Scriptures more than to any or all other sources that

every prejudiced mind must admit that mankind have been indebted for all just and worthy conceptions of God. It not only supplies a corrective and supplement to both the preceding (i.e., the outer world of nature and the moral nature within), but from its teachings respecting God, definitely understood, there can be no appeal.[51]

Robinson then argued that Christian experience is the practical testing of New Testament teaching, but "as experience, to be trustworthy, must be strictly a reflex of Scripture, this source can only be subordinate and subsidiary to that of the Bible."[52]

Side by side with this emphasis, however, Robinson affirmed that "a corrective and regulative principle in all our thinking of God is the idea of perfection" and added that "the idea of perfection evidently underlies the Scriptural conceptions of God . . . and that idea should be the controlling one, whatever the process by which our present conceptions of God are completed."[53]

It is not surprising, then, that in his treatment of the nature of God, Robinson did not appeal consistently to the revelational and philosophical spheres.

We are urged to believe in the personality of God because of the "naturalness and necessity of the idea," because the conception of personality "lies at the basis of any just conception that we can have of physical law," because denial of God's personality "involves us in self-contradiction" and "leads inevitably to the most fearful consequences" for the moral life, but there is no stress on the significance of special revelation and covenant relationship with God's people as particularly relevant to the case for divine personality.[54]

The unity of God, Robinson related, "has been thought by some to be easily established as one of the doctrines of Natural Theology."[55] After setting forth the philosophical arguments he appended the Biblical references in which the divine unity is taught, commenting that it is "more

---

[50]CT, 57. Strong interprets Robinson as giving a much greater centrality to the moral argument, and it is possible that he later moved that direction, substituting an appeal to the moral consciousness for that to logical argument (while yet regarding the latter as a valuable stimulus to the former) (Art. [1896], 170). But, as we shall see, the decisive appeal in CT is to the Scriptures.
[51]CT, 60.   [52]CT, 61.   [53]CT, 61.
[54]CT, 62-63.
[55]CT, 64.

than doubtful" that, apart from the Scriptures, such a truth could have been reached by the philosophical approach.[56]

The attributes of God, remarked Robinson, are "our modes of conceiving him."[57] But there is no sufficient reason for regarding what is known to us only in relations as on that account untrustworthy.[58] Yet the essential nature of God, as distinct from the attributes, is something of which our notion is "exceedingly dim and ill defined."[59] The essence of God is not identical "with any one, or with all, of his attributes, but . . . the common subject of them all.[60] Again, "attributes do not represent distinguishable properties in the Divine Essence;" so that "to suppose that we treat of essence . . . when we treat of attributes, is to confound God with our conceptions of him."[61] From this treatment it is clear that Robinson did not work out a satisfactory statement of the relationship between attributes and essence in the divine nature, nor did he clearly formulate the grounds for his affirmation that our knowledge of God in his relations is trustworthy, if the attributes are not to be closely related to the essence.[62]

In dealing with the divine attributes, Robinson arranged a new classification, according to the order of relations that make the attributes known, but he fluctuated between a revelational and philosophical appeal. Although the Scriptures abound in descriptions of divine omnipresence, they "do not distinctly assert, though they plainly imply, according to Jewish modes of thought, the divine Immensity in space."[63] The writers of Scripture

---

[56]"The unaided Gentile mind was ever oscillating between the pantheism of the philosophers and the polytheism of the multitude. . . . It is extremely doubtful if the Greek and Roman classical writers had any definite conceptions of the Divine unity. This truth, which to enlightened minds is now apparently so self-evident, has received recognition among men only after those reiterated declarations and that enforcement by a most protracted and painful discipline, of which the Holy Scriptures contain the details" (CT, 66).

[57]CT, 67.

[58]CT, 68.

[59]CT, 68: "The question of the relation of the substance or essence of matter to its qualities, differs from that of the relation or attributes to the essence of a personal being, by just so much as matter differs from spirit, and the intelligent volitional power of a personal being from the mechanical force of matter. We may know equally well, by one concrete act of the mind, both the substance and the qualities of matter, which are inseparable, but we apprehend being only by its modes or relations which are variable and totally distinct from itself."

[60]CT, 69.

[61]CT, 69.

[62]Robinson's treatment of the attributes, complained Strong, "yields too much to the Kantian and Hamiltonian relativity" (Art. [1896], 173) despite his insistence that the trustworthiness of all knowledge is overthrown if conceptions relatively true to us are not positively true in themselves. One of the essential differences between Strong and Robinson was in the making at this point, for Strong complained that Robinson was hampered by a wrong philosophy—Kant's distinction between the phenomenon and the unknowable *ding-an-sich*—in formulating his statement of the divine attributes. "A more modern and more correct philosophy admits no such element of inherent and eternal agnosticism. Though essence can be known only through attributes, it is still true that, in knowing attributes, we know essence. . . . The reason why we cannot perfectly know God is that we cannot perfectly know his attributes; not that knowledge of attributes does not involve knowledge of essence. We do not fully know God's attributes because he has not fully revealed them, and because we are not great enough to understand them. But we do know them in part, and in just so far we know God" (Art. [1896], 173-174).

[63]CT, 71.

set forth the divine eternity as something which they "seem to have apprehended" by an act of regression and progression which moves from past cycles of phenomenal changes through anticipated future cycles, "finding at the last stage of thought, in either direction, an existing Godhead, which, by a necessity of thought, it pronounces eternal: Romans 1:20."[64] Again,

the Universe or Cosmos, with the necessary idea of causation in mind, was doubtless the source of the conceptions of the power, knowledge, wisdom, presence, etc., of God, and it is from the study of this source that, under the guidance of the Scriptures, these conceptions can be completed and justified.[65]

The metaphysical conception of absolute omnipotence, we are told, is "only indirectly given in the Scriptures"[66] whereas that God's knowledge is infinite in degree and perfect in kind is "clearly taught . . . both by what is implied in their idea of God, and by what is distinctly asserted."[67] The Scriptures speak of an essential, personal omnipresence.[68]

The attribute of spirituality is, like that of omnipresence, suggested only on reflection, Robinson remarked.[69]

If the physical universe justify our conceptions of the power, knowledge, and presence of God, the question, whether he be material or spiritual, is also at once suggested. This question, thrust on us by the very process through which we justify our belief in the Divine existence, has been in part anticipated in treating of the Personality of God, and it only remains for us at this point, simply to assure ourselves, on the authority of Scripture, that God, everywhere present in the Cosmos, is a Spirit totally distinct from matter, independent of it, and the almighty Creator and Controller of it.[70]

Holiness was named the fundamental moral attribute,[71] both because of the testimony of conscience and of the Bible.

[64]CT, 71.
[65]CT, 72.
[66]CT, 73.
[67]CT, 74.
[68]CT, 75.
[69]CT, 76.
[70]CT, 76.
[71]CT, 77. Strong called Robinson's "greatest originality" the singling out of holiness as fundamental and supreme, an emphasis which Strong retained. Whereas Robinson had opposed this to the New England theology, with its emphasis on the divine benevolence and love of being in general, and the Old School theology, which treated holiness as the aggregate of all divine perfections, so that it had no distinct significance, Strong later opposed it to Modernist theology. That holiness is not a form of love, but love a form of holiness, Strong learned from Robinson. Wrote Strong: "This view of holiness as the fundamental attribute of God prepared the way for what was probably the most impressive and inspiring part of his teaching; I mean his idea of law as the expression of God's holiness, or the transcript of the moral nature of God. No man who sat under Dr. Robinson's instruction can ever forget the scorn with which he treated the vulgar notion of law as something devised or invented, a makeshift to meet an exigency, an arbitrary enactment for the good of the creature, founded in mere will, unmade as easily as made, suspended or abrogated by fiat even as mere fiat had given it birth. Nor can any student of his forget his sublime and perpetual insistence on moral law as the eternal and unchangeable expression of the nature of God and the relations between God and his creatures,—an expression so eternal and uncheangeable that God himself cannot change his law without ceasing to be God" (Art. [1896], 175). Added Strong: "By these conceptions of holiness and law Dr. Robinson defined his position as an Old-School man, and made it impossible that he should have any other than an Old-School view of sin" (Art. [1896], 175-176).

God's eternal purposes include "his decretive permission of the free and opposing activities of his creatures . . . as much . . . as . . . the ultimate and eternal ends to which the universe of beings and of matter alike contribute."[72] Many have rejected the doctrine of decrees "not so much because unsupported by Scripture, as on account of the supposed impossibility of reconciling it with other recognized truths."[73] But revelation and reason together pronounce the last word in such disputes:

> But in answer to all objections, it should be remembered that a doctrine is not to be rejected because it may be misunderstood, or may have been perverted; not because we may be unable, in every respect, to harmonize it with every other doctrine. The only question to be asked is, does Revelation teach it and reason justify it? If it be both scriptural and rational, it is idle to set it aside, or for any reason to attempt to evade it.[74]

The same twofold appeal to revelation and reason, without a detailed outworking of their relations, was found in Robinson's treatment of creation: "Creation is strictly a biblical idea and follows naturally, if not necessarily, from that of a personal God."[75] The Old and the New Testaments clearly reiterate the doctrine, but "whether the Scriptures teach the absolute origination of matter, its creation out of nothing, is an open question."[76] This is the most natural interpretation, though another sense is not impossible.[77] The question of the origin of matter is beyond the reach of physical science.[78] Science is competent to speak of the processes of nature, and here the theory of evolution has gained ground and "there is no need that theology should set itself in hostility" to the scientific account of such processes.[79]

> The conclusions of science may require us to modify our conceptions of the mode of man's creation, but they cannot disprove the fact of his creation; they may compel us, contrary to Jewish apprehension, to recognize the intermediation of second causes, but they can determine nothing respecting the presence of the personal agent who gives to second causes their efficiency. The most that the Darwinian theory, or that any other theory, of evolution, has yet accomplished, is to show the possible method

---

[72] CT, 83.
[73] CT, 86.
[74] CT, 87-88.
[75] CT, 88.
[76] CT, 88. "Here we have another illustration," wrote Strong of Robinson, "of his refusal to dogmatize where he regarded Scripture as teaching nothing decisive, and of his earnest effort to reach reality beneath the forms of traditional statement. To his mind it was an open question whether the Scriptures teach the absolute *origination* of matter. The Hebrew word *bara* did not seem to him to settle the question. Yet he recognized in the organic *forms* of matter the embodied thought of a creative Will" (Art. [1896], 176-177). Strong here quoted from Robinson: "Even spontaneous generation does not preclude the idea of such a creative will, working by natural law and secondary causes," a passage taken almost verbatim from Robinson's CT, 91. However, Strong's statements were sometimes more assertive, in interpreting Robinson, than the latter's writings would seem to permit. One cannot be sure whether Strong at this point reflected the direction in which Robinson's thought later crystallized, or whether Strong read Robinson from the standpoint of Strong's own convictions. After all, Robinson did, as indicated above, proceed to comment that creation *ex nihilo* is the most natural interpretation of the Scripture teaching.
[77] CT, 89.
[78] CT, 90.
[79] CT, 92.

of the Divine procedure in the creation of man; it throws no light whatever on the causative power that used the method and wrought the result.[80]

The teaching of Scripture, that man came into being by the immediate power of God, is not contradicted, as yet, by any trustworthy authority of physical science.[81]

The final cause of creation, according to the Scriptures, is "unquestionably in God himself, but this cause is not exclusive of human happiness."[82] The Scriptures further teach that nothing in nature is self-sustaining, but that God sustains and controls the universe.[83] God's conservation and government are providential, so that "all events, phenomena of matter as well as of mind, are made to occur according to his prevision and prearrangement;"[84] but this special and particular providence does not require a miraculous deflection of the ordinary courses of nature.[85] Both Scripture and consciousness aver that "our responsibility is not annulled by the sustaining providence through which we act."[86]

In treating special providence, Robinson stressed the unsatisfactoriness of Scholastic views of divine *concursus*.

> Any explanation that can be given of God's relation to the forces of nature, whether physical or vital, must be purely hypothetical; dogmatic assertion respecting them is mere presumption. Matter and physical force are indissolubly one, . . . but what may be the relation of the activities of these forces to the Divine efficiency, in the conservation and progressive movement of the world, . . . it is worse than idle to inquire. We only know that God rules over all, and that all forces and wills, in the end, are made to subserve his immutable purposes.[87]

---

[80]CT, 116.
[81]CT, 116.
[82]CT, 94, where Robinson added: "It is a matter of indifference, therefore, whether we say that God created all things for the highest good of his creatures, accomplishing thereby his own supreme glory as the final cause of all."
[83]CT, 95. "The Christian theist, accepting the biblical statement that God is the upholder of all things and the continuator of life, sees in the mechanical action of physical forces the fitting instruments through which he works; in the uniformity of his working, discerns the fixedness of his purposes and the stability of his government" (CT, 96).
[84]CT, 95.
[85]CT, 97, footnote.
[86]CT, 103.
[87]CT, 102, footnote. Strong later commented: "I do not know how much of an attraction the idealistic interpretation . . . had for Dr. Robinson. The mention of secondary causes . . . and his declaration . . . that space must have existed before the universe, would seem to show that he sought no relief from the problem of creation in the thought that matter, as ideal, may also be eternal. But, in treating of preservation and providence, he seems to verge toward the idealistic explanation. Though he denies that law is simply uniform divine action, he also denies the so-called *concursus* of God with finite causes. Though he declares that 'God's relation to the material universe is unknown and unknowable' (Strong was here quoting CT, 99, but Robinson also wrote that the Scholastic theories of *concursus* are unsatisfactory "for they rest on theories of *God's relation to both matter and mind of which we know absolutely nothing*" [CT, 102, italics supplied]) he also declares that 'matter and physical force are indissolubly one,' that 'all forces are modes of one force,' and that 'this force is personal force.' The natural is God's work. He originated it. There is no separateness between the natural and the supernatural. The natural *is* the supernatural. God works in everything. Every end, even though attained by mechanical means, is as truly God's end as if wrought by miracle.' Hence the more modern conception of the universe seems to be working in Dr. Robinson's mind, and to be coloring his thought. His readiness to recognize the working of God both in nature and in man, and his unreadiness

Robinson refused to press these dissatisfactions to an idealistic conclusion.[88] He complained that theologians have persisted in theorizing on God's relation to the universe, despite its unknowability. He criticized especially the view that

> physical phenomena are the products of God's direct personal efficiency, law denoting nothing more than his uniformity of action:—a theory which is objectionable, as being pantheistic; as degrading to God, since many physical forces are subject to the manipulations of man; as contrary to the analogy seen in God's method of accomplishing moral ends through second causes; and as contrary to the observed fact that physical force is the necessary product of matter under given conditions;—but it is a theory which had its medieval and earlier Protestant advocates.[89]

At the same time, he rejected the prevailing notions of *concursus* in Protestant as well as Catholic formulations.

> Another class, recognizing the efficiency of second causes in both matter and mind, supposes such a CONCURSUS of the Divine energy with these as not only imparts to them their own efficiency but secures its subserviency to the Divine will:—a theory resting on purely verbal distinctions, without a shadow of fact to appeal to, and contradicted by what we know of the physical world from observation and of ourselves from consciousness;—but a theory which was accepted by Augustine and Aquinas, was elaborately explained and defended by nearly all the principal Protestant writers of the 17th and 18th centuries, and perhaps more than any other, underlies the existing popular theological conception of a special revelation.[90]

Miracles are wrongly confounded with extraordinary and inexplicable occurrences, Robinson believed. The chief characteristic of a miracle is "its significancy or purpose."[91] The interposition of the Divine Will may accomplish new results, either without the slightest interference with the uniformity of law, or by modifying the action of physical and vital forces.[92] The real office of miracle, in the Scriptures, is the "certification by supernatural phenomenon of one's claim to be a messenger from God."[93] But miracles were not of themselves a proof of a divine mission, for such con-

---

to postulate a *Deus ex machina* where the 'Spirit within the wheels' would account for all the facts, seem like an unconscious anticipation of the thought of God's immanence, which is so transforming the theology of our generation" (Art. [1896], 1777-178). But, it may be asked, did Strong read this into Robinson's words?

[88] Strong does not seem to do justice to passages in Robinson which preclude an interpretation of his statements along the line of idealistic monism. "God, everywhere present in the Cosmos," wrote Robinson, "is a Spirit totally distinct from matter, independent of it, and the almighty Creator and Controller of it" (CT, 76).

[89] CT, 99.

[90] CT, 99.

[91] CT, 105. Strong emphasized that this "definition of miracle as a 'special sign from God, authenticating the claim of one of his messengers,' is confessedly intended to exclude all dogmatizing with regard to the relation of the miracle to natural law and to second causes. If the signality of the miracle be maintained, then it matters not, even if natural law itself be the perpetual working of God" (Art. [1896] 178). But it is not so apparent from a reading of CT that Robinson was concerned to eliminate secondary causation; his concern appeared rather to remove the tension between the prevailing supernatural and scientific conceptions of the universe.

[92] CT, 106. Robinson made a point of observing that "the personal will of man, even limited as it is to the use of second causes, is perpetually producing phenomena that are quite aside from the established order of nature; it surely is not impossible for the infinite power of the personal God to make such use as he chooses of the forces, physical and vital, of which he is himself the Creator, or, even, if need be, to modify their action altogether by . . . a new and overriding force of will."

[93] CT, 107.

viction depends upon congruity of the miracle and the agent's moral character and also the character of the beholder; hence, "the miracle is a certification to him only who can perceive its significance."[94] The divine commission was perceived not because of mere outward wonder, but by the moral consciousness. The existence of the church is proof of Christ's resurrection, although the church would not exist had Christ remained in the tomb. Biblical miracles were for the special benefit of immediate witnesses; their evidential value weakens as it is made dependent on testimony.[95] For us, consequently, miracles as evidence of the Divine origin and authority of Christianity "are inferior to the existence and contents of the Religion itself."[96] Hence Robinson defended miracles, but did not rest the case for Christianity wholly upon them.

The evidence for angelic existences is primarily Biblical and is "both abundant and decisive."[97] There are good and evil angels, and the latter have Satan as their leader.[98] The Scriptural references to Satan preclude viewing evil merely in terms of an impersonal principle.[99]

(2) *Anthropology*

No trustworthy authority of physical science has "contradicted, as yet"[100] the Biblical teaching that man came into being "by the immediate power of God,"[101] Robinson affirmed. The Bible views man as a compound being whose twofold nature allies him to two worlds.[102] There are New Testament hints of a trichotomic division of man's nature, but dogmatism involves the risk of conjecture.[103]

In treating anthropology, Robinson diverged from the traditional view of man's primitive state by his denial that man's created likeness to God consisted in man's moral perfection. Correct Biblical exegesis, he contended, will not sustain such a view. The redemptive work of Christ does not simply restore a lost relationship, but involves

the carrying of man forward towards the realization of an ideal perfection to which he was destined, but with which he was not at first endowed . . . in fact, the production of a new and higher type of man than the original (I Cor. 15:47-49; I Pet. 1:15, 16; I John 3:1-3).[104]

---

[94] CT, 108.
[95] CT, 109.
[96] CT, 109. Robinson added, however, that the origin of the Christian church is rooted in the resurrection miracle, and that the resurrection gave "proof of his ability to bear our penalty, and, in bearing, to survive it" (CT, 293).
[97] CT, 109.
[98] CT, 110.
[99] CT, 114. The dismissal of the Gospel accounts of demon-possession as superstition cannot be reconciled with Jesus' divine authority or the inspiration of the evangelists (CT, 115, footnote).
[100] CT, 116.
[101] CT, 116, where Robinson added: "There is a noticeable difference between the biblical phraseology descriptive of the origin of man, and that descriptive of the origin of other forms of organic life . . . Man alone is the immediate creature of God, and the bearer of his image."
[102] CT, 118. Man sustains "at once relations to the brute below him and to the angel above him. He is the only being, so far as we know, who forms in himself a tangential point between the two worlds of spirit and of matter" (CT, 118).
[103] CT, 119.
[104] CT, 120.

The Genesis account implies, by the phrase "very good," merely the fitness of man and the whole creation to the end which the Creator had in view. Moral perfection cannot be a direct creation, but is attained only through discipline and will.[105] Nor do the Scriptures teach that man's distinctive image was lost in the fall; rather, the original image was transmitted. Therefore the image of God consisted

> doubtless in that assemblage of qualities which constitutes the immutable distinction between man and the brute creation—in other words, in his personal existence as a rational, moral being.[106]

The Biblical data on the original condition of man are "few and of uncertain import."[107] Morally, man was originally innocent and sinless; rationally, "either an infant . . . or gifted with some degree of maturity, and accordingly with ideas and some kind of language which are necessarily coexistent."[108] The Scriptures warrant neither the traditional Protestant theory of an original perfect holiness, nor the modern scientific theory which

> makes man to have arisen from the lowest barbarism, and to have been originally not only a congener of the ape, but the offspring of still lower animals . . . That man, according to the Bible, was immature and untried at the outset, and consequently at the best only sinless, seems clearly enough implied in the garden that was prepared for him; nor is there anything in the New Testament implying that his first estate was more than that of innocence.[109]

While the New Testament does not directly assert that man was originally sinless, it everywhere takes for granted that he is now in a fallen state.[110] Man's sin cannot be explained either in terms of his possession of a body, or as a necessity of development, or as a concomitant of his finiteness, or as efficiently willed by God.[111] The blame for sin cannot be placed upon God, nor was it a necessity of man's development. Sin entered through man's abuse of his created free-will, without God's re-

---

[105] While Robinson denied the first man a primitive holy character, he seems to grant him right tendencies: "Originally faultless as the work of God, all man's spontaneities must have been right, and yet to develop these spontaneities into consciously elective and determinative principles of character—to secure personal worthiness to individuals, it was necessary that there should be volitional action" (CT, 123).

[106] CT, 120.

[107] CT, 121.

[108] CT, 121.

[109] CT, 122. Strong's early teaching took vigorous exception to the concessions of Robinson's anthropology. Later Strong himself, as we shall see, accepted an evolutionary view, but still insisted on a position nearer that of traditional Protestantism than Robinson's. Wrote Strong: "I have no doubt that the old orthodoxy, which Dr. Robinson was here opposing, unduly magnified the powers and virtues of the first father of our race. When Dr. South declared that 'Aristotle was but the rubbish of an Adam,' he went far beyond Scripture. But it seems to me that Dr. Robinson went to quite the opposite extreme when he made the image of God consist in mere personality, and denied to the first man any, even a germinal, holiness of character. If, when God newly creates the soul in Christ, he gives a germinal 'righteousness and holiness of truth,' then in the original creation he could also impart a tendency toward the good and a love for himself" (Art. [1896] 180-181). This emphasis on man's original righteousness characterized Strong's anthropology, in both its creation and evolutionary statements.

[110] CT, 122.

[111] CT, 124ff.

sponsibility for the abuse.[112] The existence of moral evil is inexplicable.[113] But man's fall from original sinlessness is evidenced by the Scriptures and by the reproaches of individual conscience.[114]

In consequence of the fall, man lost an "original righteousness"[115] and incurred positive evils. All painful consequences of wrong acts, whether by the constitution and course of nature or by guilt incurred by violating revealed statutes, are penal.[116] There is no distinction between penalty and consequences, between guilt and liability. Robinson at this point resisted modern theology, complaining that a distinction is maintainable only by limiting man's moral knowledge to mere Biblical statutes, by restricting human guilt to violations of such statutes, and by placing revelation over against nature in such a way as to obscure God's authorship of nature. Consequently, he declared, "all painful consequences of wrong acts must be as distinctly penal as if they had been formally threatened."[117] Penal evils resulting from the fall of man include spiritual death and physical death.[118] Man was created mortal, with provision for immortality that need not have required physical death were it not for sin. But the chief penalty is spiritual; sin is itself death, as a voluntary withdrawal from God, the source of life.

Freedom of will also was lost as a consequence of the fall.[119] Of the two elements in a free will, man retains the power of mental self-determination (that formal freedom which is a necessary condition of rational existence), but has lost "the concurrent and harmonious action of all the

---

[112]CT, 127.

[113]CT, 127. Robinson wrote: "The result could not have been purposed, nor yet unforeseen, nor yet again beyond the power of God to prevent. The origin of evil is an insoluble mystery" (CT, 127). Again: "Against the notion of a divine efficiency in the origin of evil, stands the most indubitable evidence that God is an infinitely holy and just Being; he cannot have been the author of that which is absolutely opposed to himself" (CT, 126).

[114]CT, 126.

[115]The phrase "original righteousness" suggests that Robinson did not wholly discard the idea of some positive tendencies to good in primal man: "By the fall . . . was lost an original righteousness which, but for its loss, would have been the birthright of every one of the race, and in its stead . . . were incurred certain positive evils" (CT, 128).

[116]CT, 129.
[117]CT, 183.
[118]CT, 131.

[119]CT, 132. Strong expressed the wish that Robinson, in treating of the will of man, "had more definitely set himself against determinism. He seems rather to intimate that Jonathan Edwards's argument has never been satisfactorily answered. . . . The will cannot be compelled; for, unless self-determined, it is no longer will. The consciousness of freedom must be trusted, even though we cannot reconcile it with our logic . . . Dr. Robinson does not decide the philosophical question, though it is plain that his leanings are toward determinism" (Art. [1896] 179). And yet Robinson insisted, in treating the divine decrees, that the certainty of their fulfillment does not involve a divine determinism (CT, 83-87). "For aught we know to the contrary," Robinson wrote, "the eternal purposes may have been so quadrated with human wills as to have provided for their largest conceivable freedom; indeed, the very constitution of man's spiritual nature may have been so grounded in the eternal purposes as to make the freedom of his will an essential factor in their fulfillment. The purposes may be unalterably fixed, every act of man may invariably contribute to their fulfillment, and yet every act be as voluntary and as free as if there existed no decrees to be fulfilled" (CT, 87).

powers that properly make up the human personality."[120] Separation from God involves the disintegration of man's spiritual being. Scripture and conscience attest man's present freedom "to discern and to elect, but not to appropriate, the right."[121] Conscience, as a result of the fall, no longer renders right decisions, but "now often renders false judgments and positively misleads."[122] The whole current of human life has been imparted a wrong tendency, both by example and corruption of will, so that society has become "organically evil."[123]

Sin has three aspects:

as an act, sin is a transgression of God's law; as a principle that determines the guilt of acts, it is opposition or hostility to God; as state or nature, it is moral unlikeness to God.[124]

The essence of sin is selfishness, that is, an inordinate self-love and self-seeking at the expense of the will of God.[125]

Mankind is involved in original sin, so that all men are sinners "in consequence of an inborn sinful nature."[126] Thus depravity is innate or inborn; human nature is morally corrupted or depraved.[127] Robinson appealed to the "universality, spontaneousness and absolute certainty" of sinful development as demonstrative proofs of innateness,[128] and also to the teachings of the Scriptures.[129] This depravity is not only innate but also hereditary.[130] This Robinson supported by an appeal to these considerations: the principle of heredity is the "more reasonable" view of the innateness of depravity; the evidence from analogy would indicate a formative principle working in the species; the transmission of moral, intellectual and physical traits has been established; the doctrine is Scriptural.[131]

This natural depravity is justly condemnable and punishable. Robinson held to mediate imputation in explaining the common guilt of the race; not so much a common act of the race in Adam, as man's universal and congenital depravity, is the ground of his condemnation. Each man is guilty because of his own depravity.[132] But "the words sin and guilt, when applied to an inherited nature, must necessarily have a restricted mean-

---

[120]CT, 132f.
[121]CT, 133.
[122]CT, 136.
[123]CT, 137.
[124]CT, 138. Strong later declared that in these words Robinson had "probably given us the most comprehensive and exact definition of sin that can be found in theological literature" (Art. [1896] 184).
[125]CT, 143.
[126]CT, 156. Robinson held to the traducian view of the origin of the soul.
[127]CT, 156-157.
[128]CT, 157.
[129]CT, 158.
[130]Robinson protested against both the New School and the covenant theologians (immediate imputationists): "The more rational view is . . . that in his fall we all fell, because we were all potentially—germinally in him, and because of his entire nature we, by natural descent, are all partakers" (CT, 158-159).
[131]CT, 159.
[132]Strong took serious exception to this formulation, declaring that here Robinson "diverged from the teaching of Scripture, became inconsistent with himself, and adopted a principle which burdened him greatly when he came to explain Christ's taking our penalty upon him. Dr. Robinson had granted that the consequences of the first sin are to Adam's posterity precisely what they were to Adam himself.

ing as compared with that . . . applied to our voluntary actions."[133] It is sinful and guilty in a qualified sense. This sinfulness of hereditary nature the Scriptures "seem very distinctly" to teach.[134] The human race is an organic unity sharing a common and punishable guilt.

Man's predicament is that of total depravity, so that "without Divine assistance, all men are totally incapable of an affection, volition, or act, which is acceptable to God."[135] But man is responsible despite his inability, as the Scriptures, consciousness, and experience teach.[136]

(3) *Soteriology*

The divine redemptive plan was in purpose coeternal with that of creation; the divine provision of salvation is not an afterthought.[137] The history of the world manifests a providential preparation, positively among the Hebrews and negatively elsewhere, for the coming of Christ.[138]

The origin of moral law cannot be referred only to the sovereign will of God,[139] but is found in the moral nature of God.[140] Moral law was not made, but rather, was revealed. Rewards and penalties, therefore, are not arbitrary, but are natural and inevitable consequences of man's relationship of God.[141] The law, as objective statute, was not given to man as a means of salvation, but rather for pedagogic purposes, until men should put their trust in the perfect Redeemer.[142] But the law, as subjective principle of being, reflecting the divine nature, is as immutable as God.[143] Hence the gospel does not annul the law.

The central interest of the Scriptures is the Redeemer, Jesus Christ.[144] The evidence for the deity of Christ is chiefly though not exclusively Scriptural.[145] His miracles prove His divine mission and thus his Messiahship, but not his deity.[146]

But to Adam they were certainly first guilt, and then depravity. To Adam's descendants, also, the consequences of Adam's sin came in the same order . . . Paul . . . bases God's infliction of the penalty of death, not upon the ground that all are sinful, but upon the ground that 'all sinned.' Since depravity is caused by the apostasy, we cannot be guilty of the depravity without first being guilty of the apostasy" (Art. [1896], 185).

[133]CT, 161. This mitigation of the judgment passed upon depravity, Strong declared, grew out of Robinson's failure to apply his realism consistently. "He should have considered that as Adam's act was condemnable apart from its consequences, so we, who were one with him in the transgression, have incurred guilt apart from the depravity which is a consequence of that act. . . . His theology would have been more consistent if he had been more thoroughly realistic and Pauline, and had said plainly, 'In Adam's fall we sinned all.' It is unjust to hold us guilty of the effect if we be not first guilty of the cause" (Art. [1896], 185-186).

[134]CT, 162.
[135]CT, 163.
[136]CT, 174-176.
[137]CT, 179.
[138]CT, 180-181.
[139]CT, 187.
[140]CT, 190.
[141]CT, 191.
[142]CT, 193.
[143]CT, 193-194.
[144]CT, 196.
[145]CT, 198.
[146]CT, 201, footnote.

Christ united in himself the natures of both man and God.[147] Robinson points out that leading theologians have held implicitly, though some explicitly, "that there were necessarily two wills as well as two natures in Christ, though the human was ever in subordination to the divine."[148] But the single Theanthropic personality possesses "two unmixed natures (with) unblended but interpenetrating and mutually modified attributes; but always as one and the same person with one consciousness and one will."[149] He found as a chief cause of Christological error "the assumption that if two natures, the Divine and the human, were united in Christ, some definite conception of the mode of the union is both possible and necessary."[150] Robinson thus fluctuated between the Chalcedonian and a kenosis formulation of Christology.[151] In Christ's person, two distinct natures, possessing their own unchangeable and incommunicable essence, united to constitute, not a third nature, but a single and unique personality; the Divine and human were so united, that each was preserved in the fulness of its essential perfections.[152]

Christ assumed "the common nature of the races; not the nature of the unfallen Adam; nor yet a new-created nature different alike from Adam's and our own; but the nature of those whom he came to save . . . with the exception of its hereditary depravity."[153] The assumption of human nature by a supernatural act cut off hereditary guilt and depravity but not its consequences, i. e., its penalty. Hereditary depravity is involved in a

---

[147]CT, 212.
[148]CT, 214. Robinson decided against the Damascene formula that "as in the Trinity there are three persons with one will manifested in diversity of acts, so in the person of Christ there were two wills manifested in unity of acts."
[149]CT, 218.
[150]CT, 214.
[151]It is true that Strong assigned Robinson "the great merit of being one of the first in America to unfold the doctrine of the Kenosis, or self-limitation of the Logos in becoming man. The old orthodoxy had made the person of Christ unintelligible and incredible, by maintaining our Lord's continual consciousness of his deity, and his continual use of divine powers. This was either Docetism . . . or Nestorianism. . . . Our author began his study from the oneness of Christ's person. . . . He inveighed against separating the two natures, and conceiving that our Lord spoke at one time as man and at another time as God. He maintained that this attributes unveracity to Christ, and held that our Lord spoke everywhere and always as the God-man, even when he declared that he was ignorant of the day of the end. I regard this doctrine of the single personality of Christ, and of the divine self-limitation in becoming man, as one of the noblest and most valuable parts of his teaching" (Art. [1896], 187-188). But (1) the "old orthodoxy" had itself rejected the notion of a dual personality; (2) Robinson's rejection of the doctrine of dual personality did not clearly commit him to a Kenosis as against a Chalcedonian formulation, for he insisted that both natures are fully preserved in the incarnation; (3) Robinson's insistence on "one consciousness and one will" (CT, 218) was a concession to the Kenosis view in which Robinson discarded his own plea for caution about the necessity and possibility of definitely conceiving the mode of union (CT, 214).
[152]CT, 214-215. Robinson wrote: "A variable union of the Divine with the human, or a union consisting of mere superintendence of the human by the Divine, or any other union than that of a combination of the two natures into one indivisible and mysterious person, is neither warranted by Scripture, nor reconcilable with any clear and rational conception of personality" (CT, 219). Also, "a Divine Hypostasis of the triune Godhead has so assumed a real humanity as not thereby to surrender his Divinity" (CT, 237).
[153]CT, 216.

deviation of natural descent of personal life from Adam, but Christ did not thus derive His personal life. The incarnation involved a circumscription, restriction and limitation of the Divine nature.[154] The Scriptures "represent the humiliation of Christ to have pertained mainly, though not exclusively, to his Divine nature; and to have consisted in His assumption of human nature with all the limitations and environments which it necessitated, and in voluntarily bearing in that nature all the penalties that hung over it."[155] His humiliation is that of a Divine person assuming the finite conditions of human existence and identifying himself with a race so under Divine displeasure that this identification must involve the assumption of the penal consequences of its guilt.[156]

In the exaltation, the Divine nature in conjunction with the human is exalted to the highest conceivable dignity.[157] Jesus Christ continues forever to be the Logos, the Word, the communicator, between the infinite God and finite creatures.[158]

The personality of the Holy Spirit finds its proof in the Scriptures only.[159] From this, His proper Divinity follows necessarily, because of the Biblical ascriptions and affirmations.[160]

The problem of the Divine triunity comes next into view. The numerical unity of God is one of the clearest Biblical truths; numerically and essentially, God is absolutely one.[161] The doctrine of the Trinity, however, is derived not from philosophical sources, but from Biblical data.[162] Robinson regarded the doctrine as transcending reason entirely:

> The source of the difficulty is in the inconceivability of the mode of a triune existence; the absurdity itself lies wholly in the attempt to reduce a mode of existence which transcends all our knowledge, to the level of our finite experiences.[163]

Robinson held that the absence of any genuine analogies of trinitarian being renders impossible the finding of terms to designate the divine distinctions (may be only a piece of metal!)[164] Any statements avoid Tritheism or mere Modalism with extreme difficulty. The basic proof of the doctrine of the Trinity is the New Testament. The doctrine underlay the Old Testament revelation, unperceived by its writers, but the economic revelation in Christianity articulated it.[165] The Biblical doctrine is supported by the confirmation it receives from Christian experience.[166] Robinson mentioned, with-

---

[154]CT, 217.
[155]CT, 224-225.
[156]CT, 226.
[157]CT, 228.
[158]CT, 228.
[159]CT, 229.
[160]CT, 232.
[161]CT, 235.
[162]CT, 236.
[163]CT, 236.
[164]Robinson remarked that even in Christian devotion, no experiential distinction between divine persons can be made. The protest that Trinitarianism "robs God the Father of the supreme adoration due his name, by encouraging the worship of the Spirit and the Son as distinct persons," Robinson rejected on the ground that the "economic offices of the Son and the Spirit" distinctively and always lead to the adoration of the Father (CT, 238).
[165]CT, 241-243.
[166]CT, 243. Robinson did not clearly show any independent value of Christian ex-

out approval or disapproval, the psychological argument for divine personal distinctioins on the ground that the experiences both of self-consciousness and of knowledge require an object.[167] But our knowledge of the Trinity is derived from God's historical revelation in the economy of redemption. To convert the economic titles into exact descriptions of immanent and eternal distinction, however, is to substitute graded personal distinction in the Godhead for a Trinity. On the other hand, to deny the distinctions any immanent or ontologic significance is to erect an absolute and exclusive divine unity.[168] Thus Robinson served notice that his basic interest in the Trinity is historic and economic. For that reason he treated the doctrine not in conjunction with the attributes of God, but in connection with sin and redemption.

The question of the mutual relations of the persons of the Trinity is best resolved by regarding "the titles Father, Son, and Spirit as borrowed from relations that began in the work of human redemption," yet as "representing real and immanent distinctions in the Godhead, which had existed from eternity."[169] Thus Robinson discarded the Nicene statement of eternal generation, as escaping a suggestion of derivation and subordination only in a verbal manner. There is no adequate Biblical case for eternal generation.[170] In John's Gospel, the first chapter, Christ is designated Logos prior to the incarnation, and is called Son of God only after the incarnation; the entire fourth Gospel is an exhibit of historical evidence, not of eternal Sonship.[171] The New Testament interest is mainly in the historical, and not the pre-historical Christ. Yet, Robinson insisted,

The titles Father, Son and Holy Spirit, though derived from the historical facts of the Christian economy, do nevertheless represent eternal ontologic distinctions in the Godhead. This view discards all theories of the relations and rests content on the simple facts of the case.[172]

---

perience in this regard. Indeed, in view of the above footnote quotation from CT, 238, it is difficult to see how any positive argument could thus be evolved, other than the claim that experience does not contradict the doctrine. Elsewhere he remarked that "every normal Christian consciousness responds at once to the truth of the economic Trinity as taught in the New Testament" (CT, 252).

[167] Robinson's reserve in this regard will be contrasted later with Strong's appropriation of idealistic arguments for personal divine distinctions. "Notwithstanding the absence of all trustworthy data from which to reason in respect to the relation of persons in the Trinity," wrote Robinson, "attempts are still made to construct the doctrine from the postulates of speculative philosophy" (CT, 251, footnote).

[168] CT, 239.

[169] CT, 247.

[170] CT, 248.

[171] CT, 249. Robinson confined himself mainly to the historical manifestations, avoiding a final attempt to interpret the ante-mundane mystery of the Trinity. This called forth Strong's protest: "We might well follow his example, if we did not seem to recognize in Scripture an effort to teach us something with regard to the pretemporal relations of the persons of the Trinity. . . . Only when we regard the terms Father, Son and Holy Ghost as intimations of a relation prior to all time, do we know anything of God's essential nature. Revelation is not revelation if it does not tell us something of what God is *in himself*, not simply what he is *to us*." (Art. [1896], 194, 195).

[172] CT, 250. Robinson's expansion of this is a curious example of metaphysical reserve and tension. The Bible gives no information respecting the inner divine relations except as the ultimate end of Christianity necessitates; Scripture terminology seems to have been suggested by historical phenomena rather than eternal principles beyond them. Hence the names and representations of the divine persons are

Christ's meditation between God and man is best described under the threefold offices of Prophet, Priest, and King.[173] These metaphors are not to be interpreted literally, yet represent "real and distinct offices of Christ in teaching, redeeming and controlling his people."[174]

As Prophet, Christ communicates to man the mind and will of God. But the New Testament chiefly presents Him as Priest,[175] who transacts with God for men, and becomes man's Saviour by the offering of himself as a sacrifice for the human race on Calvary. Through the Church Christ reigns preeminently as King, and by its instrumentality his empire is to become universal.[176]

The priestly office of Christ centers in the theme of atonement, which represents "in respect to God, the expiation of guilt, and, in respect to man, his at-one-ment with God." The term designates all that he accomplished for man in his life, as well as what he procured for man by his death. As to the latter,

"Nothing is more plainly or more emphatically taught in the Scriptures than that Jesus Christ died on the cross to procure for man his salvation from sin and its consequences. The saving efficacy of the death of Christ is the one idea that gives organic unity to the . . . New Testament Scriptures; and it is the appropriation of this idea in his individual life which makes a man to be distinctively a Christian."[177]

But those who agree on this fact, disagree on the method whereby Christ's death avails for salvation.

The oldest theory of atonement, that of satisfaction, which claims to be exclusively orthodox, "is preeminently theoretic" and despite any modifications is "as purely a theory as any that has ever been propounded in its stead."[178] It is more likely that Anselm held that the death of Christ was a voluntary sacrifice, rather than a vicarious punishment, contrary to opposing interpretations.[179] The forensic view of substitutionary satisfaction is objectionable because it literalizes Biblical figures of speech.

It gives a literal meaning to the words covenant, sacrifice, propitiation, atonement, and redemption, terms which, applied to the redemptive work of Christ, are manifestly metaphors, though metaphors laden with the most weighty of meanings; meanings also, which carry us beneath the machinery of government to the moral natures of Him who rules and of them who are ruled.[180]

More than this, the forensic view involves an absolute inconceivable juridical transfer of moral penalty from the consciously guilty to the con-

---

strictly economic. "But it cannot be denied, that all our necessary conceptions of God must have some underlying and essential basis of eternal reality. . . . There must, therefore, be some ontologic or immanent, and consequently eternal, distinctions in the Godhead on which are grounded the economic titles and the conceptions of personality which they suggest. . . . But what the distinctions were, what their *modus existendi*, and what their common relation to the absolute oneness of the Divine essence, the Scriptures do not inform us, and it is idle to inquire" (CT, 250, 251).
[173]CT, 252.
[174]CT, 253.
[175]CT, 253f.
[176]CT, 255.
[177]CT, 255.
[178]CT, 256.
[179]CT, 258, footnote.
[180]CT, 260. Robinson did not fully clarify what he meant by the precise non-literal meaning of the metaphors.

sciously innocent;[181] it contradicts the innate sense of justice which is not satisfied by an unqualified escape of the guilty;[182] it contradicts the established order of the invariable and inevitable penal consequences of violated law; and it is self-contradictory, for it insists both that the punishment of the sinner is absolutely demanded by immutable divine justice, and then that the immutable divine justice is satisfied by a commutation or substitution of both person and punishment.[183]

But that men are saved through the sufferings and death of Christ as representative and personal substitute before God "there seems to be the clearest evidence both in the Scriptures and in Christian education." The simple Biblical facts suggest that

> our Lord in assuming human nature became subject to its laws, limitations, exposures and penal liabilities. Having taken our nature for the express purpose of interposing in our behalf . . . he actually suffered the woes which have come, or, without his interposing help, must come, on every one of the race. He bore these as the true penal sufferings for sin. They were not transferred by literal imputation, from the race, or from any individual of the race, to him, but as one of the race, as its interposing and recognized representative, he bore them, and in bearing them triumphed over them. And to every one who has fellowship with him as a sufferer for sin, and faith in him as a personal Saviour from its power, it is divinely given to share in his triumphs.[184]

His sufferings need not have been identical with those endured by all or

---

[181] The transfer of moral penalty from the consciously guilty to the consciously innocent "contradicts the very idea of penalty," Robinson affirmed (CT, 261). Hence one's sins are laid on Christ only in the sense that one is saved by Him (metaphorically), not by a transfer of guilt or penalty.

[182] The demands of the innate sense of justice, that all wrong doing be punished, "can be fully satisfied only when penalty is so inflicted upon the guilty, in conjunction with his Deliverer, as that, by its infliction, he shall be rescued from his sin; but it is not satisfied in the unqualified escape of the guilty" (CT, 261).

[183] CT, 261-262. Robinson specifically criticized William G. T. Shedd's theory of atonement *ab intra*, a self-oblation on the part of Deity himself, by which to satisfy those immanent and eternal imperatives of the divine nature, which without it must find their satisfaction in the punishment of the transgressor, or else be outraged." Robinson protested that "an atonement made necessary to balance the character of God, could not be a gratuity to men" (CT, 260). Strong, too, objected to Shedd's formulation, but not in the interest of the view which Robinson championed; rather, he retained substitution and merged it with the newer emphases. Strong declared that Robinson "does not seem fully to apprehend Dr. Shedd's position in the matter of the relation of the divine attributes. The latter's conception of justice does not exclude the possibility of grace, since but for grace Christ never would have 'offered himself through the eternal Spirit without blemish unto God' " (Art. [1896], 190). Shedd had himself asked: "Where is the mercy of God, in case justice is strictly satisfied by a vicarious person? There is mercy in permitting another person to do for the sinner what the sinner is bound to do for himself; and still greater mercy in providing that person; and greater still, in becoming that person" (Shedd, *Dogmatic Theology*, I, 378).

[184] CT, 262. The subjectivistic emphasis, contrasted with the objective justification insisted upon by Reformation theology, here comes clearly to the fore. The guilt or penalty of humanity is not transferred to Christ, for such imputation would be immoral, would outrage the innate sense of justice. Christ assumes our penalty only in the sense that faith in Him gives us a sense of peace. Though the sense of guilt "is a personal possession which cannot be conceived of, either as being literally transferred, or as being voluntarily assumed by one for another, yet there is a clearly intelligible sense in which it may be said to have been imputed to Christ, and Christ may be said to have borne it. Thus, when a sinful man, burdened with a sense of ill-desert, finds himself consciously and peacefully trusting in Christ as his Saviour, so complete is the extinction of his feeling of remorse, that Christ may justly be said to have borne it in his stead" (CT, 264).

any saved by Him.[185] The woes which Christ suffered are thus not positive and external inflictions by God, but natural consequences of Christ's assumption of human nature; hence the sufferings would have been the same, though nobody were saved, because of his incarnation.[186] His sufferings were the necessary result of the conflict with evil with which he engaged in the flesh. To redeem, and by redeeming to purify and rescue human nature, he must bear its penalties, and endure spiritual death.[187] It is not even impossible that, in partaking of human nature, Christ also partook of the immanent and universal feeling of guilt before God.[188] While personal guilt for voluntary acts cannot be literally transferred or voluntarily assumed by another, Christ assumes it by so fully extinguishing the feeling of remorse[189] of those who trust him that there is no impropriety in declaring that Christ has borne it in their stead.[190] If Christ had actually borne our personal penalty, then salvation would be due to

---

[185]CT, 263.
[186]CT, 264: "As one of mankind, Christ, if he would save the human nature he had assumed, must have suffered what he did, whether all the race or none of the race were to be saved by him."
[187]CT, 265.
[188]CT, 264f. Strong protested this view, "that Christ was visited with penalty though he had neither depravity nor guilt. If both depravity and guilt were cut off in his case by his supernatural conception, how can he justly suffer?" (Art. [1896], 193). For Strong, guilt and penalty necessarily involve each other, but his solution was, as we shall see, even more unorthodox than that of Robinson, who resisted the view that the guilt of the race was imputed to Christ. But how much both men shared in common, as they came to the subject of redemption, is seen in Strong's emphasis that Robinson's views of holiness, law and sin logically necessitated the deity and the propitiatory sacrifice of Jesus Christ "in spite of peculiar views with regard to the method and application of the atonement" (Art. [1896], 176).
[189]Strong later conceded that "the subjective element so predominates" in Robinson's statement of the atonement "both in the pains Christ bears and in the redemption the believer experiences, that we can easily understand how Dr. Robinson was regarded by many as holding to the Socinan or moral influence theory of the atonement" (Art. [1896], 191f.). The peace which the believer experiences by trusting Christ was not, according to Robinson, the peace that Christ has borne our penalties, so as to free us from the necessity of bearing them; rather, Christ's influence upon us enables us so to bear the penal consequences of our sins through saving faith and new affections, that we survive them and escape from them as he did. The "penalty is so inflicted, upon the guilty, in conjunction with his Deliverer, as that, by its infliction, he shall be rescued from his sin; but (there is no) . . . unqualified escape of the guilty" (CT, 261). "Here, then, we have the abounding grace of God in Christ, first reclaiming a man from his sins, by imparting to him an abhorrence of moral evil and the feeling of deliverance from its hated dominion, and thus of forgiveness on account of it; and then starting him on that career of Christian living, which, through the exhaustless resources of Divine grace, shall gradually erase from his character the penal traces of his former estate, and thus carry him endlessly onward and upward" (CT, 267). Salvation is a remedial redemptive process through which the effects of a violated law are gradually reversed and finally eradicated by the working of a new law. Strong declared that this reads much like the Socinian or Bushnellian example and moral influence theories, wherein the sinner with Christ's influence works out both his own atonement and renewal. But Robinson, he grants, emphasized his rejection of those views, and insisted that the subjective change does not come from man, but from God.
[190]CT, 264: "When the believer is enabled so to appropriate to himself the sacrifice of Christ, that he may be said to have eaten Christ's flesh and to have drunk Christ's blood, then is his sense of guilt so overborne and extinguished, by a new and more powerful consciousness of release from the dominion of sin and of reconciliation with God, that Christ may be said with propriety and emphasis to have borne all his punishment and to have expiated all his guilt."

individual believers as an act of justice alone; grace and mercy would be relevant only to His work for us in His own person.[191] Rather, by His obedience and sufferings He has

> fulfilled all the moral law and borne all penalties to which the race are liable; that every individual trusting in him shall find all his own obligations fulfilled, all his personal sins and their consequences taken away, and himself put upon a career that shall bring him into a full participation in the triumphant exaltation of his Saviour and Lord.[192]

Christ thus becomes Saviour, not by an act of imputation, but rather through the control[193] which He wields over us when we see that He has borne our woes in such a way as to make full satisfaction to God and to impart to believers everlasting salvation. Robinson appealed to the Scriptures for support that

> the chief, and in some instances the exclusive, reference is to the subjective effect of Christ's redeeming work in the heart of believers[194]

and that the Scriptures have in view the final object of Christ's death rather than the method by which it avails, yet we are plainly required to regard the death as vicarious;[195] his death has redemptive efficacy. The underlying conception of the metaphors applied to his death is that of a Mediator interposing in our behalf.[196] The subjective influence of Christ's work in the believer's heart is an important, but not an exhaustive explanation, of these metaphors. The subjective redemption, in fact,

> is effected solely through the inward assurance of, and experimental acquaintance with, the objective interposing Ransomer who places himself between us and the objective wrath of God. . . . Christ, by his life and death, becomes, to every one who in loving sympathy and faith obeys him, not only a Deliverer from the dominion of sin now, but from its penalties hereafter forever.[197]

The moral influence theory of the atonement is inadequate because it rejects the thought of expiation.[198] That theory rests upon a fallacious fundamental postulate, that the mercy or benevolence of God is more central and more determinate than his justice;[199] such a view assumes

---

[191] CT, 266.
[192] CT, 266f.
[193] CT, 273: "Thus Christ is a Saviour to all who will be saved by him; not by any formal imputation of our sins to him, or of his righteousness to us, but solely through that control which he exercises over us whenever we come to understand him as the One who has borne all our woes, and so borne them as both to make full satisfaction to God and to impart to all, who will lovingly trust in him, an everlasting salvation."
[194] CT, 270.
[195] CT, 270.
[196] CT, 272.
[197] CT, 273.
[198] CT, 276.
[199] Strong emphasized that, despite Robinson's compromise of a theory of objective atonement (in which God rather than man is primarily reconciled), he "continually and vigorously protested against" the moral influence theory "in its assertions that God is primarily love rather than holiness, and that law is essentially decretive or a creation of will; while he maintained on the contrary, that it was justice which made the atonement necessary, and that the sufferings of Christ were an expiatory sacrifice for the sins of the world" (Art. [1896], 192). Robinson seems therefore to have halted midway between a clearly objective and subjective statement of the

that justice, law and penalty are strictly decretive.[200] Moreover, the Scriptures emphasize that divine forgiveness of man's sin is on Christ's account, and not because of any amendment of his life; such amendment is a consequence of the new relationship to God.[201] The governmental theory of the atonement likewise gives no satisfactory explanation of Christ's person and sufferings, for it denies that he died "in satisfaction of the penal justice of God."[202] But Robinson does not appear clearly to rise above a metaphorical satisfaction[203] of the justice of God.

The possibility of redemption from sin's power and penalty by the vicarious death of Christ "is preeminently a doctrine of Divine revelation.[204] Without revelational assurance, we could know "little, if anything, of its necessity."[205] The atonement finds its necessity in the immutable nature of God:

> God as holy, necessarily repels all sinners from his presence, and by the very act of repulsion punishes them. Whoever, therefore, should assume our nature and take his place among us as one of our race, and take it for the express purpose of redeeming us from sin and reconciling us to God, would be under the inexorable necessity of so confronting the Divine repulsion as to remove it or he could not achieve our redemption.[206]

And yet the atonement must be voluntary.[207] It was contemplated by Christ for eternity, and included in the original design of creation. The substitute needed "to secure an actual personal righteousness on the part of the redeemed," which Christ accomplished by "becoming security for the good conduct of those whose place he takes."[208] By virtue of the union of be-

---

atonement. Strong expressed his doubts that Robinson "succeeded in reconciling Christ's sufferings with the orthodox promise from which he set out. I must be allowed to record my doubts. He fails to show that either law or justice has any claim upon Christ. And yet the foundation of the system is the holiness or justice of God, and the law is the necessary and unchangeable expression of God's nature" (Art. [1896], 192-193).

[200] CT, 276.
[201] CT, 278.
[202] CT, 284. Robinson rejected the notion (against Hodge and others) that the divine nature in Christ was necessary to give dignity and worth to the sufferings of the man Jesus, on the ground that the divine nature can hardly give worth to sufferings in which it did not participate. The human nature in that event, he complained, "differed from that of ordinary men only in being conjoined with a divine nature" (CT, 285, footnote).
[203] This appears true, despite the strong statement that "if . . . we find . . . that he came into the world for the very purpose of suffering as he did, that thereby he might release from like mental sufferings all who would be saved by him, then the conclusion is inevitable that the sufferings were an actual atonement for sin, and that he made in his own person a real satisfaction to moral law and to God" (CT 296).
[204] CT, 288.
[205] CT, 288.
[206] CT, 291. Robinson protests against distinguishing between justice and mercy as if the divine nature were divided against itself. "God is always justly merciful and mercifully just. The all-inclusive necessity of the atonement is in the infinite perfections of the Divine nature. . . . Every attempt to find an ultimate basis of necessity for an atonement short of the immutable nature of God, leaves unanswered the question, why a plan of the creation should have been adopted in which that necessity was involved? and no answer can be given which does not . . . bring us to the eternal nature of him whose immutable counsels are what they are because his eternal nature is what it is" (CT, 291).
[207] CT, 292.
[208] CT, 294.

lievers with himself, Christ enables them, through saving faith and the affections he awakens in them, so to bear the penal consequences of their sins that they both survive and escape them.[209]

The efficacy of the atonement is universal, but the specific appropriation of its benefits involves the sovereign grace of God in the lives of men.[210]

In passing from the subject of the provision of redemption to that of the application of redemption, Robinson further discloses the movement of his theology away from orthodox formulations. Justification is attained solely through faith in Christ, but

> the chief point in dispute turns on the relation to Christ into which faith is supposed to bring the believer, and on what it is in that relation which constitutes the real ground of the believer's justification.[211]

Robinson rejects both the Protestant and Roman Catholic views of justification in the interest of the "plain teaching of the New Testament."[212] The Scriptural account of justification consists in "three distinct but inseparable ideas": (1) The interposition of Christ affords those who trust Him assurance of full acquittal from all their offences;[213] (2) Justification involves approval, or restitution to divine favor, of those who trust Christ; (3) Justification involves a personal fitness to be justified, for Christ's redemption takes effect in our personal justification "only by the implanting of a germ of personal righteousness."[214] Contrary to the Reformation view that justification is basically a change of attitude in God rather than a moral change in the sinner, Robinson insists that justification must be viewed "not only as God's act *for* man, but also God's act *in* man."[215] Both the objective work of Christ and subjective moral renewal are involved; man cannot attain personal righteousness by his own unaided effort. Hence

---

[209]CT, 294.
[210]CT, 296.
[211]CT, 297.
[212]CT, 299. Strong declared that as he had been unable to find in Robinson's view of the atonement in its relation to God "more than a metaphorical execution of the justice which the atonement is supposed to satisfy, so . . . (in) his view of the atonement in its relation to man, I am unable to find . . . any other than a metaphorical bearing of the penalty of human sin on the part of Christ, or any other than a metaphorical redemption of those who put their trust in him" (Art. [1896], 196).
[213]CT, 300. Note the subjectivistic note also found here: "In Christ, man finds himself pardoned—his sense of guilt removed."
[214]CT, 300. "It is Christ alone that saves us; our justification is solely on his account; metaphorically expressed, his righteousness is imputed to us, and through faith in him and in his sacrifice of himself for us, we are accounted righteous; but the literal fact is, that our relation to him as a living personal Saviour imparts to us a new religious life and a personal righteousness, without which salvation is impossible, and which in reality are the constituent elements of the salvation itself" (CT, 299).
[215]CT, 300. Protestant theologians had denied that justification had any subjective element, or that it included the beginning of a holy character, to make clear that justification was completely an act of grace, without works. They had insisted that justification is accompanied by a process of sanctification as a concomitant, but refused to merge the two in any way. Robinson indeed sometimes used this same terminology, speaking of personal righteousness as a concomitant of justification, but again he declared uncompromisingly that justification includes a moral change by which the justified become personally just. Strong commented that "in Dr. Robinson's system . . . it was necessary that there should be no merely external acts

it is one-sided to see nothing but the unconditional act of justification on Christ's account,[216] for actual justification is always accompanied by actual regeneration. God does not justify the ungodly in their ungodliness, but only in a simultaneous moral change.[217] None of the series of divine acts and human states—effectual calling, regeneration, repentance, faith, and so forth—can exist disconnectedly from the others; they are parts of an organic whole from which the renewed man may be variously contemplated.[218]

The Scriptures indubitably teach that in becoming Christians men are moved and transformed by the Divine Will, or the fact of election.[219] God sovereignly used efficacious grace in the salvation of a portion of mankind in contradistinction from all humanity. But both Scripture and conscience assure men that their damnation is their own fault. Reprobation, or absolute predestination to damnation, is "neither a sequence of the doctrine of election or the teaching of the Scriptures."[220]

By the word regeneration, the Scriptures emphasize that man in becoming a Christian undergoes a radical moral change.[221] No satisfactory psychological explanation of this change is possible, for it can be known only in its fruits, and the action of the will, from which these are derived, is the most insoluble of all psychological problems.[222] But Scripture and experience make clear that regeneration is a divinely wrought change of the moral affections so great as to constitute a new man, a creature whose moral aims are reversed.[223] Conversion is oft repeated, and hence is more synonymous with repentance than with regeneration.[224] God is the author of the regenerative change, which is rather the impartation of a germin-

---

of God, no judicial decisions apart from the beings upon whom they terminated. To him justification was a mere legal fiction. . . . Our relation to Christ, which, so far as I can see, is only an external relation of gratitude, sympathy and love, imparts to us a new religious life and a personal righteousness, which together make up the idea of salvation" (CT, 198-199).

[216]CT, 301. "The Catholic confounds the accompanying effect with the procuring cause; the unguarded Protestant honors the cause to the exclusion of the effect," Robinson complains (CT, 301). Protestant orthodoxy, he suggested, makes justification and sanctification chronologically separate and causally distinct.

[217]CT, 305. Strong saw this intimation that the exercise of will in faith is somehow the germ of personal righteousness or the faint beginning of a new obedience of our own—rather than merely the surrender of an empty soul to Christ—as "a subtle doctrine of salvation by works" (Art. [1896], 200).

[218]CT, 307.

[219]CT, 311.

[220]CT, 313.

[221]CT, 318. Strong expressed relief that Robinson's doctrine of regeneration "is so markedly able and Scriptural" (Art. [1896], 199), ascribing the new life to the Holy Spirit. Here the tendency to make regeneration a part of justification, in making the sinner's acceptance with God depend upon some beginnings of subjective righteousness, is not further worked out by Robinson. But to view justification and righteousness as the same thing from two different viewpoints, remarked Strong, "made dangerous concessions to Romanism, and paved the way for all manner of sacramental and High Church theories of Christianity" (Art. [1896], 199).

[222]CT, 320. Robinson protested against Hodge's view that regeneration involves, by immediate and absolute divine creation, the origination of "the principle of the spirit of life" just as literally as the commencement of the principle of natural life (Hodge, ST, II, 701).

[223]CT, 320. It should be recalled that the 1872 edition of CT stopped with the treatment of Regeneration.

[224]CT, 321.

ally absolute character, or of organic force which ultimately reconstructs a man's character, than the divine giving to man of a change of character.[225]

While regeneration involves a direct influence of the Holy Spirit on the heart of man, the Spirit makes use of the instrumentality of truth, and inclines him to obey the truth.[226] Regeneration viewed from the side of conversion may be tested by the evidence of a delight in the personal character, blessedness and pursuits of a Christian.[227]

Repentance and faith are inseparable from regeneration.[228] Repentance involves both a grief toward sin and an active trust in Christ.[229] Faith involves assent of the intellect to the divine declarations and consent of the heart to all divine requirements.[230] Saving faith is neither mere historical faith, or belief in historical facts, nor is it full assurance.[231] Saving faith involves the element of will, for a faith which does not issue in radical transformation will not justify.[232] Saving grace brings us into a personal union with Christ.[233]

Sanctification differs from justification only in degree.[234] Sanctification is the nurturing into fruitage of the germ of a new life implanted in the twofold but inseparable act of justification and regeneration. The denial that perfection, or absolute holiness, is attainable, should not involve a lowering beyond warrant of the true ideal of Christian character.[235]

---

[225] CT, 322. Robinson tended to empty the New Testament figures of more content than many theologians: "The metaphorical terms which designate the act itself, such as regeneration, renewal, recreation, distinctly declare the change to be wrought by some power outside of man's own will. The changed man is said to have been born again, ... raised from the dead, ... renewed, ... created anew. ... These are figures of speech which, if language has meaning, must denote the putting forth upon man of a controlling power from without and above" (CT, 323). Strong wrote: "The idea of the believer's spiritual union with the Redeemer had no special chapter given to it in Dr. Robinson's system. He did not believe in what is commonly called the mystical union, and he regarded the parable of the vine and the branches as an Orientalism. The real truth was the influence of Christ *upon* us. Our union with Christ is a union of sympathy, of gratitude, of love. The term 'union,' like the term 'substitution,' is a figure of speech which expresses the result in us of his work *for us*" (Art. [1896], 195).

[226] CT, 324.

[227] CT, 327.

[228] CT, 327.

[229] CT, 328-329.

[230] CT, 331. This precluded the possibility of infant baptism, which Robinson called "a rag of Romanism."

[231] CT, 333.

[232] CT, 335.

[233] CT, 339. Robinson developed this in two sentences: "The often recurring phrase, ... and its correlative, 'Christ in us,' cannot be satisfactorily explained by the interpretation which makes them to consist in the mere influence of truth. Such explanation does not accord with the intimacy of relationship between Christ and his disciples so often dwelt upon and so variously illustrated by Christ and the apostles" (CT, 339). But Strong was hardly satisfied with this. "I wish," he remarked, "that (the) thought of the will in faith, as not only seeing, but appropriating the personal Saviour, had led Dr. Robinson to the more spiritual conception of that union with Christ of which faith is the medium" (Art. [1896], 200).

[234] Robinson held, contrary to Reformation theology, that justification includes "a conception of a divinely provided condition of spiritual renewal, a *making* just" (CT, 340).

[235] CT, 341, 342.

Robinson held an essentially Baptist view of the Church.[236] The Church's central purpose is to proclaim the gospel and to win men to Christ, not directly to suppress vice or to regenerate society. Its aim is basically religious and spiritual, not moral and social. Baptism and the Lord's Supper are ordinances for believers, and the latter is for baptized Christians who are members of the local church. Yet Robinson decried a divisive churchism or sectarianism among Christians.

Christ is portrayed in Scripture as king no less than prophet and priest.[237] An intimate and indissoluble connection exists between the church of Christ and the kingdom of God; the church is the only visible exhibition of the kingdom.[238]

(4) *Eschatology*

The notes on eschatology in Robinson's volume of theology are mere outlines of his thought. But he emphasizes how dependent the doctrine of future events is upon Biblical revelation.[239] Christianity discloses the divine purpose of a consummation. The doctrines of eschatology rest on Scripture alone and, since they are prospective, create the possibility of some diversity of view.

Physical death, or separation of the soul from the body, comes to the believer in Christ as a transition to a higher state, whereas for the unbeliever it concludes hope and is the consummation of evil. The soul is ushered immediately, consciously, and irrevocably, according to the Scriptures, into a state of blessedness or woe.[240]

The divine consummation centers in the personal and permanent appearance of Jesus Christ, but it is almost impossible fully to interpret the prophecies relating thereto until after their fulfillment.[241] The great unanimity among theologians regarding the fact of the final personal return of Christ, coupled with great diversity regarding its preliminaries and adjuncts, are understandable.[242] At most it can be confidently affirmed that before Christ's personal coming the gospel will have achieved its widest and ablest possible results under the dispensation of the Spirit:[243]

---

[236]No notes on the subject are included in CT, but Strong reproduced the essence of notes dictated to students in Robinson's classes (Art. [1896], 201-202) and this paragraph rests upon that material. Robinson taught also Church Polity and Pastoral Theology as well as Systematic Theology. Three of his contributions relating to Ecclesiology have been printed, viz.: "The Relation of the Bible to the Church," *Madison Avenue Lectures*, pp. 387-419 (American Baptist Publication Society), also revised and reissued as a pamphlet; "Ritualism in the Church of England," *Baptist Quarterly*, Jan., 1869; *Yale Lectures on Preachcing* (Henry Holt & Co., 1883).
[237]CT, 342.
[238]CT, 343.
[239]CT, 344.
[240]Strong apparently had access to later notes, in which Robinson spoke more guardedly of personal immortality, while not denying the possibility of bodiless existence in the intermediate state (Art. [1896], 203).
[241]CT, 347.
[242]CT, 348.
[243]CT, 348. Strong remarked that Robinson held that premillennialism and detailed prophetic prediction "stultifies the system and scheme of Christianity. . . . To depend for the progress of the Church upon Christ's visible and literal return is to discredit the dispensation and power of the Holy Spirit, which Christ himself declared to be better for the Church than his own bodily presence would be" (Art. [1896], 203).

the Jewish nation will partake of the blessings of Christianity, which will come into a deadly, final conflict with false religion and secularism, and then Christ will appear suddenly and unexpectedly, followed by a simultaneous resurrection of righteous and wicked dead, the instantaneous translation of the living, and a final and irrevocable dismission of righteous and wicked to their eternal state.

The resurrection of the dead is to be accomplished by supernatural intervention. The resurrection bodies are not necessarily constructed out of the identical particles of matter which previously composed the human body; only the individuality or personal identity need be preserved.[244]

The last judgment involves a formal, visible, and universally recognized adjudication of the two great divisions of the race to their opposite destinies, but conscience will cooperate to necessitate and sanction that final discrimination.[245]

The redeemed are promised a state of future blessedness and there is "a very good degree of unanimity" in viewing this state as spatially localized, although its location is uncertain.[246] The wicked will be exposed to punishment largely as the natural result of cumulative rebellion, though not to the exclusion of supernaturally inflicted penalties.[247] The Scriptures teach us eternal wretchedness of the wicked. Such eternal punishment does not impugn divine benevolence, for the latter effectively suppresses evil and promotes the good.[248]

IV. STRONG'S 1867 AND 1868 ADDRESSES

After his post-commencement European travels, Strong was ordained to the Baptist ministry at Haverhill, Massachusetts, on August 31, 1861, and served the First Baptist Church there from 1861 to 1865.

That he was called from Haverhill to the scholarly, theologically-minded First Baptist Church of Cleveland, widely known as "the Rockefeller church," which he served until his call to Rochester Theological Seminary in 1872, is itself an indication of Strong's erudite pulpit ability.

But this is not the only suggestion preserved to us from those years, to indicate that Strong had interacted constantly and effectively with philosophical and scientific interests bearing upon the Christian message. Two addresses, titled respectively "Science and Religion" and "Philosophy and Religion," and delivered in 1867 and 1868, appear in a later collec-

---

[244]CT, 349. Robinson denied that judgment is confined to the future; there is a future culmination of the judicial process. But judgment began with the first advent, and has continued in successive manifestations of power and grace.

[245]CT, 350.

[246]CT, 350. Strong apparently referred to class statements not included in CT when he represented Robinson as having taught that believers are not suddenly perfected at death in passing into the presence of Christ. "There is no intimation of that sudden transformation at the hour of dissolution which is commonly supposed. No sinners can go there, but men may enter there who still possess defects (in the sense of incompletenesses) of character" which may be gradually removed (Art. [1896], 205).

[247]CT, 351. Moral penalty is grounded in the moral constitution of the universe, so that punishment is essentially subjective, and not merely an objective judicial infliction.

[248]CT, 352.

tion of forty-nine of Strong's addresses and sermons, issued in 1888 under the title of the second of these addresses, *Philosophy and Religion*.[249]

1. Address on "Science and Religion"

Strong's address on "Science and Religion" was delivered February 18, 1867, at the commencement of the Medical College of Cleveland, Ohio, where he cautioned his hearers that medicine shares with all pursuits of natural science "the common danger of forgetting those spiritual facts which give to its conclusions all their validity and significance."[250] Despite the tendency of scientists to be "practical unbelievers in anything but nature," mental and spiritual facts are as demonstrable as visible and material facts, though by another kind of evidence, Strong urged.

The address developed the proposition: that no system of thought merits the name of true science which "does not recognize the existence and importance of a realm of metaphysical, moral and spiritual truth, side by side with the great fields of physical inquiry."[251] Of particular interest, for this dissertation, is Strong's plea for balance with regard to the physical and psychical, as against the philosophic movements to the so-called extremes of naturalism or spiritualism:

Idealism and Materialism have alternately held sway, and the world, in the heat of controversy between them, has forgotten that the rounded globe of truth must have two poles, not one. There is truth in both, but either taken singly is false by defect.... The fatal tendency to merge matter in mind or mind in matter, and so convert the universe into one substance, can only be counteracted by a study of both.... Nature ... is different from mind or God.[252]

Strong's hostility to idealism derived mainly from the conviction that it led inevitably to pantheism.[253] Between a view which made everything nature and one that made everything God, Strong found little to choose.

The same address indicated a receptivity to evolution which, curiously, appears somewhat modified in Strong's initial theology lectures almost a decade later. Evolution, he declared, is but a mode of divine action; rather than conflicting with the argument from design, it affords "a new illustration of it,—a method of securing a result, and so the latest and best proof of a designing God."[254] The created world is pliable in God's hands,

---

[249] Referred to hereafter as PAR. In this volume, the introductory address is "Philosophy and Religion" and the second, "Science and Religion," although they were delivered in reverse order.

[250] PAR, 19.

[251] PAR, 20.

[252] PAR, 23. Strong employed terminology found frequently in his later writings with but slight variation of expression, but which is here used in support of a non-mental view of nature, e.g., "Nature is but the manifestation of God, and the laws of nature are only the fixed methods of His working. He orders and governs the universe, not for its own sake, but for the revelation of Himself" (PAR, 29).

[253] Strong's mode of argument against pantheism suggests that an idealism (like personalism) which provides for human responsibility and the possibility of moral failure by man's relative independence, would circumvent his main objections. His constant assumption appears to be that only realism avoids losing human freedom and responsibility in God. But while opposing monism of any kind, he insisted that "nature must be interpreted by our knowledge of mind" (PAR, 24) and that "personal will" affords "the only key to the interpretation of nature" (PAR, 25).

[254] PAR, 28.

Strong urged, and so miracles are possible.[255] If a sufficient end is to be gained by their performance, an end such as "the authentication of that very revelation which nature makes only imperfectly,"[256] the possibility is converted into a natural probability. Faith is acceptance of the testimony of almighty God "on evidence as accessible and as valid as that on which we accept the reality of outward phenomena."[257]

2. Address on "Philosophy and Religion"

The address on "Philosophy and Religion" was delivered May 20, 1868, before the alumni of Rochester Theological Seminary, and was subsequently published in the *Baptist Quarterly*, prior to inclusion in the volume of addresses, essay and sermons. It may be questioned whether Strong anywhere gave philosophy broader rights against religion than in this address.

Religion, as a scientific system, affirmed Strong, rests upon a basis of philosophy. For the mind "cannot content itself with theology proper," not alone because it seeks a systematic statement of its beliefs but because "it desires to know what are the proofs of revelation, and what are the evidences that a God exists from whom a revelation might come."[258]

Moreover, Strong assigned to philosophy the service of "defining and correlating the great primary conceptions of religion."[259] Theology's

doctrine of the will, and her determination of the limits of the human faculties, her application of realism to the unity of the race, and her theory of the true end of being, must all be ultimately given her by the prior philosophy with which she sets out in her investigations. Both in her account of the universe and in her account of God, theology is obliged to combine with the facts of revelation the facts of consciousness, since only through consciousness have we any personal knowledge of either.[260]

Theology, furthermore, received its status as a science, through the logical impetus of Aristotle.[261] But theology has its debt not alone to ancient philosophers, but to moderns like Bishop Butler, with his doctrine of the supremacy of conscience in the moral constitution of man; Coleridge, with his splendid but incomplete spiritual philosophy in opposition to German Pantheism; and Jonathan Edwards, with his enthronement of love as the central emphasis in a Calvinistic view of creation.[262]

---

[255] PAR, 29.
[256] PAR, 30.
[257] PAR, 30.
[258] PAR, 3. "Philosophy is the science of foundation," Strong stated. "It busies itself with the examination of the grounds of faith. It seeks to determine whether religion has a safe basis and support in the facts of consciousness" (PAR, 3).
[259] PAR, 3.
[260] PAR, 3. Strong stressed the abstract approach which philosophy makes to the concrete revelational ideas of God, providence, liberty, virtue, conscience. Philosophy analyze these, and reconciles them with the remaining facts of our mental constitution and with our observation of nature (PAR, 3).
[261] "Have you ever reflected upon the remarkable difference in form that exists between Augustine and Calvin? . . . And to what shall we attribute this advance? To nothing more or less than the influence of that Aristotle, whom Luther called 'an accursed, mischief-making heathen.' It was the study of Aristotle which first made theology a science, and rendered possible a Calvin. . . . Take away the influence of Plato and Aristotle, and you put a scientific theology where John of Damascus found it eleven centuries ago" (PAR, 4).
[262] PAR, 4-5.

But philosophy and religion share a common danger in the tendency to extremes. Theology has swung to extremes between an emphasis on divine sovereignty and human freedom, which are true but "logically irreconcilable" factors, and philosophy has swung to extremes touching the duality of matter and spirit.[263]

Strong's uncompromising hostility to metaphysical monism, invariably equated with pantheism in this period of his thought, is seen from the warning that

any theory of philosophy which is based upon a monistic hypothesis, and which denies the facts of either matter or mind, must exert a deadly influence upon theology and religion. The ultimate conclusion must be that God is the universe or that the universe is God—in other words, there is no God separate from the soul or the world.[264]

At the same time, Strong attacked "the new philosophy of Nescience" inspired by Comte, as denying the direct intuitions of human consciousness in such a way as consistently to make all science impossible:

Unless the primitive beliefs of substance, resemblance, power, which are a part of the original endowment of the mind, and which flash out from latency into living energy the moment we are brought in contact with the phenomena of the outer world . . . all science is forever impossible.[265]

Such a view, Strong protested, tears up philosophy by the roots, and "Religion must share the fate of philosophy."[266]

Essential to the perfect triumph of religion is an "impartial philosophy."[267] And a true philosophy "must be one of God's chosen weapons for subduing the world to Christ" if the triumph of Christianity is to be accomplished "in accordance with the common laws of mind."[268] The philosophic trend happily had already championed an inductive method which "begins with the fundamental facts of consciousness—the intuitive knowledge of matter, of mind, of God, and of each as distinct and differing in nature from the others."[269] The door must not be left ajar "for a subtle Idealism."[270] The clearness and power of man's intuitive knowledge of God may be "dimmed and blunted" by sin, but

still the fact remains that an intuitive knowledge of God, distorted, blunted, overlaid with a thousand superstitious fancies though it be, belongs to man as man, revealing itself in his consciousness of the Infinite around him and in his fears of the judgment before him.[271]

---

[263] PAR, 6. "In the precise proportion to which the view of mind leans to one or the other extreme," Strong remarked, "will the religious thinking of the individual and the age lean towards Materialism or Pantheism" (PAR, 7).

[264] PAR, 7.

[265] PAR, 9-10. Strong here attacked Comte's thesis that we know nothing but the phenomena of matter, and that mind lies wholly out of reach of direct observation, by the emphasis that no experience at all is possible, but for a mental potency which is prior to all experience.

[266] PAR, 13.
[267] PAR, 14.
[268] PAR, 14.
[269] PAR, 16.
[270] PAR, 16.
[271] PAR, 16.

This intuition is awakened into living power, and the soul restored to actual communion with God, by the coming of Christ.[272] The establishment of this intuition upon a scientific basis is "the test and the goal of a true philosophy."[273]

It is clear from a study of these addresses delivered by Strong in 1867 and 1868, that he resisted metaphysical monism of an idealistic no less than a materialistic sort, on the ground that the former led invariably to pantheism; that he was receptive to the view of theistic evolution, as long as the miraculous was not precluded; that he gave to philosophy broad rights as against theology—rights so broad, indeed, that it is difficult to see how, at the same time, the revelational view of God could be made a true philosophy's test and goal.

V. THE INITIAL THEOLOGY TAUGHT BY STRONG

Strong returned to the classroom, this time as teacher rather than as student, in 1872, and behind him in Christian experience there stood a decade of Baptist pastoral effort, and three strands of theological statement which, while insisting on the main doctrines of an evangelical view, yet included various shades of departure from the current orthodoxy. His divinity studies had centered, in the first place, in a commitment to an essentially Calvinistic, rather than Arminian, theology. But his studies with Robinson, while orthodox in the main, afforded both an orientation to the rising liberal thought, as well as, in certain significant respects, an occasion of compromise with it, and an incentive to state his own position in clearer affinity to or contrast with the prevailing competitive influences of the day.[274]

Doubtless the compromise elements in Robinson's thought were not as conspicuous, because not as carefully worked out, when Strong studied under him. But before Robinson left the divinity lecture room, Strong later stated, he

probably taught in the Rochester Theological Seminary a more modern system than was at that time taught in any other evangelical Seminary of any denomination whatever.... I find myself impressed anew with the boldness and independence of his views, but also with the fact that he represented consciously or unconsciously a great movement of human thought, a movement of which the Ritschlian School in Germany and the New Theology of this country are later types and manifestations.[275]

Yet it should be recalled that, with the commencement of his teaching duties, Strong deliberately turned aside from employing Robinson's theology notes, just then published, in order to overcome a complete

---

[272]PAR, 17.
[273]PAR, 17.
[274]It should be recalled also that, as Strong looked back two decades later, he recalled early impulses toward monism in Robinson's teaching that the Scriptures do not indubitably teach the absolute origination of matter, and his dissatisfaction with the Scholastic doctrine of *concursus*.
[275]Art. (1896), 206.

dependence upon the revered teacher from whom he had first studied systematic theology. Strong candidly related:

> When I began . . . as . . . successor, . . . I knew that my ways of theological thinking had been largely shaped by him. I feared, if I made use of his recently printed notes, that I should become a copyist. I resolved, therefore, to construct my own system *de novo*, without once looking at what my former teacher had written.[276]

1. The 1876 Lectures

For this reason alone, Strong's *Lectures on Theology*,[277] which appeared in 1876, hold no little historical interest.[278] The early theology of Strong was essentially evangelical, and the differences with Robinson were almost all in the direction of a more traditional and orthodox statement. There is no indication of any interest in the newer philosophies of divine immanence, and the lecture notes and reading references are without reference to Lotze.[279] It will not be necessary to give a comprehensive summary of Strong's views, but only to set forth in main outline his doctrinal insistences.

(1) *Prolegomena*

Theology was defined by Strong as "the science of God and of the relations between God and the universe."[280]

The sources of theology are natural theology and its supplement, the Scriptures.[281]

(2) *The Existence of God*

The existence of God is a first truth,[282] not derived from but developed upon the occasion of observation and reflection.[283] The Scriptures therefore attempt no proof of God's existence, but assume and declare the universality of that knowledge.[284] The intuitive knowledge of God may be confirmed and explicated by arguments from general revelation.[285] Such arguments are

---

[276]Art. (1896), 167-168.
[277]Referred to hereafter simply as LOT.
[278]The writer possesses a copy of LOT interleaved for student notes. A prefatory note affirms that "These lectures are printed, not published." The fly-leaf bears the legend of a Rochester student, "A. S. Carman, Sept. 1882-R.T.S.-'85", so that the fading but legible inked notes serve to show later modifications in Strong's thought. Carman later became a professor and his son, Prof. E. A. Carman, presented the father's text to the writer.
[279]There are perhaps a half-dozen references to Bowne's *Review of H. Spencer*, so that the limited interest in philosophical idealism appears rather along epistemological than ontological lines.
[280]LOT, 1. There was on contrastive reference to Robinson's metaphysical reserve. The possibility of theology, declared Strong, is lodged in (1) The existence of a God who has relations to the universe; (2) The capacity of the human mind for knowing God and certain of these relations; (3) God's actual revelation of himself and certain of these relations (LOT, 2-5). Strong pressed the case against Sir William Hamilton and Herbert Spencer.
[281]LOT, 9. Strong therefore was not adverse to the possibility of developing general revelation into a positive but incomplete theism.
[282]LOT, 17.
[283]LOT, 18.
[284]LOT, 21.
[285]LOT, 22.

probable, not demonstrative, but taken together furnish moral certainty.[286] The cosmological argument proves "some cause of the universe indefinitely great."[287] The teleological argument proves "an intelligence adequate to (the) contrivance" of the present harmony of the universe, but cannot assure us "whether this intelligence is creator or only fashioner, personal or impersonal, one or many, finite or infinite, eternal or owing its being to another."[288] The moral argument assures a personal, ethical Being who is the "proper object of supreme affection and service," but cannot prove God's creatorship, infinity, or mercy.[289] Strong assigned the moral argument "chief place" because it adds to the other evidences the "far wider ideas of personality and righteous lordship."[290] The ontological argument Strong dismissed as confounding ideal and real existence.[291]

Strong seemed to waver as to the cumulative value of the empirical proofs, however. On the one hand, he declared that the existence of "a Being indefinitely great, a personal Cause, Contriver and Lawgiver," had been "proved" by the arguments;[292] on the other, that "as a logical process this is indeed defective, since all logic as well as all observation depends for its validity upon the presupposed existence of God"[293] and that the bridge to God can be made only upon the assumption that "our abstract ideas of infinity and perfection are to be applied to the Being to whom argument has actually conducted us."[294] What is significant here is that, although Strong presents a revelational theology, the case for God is settled without any appeal to the significance of special revelation at this juncture. It is not that Strong denied that special revelation is required as a corrective, in view of man's sin, but that he appeared to construct the argument for the existence of God without any appeal to special divine disclosure.

Any correct interpretation of the universe must postulate, declared Strong, an intuitive knowledge of the external world, of the self, and of God.[295] But these three factors cannot be reduced to one, as materialism, idealism, or pantheism would do.[296]

---

[286] Strong's words are: "They together furnish a corroboration of our primitive conviction of God's existence, which is of great practical value, and is in itself sufficient to bind the moral action of men" (LOT, 23).
[287] LOT, 23.
[288] LOT, 25.
[289] LOT, 26.
[290] LOT, 26.
[291] LOT, 27.
[292] Since, he added, the law of parsimony requires that the conclusions be applied to one Being, not to many (LOT, 27).
[293] In an address titled "Scientific Theism" (PAR, 75-89), read before "The Club" in Rochester on February 16, 1875, Strong presented his most closely worked statement of the evidences for God. He rested his case especially on the conviction that God is the logical presupposition of any knowledge at all: "To all arguments for the existence of God, we have a still more radical objection to urge, namely that all reasoning presupposes the existence of God as its logical condition and foundation. Not only . . . the trustworthiness of the simplest mental acts . . . but the more complex processes, such as induction and deduction, can be relied upon only by supposing a thinking Deity, who has made the various parts of the universe to correspond to each other and to the investigating faculties of man" (PAR, 85).
[294] LOT, 27.

(3) *The Scriptures a Revelation from God*

The appeal to divine revelation is made by Strong, on the ground of both a psychological and historical need for it.[297] There is a presumption that this need will be met in view of "what we know of God by nature."[298]

Divine revelation is attested by miracles and prophecy.

Miracles contravene no laws of nature, but those laws cannot explain them, for miracles are produced by God's immediate agency for a religious purpose.[299] Miracles draw attention to new truth and cease when that truth has gained foothold.[300] They certify to doctrinal truth only indirectly; directly they attest the divine commission and authority of a religious teacher.[301]

Purity of life and doctrine, however, must go with the miracles to assure divine commission; miracles and doctrine support each other, and internal evidence may have greater power than external over some minds and ages. Still, the miracles do not lose their value as evidences; the authority of Christ as teacher rests upon his miracles, specifically the resurrection.[302]

Prophecy proceeds from divine knowledge to attest revelation, as miracles proceed from divine power.[303] But, like miracle, prophecy is a corroborative evidence which does not stand alone; it unites with miracle to prove the divine commission and authority of a teacher.[304]

---

[295] LOT, 28.
[296] LOT, 28. Strong had contributed an essay to the October 2, 1873, issue of *The Examiner*, under the topic of "Materialistic Skepticism" (PAR, 31-38), in which he viewed the mechanical philosophies as a natural reaction from the transcendental idealism of Hegel which had "threatened to sweep away the faith of the world" (PAR, 31). He seized on the emphasis of the later materialism that reality must be interpreted in terms both of matter and force, while regarding force as an inseparable property of matter, since "to make it a separate and independent existence would be, for the materialist, to give up the theory of matter as a cause, and to make shipwreck of his materialism" (PAR, 33). Strong urged that, because of the harmonious working of nature toward useful ends, a force both immaterial and mental must be postulated (PAR, 33), an interesting circumstance in view of Strong's later contention that matter is idea plus will. To this he added the arguments from the organization of nature and from the intuition of the priority of mind.
[297] LOT, 31.
[298] LOT, 31. Strong's argument here was curiously circular. Since God made man a spiritual being for spiritual ends, the means to secure these ends might be expected. Since God had begun an incompleted revelation, He may be expected to complete it (by special revelation?). Since other wants are supplied, it is unlikely that the highest want would be unsupplied (would man want a special revelation apart from knowledge of its possibility?). The signs of a reparative goodness in nature and history suggest a likelihood of revelation (do they suggest mercy?). The further appeal to expectations in view of other communications of divine truth in general revelation would seem to rule out, rather than to encourage, as Strong thought, the expectation of a once-for-all disclosure.
[299] LOT, 33.
[300] LOT, 35.
[301] LOT, 35.
[302] LOT, 35.
[303] LOT, 36.
[304] LOT, 37. Strong does not seem to have given any clearly worked out statement of the relationship between the compulsion of truth and miracle in the introduction of new doctrine. This difficulty was noted also in Robinson.

Strong considered it from the first to be a part of systematic theology to discuss the genuineness of the books of the Bible, and the credibility of the writers, and established this along thoroughly conservative views of authorship.[305] The supernatural character of the Scriptures is supported by their unity, their meeting of human needs, the moral system of the New Testament, the person and character of Christ, and the historical results of the proclamation of Christianity.[306]

A special divine influence was exerted upon the Scripture writers so that their productions constitute "an infallible and sufficient rule of faith and practice."[397] Inspiration has as its end result a trustworthy record. It is supernatural, plenary, and dynamical as opposed to mechanical.[308] They are a joint divine-human production incorporating the personal peculiarities of the writers.[309] The precise words were not generally communicated to them, but the thoughts were; inspiration is verbal as to result, but not as to method.[310] If errors in secular matters were proved, this would not overthrow the doctrine of inspiration,[311] but in fact no scientific or historical or moral errors exist.[312]

(4) *The Nature, Decrees and Works of God*

The works of God form a natural transition to a study of the attributes and essence of God.[313] The attributes are not merely subjective distinctions, but have an objective existence.[314] The attributes inhere in the divine essence, but the essence is known only as manifested through the attributes.[315]

Strong divided the attributes into absolute and immanent; the former belonging to God's nature independently of His connection with the universe, and the latter being involved in His relations to creation.[316] The absolute attributes are spirituality (holiness, love, truth) and infinity (self-existence, immutability, unity). The relative attributes are those related to time and space (eternity, immensity), to creation (omnipresence, omniscience, omnipotence), and to moral beings (justice, goodness, mercy). The predominant appeal, in establishing these attributes, is to the Scriptures,

---

[305]LOT, 39-45.
[306]LOT, 45-49.
[307]LOT, 50.
[308]LOT, 53.
[309]LOT, 53.
[310]LOT, 54.
[311]"It would only compel us to give a larger place to the human element in the composition of the Scriptures, and to regard them more exclusively as a text-book of religion" (LOT, 55).
[312]LOT, 55-57.
[313]It should be noted that Strong, like Robinson before him, fluctuated in an appeal to philosophical and revelational considerations. Strong remarked, however, that the rational method (via negationis, via eminentiae, and via causalitatis) "is valuable (but) it has insuperable difficulties and its place is a subordinate one. While we use it continually to confirm and supplement results otherwise obtained, our chief means of determining the divine attributes must be the Biblical method" (LOT, 62).
[314]Robinson, it will be recalled, held metaphysical reservations at this point.
[315]LOT, 61. Strong thus held a realist rather than an idealist view of the relation of attributes and substance.
[316]LOT, 62.

although a philosophical justification is sometimes also given.³¹⁷ God's nature is not subject to time, and to him, past, present and future are "one eternal now," not as being indistinguishable, but in the sense that God sees past and future as vividly as the present.³¹⁸ God's mercy is that eternal principal of His nature which "leads him to seek the temporal good and eternal salvation of those who have opposed themselves to his will, even at the cost of infinite self-sacrifice."³¹⁹

The fundamental divine attribute is holiness.³²⁰ The divine justice and mercy are reconciled in the salvation of sinful men only by the substitutionary death of the God-man.³²¹ The ground of moral obligation is the moral perfection of the divine nature.³²²

The tripersonality of God is exclusively a truth of revelation.³²³ This triunity is not merely economic and temporal, but is immanent and eternal.³²⁴ The terms "generation" and "procession" as applied to the Son and to the Holy Spirit only approximate the truth, and the impressions gained from them are to be corrected by the whole tenor of Scripture.³²⁵ While the mode of divine triunity is unrevealed and inscrutable, the doctrine contains no self-contradictory elements, and furnishes a principle of connection between all other Christian doctrines.³²⁶

God's eternal plan has rendered certain all events of the universe, past, present and future.³²⁷ The decrees are consistent with the free agency of man.³²⁸ They do not make God the author of sin, but of free agents who sin.³²⁹

The universe is a voluntary *ex nihilo* creation.³³⁰ The Mosaic account recognizes an original creation and a subsequent arrangement and de-

---

³¹⁷Strong argued that "reason teaches no change is possible in God" (LOT, 66) and that "the notion of two or more Gods is self-contradictory; since each limits the other and destroys his Godhead. . . . It is unphilosophical, moreover, to assume the existence of two or more Gods when one will explain all the facts" (LOT, 67).
³¹⁸LOT, 67.
³¹⁹LOT, 70.
³²⁰This is evidenced, Strong wrote, by the Scriptures, by our own moral constitution, and by the actual dealings of God in terms of penalty and requirement of atonement (LOT, 70).
³²¹LOT, 71.
³²²LOT, 71.
³²³LOT, 72.
³²⁴LOT, 79. The three persons have an undivided essence, Strong stated, in line with the orthodox tradition (LOT, 80). Strong commented that the term "person" is only an approximation of the truth, since it does not imply three essences in the trinity, yet it is the best approximation of the Biblical conception (LOT, 80).
³²⁵LOT, 82.
³²⁶LOT, 84.
³²⁷LOT, 86.
³²⁸LOT, 88.
³²⁹LOT, 90.
³³⁰LOT, 92. Strong deliberately set creation over against the idealistic theories: "If the world be eternal, like God, it must be an efflux from the substance of God and must be absolutely equal with God. Only a proper doctrine of creation can secure God's absolute distinctness from the world and his sovereignty over it. The logical alternative of creation is therefore a system of pantheism, in which God is an impersonal and necessary force. Hence the pantheistic dicta of Fichte: 'The assumption of a creation is the fundamental error of all false metaphysics and false theology'; of Hegel: 'God evolves the world out of himself in order to take it back into himself again in the spirit' " (LOT, 103).

velopment.³³¹ If science should "ultimately render it certain" that all present species were derived by natural descent from a few original germs which evolved from inorganic forces and materials, the Mosaic account "would not therefore be proved untrue."³³² But such derivation has not been demonstrated, and there is no reason for disbelieving that brute and human life were introduced by absolute origination.³³³ The pictorial-summary interpretation, which views the Mosaic account as a rough sketch of the creation history presented in graphic form, is most acceptable.³³⁴

God's supreme end in creation in His glory.³³⁵ The creation necessarily manifests His moral attributes.³³⁶ But we are not justified in assuming that the actual creation was the best possible or the only possible creation.³³⁷

God continually preserves His creation by a positive sustaining agency.³³⁸ But the properties and powers of nature have objective reality:

although matter and mind retain their existence and endowments only by the constant energy of God, second causes are not mere names for the great first cause.³³⁹

There is a natural concurrence of God in all operations of matter and mind so that, while God's will is not the sole force, without His concurrence no being or substance could continue to exist or act.³⁴⁰ The divine efficiency interpenetrates nature and man without absorbing them.³⁴¹ God concurs with evil acts only insofar as they are natural, and not as they are evil, acts.³⁴²

God by a continuous providential agency makes all events of the physical and moral universe fulfill the original design of the creation.³⁴³ Providence extends to particular events.³⁴⁴ Special providence is a type of particular providence which produces an impressive effect upon us,³⁴⁵ contrasted with miracles and works of grace like regeneration which are supernatural acts. God may answer prayer even by changing the sequence of nature.³⁴⁶ But since He is immanent in nature, an answer coming by natural agencies alone is equally a revelation of His personal care.³⁴⁷

The probability of angelic existences, in view of the ascending scale of created intelligences, is turned to certainty by Biblical statement.³⁴⁸ The

---
³³¹LOT, 97.
³³²LOT, 97.
³³³LOT, 98.
³³⁴LOT, 99.
³³⁵LOT, 101.
³³⁶LOT, 102.
³³⁷LOT, 102. Strong remarked: "Since the resources of God's wisdom are infinite, there may have been in the divine mind many possible systems, equally adapted to manifest his glory. We must therefore regard the present creation simply as the act of God's free and sovereign will."
³³⁸LOT, 103.
³³⁹LOT, 103.
³⁴⁰LOT, 103.
³⁴¹LOT, 105.
³⁴²LOT, 106.
³⁴³LOT, 106.
³⁴⁴LOT, 106. The theory of general providence Strong dismissed as "only a form of deism" (LOT, 109).
³⁴⁵LOT, 110.
³⁴⁶LOT, 111.
³⁴⁷LOT, 112.
³⁴⁸LOT, 114.

Scriptures preclude any view of evil except in terms of a personal being of great power who leads an organized opposition to the divine government.[349]

(5) *Anthropology*

The Scriptures negate a purely naturalistic origin of man, yet do not disclose the divine method of creation, whether mediate or immediate.[350] Psychology suggests that what chiefly distinguishes man from the beasts could not have been derived by any natural process of development, and comparative physiology does not preclude a similar view of his body.[351] The human race is descended from a single pair.[352]

The Bible supports a dichotomous view of the essential elements of human nature; man consists of body, and of spirit or soul.[353] The traducian theory of the origin of the soul seems to accord best with Scripture.[354]

Man's original state is disclosed in the Scriptures alone.[355] He was created a personal being, and hence possessed in distinction from the brute self-consciousness, God-consciousness, and self-determination, and also moral likeness to God.[356] Yet his perfection was not final and absolute, but relative and provisional.[357]

Before treating man's apostasy, Strong discussed the nature of divine law,[358] which he designated as a general expression of God's nature, and thus leaves open the possibility of grace, not as abrogating but as republishing and enforcing law.[359]

Sin is lack of conformity to God's moral law, either in act, disposition or state.[360] Ability to fulfill the law is not essential to constitute the non-fulfillment sin.[361]

The essential principle of sin is selfishness, or that choice of self as the end which is antithetic to supreme love of God.[362] Sin is universal in the human race.[363] All men possess a sinful nature, and the Scriptures refer the origin of this nature to our first parents.[364] The Genesis account of man's fall from primal holiness is historical.[365] The consequences of the fall from Adam were physical and spiritual death,[366] and positive and formal exclusion from God's presence.[367]

The transgression of the first parents constituted their posterity sinners, according to the Scriptures, so that Adam's sin is "imputed to every member of the race of which he was the germ and head."[368] Strong declared for a theory of natural headship of Adam, against the Princeton theory of federal headship and the theory of mediate imputation of Adam's sin.[369] He warned, however, that any theory of the method of man's union with Adam

is merely a valuable hypothesis. . . . A central fact is announced in Scripture, which we feel compelled to believe upon divine testimony, even though every attempted ex-

---

[349]LOT, 115.   [354]LOT, 128.   [359]LOT, 139.   [364]LOT, 148.
[350]LOT, 121.   [355]LOT, 130.   [360]LOT, 140.   [365]LOT, 148.
[351]LOT, 121.   [356]LOT, 130.   [361]LOT, 142.   [366]LOT, 150.
[352]LOT, 122.   [357]LOT, 133.   [362]LOT, 144.   [367]LOT, 151.
[353]LOT, 124.   [358]LOT, 137.   [363]LOT, 146.   [368]LOT, 151.

[369]Strong objected that the federal theory made imputation the cause of depravity, and the mediate theory made depravity the cause of imputation, whereas the Biblical account is that all men sinned seminally in Adam (LOT, 155-158).

planation should prove unsatisfactory. That central fact, which constitutes the substance of the Scripture doctrine of original sin, is simply this, that the sin of Adam is the immediate cause and ground of inborn depravity, guilt and condemnation to the whole human race.[370]

Thus mankind has lost original righteousness and has suffered the total depravity of the moral nature,[371] is obligated to render satisfaction to God's justice,[372] and subjected to pain or loss inflicted directly or indirectly in vindication of divine justice.[373] The penalty of sin is physical and spiritual death;[374] if the latter is not reversed before physical death, it passes irreversibly into eternal death.[375] Those who die in infancy are saved because they have not personally transgressed and their racial guilt is atoned for by the death of Christ.[376]

(6) *Soteriology*

The history of the race discloses a providential preparation for the provision of redemption, negatively in heathen history, and positively in the history of Israel.[377]

This redemption was to be effected through a Mediator uniting divine and human natures for purposes of reconciliation.[378] The orthodox view of Jesus Christ was promulgated at Chalcedon.[379] The attributes and powers of both natures are ascribed to the one Christ, and conversely the works and dignities of the one Christ to either nature, thus requiring an organic and indissoluble union of the two natures in a single person.[380] Strong resisted views such as that the divine Logos reduced himself to the condition and limits of human nature,[381] or that the incarnation was progressive and gradual.[382] The union of natures is necessarily inscrutable because without analogy,[383] Christ's human nature is impersonal in that it attained self-consciousness and self-determination only in the personality of the God-man; the Logos furnished the principle of personality.[384] Self-consciousness and self-determination belong to personality, and not to nature as such, and hence Christ has but a single consciousness and a single will, and this consciousness and will is never simply human, but

---

[370]LOT, 159.
[371]LOT, 162.
[372]LOT, 165.
[373]LOT, 167.
[374]LOT, 167-168.
[375]LOT, 168.
[376]LOT, 169.
[377]LOT, 171.
[378]LOT, 172.
[379]LOT, 174.
[380]LOT, 176: "Hence we can say on the one hand, that the God-man existed before Abraham, yet was born in the reign of Augustus Caesar, and that Jesus Christ wept, was weary, suffered, died, yet is the same yesterday, today and forever . . . "
[381]LOT, 177.
[382]LOT, 178.
[383]LOT, 179. "The possibility of the union of deity and humanity in one person," Strong wrote, "is grounded in the original creation of man in the divine image. Man's kinship to God, in other words, his possession of a rational and spiritual image, is the condition of incarnation" (LOT, 179).
[384]LOT, 180.

theanthropic.³⁸⁵ The divine attributes are imparted to the human without passing over into its essence, although this power was only rarely manifested because of the God-man's chosen state of humiliation.³⁸⁶ The union of the two natures in one person, necessary to constitute Jesus Christ a proper mediator between man and God, is indissoluble and eternal.³⁸⁷

The humiliation of Christ consisted in the assumption of a servant-form in which he resigned the independent exercise of the divine attributes, in His submission to the control of the Holy Spirit, and His continuous surrender of the exercise of divine powers so far as His human nature was concerned.³⁸⁸ But in becoming man He did not divest himself of the substance of his Godhead.³⁸⁹ His exaltation consisted in resumption of His independent exercise of divine attributes, in the withdrawal by the Logos of all limitations in the communication of the divine fulness to the human nature of Christ, and in the corresponding exercise on the part of the human nature of those powers which belonged to it by virtue of union with the divine.³⁹⁰ The stages of the exaltation were the quickening and resurrection, and the ascension and sitting on the right hand of God.³⁹¹

Christ's offices are represented in Scripture as threefold: prophetic, priestly and kingly.³⁹²

His prophetic work included teaching, predicting, and miracle-working, and has four stages: the preparatory work of the Logos,³⁹³ His earthly incarnate ministry, His guidance and teaching of the church on earth since the ascension, and His final revelation of the Father to the saints in glory.

His priestly office is fulfilled by His sacrifice and by making intercession.³⁹⁴

The Scriptures represent His sacrificial work as a provision originating in God's love, as an example of disinterested love to secure our deliverance from selfishness, as a ransom paid to free us from the bondage of sin, as a penalty borne in order to rescue the guilty, as an exhibition of God's righteousness, as a substitution, as a sin-offering, as a propitiation, and as a work of priestly meditation which reconciles God to men.³⁹⁵ His atonement was prefigured by the Old Testament sacrificial system.³⁹⁶ Scripture compels us to view the death of Christ as

---

³⁸⁵LOT, 180.
³⁸⁶LOT, 180. Strong added: "As the human Saviour can exercise divine attributes, not in virtue of his humanity alone, but derivatively by virtue of his possession of a divine nature, so the divine Saviour can suffer and be ignorant as man, not in his divine nature, but derivatively by virtue of his possession of a human nature" (LOT, 181).
³⁸⁷LOT, 181.
³⁸⁸LOT, 183.
³⁸⁹LOT, 183.
³⁹⁰LOT, 184.
³⁹¹LOT, 184-185.
³⁹²LOT, 185.
³⁹³"All preliminary religious knowledge, whether within or without the bounds of the chosen people, is from Christ, the revealer of God" (LOT, 185-186).
³⁹⁴LOT, 186.

a vicarious offering, provided by God's love for the purpose of satisfying an internal demand of the divine holiness, and of removing an obstacle in the divine mind to the renewal and pardon of sinners.[397]

But the Anselmic theory conceives the principle which is satisfied in a manner too formal and external, making the divine honor or majesty more prominent than the divine holiness, holds merely to an external transfer of the merit of Christ's work, and does not clearly state the internal ground of that transfer in the believer's union with Christ.[398] In its stead, Strong proposed the "ethical theory" of the atonement, which holds that the necessity of the atonement is grounded in divine holiness,[399] so that the atonement answers the ethical demand of the divine nature that sin be visited with penalty.[400] The atonement is sufficient for all men; it is limited not in extent, but in application to the elect.[401]

The priesthood of Christ did not cease with the atonement, but He fulfills the office of intercession in the presence of God.[402] By this special activity He secures, upon the ground of His sacrifice, whatever temporal or spiritual blessing comes to man.[403]

Christ's kingdom is the sovereignty not of His divine nature, but a sovereignty which He possesses as divine-human Redeemer, and by which He rules all things for the glory of God and for the execution of the divine purpose of salvation.[404]

Strong declared for the sublapsarian as against the supralapsarian order of divine decrees,[405] at the same time inverting (in view of his conviction against limited atonement) the decree to elect some and the decree to provide salvation. Strong's view of the true order, therefore, was: (1) the decree to create; (2) the decree to permit the fall; (3) the decree to provide salvation in Christ sufficient for the needs of all; (4) the decree to elect some.

God's election is that eternal act whereby, in His sovereign pleasure and not on account of foreseen merit, He chooses certain sinful men to receive special grace and be made voluntary partakers of Christ's election.[406] This involves no injustice, for the unsaved suffer only the due

---

[395] LOT, 186-187.
[396] LOT, 187-189.
[397] LOT, 189.
[398] LOT, 194.
[399] There is no doubt, however, that most contemporary statements of Anselm's satisfaction theory took this view also. Strong later acknowledged that Thomas Aquinas had supplemented the Anselmic theory in this regard (*Summa*, III, 8).
[400] LOT, 194-195. Strong held that the ethical theory escapes the objection made against "a merely commercial view of the Atonement," that satisfaction and forgiveness are mutually exclusive. "Since it is not a third party but the Judge himself who makes satisfaction to his own violated holiness, forgiveness is still optional, and may be offered upon terms agreeable to himself" (LOT, 197).
[401] LOT, 196.
[402] LOT, 198.
[403] LOT, 198.
[404] LOT, 199. He upholds the universe by a kingdom of power, the militant church in a kingdom of grace, and ultimately the church triumphant as a kingdom of glory, Strong wrote.
[405] LOT, 200.
[406] LOT, 201.

reward of their deeds;[407] nor is it arbitrary, but is the free choice of a wise and sovereign will.[408] The Scriptures distinguish between a general, external call to all men, and a special, efficacious call of the Spirit to the elect.[409] Regeneration is the divine act which, through the truth as a means, makes holy the governing disposition of the soul.[410] The Holy Spirit is the immediate agent.[411] Regeneration is wrought in conjunction with the presentation of truth to the intellect.[412] The change is instantaneous, in a region of the soul below consciousness, and hence known only in its results.[413] Conversion is a voluntary change by which the sinner turns from sin to Christ; the turning from sin is repentance, the turning to Christ is faith.[414] Repentance has intellectual, emotional and volitional elements,[415] as also does faith.[416] By faith there is constituted a union of the soul with Christ which transcends associational and moral union and is a union of life.[417] The consequences of this union are the believer's justification, sanctification, perseverance, and ultimate glorification.[418]

Justification is a judicial act by which God, on account of Christ, declares the sinner to be no longer exposed to penalty, but to be restored to favor.[419] Justification is a forensic term, and is to be accepted on the testimony of Scripture.[420] Justification is possible because it is "always accompanied by regeneration and union with Christ and is followed by sanctification."[421] Christ is the ground of our justification and faith is the instrument.[422] Sanctification is that continuous operation of the Spirit which strengthens and confirms the holy disposition imparted in regeneration.[423] This is a continuous process which is completed in the life to come.[424] The voluntary continuance of the Christian is its human side,

---

[407]LOT, 201.
[408]LOT, 202.
[409]LOT, 203. The general call is not insincere, Strong affirmed, for the inability to respond to it is not physical, but moral, in view of the settled perversity of man's will (LOT, 203).
[410]LOT, 204.
[411]LOT, 206.
[412]LOT, 206.
[413]LOT, 208. "Although man is conscious, he is not conscious of God's regenerating agency" (LOT, 209).
[414]LOT, 209.
[415]LOT, 210.
[416]LOT, 212.
[417]In this union of life, Strong wrote, "the human spirit, while then most truly possessing its own individuality and personal distinctness, is interpenetrated and energized by the Spirit of Christ, is made inscrutably but indissolubly one with him, and so becomes a member of that new humanity of which he is the head" (LOT, 214-215).
[418]LOT, 216.
[419]LOT, 217.
[420]LOT, 220.
[421]LOT, 221. Strong's notes indicate no reference at this time to Robinson's position, which seemed to confuse justification and sanctification, although Strong formulated his view to hold fast "to the Scripture distinction between justification as a declarative act of God, and regeneration and sanctification as those efficient acts of God by which justification is accomplished and followed" (LOT, 222).
[422]LOT, 222.
[423]LOT, 223.
[424]LOT, 224.

and is called perseverance.⁴²⁵ All who are united to Christ by faith "will infallibly continue in a state of grace and finally attain to everlasting life."⁴²⁶

(7) *Ecclesiology*

The church of Christ is the whole company of regenerate persons in all ages, in heaven and earth.⁴²⁷ The individual church exhibits the universal church concretely.⁴²⁸ The New Testament does not use the word "church" in any other sense,⁴²⁹ and its prevailing reference is to the local church.⁴³⁰ The church is an institution of divine appointment and also a voluntary society.⁴³¹ Strong then set forth, of course, the Baptist view of church organization and government.⁴³² Baptism by immersion and the Lord's Supper are ordinances, and are for believers only, thus manifesting a preceding union with Christ.⁴³³ Both are symbols of the substitutionary death of Christ,⁴³⁴ but the Supper expresses primarily the believer's fellowship with his Lord.⁴³⁵ Strong vigorously opposed open communion.⁴³⁶

(8) *Eschatology*

The perfection of individual Christian character and of the church as a whole is to be attained only in the world to come.⁴³⁷ The future condition of men includes an intermediate and ultimate state.⁴³⁸ Physical death results from the separation of soul and body, but this does not involve cessation of being for either sinner or saint.⁴³⁹

The case which Strong presented for immortality, although involving both philosophical and Biblical appeals, developed the former arguments with uncompromised confidence. The metaphysical argument from the simplicity of the soul shows it to be indestructible.⁴⁴⁰ The teleological argument, from the incompleteness of human development in this life, demands a hereafter for the satisfaction of human aspirations.⁴⁴¹ The inequity of rewards or punishments demands a future rectification.⁴⁴² The universal belief in immortality shows that this is an idea natural to the

---

425LOT, 226.
426LOT, 226.
427LOT, 228.
428LOT, 228.
429LOT, 228.
430LOT, 229.
431LOT, 229.
432LOT, 229-238.
433LOT, 239-249.
434LOT, 249.
435LOT, 250.
436That is, the view that baptism, as not being an indispensable term of salvation, cannot properly be made an indispensable term of communion. The practice, Strong wrote, "tends to do away with all discipline . . . (and) with the visible church . . . For no visible church is possible unless some sign of membership be required, in addition to the signs of membership in the invisible church. Open communion logically leads to open church membership . . . (which) is virtually an identification of the church with the world" (LOT, 254).
437LOT, 256.
438LOT, 256.
439LOT, 256.
440LOT, 256.
441LOT, 256.
442LOT, 257.

human mind.⁴⁴³ The Biblical teaching with regard to man's spiritual nature is decisive, but the most impressive and conclusive of proofs is the bodily resurrection of Jesus Christ.⁴⁴⁴

The intermediate state of the righteous is conscious joy, of the unrighteous, conscious suffering.⁴⁴⁵ The Roman Catholic view of purgatorial suffering is unbiblical.⁴⁴⁶ But the intermediate state is one of incompleteness, and the perfect joy of saints and utter misery of the wicked begin only with the resurrection and general judgment.⁴⁴⁷

A final, triumphant return of Christ, to punish the wicked and to complete the salvation of his people, will terminate earthly history.⁴⁴⁸ Although accompanied in the case of the regenerate by inward and invisible influences of the Holy Spirit, the second advent will be outward and visible.⁴⁴⁹ The precursors of Christ's coming include the general prevalence of Christianity throughout the earth, a corresponding development of evil, and a final spiritual struggle between these two forces.⁴⁵⁰ Strong therefore accepted a post-millennial view of Christ's second advent.

At the second coming of Christ, the resurrection of the body is to occur, involving a reunion of the body to the soul from which it had been separated during the intermediate state.⁴⁵¹ This material organism will be perfectly adapted as the outward expression and vehicle of the purified soul.⁴⁵² Scripture itself denies that all particles which exist in the body at death are present in the resurrection body, but intimate only a certain physical connection between the old and the new without disclosing its nature.⁴⁵³ The bodily identity is to consist in the organizing force which binds the old and new together in the unity of a single consciousness.⁴⁵⁴

The manifestations of God's vindicatory justice in history are to be concluded by a final and complete vindication of God's righteousness.⁴⁵⁵ The final judgment is to be an outward, visible event.⁴⁵⁶ Its object is "not the ascertainment, but the manifestation, of character, and the assignment of outward condition corresponding to it."⁴⁵⁷ The judge is to be God, in the person of Christ Jesus.⁴⁵⁸ Both men and evil angels are to be judged.⁴⁵⁹ The grounds of judgment will be the law of God known in conscience and Scripture, and the grace of Christ.⁴⁶⁰ The final state of the righteous is one of the eternal bliss,⁴⁶¹ that of the wicked, eternal punishment.⁴⁶² On the question, whether heaven is a place, Strong vacillated.⁴⁶³ As to hell, the decisive element is not the outward, but the inward

---

⁴⁴³LOT, 257. This argument appears to be stated with a good deal of circumlocution: "The popular belief of all nations and ages shows that the idea of immortality is natural to the human mind" (LOT, 257).

⁴⁴⁴LOT, 258. ⁴⁴⁸LOT, 260. ⁴⁵²LOT, 264. ⁴⁵⁶LOT, 266.
⁴⁴⁵LOT, 258. ⁴⁴⁹LOT, 260. ⁴⁵³LOT, 264. ⁴⁵⁷LOT, 266.
⁴⁴⁶LOT, 259. ⁴⁵⁰LOT, 261. ⁴⁵⁴LOT, 265. ⁴⁵⁸LOT, 266.
⁴⁴⁷LOT, 260. ⁴⁵¹LOT, 263. ⁴⁵⁵LOT, 265. ⁴⁵⁹LOT, 267.
⁴⁶⁰LOT, 267.
⁴⁶¹LOT, 267.
⁴⁶²LOT, 268.

⁴⁶³Christ's human body does not require limitation to place because deity and humanity are indissolubly united in his single person, Strong explained. "Though there may be such a place of Christ's special manifestation to his people, our ruling conception of heaven must be that of a state of holy communion with God" (LOT, 268).

state.[464] Preaching which ignores eternal punishment lowers the holiness of God and degrades the saving work of Christ.[465] The fear of punishment is not the highest motive, yet is a proper motive, for seeking salvation in Christ.[466]

2. Addresses and Essays Between 1876 and 1884

Between the first and second editions of Strong's volume on theology, he provided a number of addresses and essays which furnish added perspective on his earlier theology. The topics covered by such addresses and articles included the holiness of God, evolution, miracles, union with Christ, the will, the baptism of Jesus, inspiration, human freedom, and the two natures of Christ.

(1) *Sermon on "The Holiness of God"*

Strong preached in the University of Rochester chapel on the Day of Prayer for Colleges, January 31, 1878, delivering a sermon on "The Holiness of God"[467] which subsequently appeared serially as an article in *The Examiner* for January 26, February 9, and February 22, 1882. In this, Strong emphasized that holiness is the basic divine attribute,[468] that the universe is built upon a plan whereby the finally impenitent secure everlasting destruction from the presence of God,[469] that God's love to sinners can be properly estimated only in the light of such supreme holiness,[470] that the universe shall ultimately assemble to recognize the right of holiness to reign.[471]

(2) *Address on "The Philosophy of Evolution"*

Speaking before the Literary Societies of Colby University in Waterville, Maine, on July 23, 1878, Strong delivered an address on "The Philosophy of Evolution."[472]

By way of introduction, Strong recalled how British empiricism had been "attacked and seemingly overthrown by the transcendentalism of Germany" only to become, in turn, "the bugbear of orthodox thinkers" and then again to give way to positivism and materialism.[473]

Strong appealed now that the fundamental principle of Spencer's philosophy, false by defect, be

enlarged to take in the full compass of this intuitive deliverance of reason, and that he build his system henceforth, if he can, upon the broader truth that, as the ultimate

---

[464]Strong wrote: "If hell be a place, it is only that the outward may correspond to the inward" (LOT, 268).
[465]LOT, 271.
[466]LOT, 271.
[467]PAR, 188-200.
[468]PAR, 189.
[469]PAR, 196.
[470]"God is strangely capable at once of these two mighty emotions—hatred of the sin and love for the sinner; or, to put it more accurately, love for the sinner, as he is a creature with infinite capacities of joy or sorrow, of purity or wickedness, but simultaneous hatred for that same sinner, as he is an enemy to holiness and to God" (PAR, 198).
[471]PAR, 200.
[472]PAR, 39-57.
[473]PAR, 39.

basis and explanation of all things, there exists and persists an infinite source of energy whose nature is conscious intelligence and will.[474]

Before Spencer's forces can build up a universe, a Creator is required.[475] His theory is defective as an explanation of the origin of life and mind, as a theory of human knowledge with regard to truth and to God, and as a basis for scientific and practical morality.[476]

The Mosaic record recognizes the present order of things as the result of an originating fiat of God and of subsequent arrangement and development.[477] This principle of development in Genesis, perceived many centuries ago by Origen, Augustine and Anselm, "has not been allowed its full weight."[478] The interpreters of Scripture

have been so impressed with the unique declarations of God's absolute Creatorship that they have not sufficiently attended to the accompanying declarations of subsequent evolution according to natural law.[479]

Strong acknowledged that "we are ourselves evolutionists . . . within certain limits, and we accept a large portion of the results of Mr. Spencer's work."[480] He gave it as his judgment that the day is past "when thoughtful men can believe that there was a creative fiat of God at the introduction of every variety of vegetable and animal life."[481] The possibility of such divine acts Strong did not question, but he urged that "God may work by means, and a law of variation and of natural selection may have been and probably was the method" by which the vast majority of living forms came into being. But evolution does not furnish an exhaustive explanation of the facts. For organic life, the human soul, and the realized ideal of manhood in Christ "owe their origin, not to processes of natural law, but to direct interposition of God."[482] The facts thus require both the truth of creation, ensuring God's independence and sovereignty, and his superintendence; neither His transcendence nor His immanence is to be minimized.[483]

(3) *Essay on "The Christian Miracles"*

Strong read an essay on the theme of miracles as attesting a divine revelation, before the Baptist Pastors' Conference of the State of New York on October 23, 1878, in Binghampton. The essay, titled "The

---

[474]PAR, 42.
[475]PAR, 43.
[476]PAR, 44.
[477]PAR, 45.
[478]PAR, 45.
[479]PAR, 45. "It is the last principle which Mr. Spencer has made the characteristic of his system," Strong observed, "but the principle is not only as old as the church-fathers,—it is as old as Moses. We thank him for emphasizing a truth too much neglected. But we charge him with narrowness in excluding from his scheme the greater truth that in the beginning God created the heavens and the earth. His philosophy demands this truth for its supplement and explanation, but, since it is a truth which could come only from revelation, he will none of it. How is it that the Hebrews alone of all nations had the idea of absolute creation?" (PAR, 45).
[480]PAR, 45.
[481]PAR, 45.
[482]PAR, 46.
[483]PAR, 50.

Christian Miracles,"[484] subsequently appeared in the April, 1879, issue, of the *Baptist Review*.

Referring to the recent tendency to lay stress upon internal evidences[485] in Christian apologetics, Strong expressed the conviction that this is necessarily secondary and supplementary, and apart from an appeal to miracle is insufficient to substantiate the divine authority of the Christian system. For the Christian system includes doctrines which are beyond the power of reason to discover, or even to demonstrate once they are made known. Since the Scriptures are an unveiling of truth which is beyond our natural powers, some external proof of divine origin is requisite.[486]

Strong anticipated the objection that divine testimony to the truth of revelation might be given internally, by direct action of the divine upon the human mind, thus dispensing with the necessity of external certification. For such testimony could not be indubitably traced to a God external to the soul, and consequently the evidence of divine authorship would not be as clear.[487] Even among original recipients of revelation, outward certification was advantageous, and in the case of the multitude to whom the message was proclaimed, it was an absolute necessity.[488] Although God might make the same revelation inwardly, simultaneously to each member of the race, it is manifest that the divine method is different from this; great secular truths are first perceived by a few, and then mediated by them to the multitudes.[489]

The defense of miracles is therefore not optional for those who accept the internal evidences, "the internal and the external are so inextricably interwoven, that loss of faith in the one involves loss of faith in the other."[490] But the primary importance of external evidences must not be urged in such a way as to sunder them from the internal. Miracles do not stand alone as evidences, for power by itself cannot prove a divine commission; purity of life and doctrine must go with the miracles.[491] Miracle and doctrine supplement each other, forming parts of one whole. Granted that the internal evidence has greater power over certain minds and ages, however, miracle is "logically the prior and the more important."[492]

---

[484] PAR, 129-147.
[485] Strong cited, by way of illustration, the efforts to show the supernatural character of the Scripture teaching by appeals to the unity of revelation, the superiority of the New Testament system of morality, the conception of Christ's person and character, and the witness of Jesus to his divinity and lordship (PAR, 129).
[486] PAR, 129-130.
[487] PAR, 130.
[488] PAR, 130.
[489] PAR, 130.
[490] PAR, 131. Strong added: "However impressive the doctrine of Scripture may be, if it be accompanied by falsehood in matters of fact, it is proved thereby to have not a divine but a human origin. But facts are not merely accompaniments here—they are the centre and core of its teachings. Its main doctrines claim to be facts as well as doctrines, and to be doctrines only because they are facts. The incarnation and resurrection of Jesus Christ are valuable for purposes of doctrine, only as they are first allowed to be facts of history. But such facts as these are miracles. And therefore Christianity stands or falls with its miracles" (PAR, 131).
[491] PAR, 131.
[492] PAR, 131. "It has been well said," Strong commented, "that a supernatural fact

Strong did not rule on the question whether miracle requires a suspension or violation of natural law, or whether it dispenses absolutely with all physical means and antecedents so that the result is simply that of an immediate divine volition.[493] On whatever alternative, Strong insisted, Christian miracle might be successfully defended. But a miracle is not simply an unusual physical event, but "an extraordinary physical event in peculiar connection with the word of a religious teacher or leader."[494] Strong took exception, however, to the view that the essence of miracle is a supernatural impression of wonder engendered in the witness, whereas the external events themselves were merely explained in terms of special providence.[495]

(4) *Article on "The Believer's Union with Christ"*

The June 12, 1879, issue of *The Examiner* contained an article written by Strong under the title, "The Believer's Union with Christ."[496] Strong expressed surprise that this central theological truth should have been so little considered in treatises both on dogmatics and religious experience.[497] the believer and Christ, in a wholly orthodox manner, guarding against a false mysticism, for "the doctrine of Union with Christ . . . is taught (in the New Testament) so variously and abundantly, that to deny it is to deny inspiration itself."[498]

Strong developed this treatment of a vital and organic union of the believer and Christ, in a wholly orthodox manner, guarding against the loss of separate personality in an encounter of fellowship and cleansing from sin. There is here no trace of the later view, of a pre-incarnation union of the Logos and humanity; rather, the union of Christ with the race in incarnation, and the application of the principle of imputation, is felt to safeguard the doctrine of atonement and justification against mechanical interpretation:

The nature of our relation to Adam, in whom the old humanity as an organic unit fell, can be understood only in the light of our relation to Christ, in whom the new humanity, in its principle and germ, atoned for sin and wrought out a perfect righteousness. The atonement itself, in the aspect of it which is most difficult to reason, the just suffering for others of one who was personally innocent, has more light reflected upon it from this doctrine of our union with Christ than from any other. There is a race-responsibility which belongs to every descendant of Adam, and this race-responsibility is distinguishable from personal responsibility. Christ's corporate union with humanity involved him in that race-responsibility, and so, though he was personally pure, law

---

is the proper proof of a supernatural doctrine, but a supernatural doctrine is not the proper proof of a supernatural fact" (PAR, 131).
[493]PAR, 133.
[494]PAR, 137.
[495]Strong readily granted that one might believe in a miracle and yet consider miracles as divine works *par excellence* because they awakened more distinct thoughts of God, but he preferred "the view which holds to an immediate divine operation in the realm of nature as well as in the realm of mind, and that because of its greater fitness to accomplish the object aimed at in the miracle. That object is the giving of a sign . . . But upon the view here considered, this signality does not seem to be perfectly secured" (PAR, 138).
[496]PAR, 220-225.
[497]"The majority of Christians," Strong lamented, "much more frequently think of Christ as a Savior outside of them, than as a Savior who dwells within" (PAR, 220).
[498]PAR, 220.

STRONG'S THEOLOGY 69

could lay her penalties upon the head of our Redeemer. Christ took our guilt when he took our nature; he has delivered us from the surse of the law by being made a curse for us. . . . This connection of atonement and of justification with the doctrine under consideration relieves both of them from the charge of being mechanical and arbitrary procedures. . . . As Adam's sin is imputed to us, not because Adam is in us, but because we were in Adam, so Christ's righeousness is imputed to us, not because Christ is in us, but because we are in Christ, that is, joined by faith to one whose righteousness and life are infinitely greater than our power to appropriate or contain.[499]

(5) *Article on "The Will of Theology"*

Strong's article on "The Will of Theology"[500] appeared in the *Baptist Review* of 1880 and 1881 in several installments.

Philosophy has no more difficult problem, Strong declared, than that of the will. The interpretation placed on the testimony of consciousness to human freedom has been interpreted within the extremes of fatalism and arbitrariness.

A satisfactory view can be attained only by "new examinations of the facts of consciousness, with the added help of Christian experience and of Scriptures."[501] From the simple facts of consciousness, it may be shown that the will as a faculty of volitions is the efficient cause of mental actions; that its efficient faculty depends for its particular direction upon occasional causes, or objects or reasons for its activity; that these motives are always, ultimately, internal and not external to the mind; that internal dispositions and desires are optative states of the soul into which the will enters as a constituent element; that will therefore includes both the faculty of individual choices and states of immanent preference; that this determination of action by character suggests how freedom in executive acts "may coexist with certainty and even necessity as to their particular nature"; that man has liberty in manifesting his character, but cannot by a power of contrary choice permanently reverse his moral nature; that will's freedom is so limited by its own character and condition that man cannot justly be called a creative first cause, nor be admitted the power of contrary choice in moral and religious matters.[502] Precisely this view is that also of revelation.[503]

Consequently, the very beginnings of moral good are impossible without the activity of the Holy Spirit.[504] God alone can furnish the new motive for holiness.[505] Without a renewal of their wills, men will not and cannot accept salvation.[506]

(6) *Sermon on "The Baptism of Jesus"*

The February 12 and February 19, 1880 issues of the *Examiner* contained a sermon on "The Baptism of Jesus,"[507] which Strong had delivered

---
[499]PAR, 223-224. The emphasis that Christ is involved in race-responsibility through his *corporate* union with humanity should be especially noted, in anticipating Strong's later position.
[500]PAR, 90-113.
[501]PAR, 90.
[502]PAR, 91-98.
[503]PAR, 99-107.
[504]PAR, 112.
[505]PAR, 112.
[506]PAR, 113.
[507]PAR, 226-237.

before the Cincinnati Baptist Union. Since it bears upon the nature of Christ's redemptive union with humanity, it will be well to observe a few passages reflective of his early theological view in this regard.

Strong held that the baptism of Jesus can be explained only by an awareness that He assumed our nature, with "all its exposures and liabilities, yet without its hereditary corruption, that He might redeem it and reunite it to God."[508] The taking of human nature in the incarnation is the central point of reference. He could be the head of a new race and the source of its righteousness only "by first suffering the death due to the nature He had assumed, thereby delivering it from its exposures and perfecting it forever."[509]

(7) *Essay on "The Method of Inspiration"*

The October 7 and October 14, 1880, issues of *The Examiner* contained an essay of Strong's titled "The Method of Inspiration."[510]

In this study, Strong turned to the theology of Dorner, the German Lutheran scholar, as furnishing the key to a statement of a satisfactory doctrine of inspiration by his emphasis that "man is not a mere tangent to God, capable of juxtaposition and contact with him, but of no interpenetration and indwelling of the divine Spirit."[511] The effect of God's union with the believing soul is to put man more fully in possession of his own powers; man is never more fully himself than when God works in and through him. The Scriptures are the product "equally of God and man" by the union of the two.[512] Divinely chosen men spoke and wrote God's words "not as from without but as from within; and that, not passively, but in the most conscious possession and the most exalted exercise of their own powers of intellect, emotion and will."[513]

Strong insisted on "a possession and enlightenment of the writers in all parts of their work," yet also emphasized that it must be such "as left them in the fullest exercise of their natural powers."[514]

All parts of the Bible are inspired, but must be taken in their connection and relation to each other, Strong urged.[515] At the same time, he asserted that there are degrees of value in the Scriptures, but not degrees of inspiration.[516]

(8) *Essay on "Modified Calvinism"*

A discussion of the remainders of freedom in man was contributed by Strong, under the title of "Modified Calvinism,"[517] to the April, 1883, issue of the *Baptist Review*.

---

[508]PAR, 230.
[509]PAR, 231.
[510]PAR, 148-155.
[511]PAR, 150.
[512]PAR, 150.
[513]PAR, 150.
[514]PAR, 154. "When they wrote," he added, "they wrote in the method and vocabulary of their time, and out of their present conscious experience under the influence of the Spirit" (PAR, 154).
[515]PAR, 155.
[516]PAR, 155.
[517]PAR, 114-128. Strong quoted W. C. T. Shedd as saying that the answer to the

Strong complained that Jonathan Edwards' theory, that an act of will contrary to the soul's fundamental preference is inconceivable and impossible, is too narrow to embrace all facts, and contended that both Augustine and Calvin held "a somewhat broader and a more Scriptural view of human liberty."[518]

The highest freedom is "such an inworking of law into the heart and soul of man, that there is a spontaneous and infallible choosing" of the right.[519] Hence, there is no true freedom without God.[520] But Scripture emphasizes both divine sovereignty and efficiency and human freedom and responsibility.[521] But Paul does not urge human duty by undervaluing divine activity.[522] God is the efficient cause, however, only of all good.[523] Man is responsible for his evil nature only because he is in some proper sense the originator of it.[524]

An adequate Biblical view rejects not only the theory that man's acts are all determined from without, but also the theory that man's freedom is simply freedom to act conformably to his existing evil inclination.[525] The facts of experience, no less than the Scriptures, oppose the latter view.[526] Man is not compelled to commit the sin against the Holy Ghost, he can choose a less degree of sin instead of a greater, he can do outwardly good acts with imperfect motives, and can even seek God from selfish considerations.[527] Man's only probation is not in Adam, for there is an individual probation as well, with reference to light which is given to each.[528]

Both Augustine and Calvin held that Adam at least had a power of contrary choice, and that despite inherited human depravity, each individual has power to check and modify his evil nature in the interest of less or more guilt before God.[529] Character does not absolutely bind us. Man may choose between motives. The desire and the will always go together. Man has not lost his natural power of will, but rather the inclination to will conformably to God's law.[530] But there remains "a power to check the manifestations of evil inclination, and at least indirectly and with imperfect motives to seek its reversal."[531]

That God alone can regenerate man does not preclude human activity, for Christ does not constrain or compel.[532] Regeneration is "a work of

---

question, how much freedom is left to man in an unregenerate state, "determines a man's position in theology" more than anything else.
[518]PAR, 114.
[519]PAR, 114.
[520]PAR, 115.
[521]PAR, 115.
[522]PAR, 116.
[523]PAR, 117.
[524]PAR, 118.
[525]This latter view, Strong protested, "grants a freedom *to* action, but denies a freedom *from* action" (PAR, 118).
[526]PAR, 118. Jonathan Edwards made no attempt to explain—because he could not, on his theory—how Adam could fall from holiness, or how the regenerated Christian can ever sin, remarked Strong.
[527]PAR, 119.
[528]PAR, 119.
[529]PAR, 121-122.
[530]PAR, 124.
[531]PAR, 125.
[532]PAR, 125.

personal influence upon the sinner's affections."[533] In developing this, Strong stated the relationship in such a way as to stress that communication between spirits is here not limited to logical insight, but involves also a vital union.[534] Man's real freedom, or the power to love God with all his heart, is partially restored in regeneration, and will be perfected in future glorification.[535]

(9) *Sermon on "The Two Natures of Christ"*

On May 25, 1884, Strong preached in Sage Chapel of Cornell University on the subject, "The Two Natures of Christ."[536] Here he championed both the true deity and true humanity of Christ.

In presenting the case for Christ's humanity, Strong emphasized that Christ had a human mind as well as a human body, and

that mind was subject to the ordinary laws of human development. He grew in wisdom, as well as in stature and in favor with God and man. In his mother's arms he was not the omniscient babe that some have supposed. In his later years he suffered, being tempted, as he could not have suffered, if all things had been open to his gaze. Even to the last, it would seem that he was ignorant of the day of the end.[537]

Strong attempted no reconciliation of this denial of omnipresence to Christ's human nature, with the correlative emphasis that He possessed also a perfect divine nature. The main distinction of Jesus' manhood was its ideal[538] and life-giving quality; in Him the fallen race finds its true source of spiritual life.[539]

But Christ can suffer vicariously for humanity only because He is God as well as man.[540] Because of His divine nature He underwent a suffering absolutely infinite.[541] Strong then pressed the Chalcedonian insistence that the two natures are perfectly and eternally united in His one person.[542]

This concludes the sermons, addresses and essays prepared by Strong between 1876 and 1884, from which some significant insights into his theological position, as contrasted with its later reformulation under the influence of monistic thought.[543] It is clear that in the main Strong's views were solidly in the evangelical bracket, although he was ready to yield to a theistic evolutionary formulation, and although the relationship of special

---

[533] PAR, 125.
[534] "Nor is it (regeneration) an influence exerted only through the truth, as if man were the only agent, and moral suasion were the only method God could employ to change man's will. We repel the notion that the only communication between spirit and spirit is through truth; for this is a virtual denial of the Christian's union with Christ and of God's personal communion with the human soul. We know of an influence exerted by the orator, which is above and beyond that of the words he speaks" (PAR, 125). This is a curious passage. In all editions of his Systematic Theology, Strong took the view that the testimony of the Holy Spirit terminates upon truth.
[535] PAR, 126.
[536] PAR, 201-212.
[537] PAR, 201.
[538] PAR, 202.
[539] PAR, 204.
[540] PAR, 208.
[541] PAR, 209.
[542] PAR, 209.
[543] It was monism of the qualitative type which later influenced Strong; quantitative monism he opposed throughout his life, in the interest of human freedom and moral responsibility.

revelation and philosophy appears not to have been worked out in any detailed manner. It is clear also that, during these years, there was no favor for any monistic hypothesis; idealisms of all sorts were resisted as inevitably pantheistic.

3. The 1882-1885 Lectures

Strong's 1876 lectures, as well as his formulations of the next decade, it was evident, stood in the tradition of Protestant orthodoxy and contained little interaction with the heightened emphasis on divine immanence to be found in the idealistic philosophies. There were, in the 1876 lectures, it is true, elements quite congenial to idealistic metaphysics, such as the scope assigned to natural theology, so that the employment of rationalistic argument side by side with revelational appeal is frequently carried on, from the proofs for the existence of God to the proofs for immortality, as if the former led directly to a Biblical view, except not quite so certainly. There can be no doubt that in principle Strong insisted on the priority of revelation, though in practise his arguments quite often veer to philosophy in such a way as to expect specifically Christian conclusions from speculative study of the data. While such methodology would create a natural interest in idealistic refutations of naturalism, there is no indication that Strong was to any marked extent influenced by idealism in the formulation of his convictions; indeed, the insistence on the reality of secondary causes points in the other direction. At the same time, his cautious statement of the origin of man, suggesting in view of the evolutionary trend of modern science that the Scriptures preclude naturalism and require the view of man's initial perfection, but do not legislate on whether the divine creation of primal man was mediate or immediate, suggests a frame of mind which would welcome a new philosophy which would stress the uniqueness of man as against the naturalistic interpretations.

When one scans the lecture notes made almost a decade later by one of Strong's students in the inter-leaved copies of *Lectures on Theology* then in use, one finds little in the way of concession to the idealists. But one fact is clear, and that is Strong's constant reference to Browne's writings, and a far greater use of Bowne for illustrative and supplementary purposes in the lectures. Yet there are some signs also of slight modifications of view, although these are not exclusively in the direction of personalistic idealism.

Instead of reviewing Strong's whole theological system, already set forth in its evangelical outlines for background purposes, we shall be able to discern the modifications to better advantage simply by considering the directions in which changes are made, sometimes in the interest of a more thorough evangelical position, sometimes haltingly away from the traditional formulation in the direction of liberal theology—though not in either case under the impulse of idealistic thought—and again in what might legitimately be considered the direction of idealism.

(1) *Supplementation in the Traditional Direction*

Strong's main supplementations here indicate how solidly he stood, in the main, with a Reformation view of theology. These occur especially with reference to the relationship of miracle and revelation, the view of inspiration, the place of imputation in soteriology, the Christological views, and the restatement of the case for immortality.

Special revelation is attested by miracles, so that the ceasing of such revelation is "a reason for the ceasing of miracles," Strong emphasized.[544] "Miracle affords a full warrant that a revelation comes from God,"[545] he declared. The resurrection of Christ is therefore "the central element of Christianity."[546]

Strong clarified his earlier statement that "the Scriptures are the product equally of God and of man" to mean that they are "just as truly" the product of both.[547] Strong reiterated his earlier view that inspiration secured infallible transmission of divine truth, that the Bible is an organic whole, and that inspiration while not verbal as to method is yet verbal as to result.[548]

As to sin and redemption, Strong strengthened his views in the orthodox direction. He emphasized the reality of a state of sin.[549] At the same time, he insisted even more vigorously on the centrality of imputation for an understanding of the Biblical view of condemnation and justification. He continued, however, his attack on the Princeton theology, with its view of the federal headship of Christ, in the interest of the natural headship theory.[550] The Biblical view, he stressed, provides for degrees of guilt between original and actual sin, the final condemnation of none on account

---

[544] LOT(CN), 9. Strong urged his class to read Mozley's *Miracles* (Bampton Lectures), widely regarded as the classic statement of the traditional Protestant view. Against Pascal's view that miracle is to be judged by doctrine and doctrine by miracle, Strong quoted Mozley: "Fact proves doctrine, but not vice versa."

[545] LOT(CN), 33. Strong even strengthened his earlier view at this point, that miracles certify truth not directly but only indirectly (or a new miracle, he then said, would have to accompany each new doctrine). But Strong now affirmed that "the attestation of a foundation doctrine might serve for a whole system built upon it" (LOT[CN], 35).

[546] LOT(CN), 35.

[547] LOT(CN), 53.

[548] LOT(CN), 53. The writers were held back from the selection of wrong words, but inspiration did not generally involve direct communication of the words, Strong affirmed.

[549] Strong held that "the Old School and the New School are not so far apart when we remember that the New School 'choice' is an *elective preference* exercised . . . as soon as the child is born and reasserting itself in all the subordinate choices of life; while the Old School 'state' is not a dead, passive, mechanical thing, but is a *state of active movement* or of tendency to move toward evil" (LOT[CN], 140). Yet he emphasized that the watchword of the New School is that "all sin consists in sinning" (an atomistic theory of human nature), whereas that of the Old School is "all sin in Adam" (LOT[CN], 151). The New School held to sin as personal alone, the Old School affirmed the guilt of hereditary depravity (LOT[CN], 154).

[550] Strong reaffirmed that any theory of the method of man's union with Adam is merely hypothetical, his own view of natural headship no less than any other, but added in the interest of that view: "From . . . (the) . . . Scripture it seems not only natural, but inevitable to draw the inference that we 'all sinned' in Adam. The Augustinian theory simply puts in that link of connection between two sets of facts which otherwise would be difficult to reconcile. But in putting in that link of connection it claims that it is merely bringing out into clear light an underlying but implicit assumption of Paul's reasoning and this it seeks to prove by showing that upon no other assumption can Paul's reasoning be understood at all" (LOT[CN], 159). The class notes indicate that Strong took at least one period to dictate the exposition of Romans 5:12-19 as given chiefly by Meyer and Shedd (LOT[CN],160-161).

Strong's Theology

of original sin alone, and an original act of free will in Adam.[551] But three beliefs must be accepted on the testimony of Scripture: inborn depravity, guilt and condemnation in view of this depravity, and Adam's sin the cause and ground of both depravity and the resultant guilt and condemnation.[552] Strong emphasized that guilt and penalty are correlative.[553] Penalty primarily vindicates the righteousness of God.[554]

Strong undergirded his conviction that the atonement of Christ is substitutionary and propitiatory. He urged the reading of Shedd's essay on the atonement as "the best thing on the subject,"[555] and stressed the substitutionary implications of the Greek prepositions in the relevant New Testament passages, singling out Romans 5:12, Philippians 2 and Romans 3:24-26 as "the three most important theological passages in the Bible."[556] At the same time, Strong emphasized the difference "between holding to a substitute for penalty as Grotius did, and holding to an equivalent substituted penalty as the Scriptures do."[557] One significant development of Strong's doctrine, however, appears in the class notes. Although Strong had previously related the necessity for the atonement solely to the holiness of God, he now stressed the obligation of Christ to meet the penalty of sin in view of his organic and corporate union with humanity.[558]

In reaffirming a sublapsarian[559] view of the divine decrees,[560] Strong at the same time supported his view of election by an appeal to Shedd's insistence that the New Testament use of the word "foreknow" involves not simply prescience, but "selection with a benignant and kindly feeling toward the object."[561]

Strong strengthened the definitions of the law of God to stress that it is the nature of God expressed in the form of moral requirement, and not in any sense merely arbitrary.[562] He modified his view of free agency, defining moral freedom no longer as "power to manifest character in action" but as "self-determination in view of motive."[563] Such free agency is not inconsistent with the certainty of the result involved in the divine decrees, he reiterated.[564]

---

[551] LOT(CN), 151.
[552] LOT(CN), 159.
[553] LOT(CN), 165.
[554] LOT(CN,) 167. Penalty is not essentially reformatory, nor deterrent, nor preventative, but has a fundamental reference to vindication, Strong held.
[555] LOT(CN), 186. Strong apparently had in view Shedd's *Discourses and Essays*, 272-324.
[556] LOT(CN), 187.
[557] LOT(CN), 191.
[558] LOT(CN), 196.
[559] LOT(CN), 200. Strong now revised his earlier appraisal of Calvin, and said that sublapsarianism, and not supralapsarianism, was also the final position of Calvin.
[560] Strong now eliminated his earlier statement that the universe need not have been the best possible creation of God, and affirmed instead only that God had the best possible plan (LOT[CN], 102).
[561] LOT(CN), 201.
[562] LOT(CN), 137.
[563] LOT(CN), 88ff.
[564] LOT(CN), 90, where Strong pointed out also that Shedd regarded as unanswerable the question, how the divine permission of sin makes sin certain.

Strong's Christology remained quite unchanged, though there is a reserve and caution in some of his statements. The Chalcedonian doctrine proceeds from the natures, he emphasized, and regards the result of the union to be the person; it did not say that the Logos furnishes the ego in the personality, but John of Damascus pushed forward to this conclusion.[565] Yet Strong expressed no dissatisfaction with the traditional Christology. The Divine and the human, he remarked, are not to be regarded as foreign to each other and mutually exclusive.[566] Strong supplemented his Christology by the affirmation that the exalted Christ in heaven fills all things not in His divine nature alone, not in the sense that His human body is everywhere present, but His manhood is ubiquitous by virtue of His union with the Godhead, although the body necessarily exists in spatial relations.[567]

There are several indications of a clearer emphasis on the priority of special revelation. One instance is the declaration that while "reason shows us the unity of God, only Revelation shows us the trinity."[568] Another is afforded by the modification of philosophical arguments intended to show what might be antecedently expected of the divine being. In this spirit Strong now declared that God's mercy cannot be demonstrated *a priori*, for He did not spare the angels that sinned.[569] Again, Strong revised his references to the antecedent "probability" of the existence of angels to merely an antecedent "possibility."[570] The third example is found in the treatment of immortality.

Strong quite radically revised his case for immortality in accord with a revelational view. The Platonic argument from the simplicity of the soul "would apparently prove the immortality of the brute" also and actually shows only "the inconclusiveness of materialism and leaves the matter open for positive proof from Revelation."[571] The teleological argument is significant "only for the immortality of the righteous" and "assumes the fact of God's love and so assumes the very revelation which assures us of immortality."[572] The argument from God's justice to the immortality of the wicked is inconclusive, for "may not the judgment which conscience threatens be extinction of being—not immortality?"[573] The universal belief in immortality "shows only a general design for immortality which may be nothing more than the love of life which is necessary to self preservation."[574] It is the revelational assurance of immortality and especially the bodily resurrection of Christ which are crucial for the conviction.[575]

---

[565] LOT(CN), 174.
[566] This is an emphasis of the Chalcedonian formulation also.
[567] This emphasis likewise would have been compatible with a view that all reality is mental, but there appears no idealistic motivation for Strong's revision.
[568] LOT(CN), 73.
[569] LOT(CN), 70.
[570] LOT(CN), 114. This revision was not in the interest of doubt, but rather in the interest of the exclusively Biblical nature of the belief in angels. There is "no *a priori* argument for the existence of angels (but the doctrine is) founded primarily on Scripture" (LOT[CN], 115).
[571] LOT(CN), 256.
[572] LOT(CN), 256.
[573] LOT(CN), 257.
[574] LOT(CN), 257.
[575] LOT, 258. In treating the scientific objection to bodily resurrection, Strong no longer thought it necessary to insist that there need be any physical continuity whatever between the old and new bodies (LOT[CN], 264).

STRONG'S THEOLOGY

(2) Tendencies in the Liberal Direction

Strong's lectures now disclosed modifications in the interest of the contemporary evolutionary and higher critical views. He instructed his classes to omit the earlier treatment of the Mosaic account of creation, and now developed the creation story in terms of the nebular hypothesis of origins as the divine method—a scheme already developed in outline in his first printed lectures, where the pictorial summary view of Genesis was upheld, but with more reserve. Strong now intensified the emphasis on the mental differences between man and the brute.[576] At the same time, he accepted a long period of evolutionary development.[577]

To higher criticism Strong now granted that the Pentateuch may include documents of previous ages, and he accepted the division into Jehovistic and Elohistic documents, but insisted at the same time on Mosaic authorship.[578]

In two respects, the priority of special revelation and the significance of general revelation were not carefully worked out, and created a mood compatible with much liberal apologetic. Strong's insistence on the intuitive belief in God was formulated in such a way as to make this belief quite anticipative both of the theistic proofs and of special revelation, without the frequent evangelical emphasis on the distorting noetic effect of sin.[579] Furthermore, in treating the divine nature Strong, although insisting that the Scriptures are "the decisive authority with regard to God's attributes,"[580] tends to argue at times as if the Biblical view could be independently reached on philosophical ground.[581]

At one point the increasing emphasis on a heightened divine immanence was appropriated by Strong in such a way as to concede the possibility of error in the Scriptures and yet to insist that the influence of the Holy Spirit can safeguard the communication of the divine revelation. While the class notes do not indicate more than a passing remark on the subject, the question may be raised whether Strong might welcome an emphasis which would enable an acceptance of an evolutionary and higher critical view and yet maintain a revelational view.[582]

---

[576]LOT(CN), 122.
[577]He stated: "We are not limited to 6000 years for the period of development. (We are) not bound to any scheme for the chronology of the earth's history" (LOT[CN], 124).
[578]LOT(CN), 44.
[579]The theistic arguments, Strong affirmed, are "not a bridge to conduct us to our belief in such existence but rather the guides to a bridge already existing in intuitive belief in God" (LOT[CN], 27). But he stressed also that this intuitive knowledge is not "so complete and sufficient as to render reasoning and revelation unnecessary" (LOT[CN], 21).
[580]LOT(CN), 62.
[581]This same mood is seen in the rationalistic argument, which appears side by side with the Biblical, for the Trinity: "God's love must have an object in himself, i.e., the second Person of the Trinity" (LOT[CN], 64).
[582]The comment referred to is: "We grant that revelation, in order to attain its purpose, and generally in the first instance, is internal and subjective. We claim, however, that the same Spirit who originally communicated the truth has also secured its preservation in permanent and written form. Though this form is in itself imperfect it is sufficient *under the influence of the Spirit* to reproduce in others' minds the ideas with which the mind of the writers were at first divinely filled" (LOT[CN], 5).

(3) Glances in the Idealistic Direction

And yet the emphasis of Strong's lectures at this time, while aware of current idealist viewpoints, hardly permits the judgment that any fundamental concession to that school had been made.

That Strong followed carefully the idealist-materialist controversy is beyond doubt, not only from the references to Borden P. Bowne's writings[583] but from conscious effort either to improve the statement of his own position with a reference to the personalistic philosophy, or more clearly to differentiate it.

An instance of restatement which may have been encouraged by a spiritualistic philosophy is the deletion from Strong's original definition of God of the words "the absolutely perfect being" and the substitution of "the infinitely perfect Spirit."[584] Moreover, there was additional emphasis on the reality of the general revelation of the Logos, with more stress on the role of natural theology than most evangelical theology would readily have admitted.[585]

But consideration of Strong's general position makes clear that he had made no one-sided commitment to idealism by any means. He clearly differentiated his position from that of Bowne.[586] In the discussion of the relation of attribute and essence, he retained the Aristotelian distinction between substance and its qualities.[587] Miracle was defined still in relation to natural or secondary law; while Strong protested against miracle as superseding secondary causes, he protested also against the idealistic destruction of them.[588] The Biblical doctrine of preservation, Strong insisted, is "midway between the two errors of denying the first cause (Deism or Atheism) and denying second causes (Pantheism)."[589]

---

[583]"Bowne's idealism differs from Berkeley," Strong told his classes, "in that he believes in an energizing by God from the inside, while Berkeley believed in the energizing from the outside" (Lot[CN], 29). Bowne had now written PHS (1874), SIT (1879), and MSFP (1882).

[584]LOT(CN) 17.

[585]Strong declared that the Logos is "working even among the heathen, through such men as Confucius, Buddha, Pythagoras, who made their fellow-men better. Yet this light is so small that Scripture in general does not recognize it"(LOT[CN], 172). The available class notes do not indicate any expansion of his remarks as to the relation of general and special revelation. The usual Protestant view is that the general revelation of the Logos, while not completely destroyed, is nonetheless distorted by the noetic effects of sin. Strong may not have guarded his view here against the possibility of a minimal, but pure, revelation outside the Scriptures.

[586]Referring to the view advanced in Bowne's *Metaphysics*, that all force is due to the Divine will, Strong countered that all force "*implies*, not *is*, the Divine will" (LOT [CN], 104).

[587]Strong called attention to an "analogous necessity of attributing the properties of matter to an underlying substance and the phenomena of thought to an underlying spiritual essence, else matter be resolved into mere force, and mind into mere sensation. In short, all things are swallowed up in a vast idealism" (LOT[CN], 61).

[588]"The original act of creation was not a miracle," Strong explained, "because there was no natural law to be transcended prior to creation . . . He who created the second causes, can supplement them" LOT[CN], 33).

[589]LOT(CN), 105. The fact that Strong did not here differentiate between pantheism (which includes selves in God) and personalistic idealism (which holds that selves are outside God) suggests that he had not yet clearly distinguished Bowne's view from absolute idealism.

There were indeed areas of thought in which Strong was on the move, in such a way as would lead him to welcome the personalistic view, even if not conclusively. Both in his doctrine of the Holy Spirit, and his formulation of atonement there are clear evidences of reconstruction. He expressed to his classes a personal dissatisfaction with his statement of the role of the Holy Spirit in creation.[590] And in treating the divine provision of atonement, he now stressed a twofold necessity, lodged both in the holiness of God and in the organic and corporate union of Christ with humanity. The earlier lectures had already made Christ's liability to offer satisfaction contingent upon a covenented incarnation, but now Strong heightened the emphasis that Christ's ability to bear penalty and to make satisfaction to the divine justice were consequences of his union with humanity.[591] But, as distinguished from a later view, Strong at this time still lodged the union of Christ with humanity in the incarnation, rather than in the creation.

What makes most clear, however, that the changes in Strong's thought at this period were not motivated by personalistic idealism, is another circumstance. If there had been one central doctrine at which the issue would have been made apparent, it is in the statement of the union of believers with Christ, to which doctrine Strong at this time gave a new importance, although in a way that disclosed no personalistic influences. Strong restated at this time the logical order of the phases of Christian experience, in such a way as to make union with Christ the first and central point of reference.[592] But there is no indication in the treatment that the motivation for this change grew out of a greater emphasis in his own thinking upon divine immanence; rather, the change appears to have been made in the interest of a more coherent treatment.

4. The 1886 Lectures

The enlarged and amended edition of Strong's early lectures appeared in 1886,[593] and contained nearly four times the material in the first volume. Strong commented in the preface on the substantial similarity of the main text, but called attention to the fact that

important additions have been made to the treatment of the intuition of the divine existence, the classification of the attributes, the statement of the doctrine of decrees, the teaching as to race-sin and race-responsibility, ability or inability, the ethical theory of the atonement, and the final state of the wicked. The section on the moral nature of man (conscience and will) is new; a few minor paragraphs of the older book have been omitted; and the work has been somewhat altered in arrangement.[594]

---

[590]In his earlier notes, Strong had stated merely that the Father is the originating, the Son the mediating, and the Spirit the realizing cause of Creation. Strong explained that by "the Spirit as the realizing cause" he meant "the perfecting cause" and indicated dissatisfaction with the incompleteness of this treatment (LOT[CN], 92). Yet the lecture notes give no encouragement to any view that the dissatisfaction evidenced an interest in ethical monism. Rather, Strong held "there is nothing divine in creation but the origination of substance" and that "unlike the generation of the Son, creation brings into being a new essence that is not God" (LOT[CN], 92, 94).
[591]LOT(CN), 204.
[592]Strong remarked: "Union with Christ logically precedes both regeneration and justification, and yet chronologically the moment of our union with Christ is also the moment when we are regenerated and justified" (LOT[CN], 204).
[593]Hereafter referred to as ST(1886).
[594]ST(1886), vii.

Strong expressed his "peculiar obligation" to three living persons: President Noah Porter of Yale College, President Ezekiel G. Robinson of Brown University, and Professor William G. T. Shedd of Union Theological Seminary.[595] At the same time, the number of index references to idealists showed a marked increase, especially those to Lotze[596] and to Bowne,[597] which reflect a growing interaction with representatives of qualitative monism.

(1) *The Intuitive Knowledge of God*

In restating man's intuitive knowledge of God, Strong found among the idealists useful material which would afford a philosophic undergirding for the Biblical suggestions of an innate knowledge of the Deity. But the

---

[595] Strong said he owed his first insight into philosophy to Porter; into theology, to Robinson; and that from Shedd's writings he had for many years derived stimulus and suggestion.

[596] The numerous quotations from these writers, however, are in the interest of support for Strong's views, rather than of a modification of Strong's outlook in the direction of personalistic idealism. Strong referred seventeen times to Lotze's POR, and once each to the following of Lotze's works: M, OOM, OOP, and PP. In these references Strong appealed to Lotze's idealism for philosophic opposition to the pantheistic view that the divine knowledge requires an eternal non-ego to call forth self-consciousness (ST[1886], 260, referring to Lotze, POR, 55-69, and M, III, 191-200); quoted Lotze in support of the responsibility and freedom of the human will (ST[1886], 260, referring to Lotze, POR, 95-106, and PP, 35-50); appealed to Lotze in support of the accessibility of the human soul to the omnipresent Creator (ST[1886], 454, referring to Lotze, OOP, 142). He opposed to Lotze's views the insistence that God's holy being must be affirmed independent of his holy activity (ST[1886], 129, referring to Lotze POR, 139), and that faith is conditioned upon a right state of affections (ST[1886], 4, referring to Lotze, POR, 1-7). Strong called attention to Lotze's formulation of the ontological argument (ST[1886], 50, referring to Lotze, POR, 8-34). But that Strong did not yet regard Lotze's view as substantially different from other idealistic statements, in terms of a distinction between quantitative and qualitative monism, is quite apparent from his reference to Lotze "for the idealistic and monistic theory of creation" (ST[1886], 191, referring to Lotze, POR, 70-80). The wide appropriation of idealistic argument, to support Strong's own views, is seen in references to Hegel, Fichte and others, as well as from Lotze; Strong seems to have considered all idealism as pantheistic in spirit at this stage of his thought, despite the awareness that Lotze insisted on creation and on human responsibility and freedom.

[597] Strong's references to Bowne likewise were not in the interest of a strictly personalistic formulation. In these early years, in fact, Bowne could be appealed to in behalf of a substance philosophy, although he stood solidly in the tradition of qualitative monism, insisting that all reality is of the nature of consciousness, but created selves are not to be regarded as parts of God. Strong cited Bowne in support of the view that qualities imply the existence of a substance to which they belong (ST[1886], 4, referring to Bowne, PHS, 47, 207-217; that we have an intuitive and direct knowledge of substance (ST[1886], 54, quoting Bowne, M. 432); that the formation of a mental image is not necessary to conception or knowledge (ST[1886], 5, referring to Bowne, PHS, 30-34); that partial knowledge is not on that account invalid (ST[1886], 6, referring to Bowne, PHS, 72); that evolution and theism are compatible (ST[1886], 35, referring to Bowne, PHS, 163, 164); that knowledge of God is intuitive (ST[1886], 37, referring to Bowne, T, 79); that the hypothesis of infinite causal regress is unacceptable (ST[1886], 41, referring to Bowne, PHS, 36); that law is merely method, and not cause (ST[1886], 43, referring to Bowne, PHS, 231-247); that natural evil is compatible with theism (ST[1886], 7 referring to Bowne, PHS, 76); against the view that God's omnipresence is merely potential and not essential (ST[1886], 132, referring to Bowne, M, 136); and against the view that freedom requires the power of acting apart from motives (ST[1886], 259, quoting Bowne, M, 169).

references are introduced in a wholly supplementary manner, merely to call attention to representative thinkers who find an infinite mind implied in human knowing, and in no way suggest that the case for theism is lodged on this ground.[598]

Strong's restatement at this point, then, consisted in an enlarged treatment of the knowledge of God as rooted in a rational intuition, which logically precedes and conditions all observation and reasoning, and which chronologically rises in consciousness only upon the occasion of reflection upon the phenomena of nature and of mind.[599] Strong held that the idea of God meets all the conditions for a first truth: universality, necessity, logical independence and priority.[600] The intuitive knowledge of God's existence, he affirmed, is explicated and confirmed by arguments drawn from the universe and from abstract thought.[601] It is curious, in view of the firm emphasis on intuitive knowledge, that Strong dismissed the ontological argument as leading "only to an ideal conclusion."[602] But the empirical arguments are assigned greater significance, although the case for an infinite, personal Creator, the source of our moral laws, is "probable, not demonstrative."[603] But the theistic evidences afford moral certainty.[604] The law of parsimony requires that the conclusions of the cosmological, teleological and anthropological arguments be applied to a single Being.[605] "To this one Being we may . . . ascribe . . . infinity and perfection, the idea of which lies at the basis of the Ontological Argument," wrote Strong, "not because they are demonstrably his, but because our mental constitution will not allow us to think otherwise."[606] These circumstances afford reasons for expecting a special divine revelation of an authoritative nature.[607] Hence the essential continuity of general and special revelation is assumed not to be obscured by sin to the extent affirmed by Reformation theology.

(2) *The Classification of Divine Attributes*

Strong's reclassification of the divine attributes carried out his definition of theology as "the science of God and His relation to the universe" and his definition of God as "Spirit, infinite and perfect, the source, sup-

---

[598]Despite the incidental treatment, it is significant that Strong affirmed that "we cannot *prove* that God is, but we can show that, in order to the existence of any knowledge . . . man must assume that God is" (ST[1886], 34), and then quoted without comment Bowne's words: "Our objective knowledge of the finite must rest upon an ethical trust in the infinite" (M, 472).
[599]ST(1886), 29.
[600]ST(1886), 31-34.
[601]ST(1886), 39.
[602]ST(1886), 49.
[603]ST(1886), 39.
[604]Strong wrote: "They supplement each other, and constitute a series of evidences which is cumulative in its nature. Though, taken singly, none of them can be considered absolutely decisive, they together furnish a corroboration of our primitive conviction of God's existence, which is of great practical value, and is in itself sufficient to bind the moral action of men" (ST[1886], 39).
[605]ST(1886). 49.
[606]ST(1886), 49.
[607]Strong affirmed: "Man's intellectual and moral nature requires, in order to preserve it from constant deterioration, and to ensure its moral growth and progress, an authoritative and helpful revelation of religious truth, of a higher and completer sort than any to which, in its present state of sin, it can attain by the use of its unaided powers" (ST[1886], 58).

port and end of all things." The attributes he divided into two groups: absolute or immanent, and relative or transitive.[608] The former exist in no necessary relation to things outside of God, the latter exist in such relation.[609]

Significantly, Strong did not affirm that the order of attributes is merely a logical reconstruction of the inductive facts of Scripture. It is true that he appealed again to the Scripture as the decisive authority,[610] but he emphasizes that his arrangement "corresponds with the order in which the attributes commonly present themselves to the human mind."[611] Here again there is a methodological tendency to regard revelation and philosophy as leading to equivalent results, although the principle is rejected. The clearest support of this claim is seen in Strong's presentation of the doctrine of the Trinity, which he placed after the treatment of the divine attributes, as if the being and nature of God could be determined without a consideration of any special divine self-disclosure.[612]

(3) *The Statement of Divine Decrees*

The problem to which Strong devoted himself with reference to the divine decrees was that of affirming the certainty of all events, and yet of escaping their necessity, especially in view of man's moral deeds. Strong reemphasized that God's actual agency with regard to evil is only permissive.[613] But God's knowledge of the future is not merely a matter of foreknowledge; it is more true to hold that "he decrees his foreknowledge,"[614] for he foreknows because he has decreed. Free agency is inconsistent with necessity, but not with certainty; God's acts render the future certain, but not necessary.[615]

---

[608] ST(1886), 119.
[609] ST(1886), 120. Strong's chart listed:
"1. Absolute or Immanent Attributes:
  A. Spirituality, involving (a) Life, (b) Personality.
  B. Infinity, involving (a) Self-existence, (b) Immutability, (c) Unity.
  C. Perfection, involving (a) Truth, (b) Love, (c) Holiness.
2. Relative or Transitive Attributes:
  A. Related to Time and Space—(a) Eternity, (b) Immensity.
  B. Related to Creation—(a) Omnipresence, (b) Omniscience, (c) Omnipotence.
  C. Related to Moral Beings—(a) Veracity and Faithfulness, or Transitive Truth; (b) Mercy and Goodness, or Transitive Love; (c) Justice and Righteousness, or Transitive Holiness" (ST[1886], 119).
[610] ST(1886), 118. The rational arguments, he stated, are usually a merger of intuition and theological factors.
[611] ST(1886), 119, where Strong exp' "Our first thought of God is that of mere Spirit, mysterious and undefined, over against our own spirits. Our next thought is that of God's greatness; the quantitative element suggests itself; his natural attributes rise before us; we recognize him as the infinite One. Finally comes the qualitative element; our moral natures recognize a moral God; over against our error, selfishness, and impurity we perceive his absolute perfection."
[612] ST(1886), 144-170.
[613] ST(1886), 172.
[614] ST(1886), 174.
[615] ST(1886), 176. Strong cautioned: 1 reconciling God's decrees with human freedom, we must not go to the oth extreme (from the Arminian, who denies the certainty of human action), and reduce human freedom to mere determinism. . . . Human action is not simply the expression of previously dominant affections. . . . We therefore part company with Jonathan Edwards . . . and Charles Hodge. . . . We hold, on the contrary, that sensibility and will are two distinct powers, that

(4) *The Subject of Race-Sin and Race-Responsibility*

It will be recalled that the class notes for Strong's 1882-1885 lectures disclosed an emphasis upon imputation as the key to understanding the Biblical view of justification and condemnation. Strong made the remark to a class in 1901 that previous to his work at Rochester "there had been no attempt to explain the imputation of the sin of the race to Christ."[616] In view of the fact that in his later thought ethical monism came to play so large a part in the explanation of his view of the vital relationship of the race to the Logos, it is worthy of comment here that the 1882-1885 attempts at a fuller statement of the imputation of guilt from Adam to the race, of human guilt to Christ, and of Christ's righteousness to believing humanity, are carried forward to completer statement in this edition, although without an appeal to monism.[617]

Strong's chief concern is to defend the reality of the implication of the race in the penalty, corruption and guilt of Adamic sin, but in such a way as to deny the federal headship of Adam proclaimed by the Princeton theologians. The Princeton view, he contended, did not provide for a real union of the race with Adam as the basis of imputation, whereas Strong held that in the cases of the imputation of Adam's sin to humanity, of humanity's sin to Christ, and of Christ's righteousness to the believer, a real union constitutes the basis for the imputation.[618] Strong upheld, therefore, the Augustinian view that mankind is guilty in Adam on the ground that all men existed as one moral whole in him, and our corruption in Adam precedes the imputation of penalty and guilt to us.[619]

(5) *The Debate over Ability or Inability*

Strong reaffirmed the total inability of the sinner to turn to God or to do what is truly good in God's sight,[620] but contended also that "a certain remnant of freedom" is left to man.[621] The sinner can avoid sinning against the Holy Ghost, can choose the lesser sin, can refuse entirely to yield to some temptations, can do outwardly good acts from imperfect motives, and can seek God from motives of self-interest. But he cannot "by a single volition bring his character and life into complete conformity to God's law," nor can he "change his fundamental preference for self and sin to supreme love for God," nor "do any act, however insignificant, which shall meet with God's approval or answer fully to the demands of the law."[622] Freedom of choice within the affirmed limits, declared Strong, is "by no means incompatible with complete bondage of the will in spiritual things."[623]

---

infallibility are occasions but never causes of volitions, and that, while motives may infallibly persuade, they never compel the will" (ST[8186], 178).
[616]ST(1896)CN, 309.
[617]It is not until the fifth edition of ST(1886), referred to as ST(1896), that Strong adopts the principle of ethical monism and applies it to the doctrines of preservation and the atonement.
[618]ST(1886), 309.
[619]ST(1886), 328-334.
[620]ST(1886), 342.
[621]ST(1886), 342.
[622]ST(1886), 342.
[623]ST(1886), 344.

(6) *The Ethical Theory of the Atonement*

Strong reiterated that Christ's death is a propitiatory sacrifice, the first and main effect of which is upon God, in view of the demand of divine justice or holiness, the satisfaction of which is the necessary condition of God's justification of the believer.[624] But the relation of the atonement to humanity in Christ, which Strong had already developed in his class notes of 1882 to 1885 in such a way as to stress the obligation of Christ to meet the penalty of sin in view of his organic and corporate union with the race, was now developed.[625] Christ's union with humanity obligated him to suffer for men since, being one with the race, he then had a share in race-responsibility to divine law and justice.[626] The organic unity of the race has involved each member since Adam in the consequences of depravity, guilt and penalty, but the supernatural conception of Christ purified his nature, so that he was exposed to guilt and penalty, but not to depravity. He assumed no personal guilt, but solely the guilt of Adam's sin; he can justly bear penalty, because he inherits guilt. "Once born of the Virgin, once possessed of the human nature that was under the curse," wrote Strong, "he was bound to suffer."[627] Since his guilt is not personal, but the guilt of common racial transgression in Adam, "he who is personally pure can vicariously bear the penalty due to the sin of all."[628]

The problem which Strong sought to solve in this statement was, how can the innocent justly suffer for the guilty? Quite clearly, he was reaching for a ground of real union between Christ and humanity, as an alternative to the federal theory that Adam and Christ stand related primarily in a representative manner, in an application of the principle of imputation. While Strong at this time found the ground of union in the incarnation, it is clear that his mood at this point would be very hospitable to the suggestion that there is a more basic union of the Logos and humanity, on the pattern of ontological monism.

(7) *The Final State of the Wicked*

Strong did not change his view of the eternal punishment of the lost, but strengthened it against the theories of universal restoration and annihilation, which were being widely opposed in that decade to the traditional view.[629] He gave eternal punishment more of an inner basis, holding that a correct view of the will supports the view that the moral condition in which death finds men is their eternal condition.[630] The impenitent sinner makes for himself a character which, while not rendering the continuance of sinful action necessary, renders it certain apart from divine

---

[624] ST(1886), 411.
[625] ST(1886), 412-421.
[626] ST(1886), 412.
[627] ST(1886), 412.
[628] ST(1886), 412.
[629] ST(1886), 587-600.
[630] "Suffering has in itself no reforming power," Strong affirmed. "Unless accompanied by special renewing influences of the Holy Spirit, it only hardens and embitters the soul. We have no Scripture evidence that such influences of the Spirit are exerted, after death, upon the still impenitent" (ST[1886], 591).

grace.[631] The everlasting punishment of the wicked is not inconsistent with, but is a revelation of, God's justice.[632]

5. The 1888 Volume, *Philosophy and Religion*

Consideration has already been given to numerous sermons, essays and articles prepared by Strong, and later included in the volume *Philosophy and Religion*, which appeared in 1888. Included in this volume were four essays which were written specifically for this publication. They bore the titles "Modern Idealism," "The New Theology," "Dante and the Divine Comedy," and "Poetry and Robert Browning." Also included were numerous writings which had never before appeared in print, and of these, a sermon on "The Necessity of the Atonement" is of interest for this study. The essays on Dante and Browning are significant in that they indicate that Strong already was pursuing a study of the religious views of great poets, which later resulted in works on that theme.

(1) *Sermon on "The Necessity of the Atonement"*

Strong's sermon on "The Necessity of the Atonement"[633] stressed that the world could not be redeemed without the sufferings of Christ for two reasons:

first, bcause there is an ethical principle in God's nature which demands that sin shall be punished . . . secondly, because Christ stands in such a relation to humanity that what God's holiness demands, Christ is under obligation to pay, longs to pay, inevitably does pay, and pays so fully, in virtue of his twofold nature, that every claim of justice is satisfied and the sinner who accepts what he has done in his behalf is saved.[634]

It is to Christ as obligated to make atonement to which Strong directed attention.

Many persons who concede that God can justly demand satisfaction, Strong pointed out, cannot see how the suffering of the innocent can justly replace that of the guilty, that is, how Christ can justly make satisfaction. Of this view, which recognizes no obligation on the part of Christ to suffer, Strong remarked:

I am persuaded that light can be thrown upon this particular point in the great doctrine. We shall understand the necessity of Christ's sufferings, when we consider what Christ was, and what were his relations to the race.[635]

In the subsequent formulation of his view, Strong listed Christ's obligation to suffer for men as being one of the results of his union with humanity.[636] There is nothing to indicate that Strong had in view any preincarnation union of the Logos and mankind; rather, he stressed that Christ's union with humanity "put him under obligation to suffer for the sins of men" in such a way as to designate the incarnation as the time of union.[637] Strong explained:

---
[631]ST(1886), 591.
[632]ST(1886), 594.
[633]PAR, 213-219.
[634]PAR, 213.
[635]PAR, 213.
[636]PAR, 213.
[637]PAR, 215.

being one with the race, he had a share in the responsibility of the race to the law and the justice of God—a responsibility not destroyed by his purification in the womb of the virgin. . . .[638]

Christ "recognized the organic unity of the race, and saw that, having become one of the sinning race," Strong added, "he had involved himself in all its liabilities, even to the suffering of death, the great penalty of sin."[639] That the obligation of Christ to suffer was not conceived at this time by Strong to derive from a pre-incarnate union with humanity is plain from the statement that:

> he might have declined to join himself to humanity, and then he need not have suffered. He might have sundered his connection with the race, and then he need not have suffered. But once born of the Virgin, and possessed of the human nature that was under the curse, he was bound to suffer.[640]

While the problem of justifying the sufferings of Christ for the innocent seemed now to press upon Strong, it is clear that the view of an incarnate union with humanity seemed a sufficient explanation. But Strong sought to supplement the traditional view that an imputed guilt furnished the explanation of Christ's sufferings. The doctrine of atonement, he pointed out,

> needs such an actual union of Christ with humanity and such a derivation of the substance of his being by natural generation from Adam as will make him, not simply the constructive heir, but the natural heir, of the guilt of the race. . . . Christ, then, so far as his humanity was concerned, was in Adam just as we were, and, as Adam's descendant, he was responsible for Adam's sin like every other member of the race; the chief difference being that, while we inherit from Adam both guilt and depravity, he whom the Holy Spirit purified, inherited not the depravity but only the guilt. [641]

Consequently, Strong asserted a union of Christ and the race sufficient to obligate the provision of atonement, by affirming that "guilt was not simply imputed to Christ; it was imparted also."[642] The question which would soon present itself was, did not the incarnation union with humanity have its roots in an even deeper, pre-incarnation union?

(2) Essay on "The New Theology"

The trend to an inner, spiritual interpretation of Christian doctrine, in the theological movements contemporary with Strong, was evaluated in his essay on "The New Theology,"[643] which appeared in the January, 1888, *Baptist Quarterly Review*.

The newer emphasis on divine immanence which characterized the New Theology,[644] Strong reported, was "derived from idealistic sources, and is distinctly Berkeleian and Hegelian in its spirit," although many con-

---

[638]PAR, 213-14. "If Christ had been born into the world like other men, he too would have had . . . to bear, first, the burden of depravity, and secondly, the burden of guilt. . . . The purging away of all depravity did not take away guilt, in the sense of just exposure to the penalties of violated law. . . . Justice still held him to answer for the common sin of the race" (PAR, 214).
[639]PAR, 214.
[640]PAR, 214.
[641]PAR, 215.
[642]PAR, 218.
[643]PAR, 164-179.
[644]Strong also designated this as "a theology of exaggerated individualism" (PAR, 164).

temporary theologians were not consistently applying the idealistic principles.[645] Strong expressed the new mood:

Internal revelation is substituted for external; all men are conceived of as more or less inspired; the boundaries between the natural and the supernatural are broken down. Some recent writers pride themselves on having discovered anew the thought which made the early church so devoted and yet so active—the thought that in God we live and move and have our being, and they ascribe the decline of Christianity to the fact that Augustine and Calvin lost sight of it, and looked upon God, after a deistic fashion, as a mechanical contriver of the universe and a worker upon it from without. As if some of the noblest utterances of this great truth of God's immanence had not proceeded from Augustine's and from Calvin's lips.[646]

Strong granted that divine immanence did not receive sufficient attention from Butler and Paley, and that it should be given proper emphasis, and the new light thrown upon it by contemporary thought should be welcomed. "But, then," he added,

"let us equally remember that God not only speaks with the still small voice in the constitution of man and in the course of human history, but also by outward miracles of healing and resurrection, by the incarnation and death of his Son, and by the external revelations of Scripture. God's immanence is a vast truth; but we must not let it hide from our eyes the other truth of God's transcendence. He who is 'in all,' and 'through all,' is also 'above all'; and, if he had not by miracle proved his transcendence, we probably should never have believed in his immanence."[647]

The influence of idealism upon the New Theology, Strong said, came through the identity-system of Jonathan Edwards. The radical error in Edward's philosophy, he added, was "his denial of substance."[648] The mental unity of divine ideas was taken as itself constituting the reality of things. Such a view, Strong insisted, could not avoid pantheism:

No such things as physical forces exist. Nature become a mere phantom, and God is the only cause in the universe. It seems plain to me that this doctrine tends to pantheism. If all natural forces are merged in the one all-comprehending will of God, why should not the human will be merged in the will of God also? Why should not mind and matter alike be the phenomena of one force which has the attributes of both? Such a scheme makes supernatural religion impossible, for the reason that nature is denied, and everything—that is to say, nothing—becomes supernatural. How shall we save the sense of sin, if every sinful thought and impulse is the result of the divine efficiency? And, finally, how shall we save the character of God, if he is the direct author of moral evil?[649]

Strong scored especially the relationship between Christian consciousness and the Scriptures, as required by the New Theology. While not formally setting the Scriptures aside, or assigning them an inferior authority, it sets them side by side with the intuitions and experience of the believer, he protested. The idealistic scheme "depreciates the outward revelation, with the intent of exalting the inward."[650] Its motivation is "a

---
[645]PAR, 167.
[646]PAR, 167.
[647]PAR, 167.
[648]PAR, 168.
[649]PAR, 169. It is curious how often Strong rejected idealism on the ground that it led invariably to pantheism. Given such a mood, an idealism which was not pantheistic in the sense that selves are not parts of God, would remove his most frequent objection.
[650]PAR, 170. This emphasis, Strong pointed out, "connects itself very naturally with . . . the illumination-theory of inspiration, which regards inspiration as merely an in-

spirit of scientific unity," by which it appears constrained to argue, from the presence of something of the nature of inward revelation, to the position that all revelation is necessarily inward. He added:

> Christian consciousness becomes the only medium of receiving religious truths. The intuitions of the Christian are the final test. And so we have Christian preachers declaring that they will preach no doctrines which they have not realized in their own experience, and private Christians asserting that what they cannot understand they will not believe.[651]

Consciousness, Strong warned, is a con-knowing, not a new or collateral source of truth but a con-knowing of truth about God "in connection with and by means of his written word."[652] The Christian's spiritual perception is always somewhat imperfect and deceptive by virtue of remaining depravity, so that the ethico-religious consciousness is, without rectification by express divine revelation, "utterly untrustworthy."[653] Nor does an appeal to the Holy Spirit warrant attributing to Christian consciousness an "authority aside from or co-ordinate with that of Scripture."[654] The moment Christian experience is exalted into a source of Christian doctrine, the Scriptures, which constitute the only safe foundation for Christian experience, are undermined.[655]

Strong traced responsibility for the newer emphases to an insistence on the immanence of God to the exclusion of his transcendence.[656] That encouraged not only an internal view of revelation, but emphasized the extra-temporal Christ or eternal Logos who upholds all things in such a way as to "forget that the historical manifestation of Christ is in the Scriptures declared to be the only ground of hope for sinners."[657] It substitutes an inward for an outward view of Jesus' atonement, for it begins with the assumption that no principle in the divine nature needs to be propitiated. Man, not God, needs to be reconciled, on this approach; the atonement exhibits God's love, convincing sinners that no obstacle to forgiveness exists on God's part, instead of satisfying divine justice.[658] Along with this, the New Theology champions the notion of a second probation.[659] The existence of Christ as eternal Logos, beyond the bounds of his historic work, is urged against the teaching of the guilt of the heathen.[660] But this

---

tensifying and elevating of the religious perceptions of the Christian, the same kind, though greater in degree, with the illumination of every believer by the Holy Spirit; and which holds, not that the Bible is, but that it contains the word of God—not the writings, but only the writers being inspired" (PAR, 170).

[651] PAR, 170.
[652] PAR, 171.
[653] PAR, 171. Strong wrote: "Where revelation speaks, there Christian consciousness may safely speak; where that is silent, the latter must be silent" (PAR, 171).
[654] PAR, 171.
[655] PAR, 172. "The logical result," Strong warned, is "the teaching that only inspiration is Christian experience, and that all Christian experience is inspiration. We shall then cherish a thousand blind hopes for which revelation furnishes no solid basis; but with these hopes will come a thousand vagaries of doctrine, and finally both the vagaries and hopes will be succeeded by the uncertainty, the unbelief, and the despair, into which an unbridled rationalism plunges the soul" (PAR, 172).
[656] PAR, 172-173.
[657] PAR, 173.
[658] PAR, 173.
[659] PAR, 174.
[660] PAR, 176.

overlooks that Christ's supra-historic manifestation is granted to the heathen in this life, and that all natural conscience and religious ideas, so far as true, are derived from him, and yet the heathen are without excuse because of their sin against light. Men do not need to see the cross on which Christ died in order to reject him. The Scripture states the limits of divine mercy, and whatever heathen are saved must cast themselves as helpless sinners upon God's plan of salvation, dimly prefigured in nature and providence.[661]

(3) *Essay on "Modern Idealism"*

Doubtless the most significant essay written by Strong for the volume on *Philosophy and Religion* is the one which remains for our examination, titled "Modern Idealism,"[662] which appeared also in the January, 1888, issue of *Bibliotheca Sacra*. Its special interest derives from the fact that it furnished so unqualified an indictment of a "one substance" theory of reality, so short a time before Strong declared for ethical monism.

Strong's essay was devoted to an examination of the view which "regards ideas as the only object of knowledge and denies the independent existence of the external world."[663]

Kant circumvented the logical descent of Berkeleian to Humean philosophy, by going back to Locke and insisting that all sense-perception involves elements not derived from sense—but he erred in claiming for such intuitions as space, time and cause only a subjective existence and validity.[664] Kant's failure to see that the mind, in cognizing the qualities of objects, cognizes also a substance to which the qualities belong, led Fichte to reduce all knowledge to knowledge of self.[665] Hegel revived and carried to its extreme the idealistic principle which Kant purposed to check.[666]

Strong explained the influence of Hegelianism upon later philosophy in terms of the gratification which monism affords to the speculative intellect. He granted that "omniscient idealism has been a valuable counterweight to the agnostic materialism" of the day.[667] But the view "requires of its consistent defenders," of which Strong suggested there are few, "a rejection of the facts of history and of our moral nature."[668]

---

[661]PAR, 177. Strong used firm language in indicting the leaning of the new immanentism toward a second probation of the heathen: "In this great controversy between God and the sinning children of men, let us put ourselves upon the side of God and not upon the side of his enemies. Let us declare God to be true, though we have to call every man a liar" (PAR, 176).

[662]PAR, 58-74.

[663]PAR, 58.

[664]PAR, 59-60.

[665]PAR, 60.

[666]PAR, 61.

[667]PAR, 61. "Together with the evolutionary hypothesis of the origin of the world, it has found able advocates in Caird, Green and Seth, in Great Britain, and in Harris, Bowne and Royce in America" (PAR, 61).

[668]On this view, Strong complained, "sin is a necessity of finiteness and progress. Even Jesus, as he was a man, must be a sinner. The sense of remorse and the belief in freedom are alike illusions. It can hold no view of God which regards him as a veritable moral personality, or as the author of a supernatural revelation. Conscience with its testimony to the voluntariness and the damnableness of sin, as it is the eternal witness against Pantheism, is also the eternal witness against the Idealism of Hegel. We may believe that the utter inability of Hegelianism to explain

The indictment of idealism here, as always in Strong's earlier statements, is coupled with an indictment of pantheism. Strong distinguished Lotze by a view of idealism which regards idea as in the divine Intelligence, to which the perceiving mind is intimately present, and in which the perceiving mind views it, but there is no differentiation of his position from pantheistic idealism in general.[669] Strong's attacks are concentrated, therefore, against quantitative monism, with its contention that all reality is reducible numerically to God—a thesis to which personalistic idealism also was opposed.

Strong conceded that the objective idealisms are not subject to many of the attacks which could be pressed against subjective idealisms.[670]

But he offered vigorous objections to objective idealism also. It rests upon "the exceedingly precarious assumption" that the mind knows "only *ideas*, while Natural Realism has in its favor the universal belief of mankind that we know *things* as well."[671] Furthermore, idealism is inconsistent, for it must admit that "in knowing ideas the mind knows self" and "self-consciousness is a witness to the existence of a permanent somewhat underneath all ideas, and which all ideas presuppose,"[672] so that idealism is driven to grant the existence of something before ideas and more than ideas, that is, the self. Moreover, objective idealism unavailingly tries to maintain at the same time the purely ideal character of the external world and "that the object perceived is different from the act of perception."[673] In addition, idealism affords "no proper account of the distinction between the non-ego in the shape of ideas and the non-ego in the shape of our bodily organism" and thus ignores the distinction between the body and the idea of the body.[674]

---

or even to recognize the ethical problems of the universe is the chief reason for the recent cry, 'Back to Kant!' by which the younger thinkers are summoned to return to the feet of a master who at least recognized a moral law and a God who vindicates it" (PAR, 61).

[669]PAR, 63.

[670]Objective idealism "regards ideas as something distinct from the cognition of them; it may even hold that these ideas are themselves extended, and that they have all the qualities which we now attribute to the material and external object. May not God suggest ideas *to* me, which are not *in* me nor *of* me? . . . While it is objective to man, it is subjective to God. So, it may be argued, does the universe exist. God's ideas constitute its reality, its permanence, its stability" (PAR, 65).

[671]PAR, 66. "Certainly the presumption is," Strong wrote, "that the universal belief of mankind is a correct one; and this belief is not to be surrendered until it be shown self-contradictory. To say that things *are* ideas, is to common sense a yet greater absurdity" (PAR, 66).

[672]PAR, 66.

[673]"If objective idealism be not resolved into subjective idealism, if non-egoistic idealistic idealism be not resolved into subjective idealism—then the existence of the object cannot be dependent upon the percipient act, its *esse* cannot be *percipi*. Its intellectual existence . . . is contingent upon the existence of a perceiving intellect. But this is only to say it cannot be known without knowledge. . . . The error of the theory is in confounding intellectual existence, or the existence of the object as known, with its real existence" (PAR, 67).

[674]PAR, 67. "This belief in the existence of a real in distinction from a merely ideal body, a body that is extended and external to the mind, is the most primary and important fact of sense-perception," Strong affirmed. "Here . . . Natural Realism has a stronghold from which no speculative Idealism can ever dislodge it. . . . The latter (realism) represents the facts of our experience, while the former (idealism) contradicts them" (PAR, 67, 68).

The new idealism seeks to avoid solipsism, Strong added, by taking refuge in the consciousness of God and "making that the guarantee for the objective existence of our fellowmen."[675] But the same principle which removes all guarantee of our fellow-men at the same time destroys any guarantee for the existence of God.[676]

Strong attacked the monistic conception of the universe espoused by idealism. He wrote:

> It claims to be a 'one-substance' theory, although it should in consistency call itself a 'no-substance' theory instead. It repudiates the doctrine of two substances, matter and mind, because it cannot understand how mind should ever in that case be able to know matter. Materialism declares that mind knows matter because mind is matter; idealism declares that mind knows matter because matter is mind. The one is just as much an arbitrary assumption as is the other. Both are *argumenta ad ignorantiam*. Because we cannot explain *how* we know that which is other than ourselves, shall we deny that we *do* know things and beings other than ourselves?[677]

Since idealism must recognize the action of will upon matter, argued Strong, it ought not to be reluctant to recognize an action of the intellect upon matter.[678]

After exhausting philosophical criticisms of idealism, Strong asked that the view be judged "by its probable influence upon Christian faith."[679] He called attention to logical tendencies of the system, which would ultimately make themselves felt.

The first tendency listed, that of merging all things in God, shows how exclusively Strong viewed idealism in pantheistic terms at this time. "Instead of tracing all things to one source," Strong affirmed, "it prefers the shorter and easier method of asserting that all things are but forms of one substance."[680]

Secondly, idealism destroys all distinction between the possible and the actual, Strong complained. A possible universe, in God's thoughts, is already an actual universe, just as an actual universe, in God's thoughts, is a possible universe.[681] The universe is as eternal as God's thought of it, for the divine thought is the universe. Strong protested:

> Second causes do not exist; for, as things are but the ideas of God, all changes in these things are but the direct effects of a divine efficiency. All causal connections

---

[675] PAR, 69.

[676] PAR, 69. "If we know only ideas in the case of our fellow-men," Strong argued, "we can know only ideas in the case of God" (PAR, 69-70). This yields "a consciousness, with no being to *be* conscious; consciousness without a self; universal thinking without a thinker—ah, it is our old Hegelian acquaintance: thinking thinks!'" (PAR, 70).

[677] PAR, 70.

[678] "If I can *move* something outside myself, why can I not *know* something outside myself?" Strong asked. "It seems absurd to suppose that I *produce effects* only upon an ideal world when I exert my powers of volition—why is it not equally absurd to suppose that I *know* only an ideal world when I exert my powers of sense-perception?"

[679] PAR, 71.

[680] PAR, 71. "The conception of a God who *is* all, seems to it preferable to that of a God who *creates* all. In this, the doctrine runs directly counter to the Scripture teaching that 'in the beginning God created the heaven and the earth,' and so removes the barrier which God himself has set up against a pantheistic confounding of himself with his works" (PAR, 71).

[681] PAR, 71-72.

between different objects of the universe are at an end. No such things as physical forces exist. Nature becomes a mere phantom, and God is the only cause of all physical events. Sciences become at once not the study of nature, but the study of God.[682]

Thirdly, idealism destroys all distinction between truth and error, Strong contended. If ideas are the reality, how can false ideas exist, he asked, since the objects are presumed to be mental.[683] Moreover, since all motives are ideas, and all ideas are due to direct divine causation, the necessitarian can insist that the soul has no permanent existence of its own and no freedom to furnish a basis for responsibility.[684]

Fourthly, idealism cannot safeguard the identity of personal beings. If man's body, so far as objective to him, is an idea of God, then his soul likewise "may be a mere idea of God also."[685]

Fifthly, the Christian doctrine of redemption is by-passed when once sin is viewed as a natural necessity and ideas are regarded as the only real objects of knowledge:

It is no longer necessary to believe in an external revelation of God's will. Internal revelation, Christian consciousness, the direct presentation to our minds of new ideas from God, takes the place of outward Scripture, or assumes coordinate importance and authority with it.[686]

Nor is it necessary, on idealist premises, to distinguish clearly between ideal characterization and real history, and consequently the historical Jesus, his atoning death, resurrection and ascension, may be conceived ideally.

Historical testimony becomes of little account when it contradicts a preconceived theory; the idea is better than the fact—for the fact itself is only an idea.[687]

Idealism fluctuates therefore between the self-deification of solipsism and a morality-abolishing pantheism, Strong summarized. In the concluding evaluation, he indicted the new view in the harshest terms. Concerning the idealist, remarked Strong, "I know of no better remedy for his

---

[682]PAR, 72.
[683]PAR, 72. It is significant that Strong assumed that idealism necessarily involved not only quantitative monism, but also epistemological monism; actually, personalistic idealism rejected both in the interest of qualitative monism, numerical pluralism, and epistemological dualism. Strong asked: "Is it not beyond dispute that we have ideas which do not correspond to the objective truth? Are *these* realities also? and is God the author of them? . . . Is it not plain that no explanation is possible that identifies the idea with the object? Does not this abolish the distinction between truth and error, and make both our right and our wrong the direct product of the divine will?" (PAR, 72).
[684]PAR, 72. "What we call the moral law is nothing but the presentation of a sublime divine idea," Strong suggested, in evaluating idealism, "and what we call sin is nothing but the presentation of another divine idea which is given us simply to contrast with, and to emphasize, the first. Both evil and good are purely ideal. . . . The freedom to choose the good and to refuse the evil—this does not exist; for this would imply the existence of a substance separate from that of God" (PAR, 72-73).
[685]PAR, 72. The context makes clear that Strong's use of the word "may" here does not imply a wavering in his identification of idealism with quantitative monism. The "may" does not express doubt, but is consequential. Strong added: "With the evidence of personal identity the evidence of personal immortality is lost also" (PAR, 73).
[686]PAR, 73.
[687]PAR, 73.

disease than the acceptance of the Lord Jesus Christ."[688] As at the Reformation, by reception of Christ, men had been delivered from their skepticism of the existence of objective truth and righteousness, and of God himself, "so now in the individual heart, again and again, the reception of Christ, giving the first sense of reality within, leads the soul outward to the recognition of a real world and of a real morality outside of it."[689]

6. The 1889 Lectures

In 1889 appeared the second edition[690] of Strong's *Systematic Theology*. In the preface, Strong wrote that he had subjected the first edition

to a thorough revision, and now sends it out with its *errata* so far as possible corrected with many slight improvements of statement, and with more than seven hundred new references, quotations, or brief additions to the substance of the work.[691]

But an examination of the work, coupled with Strong's failure to indicate any important theological changes, and the fact that the paging of the old edition is almost uniformly preserved, except in the indexes, supports the conviction that there was in this period no substantial change of viewpoint.

7. The 1890 Lectures

Nor does there appear any significant development in Strong's thought by the time of the third edition[692] of his work a year later. That edition Strong himself described in the preface as "a reprint, with slight alterations, of the second."[693] Strong expressed appreciation of the notice given his work in England as well as in America, but there is no indication of substantial theological change in the third edition.

8. The 1892 Lectures

The demand for a fourth edition[694] of Strong's work resulted, he commented in the preface, in a publication in 1892 "once more substantially without change from the second edition."[695]

Before Strong brought out another edition of his work, his theological perspective had radically changed. The 1896 edition of his *Systematic Theology*,[696] no less than a series of articles which appeared before that volume, indicate his espousal of a new philosophical principle. But it is clear from the consideration of Strong's writings prior to 1892 that ethical monism, as he came to designate his later viewpoint, was at most a marginal interest. Both in his conversion experience and in the Christian home in which he was raised was discerned the influence of the evangelist Charles G. Finney. His seminary studies at Rochester, under Ezekiel Gilman Robinson, afforded no encouragement in the direction of a thorough-going spiritualistic view. Strong's studies under Robinson in 1858 and 1859 were in the earlier days, before his teacher had worked out a final system. When Strong began teaching in 1872, he had worked out his lectures, as we have seen,[697] independently of Robinson's writings, in order not to stifle the creative urge. The curious fact, in view of the partial concessions

---

[688]PAR, 74.
[689]PAR, 74.
[690]ST (1889).
[697]*Supra*, 83-84.

[691]ST (1889), x.
[692]ST (1890).
[693]ST (1890). xi.

[694]ST (1892).
[695]ST (1892), xi
[696]ST (1896).

made by Robinson in the liberal direction, is that Strong's teaching from the beginning stood more firmly in the evangelical tradition. Strong's treatment of the divine attributes and of the Trinity disclosed less metaphysical reserve, his early view of the Scriptures was higher than Robinson's, his view of man's primitive state involved a primal perfection rather than the primal innocence which Robinson upheld, his view of atonement protested against the subjectivistic factors in Robinson's statement which seemed to jeopardize an objective substitution, and declared also for forensic justification as against Robinson's tendency to incorporate elements of sanctification in this experience. The openness of Strong to the Darwinian theory, from the very first, was encouraged by Robinson's attitude that science at most could determine the method of divine creation, and that there was no need for theology to place itself in hostility to scientific findings. Robinson, however, had refused to concede the case for animal ancestry.[698] Strong expressed the view that had Robinson written his theological effort a quarter century later, he would not have hesitated to affirm man's descent from the brute.[699] As Strong moved to a pictorial interpretation of the Genesis account, and accepted also the theistic evolution of man, he came also to raise more critical questions about the infallibility of Scripture in the areas of history and science, yet was reluctant to concede error even in these areas, although he expressed appreciation of the spirit of reverent criticism found in Robinson's approach. Neither Robinson nor Strong had worked out carefully the relationship between general and special revelation, though both affirmed the priority of Biblical disclosure, and both assumed, that, despite the noetic distortion of sin, the continuity of general and special revelation is apparent. There was therefore a deep interest, seen especially in Strong's voluminous quotations from contemporary sources, in the speculative theisms of the day. But at one point they agreed wholly, as far as the published lecture notes tell the story: there was in the writings of neither Robinson nor of Strong any special enthusiasm for the contemporary idealisms, so far as a monistic view of substance is concerned. Robinson was non-committal in such a way as to preclude assigning to him an openness tc the newer emphasis on a more complete divine immanence, whereas Strong's proclamation of ethical monism did not come until after the 1892 revision of his work.

Two years later, in 1894, at least three events vitally significant for this study took place. In terms of them we may consider Strong's espousal of ethical monism.

---

[698]Robinson wrote: "The supposition of an original savage condition, but little if any removed from the level of the more intelligent brutes, is a mere conjecture, unsupported by any decisive evidence, besides being wholly contrary to the Scriptures" (CT, 122).

[699]Strong's statement was: "One may question . . . whether the Scriptural argument against man's descent from the brute would have seemed to him too conclusive, if this chapter had been written a quarter of a century later, when the Darwinian theory is so generally accepted, and when evolution is regarded by so many theologians as the method of creation pursued by the immanent God" (Art. [1896], 182). The emphasis on divine immanence should be noted.

CHAPTER III

THE LATER INTERACTION WITH PERSONALISTIC IDEALISM

The year 1894 marks a turning-point in Strong's theology. The importance of the ideological change could hardly be discerned two years later, when the fifth edition of Strong's theological system appeared, with the brief statement in the preface that

> for substance . . . the book remains unchanged—but with four exceptions . . . where the principle of Ethical Monism is adopted, and application of it made to the explanation of the doctrines of Preservation and of the Atonement.[1]

That the changes in the interest of ethical monism should be confined to "four exceptions" in a prevailingly orthodox system suggested, both to evangelical and non-evangelical theologians, that Strong had not yet discerned the implications of the new immanentism. But the public change in Strong's theological views came midway between the 1892 and 1896 editions of his theology, and can be dated more precisely in 1894.

In the latter year, three significant occurrences may be noted. The death of Ezekiel Gilman Robinson, Strong's predecessor, occurred on June 13, 1894. Several months previously, Strong read for the first time Robinson's *Christian Theology*.[2] In his contribution to a memorial volume, Strong affirmed that he had constructed his system "without once looking at what my former teacher had written" and added that "in fact, the pages of his work have only, within a few months, been in my hands for careful scrutiny."[3] Also in 1894 Strong began contributing to *The Examiner*, a Baptist publication in its eighty-first year, a series of articles which he cautiously characterized as tentative and which, upon their later inclusion in 1899 in a published volume, titled *Christ in Creation and Ethical Monism*,[4] he qualified as "a series of guesses at truth," although a more positive attitude toward the views is quite apparent in their presentation.

---

[1] ST(1896), x. Strong was not alone, in the world of theology and philosophy, in misunderstanding the significance of revisions made in a new edition. The revisions made by Kant in the second edition of his *Critique* constitute a striking instance of this. It is not safe to trust an author's own appraisal of the significance of changes in his thought.

[2] E. H. Johnson, who edited Robinson's autobiography and the supplement and critical estimates which appeared in the memorial volume (EGR) to which Strong contributed the essay, "Ezekiel Gilman Robinson as a Theologian," stated in the preface: "In the spring of 1893 Dr. Robinson was prevailed upon to begin the dictation of an autobiography. At the same time the contributors and the topics for a memorial volume were agreed upon substantially as they now appear" (EGR, iii).

[3] Art.(1896), 168.

[4] Referred to hereafter as CCEM. The second essay in this volume, captioned "Ethical Monism," is taken from *The Examiner* in 1894, and the third essay, captioned "Ethical Monism Once More," from *The Examiner* in 1895.

It is the more remarkable that in 1896, when Strong's memorial appreciation of Robinson was published, he wrote:

> I am humbled to find how much of my own thinking that I have thought original has been an unconscious reproduction of his own. Words and phrases which I must have heard from him in the class-room thirty-five years ago, and which have come to be a part of my mental furniture, I now recognize as not my own but his. And the ruling idea of his system,—that stands out as the ruling idea of mind; I did not realize until now that I owed it almost wholly to him.[5]

For the organizing principle around which Strong now constructed his theological system was ethical monism, which Strong came to champion not only as "the philosophy of the future"[6] but also the "hidden ground of unity"[7] of diverse creeds and theologies.

The facts so far before us are these: (1) In 1894 Strong contributed to *The Examiner* the first articles in a series devoted to monism,[8] (2) In 1894 he read Robinson's *Christian Theology*, some months prior to Robinson's death that same year; (3) In Strong's contribution to the volume memorializing Robinson, Strong made the striking assertion that the ruling idea of his own system had been, quite unconsciously, absorbed from Robinson.

The further complication is that (4) this dissertation makes it quite clear that Robinson, in his published writings, did not commit himself to monism, but rather, resisted it. Strong nowhere refers, in his memorial essay, to statements made by Robinson outside his *Christian Theology*, and since his theological impression of Robinson is formed almost exclusively from the latter's writings, the question is not inappropriately raised whether Strong did not subconsciously infuse into Robinson's structure a meaning which Robinson's words cannot be made to bear directly. The question naturally arises whether Strong's evaluation of his debt to his teacher—

> to my teacher and predecessor I owe more than I owe to any one else outside of my own family circle; and since this indebtedness must color all my judgments, it will be best to state frankly, at the start, what the debt was; the reader can then make what allowance he chooses for the personal equation.[9]

—contained a somewhat unjustifiable element of enthusiasm with relation to ethical monism. It is a curious circumstance, that, in *Christ in Creation*

---

[5] Art.(1896), 168.
[6] CCEM, 22.
[7] CCEM, 22.
[8] Already in the opening address delivered May 26, 1893, by Strong, as president of the American Baptist Missionary Union, on "The Decree of God the Great Encouragement to Missions," one finds the immanentistic emphasis on the order and regularity of the universe and history, rather than the miraculous, as especially disclosive of God: "I am bound to see Christ in nature, executing the divine will and revealing the divine wisdom in the unfailing regularity of physical law. . . . Human history is in like manner Christ's execution of the eternal purpose of God. . . . All reason and conscience, all science and philosophy, all civilization and education, all society and government, in short, all the wheels by which the world moves forward toward its goal have a living spirit within the wheels, and that living spirit is Christ, declaring, unfolding, and executing the decrees of God. Christ, the Son of man, is the throbbing heart of humanity" (CCEM, 272-274) . . . "Even now the government is upon Christ's shoulder. He is conducting the march of civilization. He is turning and overturning the systems of philosophers and the thrones of kings" (CCEM, 282).
[9] Art.(1896), 163.

and Ethical Monism, in replying to critics of a monistic position, it was not to the precedent of Robinson, but rather to the writings of Lotze, Ladd, Upton and Bowne, to whom Strong appealed, and whom he most frequently quoted in the sections of his *Systematic Theology* revised in the interest of the newer view.

One other clue is given, in Strong's final literary work,[10] to an influential source of his thought, especially on the doctrine of atonement, as it came to be modified in these later years.

In this connection, Strong disclosed that he had resisted the federal theology from seminary days.[11] To explain imputation on the ground of God's covenant with Adam and with Christ, Strong protested, "seemed to involve God in a merely forensic process, to make him a God of expedients, to reduce divine justice to bookkeeping, to ignore all truth and reality in God."[12] Strong suspended judgment on the subject, seeking further light.[13] His view of a realistic union between Adam and humanity, as the basis of imputation, was encouraged by a mystical experience of union with Christ, during his early pastoral experience.[14] Strong stated:

My federalism was succeeded by a *realistic theology. Imputation is grounded in union*, not union in imputation. Because I am one with Christ, and Christ's life has become my life, God can attribute to me whatever Christ is, and whatever Christ has done. The relation is *biological*, rather than forensic.[15]

This discovery was not original, Strong explained, for "many so called 'mystics'" had made it previously, and it transformed "a theology of technicalities into a theology of life."[16]

Strong disclosed that, in the application of a principle of life rather than of legal figures to the relationship of the race to Adam, he had been encouraged by

the reading of an old book by Baird, entitled "The Elohim Revealed," in which God's imputation of Adam's sin to all his descendants was explained as a simple recognition of their natural inheritance from him or an enfeebled and perverse will.[17]

To this Strong added the idea of subliminal tendencies constantly striving against the good, and also that of an eternal divine act which summed up and judged humanity as a race.[18]

---

[10] Strong, WSIB, 92.
[11] Robinson, Strong's former pastor and theology teacher, opposed it, as we have already seen, but Strong stated in WSIB that "the preaching to which I listened when a child, and the instruction of the theological seminary which I afterward received, emphasized the doctrine of the Covenants, and answered objections by referring the objector to the unsearchable wisdom or sovereignty of God" (WSIB, 86). Strong either heard it from other seminary professors, or Robinson may have changed his viewpoint. What makes the latter unlikely is that Strong's criticisms of Robinson's view of the atonement were almost all along the line of his endangering of its true objectivity. But Strong reported clearly: "I entered the theological seminary, and there encountered the full strain upon my faith of the federal theology" (WSIB, 89).
[12] WSIB, 86.
[13] WSIB, 89.
[14] WSIB, 90.
[15] WSIB, 91.
[16] WSIB, 92.
[17] WSIB, 92.
[18] WSIB, 93.

But this left "the great problem of theology"—that of explaining divine imputation of humanity's sin to Christ.[19] Strong disclosed that he had "privately consulted Dr. Shedd" and that "he could only call it a mystery of God."[20] In his dissatisfaction, Strong "wanted to find some union of Christ with humanity which would make this imputation also realistic and biological."[21] He added:

I have found it, and have expounded it, in my book entitled, "Christ in Creation." It is my chief contribution to scientific theology; and though I claim to have thrown new light on the doctrine of God's law, and of union with Christ, it is by my explanation of God's imputation of all human sin to Christ that my theology must stand or fall.[22]

It is apparent then that Strong, in inquiring into the statements of the new immanentism, would be attracted by a view which grounded the union of Christ and humanity more intimately than a linkage of Christ to the race and its guilt only in terms of imputation by divine covenant and a consequent incarnation. At the same time, Strong would resist any viewpoint which destroyed human freedom and responsibility; pantheism he regarded as the enemy of all true religion. From the motivations influential in Strong's thought at this period, it is clear that he would give favorable hearing to an idealism which combined qualitative monism and numerical pluralism, and this was the distinctive mark of personalistic idealism. These terms call for precise definition, in view of Strong's use of the phrase, ethical monism.[23]

Strong appears to have originated the phrase "ethical monism." While much of the philosophical emphasis to which he applied the nomenclature is, in its broad outlines, harmonious with the teaching both of Lotze and Bowne, it is unlikely that they would have encouraged the use of such a designation for the viewpoint. Both Lotze and Bowne doubtless would have avoided the word "monism" as obscuring the pluralistic emphasis of their systems:[24] Bowne, indeed, sometimes set himself against all monisms as

---

[19] WSIB, 93.

[20] WSIB, 93.

[21] WSIB, 93. From the beginning of his teaching of theology, Strong propounded an "ethical theory of the atonement" which insisted on an objective propitiation, but protested against the formality and externality of the Anselmic view, which Strong labelled as commercial. But until now, Christ's union with humanity had been viewed as being established by the incarnation.

[22] WSIB, 93.

[23] The word *monism* designates the view that all reality is one, whether qualitatively in kind or quantitatively in number. The emphasis on qualitative monism, but not quantitative monism, is common both to Strong and the personalistic idealists; Strong used the designation of ethical monism to guard against a quantitative monism, just as personalism insisted on a combination of qualitative monism with numerical pluralism. The views of Strong and Bowne are monistic only in the qualitative sense (the universe has a fundamental unity in terms of ultimate spiritualistic reality); they are not—Bowne actually, and Strong unquestionably in intent—monistic in the quantitative sense (the reduction of all reality ultimately to one being or thing, rather than to a manifold of beings). This distinction must be kept in mind because Bowne's criticisms of monism are launched against quantitative monism, whereas Strong's espousal of ethical monism repudiated, in intent, quantitative monism. The distinctive use of these terms is formulated by Calkins, PPP, 9.

[24] The pluralistic note in Lotze, although finally winning out, is not without compromises. Lotze had been influenced by Leibniz, but was more impressed by the

if the word necessarily involves the notion of quantitative monism as well as qualitative monism, and has been credited with introducing the term "pluralism" into the United States. But all three thinkers were aligned on the side of qualitative monism, insisting that the fundamental nature of reality is spiritual. This phase of his theory, as we shall see, Strong further designated as "metaphysical monism." The failure to qualify the metaphysical structure in terms of pluralism, at this juncture, raises the question whether, in point of fact, Strong's view did not yield to more of a monistic emphasis, whatever his intentions, than personalistic idealism permits; the question will, at any rate, serve to heighten interest in the relevant statements afforded by Strong's theology.

But it was by the term "ethical" that Strong intended to safeguard the pluralistic nature of his system. The only metaphysical monism to which he could subscribe, he emphasized, was one which made room for "psychological dualism"—or the relative independence and moral freedom of finite, created persons.[25] By this term, he signified his renunciation of pantheism, and the enthronement of a view of man's moral and spiritual relationship with God which would permit a view of man's sinfulness without involving Deity in sin. For this ethical emphasis in his view, Strong found abundant encouragement in Lotze and Bowne. Lotze had championed the demand for human freedom as absolutely fundamental to the religious character of his world view.[26] Bowne had devoted a chapter of his work on theism to "The World-Ground as Ethical," and had made the moral argument, coupled with the unitary intelligence of experience, the central ingredients of his argument for the existence of God, in such a way as to emphasize human freedom and responsibility.[27]

While the exact manner in which the influences of personalistic idealism made themselves felt in Strong's thinking are not known to us, it is clear that he was familiar with the work of Lotze,[28] Ladd and Bowne. He quoted

---

unity of the universe than by its variety, contrary to Leibniz' multitudinous, windowless monads. In some moods Lotze closely approached absolutism and a monistic view, but his unstable tension between quantitative monism and pluralism ends with greater emphasis on pluralism. This ambivalence in Lotze, however, coupled with the circumstance that Bowne had not yet formulated his final and definite statement at this time, will help to explain elements in Strong's position which appear to fluctuate between quantitative monism and pluralism.

[25] E. S. Brightman, in a note to the writer, has pointed out that this terminology of "psychological dualism" to refer to created selves as not being parts of God is unknown to occidental philosophy, but that it is found in Hindu thought. Whether Strong's pluralism goes the entire distance of holding that there are many selves or persons in the universe, no one of which is a part of any other, in view of a repeated emphasis on all reality as a finite, graded manifestation of God, remains to be seen.

[26] Lotze demanded man's formal freedom "because we regard it as the *conditio sine qua non* for the fulfillment of ethical commands, whose obligatory majesty we consider to be the most absolute certainty and the one that needs no derivation from any other source whatever" (OPR, 100).

[27] Bowne, POT, 211-240. Knudson wrote: "The very idea of creation excludes . . . a dualistic conception of the relation of God to the world. The only dualism permissible on the theory of creation is an ethical one, and this would apply only to free beings and their relation to God" (DOR, 26).

[28] Lotze's *Mikrokosmus* first appeared from 1856-64. The translation was first begun by a daughter of Sir William Hamilton, but she did not live to complete the task, taken up by E. E. C. Jones and completed in 1885. George T. Ladd of Yale was

and cited them frequently, at first invoking them, along with many others, when their affirmations were favorable to traditional theism, or when stating his view in contrast, but now he enlisted them as mainstays of a view similar to the ethical monism which he himself projected.[29] Strong appealed frequently to Lotze, and to Ladd,[30] but especially his appeal to Bowne[31] establishes the connection in his own writings.

If the precise influences which molded Strong's thought are hidden from us, the effect of the newer emphasis on divine immanence are set forth in print, for all to see. Since the primary interest of this study is the ideological rather than the historical element, which is shadowed by an element of uncertainty, it will be appropriate now to proceed to the public utterances and the initial articles contributed by Strong to religious periodicals, in the interest of the newer view.

Strong's interest in ethical monism came to incidental expression in his public addresses on special occasions, but it was not until the appearance in *The Examiner* on November 1, 1894, of the article on "Christ in Creation" that a somewhat systematic presentation of his views was given.

Almost coincident with the appearance of the first article, Strong, on May 27, 1894, delivered his presidential address at the eightieth anniversary of the American Baptist Missionary Union, on the theme "The Love of Christ the Great Motive to Missions." Strong pointed out that the doctrine of divine immanence was transforming contemporary theological thought.[32] "Law is only perpetual miracle," he affirmed, and "evolution is nothing but the method of God." But the world has yet to learn the great truth that "the God who is so near it, who constitutes its very life, and who is carrying forward its historic development, is none other than Christ."[33]

---

the translator or translation editor of others of Lotze's works, *i.e.*, OPR, OOM, and OPP. Bosanquet, who translated Lotze's *Metaphysik* in 1884, was influenced by Lotze's monism, rather than by the pluralistic elements in his thought, and declared for impersonalistic absolutism. Royce, another of Lotze's pupils, championed personalistic absolutism. But Lotze clearly held that whatever asserts itself as a self is outside God (MET, 229).

[29]Personalistic idealism, while insisting that all reality is of the nature of consciousness, affirms that selves are not parts of God, but are created relatively independent, with moral freedom and responsibility. A central issue will be the similarity or dissimilarity of the pluralism ("psychological dualism") affirmed by Strong, and the pluralism of personalistic idealism.

[30]Strong quoted Ladd frequently as an exponent of the newer view, but his son, John Henry Strong, has confirmed the impression that Bowne was more influential than Ladd in his interaction with the personalistic view. The son had studied under Ladd at Yale, and the father eagerly scanned the class notes taken in Ladd's course on Lotze's MET, and for that matter, the notes on the last course offered by Noah Porter, in which the son was enrolled. But the elder Strong read Bowne's writings avidly; he seldom spoke of Ladd, frequently of Bowne. Ladd had studied under Lotze, was as productive as Bowne, but not nearly so influential.

[31]Bowne had dedicated to Lotze, under whom he had studied in 1873-74, the first edition of his MSFP in 1882, "in grateful recollection to the memory of my friend and former teacher," and had ventured the remark that it was "substantially Lotzean." The writer has found no evidence that Strong and Bowne were personally acquainted. Bowne's friendship included the outstanding Methodist systematic theologian of his day, Henry C. Sheldon, and Bowne knew of Shedd, for he often quoted Shedd's statement that "a system is its own best argument and defense."

[32]CCEM, 291.

[33]CCEM, 291-292. Strong stated "Incarnation and atonement, and resurrection and regeneration are, so to speak, processes of artificial selection which counteract

Concerning his theme Strong emphasized "not simply our love to Christ, not simply Christ's love to us, but rather Christ's love *in* us, going out toward the lost."[34] The law of love, he declared, is

a law of life . . . It is no arbitrary demand but is grounded in the nature of things . . . it is only the expression of the organic relation which Christ sustains to humanity and humanity sustains to Christ.[35]

Strong then affirmed the organic union of Christ and humanity to be a Biblical truth, and proceeded to make plain that he meant not merely a vital mystical union of believers with Christ, but a substantial union:

I mean nothing less than this, that all men everywhere, saints and sinners, Jews and Gentiles, since the incarnation and before the incarnation, are bound to Christ, and Christ is bound to them, by the ties of a common life. We are familiar with the thought that Christ is the Head of the church, that all regenerate souls constitute his body, that he lives and dwells in every true believer. But there is a prior union with Christ which Scripture declares to us but which we have strangely neglected. Christ is also the natural head of universal humanity; in him . . . were all things created . . . and in him . . . all things, including humanity, consist or hold together from hour to hour. . . . Have we thought of Christ's life as animating only believers? That is true of Christ's spiritual life. But there is a natural life of Christ also, and that life pulses and throbs in all men everywhere. . . . . The whole race lives, moves, and has its being in him; for he is the soul of its soul and the life of its life. There is an organism of humanity as well as an organism of the church, and Christ is the center and life of the one as he is the center and life of the other.[36]

Strong appropriated the idealistic emphasis on the objective reality of social institutions in such a way as to identify the "larger life" or the organic unity of mankind with the immanent Christ. The organizing principle of mankind is Christ, as the whole in which all individual members participate.[37] But Strong made clear, at the same time, that he did not intend an

---

the natural selection of sin and death by the law of the Spirit of life in Christ Jesus" (CCEM, 293).

[34] CCEM, 287.
[35] CCEM, 287.
[36] CCEM, 287-288.
[37] CCEM, 289. That Christ is the soul and life of humanity is an emphasis far more reflective of absolute than of personalistic idealism, but Strong precludes taking it fully in that sense and gives the emphasis, as we shall see, a pluralistic turn. The vigorous monistic expressions, which at times suggest numerical as well as qualitative monism, may reflect the influence upon Strong of the medieval mystics, whom he read often. His interest in mysticism dated back to his early preaching at Haverford where, despairing because he feared that he had "preached himself out," Strong went for a walk in the country. His son, John Henry Strong, told the writer the details of the experience which ensued. While Strong was meditating, "the thought of his union with Christ burst upon him" and he went back to his church in the spiritual power, and a revival spirit hovered over the church. From then on, Strong's interest in the mystics was whetted; he owned the two-volume life of Madam Guyon. But he resisted pantheism in the mystics as everywhere else. The lack of significant reference to the mystics, in affirming his espousal of ethical monism, would suggest, however, that Strong's major urge toward the new view came from philosophical idealism in the Lotze-Bowne stream. But the reference to the mystics as having removed the mechanical aspects of the doctrine of atonement (WSIB, 92; cf. *supra*, 97), is significant. The fact that Strong gave the doctrine of the believer's union with Christ a non-pantheistic statement, however, is equally so. And even Lotze had written that "Creator and created blend in a community of life, for the dim profundity the noblest mysticism scarce offers adequate expression." (M, II, 400), although he insisted, of course, that "created beings" are "something that is not God Himself" and constitute a "more lustrous

immanentism of the Hegelian type, in which all persons are parts of a divine person, any more than Spencer's emphasis on a merely physical unity in which individual members passively execute the impulses communicated to them from the inscrutable power which they partially manifest.[38] The organic unity with Christ is not such that it destroys free will:

> though created and upheld by Christ, every man is endowed with that priceless heritage, free-will, and he can use his free-will in resisting, instead of obeying, the law of holiness which reigns supreme.[39]

The insistence on the immanent Christ as the organizing principle and ultimate reality of all existence, furnishing the natural ground of the organic union of mankind, and yet also on the possibility of free moral and spiritual revolt against Christ, is here clearly set forth. The more precise outworking of these factors is given, in a somewhat systematic statement, in the articles contributed by Strong to the religious press of that day.[40]

I. THE 1894-1895 "EXAMINER" ARTICLES

The 1894 and 1895 issues of *The Examiner* carried a series of articles[41] by Strong, setting forth what he regarded as the meaning of the new immanentism for evangelical theology.

1. "Christ in Creation"

The introductory article, titled "Christ in Creation,"[42] appeared in *The Examiner* early in 1894. In it, Strong expressed his conviction that the redemptive work of Christ cannot be understood properly apart from a consideration of "his relation to the universe of which we form a part."[43]

Before developing his position, Strong was careful to point out that the doctrine of the Trinity is assumed, and with this the peculiar office

---

manifestation" of the other (i.e., than nature) element in God that is more peculiarly Himself" (M, II, 397).

[38] CCEM, 289.

[39] CCEM, 289-290.

[40] It may not be superfluous to remind the reader that by monism Strong intends only qualitative monism, as the companion word "ethical" is intended to emphasize. The spiritual nature of all reality does not mean, for him, that reality is numerically one; rather, mankind has a created, relative independence, which secures human freedom and responsibility. Whether Strong was as careful as contemporary personalistic idealism in the statement of this pluralism is not of concern at the moment; his overt rejection of absolute idealism is clear.

[41] These articles form the opening chapters of CCEM.

[42] CCEM, 1-15.

[43] CCEM, 1. There are but two references to significant contemporary thinkers preoccupied with this theme, one each to Borden P. Bowne and Charles Darwin and, since in both cases Strong expressed an element of disagreement within a common intensified emphasis on divine immanence, the references afford no final clue as to the direct influences at work in molding Strong's thought. But the disagreement with Bowne is simply by way of identifying Christ as the Logos.

of the second person as the revealer of God.[44] The second person, called the Word of God, is intimated by Scripture as constituting

> the principle of objectification, consciousness, intelligence within the divine nature, and the principle of expression, manifestation, revelation, by which God is made known to other beings than himself. Christ, then, is the Reason, Wisdom, and Power of God in exercise. The Father by himself is the divine nature latent, unexpressed, unrevealed. . . . In eternity Christ, the Word, is God's truth, love, and holiness, as made objective and revealed to himself. In time Christ, the Word, is God's truth, love, and holiness, as expressed, manifested, and communicated to finite creatures.[45]

Strong left no doubt that his espousal of a monistic philosophy in no way involved for him the rejection of belief in an ontological Trinity.

The concentration of theology on providence and redemption as the work of Christ has obscured, Strong suggested, the fact that creation is likewise His work.[46] Creation is "the externalization of the divine ideas through the will of Christ."[47] The universe once existed in him, as the reason of God, as "a merely intelligible and ideal world—a *cosmos noetos*, to use the words of Philo."[48] But the universe became in him, as the power of God, "an actual, real thing, perceptible to others."[49] Christ is both the creator and sustainer of the universe; His steady will constitutes its law and makes it a cosmos rather than a chaos.

The grounding of creation in the doctrine of the Trinity avoids that "pernicious form of modern idealism"[50] in which the universe is viewed as having only a logical existence, and pantheism which regards the divine self-consciousness and spiritual life as incomplete, and makes the universe necessary to God.

Subjective idealism views God as mind or thought, but not as will; hence it yields "a merely logical, but not real, existence."[51] It is powerless to explain the difference "between thoughts and things, between the idea and its realization."[52] But "there is free divine self-determination,"[53] and it follows that

> the universe is not a merely necessary evolution of divine ideas. Christ is the power as well as the wisdom of God. . . . In God there is a principle of will as well as a principle of reason. . . . The plan is not the building; decrees are not the universe. Executive volition is also necessary. . . . Creation is his (Christ's) free and sovereign act, urning ideas into realities, making objective what was only subjective before. While the plan of creation is the product of his reason, the actual world is the product also of his will.[54]

This emphasis on Christ as the principle of self-consciousness and of self-determination in God precludes pantheism no less than "a will-less and soul-less idealism."[55] Whereas pantheism regards God as exhaustively revealed in the universe, an adequate view affirms God's transcendence no less than His immanence.[56] "The Scriptures furnish . . . the antidote to

---

[44]CCEM, 2. Strong did not intend to suggest that this can be ascertained apart from the Scriptures, however, for he added: "In the divine Being there are three distinctions, which are so described to us in Scripture that we are compelled to conceive of them as persons" (CCEM, 2).
[45]CCEM, 2. [48]CCEM, 3. [51]CCEM, 4. [54]CCEM, 3-4.
[46]CCEM, 2. [49]CCEM, 3. [52]CCEM, 4. [55]CCEM, 4.
[47]CCEM, 3. [50]CCEM, 3. [53]CCEM, 3. [56]CCEM, 4.

this systematic identification of God with nature," Strong wrote, "by telling us that Christ is *before* all things and that *in* him all things consist."[57] But it is not only the denial of divine transcendence in pantheism against which Strong protested, but also its "denial of any consciousness and will in God distinct from the consciousness and will of finite creatures."[58] Whether pantheism holds that God comes to consciousness only in man or that man comes to consciousness only in God, they remain reverse sides of the same reality, and it is impossible to save significance for the concepts of human freedom, responsibility, sin and guilt in man. On the contrary, Strong affirmed, "over against the personal God there are personal beings."[59]

It is apparent, then, that Strong outlined his view, before proceeding to the question of metaphysical monism, with an insistence that (1) Christ is the principle of reality of all things; (2) the physical universe has a real, not merely a logical existence, and represents the externalization of the divine ideas by an act of will; (3) Christ continues as the constant support of the universe, so that the processes of nature and history are simply His will manifested; (4) the doctrine of the Trinity safeguards against pantheism, by insisting upon divine transcendence as well as immanence; (5) human persons are not parts of God, but in view of human freedom, responsibility, sin and guilt, are created realities outside God.

Proceeding to the relation of Christ and nature, Strong pointed out that the old conception of a world of blind, inert matter had been rendered untenable by modern physics and psychology. The qualities of matter "exist only for intelligence. We do not know it except in connection with the sensations which it causes."[60]

Matter, therefore, is spiritual in its nature. By this I do not mean that matter *is* spirit, but only that it is the living and continual *manifestation* of spirit, just as my thoughts and volitions are a living and continual manifestation of myself. It does not consist simply of ideas, for ideas, deprived of an external object and of an internal subject, are left suspended in the air.[61]

But the external object, which affords reality to the ideas and thus renders nature real, is not an underlying substance in the Aristotelian-Thomistic sense, but rather the will of Christ:

Matter exerts force, and is known only by the force which it exerts. But force is the product of *will*, working in rational ways, and will is an attribute of *spirit*. The system of forces which we call the physical universe is the immediate product of the mind and will of God, and since Christ is the mind and will of God in exercise, Christ is the Creator and Upholder of the universe.[62]

Nature is a "series of symbols" setting forth hidden divine truth, and since Christ alone can reveal this truth, the world "is virtually the thought of Christ, made intelligible by the constant will of Christ."[63]

---

[57]CCEM, 5.
[58]CCEM, 5.
[59]CCEM, 6.
[60]CCEM, 6.
[61]CCEM, 6.
[62]CCEM, 6-7. Although Strong began with the Biblical assumption that Christ is the creator and sustainer of the universe, ought he not to have closed this statement by affirming—consistently with his position—that "Christ *is* the substantial reality of the universe"?
[63]CCEM, 7.

Nature is the omnipresent Christ manifesting God to creatures. . . . When the storm darkens the sky, the Hebrew poet can leave out of mind all the intermediate agencies of moisture and electricity, and can say, "The God of glory thundereth."[64]

The interaction between individual things can be explained only when all are embraced "within a unitary Being who constitutes their underlying reality."[65] It is Christ's constant will that "gives life and stability and order" to the universe."[66]

Christ is the answer to the epistemological, no less than to the ontological problem. Just as He is the principle of cohesion, attraction and interaction in the physical universe, so He holds together the intellectual realm, and is the assurance that sense-perceptions correspond to objective facts, that we actually communicate with other intelligent beings besides ourselves, and that there is truth apart from our individual impressions of it. Knower and known must be connected by a being "which constitutes the ground of their existence."[67] We know in Christ, as well as live in Him, for He is the principle of communication between man and God and man and the universe.[68] He is the principle of induction, permitting us to argue from one part of a system to another.[69] We can say not only that God geometrizes, and that nature's laws are God's habits, and with Bowne that "the heavens are crystallized mathematics," but "we may find in Christ the mathematician."[70]

The universe is a thought; behind that thought is a mighty thinker, and that thinker is Christ, the wisdom and the power of God. . . . Since he is himself the truth of God, as well as the revealer of it, the universe with all its law and rationality is Christ, just as much as your body, your face, your speech, are you.[71]

The plain implication of this, Strong held, is that Christ is "the principle of evolution."[72] Because Christ is the "omnipresent life and law of the world,"[73] the universe is a rational, useful, progressive evolution which combines general uniformity with occasional unique advances.[74]

Christ gives "moral unity" to the system of things.[75] The law of love and holiness expresses the natural bond which unites the universe to the source of its life and blessedness. I am bound to love my neighbor as myself, because "my neighbor *is* myself—that is, has in him the same life of Christ, made intelligible by the constant will of Christ."[76]

From this it is evident that the old theistic proofs, which led from effect to cause, have been displaced by a new argument, which moves not

---

[64]CCEM, 7.
[65]CCEM, 8.
[66]CCEM, 9.
[67]CCEM, 9.
[68]CCEM, 10.
[69]CCEM, 10.
[70]CCEM, 11.
[71]CCEM, 10. The words "as much as" are here significant. Do they preclude interpreting the quotation as encouraging the identification of nature as a part of God?
[72]CCEM, 10.
[73]CCEM, 11.
[74]CCEM, 11.
[75]CCEM, 12.
[76]CCEM, 12.

from the universe to an outside Architect, but sees God as the immanent presupposition of the present order.[77] The universe, narrowly inspected, reveals in its laws and arrangements only mechanism, but looked at more broadly, yields "a marvelous impression of system, of mind, of wisdom, of benevolence."[78] Nature is the constant expression of the living God, and this living God, disclosed in nature, is "none other than Christ."[79]

Nature is *not* his body, in the sense that he is *confined* to nature. Nature *is* his body, in the sense that in nature we see him who is *above* nature, and in whom, at the same time, all things consist.[80]

In summarizing Strong's view of nature, one finds, then, the following emphases: (1) Christ is not only the logical and moral unity of the world, but he is the principle of orderly evolution; (2) Nature is not nonmental stuff, but is a force-world in view of the externalization of the divine ideas by the constant will of Christ; (3) Nature is a partial and temporary manifestation of the transcendent God; (4) The evidence for God is found most conspicuously not in the miraculous, but in the orderly system of nature, which is the direct disclosure of the constant will of Christ, the creator and sustainer of the universe.

2. "Ethical Monism"

A second article appeared in *The Examiner* in November, 1894, under the title of "Ethical Monism."[81] In it, Strong sets forth the motivations to such a view, and also the terms in which it is to be differentiated from pantheistic views.

All departments of modern thought—including physics, literature, theology, and philosophy—were moving to monism.[82] Strong cited scholars from various fields, carefully pointing out that in many cases the movement was toward "a monism without transcendence, a monism which sees no God before, beside, and above the universe."[83] Not only physicists like Thomas C. Chamberlin, the dean of the College of Science at the newly-founded University of Chicago, but poets like Robert Browning held to but one substance or principle of being, viewing the universe as "a universe of spirits."[84] In theology, J. A. Dorner had declared that the great

---

[77]CCEM, 12-13. The old argument, Strong wrote, "had the disadvantage of not being able to show that the universe, at least so far as its substance is concerned, ever had a beginning. . . . The new argument avoids this difficulty. It takes the analogy of the soul and its relation to the body. . . . I do not need to go back to the origin of nature to prove the existence of God, any more than I need to go back to my brother's birth to prove that there is a soul behind that kindly face of his" (CCEM, 12-13).
[78]CCEM, 13-14.
[79]CCEM, 14.
[80]CCEM, 14. Strong added: "Nature is an expression of the mind and will of Christ, as my face is an expression of my mind and will. Rhetorically, I can identify nature with Christ, just as I identify my face with myself. But, then, let us remember that behind and above my face is a personality, of which the face is but the partial and temporary manifestation of the Christ who is not only *in* all things, but *before* all things and *above* all things" (CCEM, 14-15).
[81]CCEM, 16-51. This appeared in three parts, in the November 1, 8, 15, 1884, issues of *The Examiner* (Vol. 72, Nos. 44, 45, 46).
[82]CCEM, 16.
[83]CCEM, 16.
[84]CCEM, 17.

discovery of the present age is the essential unity of the divine and human. In science, the doctrine of evolution is an attempt to meet the demand for unity. But primarily, the monistic tendency is philosophical, and in various forms "holds at present almost undisputed sway in our American universities."[85] Strong cited Harvard, Yale, Brown, Cornell, Princeton, Rochester, Ann Arbor, Boston and Chicago as centers of the new monistic philosophy.

Monism was therefore "the ruling idea" of the times, and it is essential that the Christian movement hold the right attitude toward it.[86] Strong's inclination was to "welcome the new philosophy as a most valuable helper in interpreting the word and works of God."[87] Strong urged: "Let us tentatively accept the monistic principle and give to it a Christian interpretation."[88] He confessed that he had come to believe this "universal tendency toward monism . . . a mighty movement of the Spirit of God . . . preparing the way for reconciliation of diverse creeds and parties by disclosing their hidden ground of unity."[89] Strong ventured the belief that his view, which "furnishes to both philosophy and theology their greatest desideratum—an Ethical Monism,"[90] had been a late insight because of a providential divine propaedeutic.[91]

Strong's interest in monism did not imply by any means a drift to pantheism. In fact, one of the specific reasons adduced by Strong for giving a Biblical turn to the monistic approach was that the new movement, if Christian theology does not "capture it for Christ, we may find that materialism and pantheism perversely launch their craft upon the tide and compel it to further their progress."[92] To work out a Christian monism appears the more necessary in view of the fact that

> there are forms of monism which do not conserve man's ethical interests, but on the other hand sacrifice man's freedom and God's transcendence in the effort to secure scientific unity.[93]

It was against monism of the pantheistic sort that Strong invoked the philosophy of Lotze, as shaping the monistic tendency in many quarters in a non-pantheistic direction:

> no thinker of recent times has had greater influence in this direction than has Lotze. He is both monist and objective idealist. Yet he holds with equal tenacity to the distinction between the divine personality and the human personality, and declares that "where two hypotheses are equally possible, the one agreeing with our moral needs and the other conflicting with them, nothing must induce us to favor the lat-

---

[85] CCEM, 21.
[86] CCEM, 22.
[87] CCEM, 22.
[88] CCEM, 22.
[89] CCEM, 22.
[90] CCEM, 50.
[91] "The full acknowledgment in theology of this doctrine of one substance has been delayed, for the same reason that the Trinity was not more clearly revealed to the Old Testament saints—preparatory doctrines needed to be taught first. . . . So the teaching of human personality, freedom, responsibility, sin, has had to precede the teaching that man is of one substance with God, because, otherwise, consubstantiality would have been interpreted as pantheism" (CCEM, 50).
[92] CCEM, 22.
[93] CCEM, 23.

ter." He intends his monism to be an Ethical Monism by which I mean simply a monism that conserves the ethical interests of mankind.[94]

If God is the source of all finite activity, Strong inquired of pantheistic monism, what room is left "for freedom or responsibility or sin or guilt in men?"[95] He indicted any view which yields "a God without moral character," who may well be designated no God at all, or which regards the universe as an exhaustive expression of God.[96] As against monisms which do not seem to be ethical, he declared:

Monism will be the philosophy of the future, but it will be monism of another sort, a monism which makes sin and Christ the Saviour from sin starting points and fundamentals of the system, instead of virtually explaining both of these away.[97]

Strong's objections to pantheistic monism were unqualified. They reduced, however, to his insistence upon a divine transcendence over the universe and upon placing human selves outside of God in such a way as to avoid a reduction of the seriousness of sin.

The denial that the physical universe exhausts God, or constitutes a complete manifestation of him, placed Strong consciously against many contemporary expressions of the monistic philosophy, even against some exponents[98] to whom he had appealed in the first place to show how widespread was the tendency to monism in his day. To the pantheistic mood, he opposed the Scripture emphasis that God is "above" as well as "in" and "through" all things.[99] The evolutionary principle is irrational, affording

no guarantee of useful progress in the history of life, unless it is the method of an intelligence and will, not only immanent in the system, but also transcendent, and continually importing into the system new increments of energy.[100]

Strong hinted that the doctrines of transcendence required some revision, on the monistic approach,[101] but he insisted that the only sufficient antidote to pantheism is the Biblical doctrine of creation, grounded in the doctrine of divine triunity:

the phrases "before the world was," "before the foundation of the world," imply that the universe had a beginning, and the declaration that God and Christ were "before all things" implies that "things" are not a part of God or necessary to God. To make

---

[94]CCEM, 20-21. "An Ethical Monism recognizes all the truth there is in pantheism, without including any of its errors. It recognizes God as the all-inclusive life of the universe, while it adds the truths which pantheism ignores—God's personality and transcendence" (CCEM, 49).

[95]CCEM, 24.

[96]CCEM, 24. In such a view, Strong emphasized, "Nothing could be but what is. It is difficult to see how anything can be in the future but what now is; in other words, how evolution itself can be possible. And if there be no transcendent element in God, how can there be any transcendent element in man? how can man possibly be different from what he is? how can his sin be anything more than the necessary product of his environment?" (CCEM, 24).

[97]CCEM, 24-25.

[98]Strong singled out Hill's *Genetic Philosophy* and Schurman's *Belief in God* as disclosing a monism which virtually excludes divine and human freedom.

[99]CCEM, 17.

[100]CCEM, 20.

[101]CCEM, 17: "Now we readily grant that the transcendence of God does not imply God's existence in space outside the universe—that would be to imagine a second universe which contained the first."

God dependent upon his universe is to ignore the Trinity, to deny that God is sovereign and self-sufficient, and to put the finite *world* in place of the eternal *Word*.[102]

The denial that man is part of God Strong opposed deliberately to the pantheistic compromise of the freedom of man:

> the Ethical Monism . . . for which I contend, is not deterministic monism; it is the monism of free-will, the monism in which personality, both human and divine, sin and righteousness, God and the world, remain—two in one and one in two—with their antagonisms as well as their ideal unity.[103]

Determinism, Strong complained, obscures the need of atonement because it blunts the sense of responsibility, and it obscures the possibility of atonement because it blunts the sense of freedom in man and God.[104] Yet Strong stressed that he did not regard ethical monism as "contravening any article of the Christian faith."[105] To the contrary, he felt that it offered a viewpoint from which Christian doctrines may be studied "more broadly, profoundly, and successfully."[106] For illustrative purposes he singled out immortality,[107] divine sovereignty and human freedom,[108] the person of Christ,[109] prayer,[110] miracle[111] and prophecy, the problem of the resurrection,[112] Christ as universal judge.[113] Therefore Strong appealed to the example of the poet Browning, as including both man and nature in a monistic view, and insisting on an identity of the human spirit with God, and yet

---

[102] CCEM, 27. Apparently the statement that nature is not a part of God, in view of the insistence that "there is but one substance—God" (CCEM, 45), is intended only to stress divine transcendence and the possibility of more than one manifestation of the same substance.

[103] CCEM, 27.

[104] CCEM, 25. "Sin and salvation are both lost sight of. Neither the fall nor the guilt of the fall is any longer intelligible; neither incarnation nor resurrection *is* any longer credible" (CCEM, 26).

[105] CCEM, 41.

[106] CCEM, 42.

[107] "If Christ be the principle and life of all things, then the immortality and value of man's soul are comprehensible" (CCEM, 42).

[108] Divine sovereignty and human freedom lose their ancient antagonism if the divine working-in-us is held in view (CCEM, 42).

[109] On the monistic approach, Christ "in taking our humanity only limits himself by a special and permanent assumption of that which was never foreign to him" (CCEM, 42).

[110] "The efficacy of prayer is intelligible . . . since Christ, who is with his people always . . . is the connecting link between them and the whole physical and moral universe, which he 'upholds by the word of his power' " (CCEM, 42).

[111] Miracle and prophecy are relieved of difficulties "when we remember that nature is a manifestation of the mind and will of Christ, and that it is as plastic in his hand as is your thought to you, the thinker of it. Jesus can ascend into heaven from the hillside at Bethany, and he can come again in the clouds so that every eye in every part of the earth can see him; for hillside and clouds and heavens are nothing but manifestations of him" (CCEM, 43).

[112] "The problem of the resurrection can no longer stumble us; all physical things are but the expression of his mind and will; since he is the resurrection and the life, all that are in the tombs can hear his voice; he can raise both just and unjust, for body and spirit alike 'consist,' or hold together, only 'in him' " (CCEM, 43).

[113] Christ can be the judge of all "for he has been the sustainer of all human life . . . the observer of every human act and of every human thought. . . . The reaction of the natural laws of man's being, administered as they are by the Christ to whom all creatures and things are naturally united, is itself 'the wrath of the Lamb' " (CCEM, 43).

avoiding an absolute identity.[114] Likewise the theologian Dorner, while insisting that the divine and human are connected magnitudes, is no pantheist.[115] Not a monism which fails to conserve ethical interests, but only an ethical monism, which "maintains both the freedom of man and the transcendence of God"[116] finds Strong's endorsement.

But why should any monistic theory whatever be conceded? Strong granted that the new philosophy "must approve itself to reason, conscience, Scripture, before it has earned a right to supplant the old."[117] But demonstration, either mathematical or logical, is here out of question; the only proof admitted by the nature of the subject is inductive evidence of a simpler, more complete explanation.[118] The monistic philosophy

> rests its claim to acceptance upon its ability to solve the problems of nature, of the soul, and of the Bible, more simply and completely than the theory of dualism ever could. The test of truth in a theory . . . is not that it can be itself explained, but that it is capable of explaining other things.[119]

As in his initial article Strong had endeavored to show that a Christian monism furnishes the best solution of the interactions of the physical and the intellectual universes, so now in the second article he sought to show that it also best explains the facts of the moral universe. Browning and Dorner had merely set monism and morals side by side, Strong held, without showing the nexus, whereas a monistic view does not preclude a realistic view of sin. For Christ

> is of the substance of God, yet he possesses a distinct personality. If in the one substance of God there are three *infinite* personalities, why may there not be in that same substance multitudinous *finite* personalities? No believer in the Trinity can consistently deny the possibilty of this.[120]

The test of this doctrine, Strong confessed, "must be its ability to explain the fact of sin."[121] To the question, "How can the substance of God ever become morally evil?" he replied:

---

[114]CCEM, 18. Strong added that "Browning does not attempt to explain how unity of substance between God and man is consistent with freedom, sin, and guilt in the finite creature. Yet he believes in these last as firmly as in the first. . . . In other words, the poet is a monist, but an Ethical Monist; a believer that God and man are of one substance; but a hater of pantheism, which denies God's transcendence and separate personality" (CCEM, 19). Likewise the "higher pantheism" of Tennyson, affirmed Strong, "is not pantheism at all, for it recognizes the great truths which pantheism denies, the separate personality of both man and God, and God's infinite exaltation above the universe which only partially manifests him; in other words, the higher pantheism rightly understood is only Ethical Monism" (CCEM, 49). Possibly Strong was already gathering material for his later volume on *The Theology of the Great Poets* (1897).

[115]CCEM, 20.
[116]CCEM, 25.
[117]CCEM, 29.
[118]Strong did not explain what relationship the appeal to coherence has to an appeal to revelation, although he did not oppose the two. In this same essay he volunteered: "If it can be proved that the Scriptures, either directly or by implication, teach the opposite doctrine, I shall be the first to confess the vanity of my reasoning and to return to the common view. But prolonged examination of the Bible leads me to believe that monism is itself the Scripture doctrine, implicitly taught, not only by John and by Paul, and I therefore provisionally accept it" (CCEM, 47).
[119]CCEM, 29-30.
[120]CCEM, 30.
[121]CCEM, 33.

it was not morally evil at first. God has limited and circumscribed himself in giving life to finite personalities within the bounds of his own being, and it is not the fact of *sin* that constitutes the primary difficulty, but the fact of *finite personality*. When God breathed into man's nostrils the breath of his own life, he communicated freedom, and made possible the creature's self-chosen alienation from himself, the giver of that life. While man could never break the natural bond which united him to God, he could break the spiritual bond, and could introduce even into the life of God a principle of discord and evil.[122]

Thus creation affords each intelligent and moral agent the power to isolate himself from God spiritually, though he is naturally joined to God. This divine permission of the sin of finite creatures is God's ineffable act of self-limitation.[123] But the explanation of this permission is likewise found in Christ, for the decrees of redemption and apostasy are equally old, so that God ordained both sin atonement and a way of escape from sin.[124]

But the new view, that the ceaseless energy of the physical universe actively manifests God, seemed to require also a new statement of the doctrine of atonement, for the once-for-all events must now find less disjunction with the general divine activity than in the traditional theology. Therefore Strong formulated "what has not been clearly perceived in theology hitherto, that Christ's atonement is not made merely when he becomes incarnate and dies upon the cross."[125] The outward, visible union with humanity involved in his sacrificial death

is only the culmination and manifestation of a previous union with humanity which was constituted by creation, and which, from the moment of man's first sin, brought suffering to the Son of God.[126]

He was both able and obligated to bear man's penalty. He "could pay man's penalty, because he constituted the essence of man's nature."[127] Humanity is so bound to Christ that the whole organism must suffer together. From the very beginning of man's existence, Christ has been in natural union with humanity, and the whole must suffer in the self-inflicted injury of the part.[128]

The sin of finite creatures must be visited with penalty by a holy God.[129] Since God is the very life of humanity, He must "take upon his own heart the burden of shame and penalty that belong to his members."[130] Strong quoted approvingly a statement from D. W. Simon:

---

[122] CCEM, 33.
[123] CCEM, 34.
[124] CCEM, 34.
[125] CCEM, 34.
[126] CCEM, 34.
[127] CCEM, 41.
[128] Bowne, too, developed the demand for an economy of grace from the form and nature of human development, and later affirmed that "God is bound to be the great Burden-bearer of our world because of his relations to men" (SIC, 144). But in Bowne's thought, the atonement as a fact of experience and life supplanted entirely any substitutionary development of the doctrine along the lines of propitiation.
[129] CCEM, 35. Hence Strong rejected Horace Bushnell's view that Christ suffers in and with his creatures out of merely sympathetic love. "The real reason and ground of suffering in God's moral antagonism to unrighteousness," wrote Strong, is that He is the very life of humanity (CCEM, 35).
[130] CCEM, 35.

if the Logos is generally the Mediator of the divine immanence in creation, especially in man; if men are differentiations of the effluent divine energy; and if the Logos is the immanent controlling principle of all differentiation—*i.e.*, the principle of all *form*,—must not the self-perversion of these human differentiations react on him who is their constitutive principle?[131]

R. W. Dale likewise, Strong emphasized, held Christ responsible for human sin because he is naturally one with mankind, as the upholder and life of all. The necessity for the atonement is thus grounded in the creatorial relationship of Christ to humanity. "As God's righteousness compels him to inflict punishment, so Christ's union with all men by creation compels him to bear it,"[132] explained Strong.

Consequently, there is nothing arbitrary about the innocent's suffering penalty for the guilty, for the process is simply natural law and actual fact:

it is impossible that he who is the natural life of humanity should *not* be responsible for the sin committed by his own members. It is impossible that he should *not* suffer, that he should *not* make reparation, that he should *not* atone.[133]

But the atonement is not a momentary event in history. The incarnation and historical atonement are object-lessons manifesting to sense what the pre-incarnate Logos has been doing ever since man's first sin.[134] They are only "the outward and temporal exhibition of an eternal fact in the being of God, and of a suffering for sin endured by the pre-incarnate Son of God ever since the fall."[135] Patriarchs and prophets were redeemed not so much by the retroactive effect of a future atonement as by the present effect of an atonement even then in progress. The cross reveals the heart of the eternal, summing up and expressing Christ's very being. Although Christ began to endure the wrath of God against sin from the very first moral disobedience of man, the historical atonement is the conquest of sin and death, so that by it the satisfaction of justice culminates in redemption. The eternal atonement is not such a conquest. The historical atonement is not merely a manifestation, but is "the objectification of the eternal suffering love of God, and at the same time the actual deliverance of our nature from sin and death by Jesus Christ."[136]

If Christ's creatorial union with the race explains both the necessity of his atonement and its foundation in justice, it shows also how his redemptive work inures to the benefit of humanity.[137] It is not difficult to see how those who become spiritually one with him partake of the justifica-

---

[131] D. W. Simon, *The Redemption of Man*, 321 (quoted in CCEM, 35).
[132] CCEM, 35-36. Strong enlisted Biblical passages in support of his view: "'It must needs be that Christ should suffer,' for only thus could 'God himself be just and the justifier of him that hath faith in Jesus'" (CCEM, 36).
[133] CCEM, 37.
[134] CCEM, 36. Strong added: "Christ . . . conducts the march of human history. . . . He is the author, the subject, the end of the Old Testament revelation, and the New Testament is simply his emerging from behind the scenes, where he has been invisibly managing the drama of history, to take visible part in the play, to become the leading actor in it, and to bring it to its *denouement*. The curtain has not fallen, and it will not fall until the end of the world. But that appearance of the incarnate, crucified, risen and ascending God has given to us the key to human history" (CCEM, 36).
[135] CCEM, 37.
[136] CCEM, 38.
[137] CCEM, 38.

tion he provides. But his natural union with the race furnishes also an explanation of the salvation of infants and the mentally deficient, or those who never come to moral consciousness in this life. For man's natural and unconscious union with Christ secures him the benefit of Christ's redemption from hereditary and unconscious sin.[138] The emphasis on the natural union of Christ and humanity avoids the usual evangelical emphasis that men are somehow out of Christ and need to get into relation with Him, whereas rejection of Christ is a refusal to remain one with Him.[139] The divine image which humanity shares with Christ, who is the Logos or divine Reason indwelling humanity and constituting the principle of its being, is never wholly lost, yet it is "completely restored in sinners when the Spirit of Christ secures control of their wills and leads them to merge their life in his."[140]

This redemptive work of Christ is world-wide. While peculiar communications of His truth were made to the Hebrew nation,

all truth, whether made known by reason, conscience, or tradition, is Christ's communication to mankind. Heathen religions, so far as they convict of sin and lead to trust in God's mercy, are Christ's revelation. Because "all things consist in him," the heathen come already in contact with Christ, sin against light, have a just probation, are without excuse, need no further trial.[141]

In a resume of his monistic doctrine, here summarized, Strong called attention to the following features: (1) There is but one substance—God; (2) The only complete and perfect expression of God is the eternal Word, known in His historic manifestation as Christ; (3) The universe is Christ's finite and temporal manifestation of God;[142] (4) Matter is Christ's self-limitation under the law of cause and effect; (5) Humanity is Christ's self-limitation under the law of free-will, with its correlate, the possibility of sin; (6) The incarnation and atonement are Christ's self-limitation under the law of grace; (7) God is triune, and is transcendent as well as immanent;[143] (8) Evolution is the common divine method, with room for supernatural incarnation, resurrection and regeneration; (9) There are no second causes in nature;[144] (10) Finite spirits are the second causes;[145] for they have

---

[138] CCEM, 38. "Every other doctrine of infant salvation," Strong wrote, "fails to meet the objection that guilt is taken away from none but those who are in (spiritual) union with Christ" (CCEM, 38).

[139] CCEM, 39, where Strong quotes Simon approvingly in this connection.

[140] CCEM, 40.

[141] CCEM, 40-41.

[142] "The universe is not itself God—it is only the partial unfolding of God's wisdom and power, adapted to the comprehension of finite intelligences," Strong pointed out. "It has had a beginning—the world is temporal, while the Word is eternal. All expression or manifestation of the infinite and eternal Word under the forms of time and space must be a self-limitation" (CCEM, 45).

[143] "My doctrine maintains," Strong explained, "the transcendence of God, though it regards transcendence as not necessarily outsidedness in space, but rather inexhaustibleness of resource within" (CCEM, 45).

[144] "The forces and laws of nature are the habits or generic volitions of God," Strong affirmed (CCEM, 46).

[145] Of finite persons, Strong declared: "Having freedom, they do not reproduce in particular acts a generic volition of God; they may set their wills in opposition to God. That these finite spirits are circumscriptions of the divine substance and have in them the divine life shows the infinite value of their being; but it also shows the dreadfulness of their sin when they morally sunder themselves from

freedom, yet are related to the personality of God "some-what as the persons of the Trinity are related to the one all-inclusive divine personality";[146] (11) The union of Christ with all men, by creation, involves Him in responsibility for their sin, even though He is absolutely holy; (12) This natural union of all men with Christ provides a just ground for the sufferings of the innocent in behalf of the guilty;[147] (13) Sin constitutes a moral revolt of such magnitude that man's natural union with Christ is consistent with the eternal punishment of those who reject the spiritual union proffered by grace.[148]

In the course of this same essay, Strong had developed incidentally the differences between ethical monism and idealism, a theme to which he recurred in the third article of this series contributed to religious periodicals. For that reason, it seems advantageous to treat this aspect of his thought as a unit, while giving a summary of the third essay, indicating, where possible, the precise source of the various emphases which Strong set forth in this connection.

3. "Ethical Monism Once More"

The third article in this series from Strong's pen appeared in *The Examiner* in October, 1895, and bore the caption, "Ethical Monism Once More."[149]

This essay appears to have been written in view of reactions to Strong's previous articles, for he took note of "the candid and generous treatment" accorded his essays, and at the same time protested that he had been "somewhat misunderstood."[150] Consequently, this further effort was intended "to remove misapprehension, while at the same time applying the new principle in one or two new directions."[151] The criticisms of Strong's position which arose from a clear understanding of his views may be postponed, with good effect, to the next chapter of this dissertation, but such disagreements which derive from a misunderstanding of Strong's position,

---

God. . . . Christian or Ethical Monism . . . maintains the reality and guilt of sin as well as the possibility and reality of grace" (CCEM, 46).

[146] CCEM, 45. The intent of this passage is to safeguard the reality of both divine and human personalities as against pantheism.

[147] Strong did not explicitly state this point in his resume, but it was assumed in the comment that: "The union of all men with Christ, by creation, shows us how certain benefits of his redemption, such as justification from hereditary and unconscious sin, may inure to all, while justification from conscious and personal sin may inure only to those who become one with Christ by faith" (CCEM, 46).

[148] "That all men are naturally the offspring of God, and in a subordinate sense partake of the divine nature in Christ," wrote Strong, "no more proves the future annihilation of all impenitent sinners or the future restoration of all men, than it proves the present annihilation of all sinners or the present restoration of all men. Ethical Monism holds to one substance; but it also holds to free-will, and the very dignity of man's origin makes his self-perversion the more awful. If he can resist God here, he can resist him forever, and the very fact that God breathed into man the breath of life may only result in an immortality of misery to him who has devoted that breath of life to the pursuit of evil" (CCEM, 46-47).

[149] This appeared in three parts in the October 17, 24, 31, 1895 issue of *The Examiner* (Vol. 73, Nos. 42, 43, 44).

[150] CCEM, 52.

[151] CCEM, 52. The "new directions" are the implications of ethical monism for evolution and for atonement.

STRONG'S THEOLOGY   115

in so far as they provoked him to a fuller statement of it, will be dealt with at once.

Strong emphasized in this article that ethical monism is "dualistic monism"[152] and that dualism "is a permanent and fundamental truth"[153] and "the more practical, the more valuable"[154] term. Two sorts of dualism Strong willingly accepted: the dualism of matter and mind[155] and the dualism of man and God.[156] These two, since both postulate a soul distinct from matter on one hand and God on the other, "are only aspects of one truth, and I name that truth psychological dualism."[157]

In an effort to distinguish his view from idealism, Strong here developed the remarks in his previous essay, to stress the inconvertibility of matter and mind. In the third, as in the second essay, he insisted that

although idealism is not the whole truth, it is a part of the truth, and it has given us a far better conception of matter than . . . (that) of a self-subsistent yet dead somewhat, outside of God. Matter is not dead but living; it is spiritual, in the sense of being the manifestation of spirit. . . . Nature is the manifestation of God under the law of cause and effect[158]. . . . Matter is but the projection or continuation of God's regular and automatic activity.[159]

This emphasis is contained also in the prior essay, but at the same time, there as here, Strong proceeded to differentiate his position from idealism in various forms. Disavowing any intention "to favor idealism any more . . . than materialism,"[160] he insisted that the universe is not merely ideational, but is also of the nature of will, objectified in terms of force. Both Berkeley and Hegel are disowned; Berkeley because he denied substantial[161] existence to the physical universe as distinct from spirits,[162]

---

[152] CCEM, 53.
[153] CCEM, 53.
[154] CCEM, 53. "Whatever else we may be . . . we must be dualists through and through, and we must never give up our dualism, because dualism is not only the necessary condition of ethics, but is also inseparably bound up with many, if not all, of those great truths which constitute the essence of the Christian scheme" (CCEM, 53).
[155] CCEM, 53. "Matter and mind are two and not one; mind is not matter, matter is not mind; the two are inconvertible" (CCEM, 53).
[156] CCEM, 53. "God and man are two and not one; man is not God and God is not man; the two are personally differentiated from each other" (CCEM, 53-54).
[157] CCEM, 54.
[158] CCEM, 55.
[159] CCEM, 57.
[160] CCEM, 28.
[161] Strong's insistence on a dualism of mind and matter, then, was not in the interest of a non-mental view of matter, but rather of an insistence that matter, although a manifestation of the divine ideas externalized by an act of will, has substantial reality of a sort. Personalistic idealism today has abandoned a substance philosophy. Bowne's rupture with a substance philosophy is attested by his affirmation that "substance is a myth"; he repudiated "the substratum-notion as the product of sense-bondage" (MSFP, 375). But in formulating the doctrine of the soul, Bowne fluctuated still between a self-psychology and a substance-psychology, declaring that the soul is transcendent to all consciousness (M, 380).
[162] CCEM, 28: "Berkeley held that the physical universe exists only *ideally;* it consists of the ideas of God, made permanent and visible by the divine will; only spirits—the human spirit and the divine spirit—have *substantial* existence. But the modern doctrine of evolution renders this idealism no longer tenable. The rock, the vegetable, the brute, all shade into another by imperceptible graduations, and even man is acknowledged to have developed from lower orders of being. . . . We cannot draw the line that Berkeley drew, between man and the brute. . . . And since we cannot deny that man is spirit, and has substantial existence, we must affirm that nature is spirit, and has substantial existence also."

Hegel because he "identified being with thought, and held that thought thinks."[163] Strong preferred to say:

being *has*, not *is*, thought and volition; and will *may*, not *must*, initiate a finite universe of which extension is an attribute. The universe is not necessary, but free; it is the manifestation of an infinite mind and will; it may be traced back to a beginning; creation is a conception not only scientific, but indispensable; development, or evolution, is the product of free intelligence.[164]

This insistence that ethical monism is "neither idealistic nor materialistic" is found also in the third essay. While matter is not inert stuff, but is spiritual, yet "it is not simply the thought of God's reason, but the product of his will."[165]

Materialistic idealism improved upon the old materialism by holding that the universe consisted of force and of ideas; but we perceive that ideas can only belong to mind and force can be exerted only by will.[166]

Matter is known to us only as force, and force is produced by will.[167] The effects we call nature "we are compelled to attribute to some producing agency analogous to our own"[168] and no designation for this agency is "so simple or intelligible as the will of God."[169] But the divine ideas, externalized by an act of will and constituting the space-time universe, do not exhaust God's thought or power, nor is the universe co-eternal with God.[170]

The dualism of matter and mind is thus justified by an appeal to the element of force, requiring the divine will, and constituting at the same time the spiritual substantiality of matter, as against a purely logical notion. But Strong no sooner insisted upon this dualistic statement, than he

---

[163]Strong commented: "Spinoza was nearer right when he called both thought and extension opposite manifestations of being or substance. But Spinoza was wrong in putting extension on the same level with thought, and regarding it as equally primary and necessary. Both Hegel and Spinoza ignored the element of will, and denied freedom. Hegel recognized development while Spinoza had no place for it in his system" (CCEM, 31).

[164]CCEM, 32.

[165]CCSM, 55. It may be recalled that Bowne adopted the term Personalism in order, against Idealism in general, to emphasize volition as well as idea in the explanation of reality.

[166]CCEM, 68. Pantheism agrees on this point, Strong conceded, but "declares that the universe is simply immanent and impersonal mind and will. Our reply is that spirit in man shows that the infinite Spirit must be personal and transcendent mind and will" (CCEM, 68).

[167]CCEM, 69.

[168]CCEM, 69. "It does not matter that my volition is not itself physical force; it is enough that it is a cause. If physical forces are causes, then I must believe that they too are essentially exertions of will, and since they are not exertions of my will, I must call them exertions of the will of God" (CCEM, 69).

[169]This mode of argument indicates that Strong readily shifted his theology from a revelational to an experimental base, arguing for a transcendent God not on the basis of special revelation, but on philosophical grounds.

[170]"Pantheism recognizes the immanence of God, but there it stops; since it sees in God no freedom and no reverses of power, transcendence is inconceivable and impossible," Strong protested. "Pantheism shuts up God in the universe; nay, the universe is his everlasting prison; for the reason of God from eternity past has worked and could work in no other than this dynamic way. Matter is eternal, and has no more had a beginning than God himself. It is identical with God, for matter is no more the expression of God than God is the expression of matter. Now against this doctrine that the universe is as great as God, as eternal as God, dualistic monism utters its continual protest" (CCEM, 63).

STRONG'S THEOLOGY   117

stressed with equal vigor that the dualism does not preclude a more elemental monism. But, since this monism was invoked as basic to both the dualism of matter and mind, and also the dualism of human and divine personality, it will be best, before examining the monistic element, to bring into view the second kind of dualism which Strong championed.

This second type of dualism was, as Strong made clear also in his earlier essays, that of infinite and finite persons. As against pantheism, which affirms either that God has personality in a manner that makes human personality delusive, or that man has personality in which God alone comes to consciousness, ethical monism declared for the "separate personality of man and the absolute transcendence of God."[171]

But the two sorts of dualism, of matter and mind and of man and God, aspects of what may be termed psychological dualism, are nonetheless "perfectly consistent with philosophical or metaphysical monism."[172] Such dualism and monism are not contradictory, for they are asserted in different respects; monism affirms that the dualistic realities of matter and mind, man and God, "have underground connections and a common life, because all things, humanity included, live, move, and have their being in God."[173]

The duality of matter and mind is not absolute and unqualified, else all interrelation and interaction between them would be impossible; without a monistic reference, the relation of the two is an insoluble mystery.[174] That matter and mind are inconvertible does not disprove monism, for their interaction proves that the two have "a common ground and principle of being."[175] That God has decreed "that mind and matter, the two manifestations of himself which constitute the universe, should be eternally inconvertible," is no disproof of monism but is a link in proving the contrary.[176] The opposition to monism grows out of an "antiquated conception" of matter which is made "the touchstone of a true philosophy."[177] That view

regards matter as a dead somewhat, outside of God, while mind is a living somewhat, outside of God, and then it wonders how the two get on so well together. Let these absolute dualists reflect for a moment that no dead thing can be a cause, and

---

[171]CCEM, 60-61. Pantheism is monism "coupled with two denials: the denial of man's separate personality and of God's transcendence," Strong wrote (CCEM, 61).
[172]CCEM, 54.
[173]CCEM, 54.
[174]CCEM, 54.
[175]CCEM, 55. Strong added: "The very fact that matter and mind are inconvertible makes their interaction utterly inconceivable and impossible, unless they exist in a unitary Being who is not only their author, but who furnishes the constant bond of connection between them" (CCEM, 55).
[176]As soon as matter and mind are understood to be manifestations of God, explained Strong, we dispose of "the notion that their inconvertibility is inconsistent with monism" (CCEM, 56).
[177]CCEM, 55. The contrast between Strong and Bowne at this point will be clear if it is remembered that Bowne insisted that "a thing is to be viewed as real and substantial not because it has a kernel of substance in itself, but because it is able to assert itself in activity. Things do not have being or substance, but they act, and by virtue of this activity they acquire the right to be considered as existing" (MSFP, 375). Strong, however, appears to have insisted that the reality of the physical universe is substantial (*in addition to* its status as divine idea volitionally externalized), and then to have denied that activity constitutes the substantiality of things, yet rejected a realistic view. Idealism he then criticized from

that no finite living thing can come into communication with that which is around it, except as that communication is mediated by a common intelligence and life.[178]

Nor will it do to hold that the universe is explicable by the merely external divine governance and control, as "if God made this a universe by simply watching over it."[179] The old materialistic and deistic explanations have been rendered untenable by modern philosophy, which has made the issue plain; either the bond between God and the universe must be closer, or we cannot believe logically in a universe or in God.[180]

Nor is the duality of human and divine personality absolute. While God's personality and man's personality "stand over against each other, so that there is always the possibility of communion on the one hand and of antagonism on the other,"[181] yet both consciousness and conscience witness that "we are bound to one another and to God by the ties of a common mental and moral life."[182] All humanity shares a common light, which is the heritage of the race, and does not belong to the individual alone:

the higher reason, the perception of beauty, the moral ideals of mankind, have a universal character, and are not products of the single soul. There is a light that lighteth every man, and that light is none other than Christ, the light of the world. We have a natural, intellectual, and moral union with him in whom all things, including humanity, were created and in whom all things consist.[183]

The opposition to monism leaves the interaction of mind and mind unexplained, even as it was unable to explain physical interaction.[184] That many human wills are capable of independent activity does not mean that they may not have "in God the ground of their being."[185] Strong appealed at this point, as in his earlier essay, to the doctrine of the Trinity for "a hint of the possible solution" of how the insistence on monism as to substance could be combined with an insistence on dualism as to personality.[186]

---

a movable perspective—sometimes for not doing justice to the volitional manifestation of certain divine ideas in creation, and again (as in the criticism of Berkeley) for including both ideational and volitional elements but not doing justice to the spiritual substantiality of the universe (which is not more carefully defined).

[178] CCEM, 55. Strong did not hesitate to develop, in his second essay, "Ethical Monism," the implication that since Christ is the all-inclining consciousness, "our very bodies are manifestations of his thought and purpose. Christ dwells naturally in every man's physical frame, and in sinning against our own bodies we are actually crucifying Christ and putting him to an open shame" (CCEM, 32). Earlier in the same essay he stated: "If matter, moreover, be merely the expression of spirit, then the body, as an object of consciousness, may well be only the reverse side of what we call the consciousness of the object. Since the all-including consciousness is that of Christ, our very bodies may be manifestations of the thought and purpose of Christ" (CCEM, 31).

[179] CCEM, 68.
[180] CCEM, 68.
[181] CCEM, 58.
[182] CCEM, 58.
[183] CCEM, 60.
[184] "The influence of our finite intelligence upon another finite intelligence presupposes the existence and cooperation of an infinite Intelligence in which all finite intelligences have their being. And what are conscience and Scripture but means by which this same Intelligence lifts us up out of the region of his universal and eternal truth?" (CCEM, 60).
[185] CCEM, 61.
[186] "In the one divine substance there are three consciousnesses and three wills, or in other words, three persons. And yet we do not conceive of the Godhead as divided into three parts. The whole of the divine essence resides in the Son and in the

Psychological dualism is compatible, therefore, urged Strong, with the existence of but

> one substance, one underlying reality, the infinite and eternal Spirit of God, who contains within his own being the ground and principle of all other being.[187]

The logical and vital relations characterizing the universe are impossible apart from "a rational Spirit whose omnipresence unifies what otherwise would be fragments" and which is at the same time "an Intelligence and Will who orders their ongoings" and "an infinite Life who constitutes the principle of their existence and the ground of their being."[188]

Strong now disowned the view that metaphysical monism involves the pantheistic notion that nature is a part of God. In this regard, he urged two considerations: his critics misunderstood in a realistic sense his use of the word "substance" and, further, he did not deny the transcendent miraculous.

The universe is a manifestation of God, emphasized Strong, but it is not God. All things, persons, nations, worlds, are "only the partial, temporal, graded, finite unfoldings of a Being infinitely greater than they."[189] God infinitely transcends any single thing in the universe, and the whole universe put together, although it finds its principle of existence and ground of being in Him.[190] When it is urged that God is the one substance, the term should receive its meaning not from "the old and outworn Hamiltonian philosophy" but should be given "the sense which it has acquired in Lotze and the modern idealists."[191] Strong urged:

> to interpret my word 'substance' after a materialistic fashion, as if I meant that God occupied space and divided himself up into parts, carving men and nature out of his own physical being, is to attribute to me a view against which my whole scheme of thought is a protest. The infinite One does not consist of parts, nor are finite and material things parts of the infinite One. As my volitions are manifestations of my mind, but are not parts of my mind, so the works of God are manifestations of God, but are not parts of God.[192]

Strong, therefore, resisted any suggestion that the universe is a part of God, and expressed constant disapproval of the use of such terminology. The universe represents certain of the divine ideas objectified by the divine will, but the whole-part conception is less true to the relationship of nature and God than is the substance-manifestation concept.

> Holy Spirit just as fully as it resides in the Father. There is an abstract possibility of severance between the will of the Father and the will of the incarnate son, and Christ says, 'Not my will but thine be done.' My contention is that what was only abstractly possible in the case of the Son of God has become an actuality in the case of sinful men, and that the actual sin of men cannot be regarded as incompatible with a Christian monism by any who grant that Christ had an independent will while yet he was of the same substance as the Father. And yet I do not regard the doctrine of the Trinity as furnishing *more* than a hint of the possibility of multitudinous finite personalities within the bounds of God's being. . . . I claim only that in the Trinity we have plural self-consciousness, though the essence of God is one; while in man's single nature we have consciousnesses and volitions that are not only independent but abnormal" (CCEM, 62-63).

[187] CCEM, 65.
[188] CCEM, 67.
[189] CCEM, 64.
[190] CCEM, 64.
[191] CCEM, 64.
[192] CCEM, 64-65.

It is well to note that just as Strong's statement of the substantiality of the physical universe appears ambivalent, so too, his account of the relationship of finite selves to God is not wholly clear. As he distinguished mind from matter, only to resolve the distinction in terms of spiritual substantiality (without making clear what, if anything, is involved in such substantiality, beyond the externalization of certain divine ideas by an act of will), so he distinguished finite created selves from the Creator in the interest of human freedom and moral responsibility, only to insist not only upon a common rationality and morality, but upon a common life and natural union. At this point Strong appears, whatever his intentions, to have compromised the psychological dualism upon which he insisted. Whereas contemporary statements of personalistic idealism insist here upon a quantative pluralism, Strong drew back from pluralistic to more monistic ground.[193] It is significant that Strong appealed not to Bowne, but rather to Ladd, at this juncture of his thought, quoting the Yale philosopher as follows:

> Dualism is not the final word, not the ultimate solution of the problem of body and mind, or of nature at large in their complex relations to each other. Nature and body and mind cannot be left by the mind itself in this condition of separateness. . . . This dualism . . . must undoubtedly be dissolved in some ultimate monistic solution. The Being of the world, of which all particular things are but parts, must then be so conceived of as that in it can be found the one ground of all inter-related existences and activities.[194]

In the immediate context, however, Strong singled out Lotze as providing the incentive for the recent statements of dualistic monism, and suggested that Ladd's view was in essential harmony with the German thinker's philosophy. But the pluralistic turn found in Lotze, and developed by Bowne, appears to have been missed in the return from psychological dualism to a basic monism. The identification of humanity, no less than of the physical universe, as a finite, graded manifestation of God, would appear to take back much of the pluralistic emphasis.[195] Despite this, however, Strong left no doubt that human freedom and moral responsibility were not in any way to be compromised.

In applying monism to the regularity of nature, Strong emphasized further that he believed in a divine transcendence which does not preclude the benevolent miraculous, and therefore did not hold a pantheistic view of the physical universe. The laws of nature are, indeed, the habitual methods

---

[193]The deterministic factor here seems to be the stress assigned by a thinker to the unity of the universe. Not only Josiah Royce and F. H. Bradley, who stood in the absolutistic tradition, but Lotze, who maintained that selves are outside of God, gave central emphasis to the unity, whereas Bowne stated more emphatically the relation of the causality of the One and the many. Strong is concerned to deny that the many have any proper existence in themselves, and yet to deny that they are modes of the One (against Spinoza, Bradley, Royce). Lotze held that the One and the many selves are ontologically distinct yet coordinated, along the lines of organic pluralism; Strong shared this insistence on the independence of selves, but within a more fundamental insistence on monism.

[194]CCEM, 57. The source of the quotation from Ladd is not given.

[195]Some contemporary personalistic idealists identify nature as a part of God, while insisting upon a radical pluralism; Brightman is the outstanding example. Strong denied that nature, as well as that man, is a part of God, but identified both the physical universe and humanity as finite, graded manifestations of God.

by which Christ manifests himself,[196] and what we call second causes are but "secondary workings of the great First Cause."[197] Evolution from lower to higher is the rule of this habitual method.[198] But this does not preclude the miraculous:

There are two methods in the exercise of his will: first, the absolute, unique, initiatory method; secondly, the relative, regular, automatic method.[199]

Strong affirmed belief in a God who is in the evolutionary process, and manifests himself through it, and who is nonetheless unexhausted by the process, and reinforces it at times in a miraculous manner, contrary to Darwinianism and materialistic evolution.[200] But miracle, he emphasized, is "no more than divine than is law, and the ordinary operations of nature are workings of God just as much as is the raising of the dead."[201] In view of this, Strong urged that the so-called discontinuities in history and nature be viewed as divine activities from within, rather than from without, though nonetheless miraculous:

Let us look upon the breaks in the orderly progress of the world, such as the introduction of vegetable life, of animal life, of man, of Christ, together with conversions like that of Paul, and reformations like that of Luther, simply as movements of the Spirit of God from within.[202]

In this manner, God's transcendence is still insisted upon, but it is viewed as "inexhaustibleness of resource rather than as mere outsidedness in space,"[203] even though the successive creative acts are interpreted from the standpoint of divine immanence.

It is clear that in Strong's application of monism to evolution, there is frequent appeal to the regular as furnishing a clue to the interpretation of the novel. The principle of evolution sheds light on the development of

---

[196] CCEM, 71.
[197] CCEM, 71. "It is a great gain to religion," Strong commented, "to learn that second causes are but secondary workings of the great First Cause. Ethical Monism finds this Cause in Christ—it is he alone who makes this a universe" (CCEM, 73).
[198] "The transcendent God is working through Christ in the whole creation and revealing himself according to an ever-unfolding plan. Creation is just as much his act as it was before, but it is creation *from within*, if I may use a spatial term of that which has no relation to space. Why can we not believe in a God who creates from within as well as in a God who creates only from without?" (CCEM, 71).
[199] CCEM, 70. "God's habitual actions . . . are not a bar to unique and exceptional action. As nature was due in the beginning to an act of absolute origination, so the God who originated nature is not shut up to nature; he can transcend nature; he can substitute new beginnings for old regularities; he can transcend nature by miracle, and law by grace. Incarnation and resurrection are perfectly possible and credible, if we once grant that God's will is capable of a twofold activity analogous to our own" (CCEM, 70).
[200] CCEM, 71.
[201] CCEM, 71.
[202] CCEM, 71-72.
[203] CCEM, 72. Strong affirmed: "I do not deny creation; I believe in it with all my heart. The world has had a beginning, and it is the work of God's sovereign power in Christ. But I no longer conceive of the successive acts of creation as the beginning into being out of nothing of new substances that are outside of and different from God. I believe in creation, but I have a new conception of the method of creation. I interpret it from the point of view of God's immanence, and I regard transcendence as inexhaustibleness of resources rather than as mere outsidedness in space." (CCEM, 72).

the race in its renewal by divine grace, no less than in its apostasy. "The regularities of natural law are teaching us something of the solemn uniformity of moral law," Strong explained.[204] The overall plan required by the heightened immanentism removes a radical discontinuity between man and the animals;[205] if the divine element in man is recognized, a divine element may also be discerned in the brute beasts. "The animal nature in man is a good thing," Strong affirmed, and "it becomes evil only when it rebels against the higher nature and subjects that higher nature to its control."[206]

Strong insisted, however, that he accepted ethical monism not "for the sake of its Christian explanation of evolution" but rather "because of the light which it throws upon the atonement."[207] For it provided an answer to the question, how Christ could justly bear the sins of mankind, which was at the same time an alternative to the theory of "an external and mechanical transfer of guilt" in view of the emphasis on natural union of Christ and humanity which obligated Him to make atonement.[208] Strong did not add anything new, in this application of monism to the atonement, to his expressions in the previous essays,[209] in which he had already insisted that the historical atonement was the reflection of a super-historical divine suffering, although Strong concluded this third essay with a discussion of the objections which had been offered to his explanation of the atonement. It will avoid unnecessary duplication, however, to postpone consideration of these objections in the subsequent chapter, devoted to the evaluation of Strong's monism.

The emphases of Strong's third article may be summarized as follows: (1) essential to the Christian view is a psychological dualism which insists on the inconvertibility of (a) mind and matter, and (b) divine and human personality; (2) matter, while spiritual, is not reducible to idea, but to the divine thought externalized by an act of will; (3) created human persons

---

[204]"Darwin acknowledged that natural selection might lead downward as well as upward, and so we have human history witnessing to a gradual deterioration of early religions and of early morality. Huxley declared that the moral and religious development of the race requires the bringing in of principles that antagonize and reverse its natural tendencies, and this is precisely what is made known by revelation as the method of Christ. The law of the Spirit of life in Christ Jesus frees us from the law of sin and death, and a new and holy evolution begins, the power and principle of which is the Son of God. Why should we regret the publication and acceptance of the doctrine of evolution, if it reveals to us the method of Christ's working both in nature and in grace?" (CCEM, 74).

[205]CCEM, 77. "It is no more beneath God's dignity thus to *manifest* himself in nature and in the brute than it was on the old theory for him to *create* nature and the brute. In fact the difference between the old theory and the new is not a difference in the interpretation of the facts" (CCEM, 78).

[206]CCEM, 77.

[207]CCEM, 78.

[208]CCEM, 78: "It was a great day for me when I first saw that there was a natural union of Christ with all men which preceded the incarnation—that all men in fact were created and had their being in him, and that therefore he who was the ground and principle of their life, though personally pure, must bear their sins and iniquities."

[209]There, as here, Strong urged that "the incarnation and suffering of the Son of God in history were only the manifestation and visible setting forth in time and space of a great atonement by the lamb who was slain from the foundation of the world. It was through the eternal Spirit that he offered himself without spot to God, and his historical suffering redeemed the race only because it was the manifestation of an everlasting fact in the being of God" (CCEM, 79).

stand over against divine personality with the capacity for fellowship or for moral revolt; (4) psychological dualism does not preclude a more fundamental metaphysical monism, so that the infinite and eternal Spirit of God is the substance of all things, which are graded and finite manifestations; (5) the regularity of nature, according to the method of evolution, is the habitual volition of Christ, but this does not preclude special reinforcement, viewed as a novel activity *within* the process by the transcendent (inexhaustible) God; (6) the regularity of the process of nature furnishes illumination for the understanding of the process of grace; (7) the atonement by Christ is just because it comes from Him, although innocent, as from one obligated to make it in view of his natural union with humanity.

II. Address to the 1895 Graduating Class

That Strong personally viewed ethical monism as something more than "a series of guesses at truth" is seen from his remarks to the 1895 graduating class:

> It is quite possible to confound our present conceptions of the truth with the truth itself, and to cherish an attitude of hostility to every new interpretation and discovery. . . . I counsel you rather to bring forth things new as well as old. . . . Without openness of mind you will see little that is new, and when you do see it you will be prejudiced against it. You will regard all science and philosophy and literature and art as anti-Christian, and your narrowness will prevent the acceptance of Christianity by those whom you would most desire to influence. . . . When the new challenges your attention I would have you ask, not "What is there here that I can contradict and oppose?" but rather "What is there here that I can accept and utilize?" I would have you ready to recognize and welcome truth, from whatsoever source it comes.[210]

That Strong's thoughts were motivated by his commitment to the new immanentism is clear from the references to Christ as the ultimate principle of philosophy and science. "Science, philosophy, and history . . . are themselves Christ's subordinate methods of teaching the world,"[211] he affirmed. "Christ is larger than all our conception of him. He embraces in himself all the truth of nature as well as all the truth of special revelation."[212] Again,

> he who limits his view of Christ to the work of Christ incarnate, and refuses to believe in him as the pre-incarnate Logos, will necessarily be prejudiced against a large portion of Christ's truth. He who sees Christ in redemption . . . but fails to recognize Christ in creation . . . will be apt to shut the book of nature because at some points it seems at first sight hard to reconcile with the book of Scripture.[213] . . . Evolution is but the method of the immanent Christ.[214] . . . The world, with its misery and sin, is larger to us than it was to our fathers. But then we have a larger view of Christ than they ever had. . . . John Calvin thought of nature and history as under control of the Evil One, and to be delivered only at Christ's second coming, while we know that Christ is now swaying the sceptre of universal empire.[215]

One discerns here the implications for Strong's theology of the immanentistic emphasis, lodging the case for the divine origin, support and goal of the

---
[210]CCEM, 476-477.
[211]CCEM, 477.
[212]CCEM, 477-478. Strong refers also to "the occasional grains of truth that are hidden in the chaff of heathen teaching" (CCEM, 478).
[213]CCEM, 478.
[214]CCEM, 479.
[215]CCEM, 479-480.

universe not so much in special revelation as in monistic metaphysics, which Strong felt made room at the same time for special revelation.

Strong's remarks to the 1895 graduates, however, were mainly the reflection of a new note which had come to the fore in his many public addresses, often given at strategic Baptist occasions to which he was invited as the Rochester president.[216] Now in one direction and now in another he sought, as opportunities presented, to outline the implications of monism for evangelical theology. For this reason, the chronological interest in his formulations must yield to the broader effort to formulate the effect of monism on the whole of systematic theology, which came to its fullest expression a decade later with the final revision of Strong's *magnum opus*. Before that, however, the fifth edition and revision of his 1886 lectures made its appearance in 1896.[217] In view of the fact that Strong's *Christ in Creation and Ethical Monism*, which appeared in 1899, included not only the 1894 and 1895 articles contributed to *The Examiner*, but a number of other essays and addresses in which, as we shall see, some application of monism to cardinal problems of theology was made, it is curious that the 1896 revision of Strong's systematic theology lectures restricted the application of the principle "to the explanation of the doctrines of Preservation and of the Atonement."[218]

III. THE 1896 LECTURES

The preface to Strong's fifth revised edition of his theology lectures called attention to four instances—"on pages 51, 203, 205, and 413, where

---

[216] Strong's address on "Christ and the Truth," delivered November 15, 1895, at the inauguration of B. L. Whitman, D.D., as president of Columbian University, Washington, D. C., emphasized that "we cannot limit the teachings of Christ to Christendom. . . . Even before Christ came in the flesh, every ray of conscience or aspiration that ever illuminated mankind proceeded from him. . . . Special revelation brings us in contact with the personal source of truth, and so opens our eyes to see the living essence of truth. . . . All truth in physics, psychology, ethics, history, is a part of his revelation of God. . . . No single truth is rightly understood except in its relation to Christ" (CCEM, 104-105).

[217] Referred to hereafter as ST(1896). B. B. Warfield commented that "a particular interest attaches . . . to this new edition . . . from a surprising *vote face* which has been executed by its author, in the interval between the issues of the fourth and fifth editions, on one of the most fundamental questions which can underlie a system of theology. We refer to his adoption of the theory of the universe which he calls 'ethical monism,' as announced by him in a series of articles in *The Examiner*. . . . Hitherto not only had Dr. Strong not betrayed any sympathy with a monistic conception of things, but he had strongly opposed it, as well in the appropriate messages of his *Systematic Theology* as in a clear and one would think conclusive article entitled 'Modern Idealism' printed in *The Bibliotheca Sacra* so late as January, 1888" (Warfield, Rev. [1897], 357).

[218] ST(1896), x. Between 1894 and 1896 Strong delivered the following addresses, subsequently included in CCEM, dealing somewhat with monism and theology: May 27, 1894, "The Love of Christ the Great Motive in Missions," opening presidential address at the 80th anniversary of the American Baptist Missionary Union, Saratoga, N. Y., (CCEM, 284-296); May 28, 1895, "The Holy Spirit the One and Only Power in Missions," opening presidential address at the 81st anniversary of the American Baptist Missionary Union, Saratoga, N. Y., (CCEM, 297-313); November 15, 1895, "Christ and the Truth," address at the inauguration of Dr. B. L. Whitman, D. D., as president of Columbian University, Washington, D. C. (CCEM, 102-112).

STRONG'S THEOLOGY 125

the principle of Ethical Monism is adopted"[219]—which mode of statement hardly discloses the theological inversion involved in his new position.

The first of these references involved merely the listing of ethical monism as the only satisfactory alternate to the attempts to explain the universe made by materialism, materialistic idealism, and pantheism. Only a two sentence summary of the view was given,[220] with no detailed development of the position.[221] But the definition of materialism was now revised in the interest of monism. Whereas, in former editions, it was explained that the element of truth in materialism "is the reality of second causes" and that its error "is in mistaking these second causes for first causes,"[222] now Strong wrote that the truth in materialism is the reality "of the external world" and its error is in regarding the external world "as having original and independent existence, and in regarding mind as its product."[223] Sentences approving the ontology of monists like Herschel, Wallace and Bowne appeared[224] in introducing quotations from their works, and replaced the refutation of monistic views which had appeared in the fourth edition.

Two of the remaining references were to minor changes made in the treatment of the doctrine of preservation. The first of these deals with the nature of so-called secondary causation, and the second with the relation of Strong's view to that of continuous creation.

Second causes in nature, Strong affirmed, may be regarded as "only secondary, regular and automatic workings of the great first cause."[225] His argument takes the following form: Form implies a will which, directly or indirectly, it expresses. We know of force only through exercising our own wills. Since we have direct knowledge only of will as a causal agency, the causes of nature may be traced only to the divine will.[226] The circumstances that our will is often powerless does not deny that force is to be identified with will, but only that it cannot be identified with human will; in God, will and force are one.[227]

---

[219] ST(1896), x.
[220] Strong explained that according to this view, the universe is a "finite, partial, graded manifestation of the divine Life; Matter being God's self-limitation under the law of necessity, Humanity being God's self-limitation under the law of freedom, Incarnation and Atonement being God's self-limitations under the law of grace. Metaphysical Monism, or the doctrine of one Substance, Principle, or Ground of Being, is consistent with Psychological Dualism, or the doctrine that the soul is personally distinct from matter on the one hand and from God on the other" (ST[1896], 51).
[221] Class notes which were written in an inter-leaved copy of ST(1896) a few years later, probably in 1901, show that Strong supplemented the brief statements in the 1896 revision with extensive comment along the line of the three articles contributed to *The Examiner* (ST[1896]CN, 55).
[222] LOT, 28.
[223] ST(1896), 51.
[224] ST(1896), 55.
[225] ST(1896), 203.
[226] ST(1896), 203, where Strong referred to Herschel, Murphy, the Duke of Argyll, Wallace, Bowen and Martineau for modern theories identifying force with divine will.
[227] Strong deliberately placed this view over against that of Hodge, the Princeton theologian, who wrote: "Because we get our own idea of force from mind, it does not follow that mind is the only force. That mind is a cause is no proof that electricity may not be a cause. If matter is force and nothing but force, then matter is noth-

In developing the doctrine of preservation, Strong accepted the view, rejected by him in the earlier editions, that the forces of the universe and the will of God are to be identified, although divine transcendence is not denied.[228]

Preservation requires a God who is beyond nature as well as in nature. It steers a middle course between the error of continuous creation, which denies that "the Substances of the universe have a real existence and a relative independence,"[229] and the error of deism, which denies that "these substances retain their being and their powers only as they are upheld by God."[230] Nature, like the human will, both has its being in God and yet is at the same time independent in its dependence.[231] Strong pointed out that Jonathan Edwards held to God as the only cause of all natural effects, but combined this with belief in continuous creation. "The element of truth" in the latter doctrine, Strong remarked,

is its assumption that all force is will. Its error is in maintaining that all force is divine will, and divine will in direct exercise. But the human will is a force as well as the divine will, and the forces of nature are God's secondary and automatic, not his primary and immediate, workings.[232]

Strong emphasized that we cannot see the dividing line between the action of the first cause and the action of second causes, but "both are real, and each is distinct from the other, though the method of God's concurrence is inscrutable."[233]

The other revision made by Strong in this volume came in the application of monism to the doctrine of atonement. Here the statement of Christ's creational union with humanity as obliging him to make provision of atonement reflects the tenor of *The Examiner* articles already considered:

If it be asked whether this is not simply a suffering for his own sin, or rather for his own share of the sin of the race, we reply that his own share in the sin of the race is not the sole reason why he suffers; it furnishes only the subjective reason and ground for the proper laying upon him of the sin of all. Christ's union with the race in his incarnation is only the outward and visible expression of a prior union with the race which began when he created the race. As "in him were all things created," and as "in him all things consist," or hold together (Col. 1:16, 17), it follows that he who is the life of humanity must, though personally pure, be involved in responsibility for all human sin, and "it was necessary that the Christ should suffer" (Acts 17:3). This suffering was an enduring of the reaction of the divine holiness against sin and so was a bearing of penalty (Isa. 53:6; Gal. 3:13), but it was also the

---

ing, and the external world is simply God. In spite of such argument, men will believe that the external world is a reality—that matter is, and that it is the cause of the effects we attribute to its agency" (Hodge, ST, I, 596).

[228]ST(1896), 204.
[229]ST(1896), 204.
[230]ST(1896), 204.
[231]"If God can disjoin from himself a certain portion of force which we call man's will, while yet that will is dependent upon God for its continued existence, then God can also disjoin from himself a certain inferior portion of force which we call magnetism, while yet that magnetism is dependent upon him for its continued existence. The same principle which leads to the confounding of natural forces with divine will would logically require the confounding of human will with divine will" (ST[1896], 204).
[232]ST(1896), 205.
[233]ST(1896), 207. The force of this is to deny that God's action in second causes supersedes these second causes, possibly in such a way as to make room for supernatural events which are irregular and of the nature of miracle.

voluntary execution of a plan that antedated creation (Phil. 2:6-7), and Christ's sacrifice in time showed what had been in the heart of God from eternity (Heb. 9:14; Rev. 13:8).[234]

By this transition of thought, Strong discarded the passage found in the earlier edition of his theology lectures which found the "link of connection between Christ's personal innocence and the bearing of the sins of the world" in the doctrine of imputation, and substituted a view which involved Christ in the guilt of the race. Strong declared that this treatment is intended "to meet the chief modern objection to the atonement,"[235] that God is so just that he must punish sin, and yet so unjust[236] that he could punish it in the person of the innocent.

Christ's submission to John's baptism was not alone a consecration to death, Strong explained, but "also a recognition and confession of his implication in that guilt of the race for which death was the appointed and inevitable penalty."[237] This guilt itself needed atonement. Through the retroactive efficiency of Christ's atonement and upon the ground of it, "human nature in him was purged of its depravity from the moment that he took that nature,"[238] so that Christ justified himself as well as others; upon the ground of His atonement, believers before and after His advent were justified. That Christ had guilt, however, did not involve Him in depravity, for both in civil law and in the justification of the sinner the two are distinguished. Consequently, "Christ takes guilt without depravity, in order that we may have depravity without guilt."[239] Had Christ been born by ordinary generation, He would have had depravity and penalty as well.[240] But in His supernatural birth, the human nature which He assumed was purged from its depravity, but this purging "did not take away guilt, or penalty."[241]

At this point, an unreconciled element appears in Strong's presentation. Whereas, in his application of monism to the atonement, he held that Christ as the creator of humanity was involved in a natural race guilt, and that in this respect the atonement came in some respect as something due from him, yet Strong—probably in an effort to retain the emphasis on the atonement as a provision of divine grace—emphasized still in this fifth revision that Christ "might have declined to join himself to humanity, and then he need not to have suffered."[242] But in his articles in *The Examiner* he had stressed that Christ suffered from the time of the first human sin.

---

[234]ST(1896), 413.
[235]ST(1896), 413.
[236]As Greg had put it, in *Creed of Christendom*, 243.
[237]ST(1896), 416. "If it be asked whether Jesus, then, before his death, was an unjustified person, we answer that, while personally pure and well-pleasing to God (Matt. 3:17), he himself was conscious of a race-responsibility and a race-guilt which must be atoned for . . . ; and that guilty human nature in him endured at the last the separation from God which constitutes the essence of death, sin's penalty. . . . As Christ was man, the penalty due to human guilt belonged to him to bear; but, as he was God, he could exhaust that penalty, and could be a proper substitute for others" (ST[1896], 416).
[238]ST(1896), 416.
[239]ST(1896), 416.
[240]ST(1896), 412.
[241]ST(1896), 416.
[242]ST(1896), 412.

Furthermore, although Strong had emphasized that even humanity in sin has its ground of being in the Logos, yet here he affirmed that Christ "might have sundered his connection with the race, and then he need not have suffered."[243] By the union with humanity in the incarnation, Christ took upon himself the guilt of Adam's sin,[244] which belongs, prior to personal transgression and apart from inherited depravity, to every member of the human race deriving his life from Adam. Christ can justly bear penalty, because He inherits guilt which is not personal but rather the guilt of the common transgression of the race in Adam, and so, being personally pure, He can vicariously bear the penalty due to the sin of mankind.[245]

What then are the emphases found in the theology lectures, not already noted in connection with articles in *The Examiner*? For one thing, one is impressed with the fact that, in Strong's application of monism to his systematic theology, the changes were not more sweeping. The circumstances contributory to this, however, cannot now be reconstructed beyond question. Could it have been a matter of convenience, such that the demand for a new edition of his theology was so pressing that he felt it better to make minimal changes, in the hope of adequate reconstruction at a later date? Or were there still areas of Christian theology for which the implications of monism were not yet fully apparent to him? It will be seen that, in the final revision of his theology lectures a decade later, he frequently left the old and the new approaches side by side, sometimes unreconciled, sometimes declaring the new to be clearly preferable, and usually affirming the new to be advantageously inclusive of the old. But in the 1896 lectures, monism was applied only to the doctrines of preservation and atonement. And the significant elements, not found in *The Examiner* articles, appear to be: (1) a readiness to speak of the laws of nature as "second" or "secondary" causes, but in the sense that they are regular and automatic workings of the first cause; (2) the retention of the notion of "substances" in the universe, although this is possibly due to a failure to make sufficient revision in the context of the presentation of the monistic view; (3) the coupling of the insistence on Christ's creatorial union with the race as furnishing the subjective reason and ground for His atonement for the sin of the race, in which He is guilty, though personally pure, with the insistence that (a) this guilt was itself atoned for on the cross; (b) Christ experienced

---

[243] ST(1896), 412. The context here, however, makes it quite clear that Strong wrote these words not from the viewpoint of monism, but from the viewpoint of the incarnation as involving the specific identification with the race, but that he did not revise this in accord with his later views. Whether the failure to revise was merely an oversight or, as suggested above, a failure to work out the relation between an atonement viewed at the same time as in some sense an obligation on his part and yet also an act of divine grace, is uncertain. Strong added to the words quoted: "But once born of the Virgin, once possessed of the human nature that was under the curse, he was bound to suffer. The whole mass and weight of God's displeasure fell on him, when once he became a member of the race" (ST[1896], 412). On the following page, in the interest of monism, Strong urged that Christ's incarnational union with the race is only an outward, visible expression of a prior creatorial union (ST[1896], 413).

[244] The suggestion of the monistic view, elsewhere applied, was that Christ assumed this guilt automatically, as the Creator who is substantially one with humanity, at the moment of the Fall.

[245] ST(1896), 412.

guilt and penalty but not depravity; (4) the joint insistence on Christ's guilt in virtue of a creatorial union with sinful humanity as furnishing a ground of obligation for atonement, though He is personally pure, and on the atonement as a gracious divine provision, which Christ might have withheld were it not for the redemptive plan of God.

IV. THE 1896 ESSAY ON ROBINSON'S THEOLOGY

Before considering essays which appeared subsequently to the fifth revision of his theology, and contained in the 1899 volume on *Christ in Creation and Ethical Monism*, it will be necessary to consider briefly an article not contained therein, but which appeared likewise after the 1896 theology, and to which reference has already been made in an earlier chapter of this dissertation.

When the Robinson memorial volume appeared in 1896, containing Strong's contribution on "Ezekiel Gilman Robinson as a Theologian," it contained numerous references made by Strong to tensions in his former teacher's theology which, to Strong's mind, could be removed best along the lines of the ethical monism now so prominent in Strong's thinking.[246] In taking exception to Robinson's treatment of the doctrine of the Trinity, of imputation, and of atonement, Strong appealed to the monistic view for the resolution of dissatisfactions with Robinson's statements.

In criticism of Robinson's view of the Trinity, which while not denying an ontological significance yet tended to be preoccupied with the economic aspect, Strong took as a point of departure an emphasis in accord with the influence of idealistic thought. "There is a 'larger Christ' whom recent theology is coming to discover, and this 'larger Christ' is enabling us better to understand the work of the Christ incarnate,"[247] he remarked, in pleading for a fuller statement of the essential nature of God. At the same time, by emphasizing against Robinson that genuine revelation must carry us to knowledge "of what God is *in himself*, not simply what he is *to us*,"[248] Strong suggested that here too, Robinson was overinfluenced in the direction of metaphysical reserve by concessions in the Kantian direction. But what is important is that Strong's overcoming of that reserve comes by the invocation, against Kant, of the spirit of modern philosophical idealism. It is to the "larger Christ" which the theology contemporary with Strong had invoked, that he looked now for a more satisfactory doctrine of the Trinity.

While Strong criticized Robinson's treatment of the Trinity "not . . . in its ordinary place immediately after his account of the attributes of God, but (after) . . . the doctrine of sin and the person of Christ"[249] as reflecting an inadequate concern with an ontological statement of divine being, the fact that Strong suggests that the doctrine is rightly treated

---
[246]This factor might itself suggest that the monistic principle as Strong applied it does not have its precedent in Robinson.
[247]Art. (1896), 194.
[248]Art. (1896), 195.
[249]Art. (1896), 195. Robinson's method, Strong complained, seemed to imply "that the Trinity is not so much the foundation as it is the result of the later doctrines of theology" (195).

"immediately after" the statement of divine attributes—as he himself does consider the theme—is itself disclosive of a theological trend with which he finds himself in sympathy, and according to which the divine attributes apparently may be sufficiently established without a consideration of a divine self-disclosure of triunity.

Strong also fastened upon Robinson's fluctuation between objective and subjective statements of the doctrine of atonement as evidence of a grasping for a clarifying principle which Robinson had not attained, and which the doctrine of immanence supplied.

God in Christ is immanent in humanity. If all good in man is the work of Christ, then a seemingly subjective theory of the atonement may have an objective side or aspect. What before appeared to be simply man's work is God's work, now that we see all but sin to come from God. Unless some such principle be assumed, I find it difficult to acquit Dr. Robinson of inconsistency, and impossible to deny that the Old School doctrine with which his theology began evaporated, as he went on, in the fire of criticism. I am unwilling to grant that he was conscious of inconsistency. I prefer to say, therefore, that . . . he unconsciously admitted to his system ideas which he did not himself work out to their logical conclusions. . . . Was Dr. Robinson . . . building better than he knew, and preparing the way for a more modern theology?[250]

Consequently, Strong even suggests in that Robinson's mind "there was some principle of reconciliation which was consciously or unconsciously working, though it was unexpressed."[251] That principle, for Strong, was included in and best stated by ethical monism.

It will be recalled that Robinson objected to forensic substitution and especially the notion of "an absolute justice in God, which his mercy could satisfy or not" and consequently took issue with Shedd's theory of the atonement. Strong, however, refused to eliminate the element of divine propitiation, and contended that Shedd's view can be made tenable, but only by introducing a further principle, that of the union of all men with Christ by creation. This principle alone can make Christ's substitution consistent with justice, he affirmed.[252]

If Robinson had denied that the guilt and penalty of human sin were imputed to Christ, and insisted that the Christ endured penalty but neither depravity nor guilt, Strong insisted on both an imputed and imparted guilt, as well as penalty. Both theologians denied that the incarnation involved Him in depravity, in view of His supernatural conception. But Strong sought a principle to justify the imputation of penalty to Christ, and found it in a natural union of the Logos and humanity.[253] He quoted:

As, in the case of hereditary depravity, God's procedure in charging upon us guilt can be justified only upon the Scriptural ground that we were seminally and organically one with our first father in the transgression; so the visiting of the penalties of the race upon Christ our Lord can be justified only upon the ground that he, too, was heir with us to the same guilt and condemnation, even though depravity was cut off by his immaculate conception in the womb of the Virgin. And if any ask how thus becoming one of the race can load him with anything more than his portion of the common guilt of the fall, I answer that he was "the root," as well as "the offspring, of David," and that since all men, as well as all things, were created

[250]Art. (1896), 197.
[251]Art. (1896), 197.
[252]Art. (1896), 196-197.
[253]Art. (1896), 190.

and upheld by him, there naturally and inevitably rested upon him who was their life the burden and responsibility of the sins of his members.[254]

V. THE 1889 VOLUME: *Christ in Creation and Ethical Monism*

Strong wrote the preface for the fifth revision of his 1886 theology on January 1, 1896. Between that date and the appearance in 1899 of *Christ in Creation and Ethical Monism*, the opening chapters of which are a reprint of the articles[255] in *The Examiner*, he delivered a number of addresses[256] involving the application of monism to theology which are also included in the volume, along with similar addresses already referred to,[257] delivered prior to 1896, and several chapters apparently prepared specifically for inclusion in this volume.[258] Also contained in the volume are a number of sermons preached on distinguished occasions and Strong's addresses to graduating classes from 1888 to 1899, none of which bear in any essential way on the specialized interest of this study, except in the case of one commencement address to which reference has already been made.[259]

The essays in *Christ in Creation and Ethical Monism* which bear on the application of monism to theology will now be considered briefly.

1. Address on "Modern Tendencies in Theological Thought"

Strong delivered the address at the convocation of the University of Chicago on October 1, 1896, on the theme, "Modern Tendencies in Theological Thought." Here he employed the widely-invoked theological formula "back to Christ" in a "larger and deeper sense," urging a return

to Christ as to that which is original in thought, archetypal in creation, immanent in history; to the Logos of God, who is not only the omniscient reason, but also the personal conscience and will, at the heart of the universe.[260]

Back to Christ as Logos, back to the ante-mundane life of the Son of God, for an understanding of reality, was Strong's emphasis.

---

[254]Art. (1896), 193-194.
[255]*The Presbyterian and Reformed Review* singled out the appearance of CCEM as affording additional background against which the changes in Strong's thought could be discerned more intelligently. An anonymous reviewer commented: "As was pointed out in our notice of the fifth edition of the *Systematic Theology*, Dr. Strong had experienced since the issue of the fourth edition a somewhat radical change of fundamental conceptions, marked in the fifth edition only by a few alterations in the text that did not much signify. The present volume puts in permanently accessible form the more extended discussions in which he had announced and defended his change of view: and naturally enough these important essays, as they give character, are allowed to give title also to the volume. . . . The accession of so winning a writer to the ranks of the ethical monists is a circumstance of first-rate importance to them" (Anon., Rev. [1901], 325-326).
[256]These include not only the addresses to the successive graduating classes, but the following: "Modern Tendencies in Theological Thought" (CCEM 137-162); "The Fall and the Redemption of Man in the Light of Evolution" (CCEM, 163-180); "Fifty Years of Theology" (CCEM, 181-208).
[257]Cf. *supra*, 33-34.
[258]These are: "God's Self-Limitations" (CCEM, 87-101); "The Authority of Scripture" (CCEM, 113-136); "The Scriptural Doctrine of Eternal Punishment" (CCEM, 422-439).
[259]Cf. *supra*, 34-35.
[260]CCEM, 141.

Evolution is the divine method, and only discloses the nature of the involution which preceded it.²⁶¹ But the regularity of nature does not preclude surprising and unique divine acts.²⁶² Human knowledge enlightened by love both recognizes and defends the rationality of a divine incarnation in Christ and an atonement for man's sin by the "original author and the continuous upholder" of human life.²⁶³

As against deism, Strong upheld "Christ, the Life of Nature."²⁶⁴ The pattern of argument was not new. Since energy dissipates, force must be viewed as an exercise of will. The system of things, or universe, requires the postulation of an omnipresent reason and will. In identifying this omnipresent reason and will with the Redeemer, the Christian but follows the lead of the Scripture, where the full and complete identification is made with Jesus Christ. The recognition of Christ as the life of nature provides the "guarantee that theology and science will come to complete accord."²⁶⁵

As against atomism, which disregards the organic unity of mankind and its connection with God, and regards men only as individuals, Strong upheld "Christ, the Life and Humanity."²⁶⁶ Evolution, sociology and political ethics concur in the organic emphasis.²⁶⁷ But modern thought erroneously lays the blame for sin upon the Creator, instead of regarding it as self-perversion, when sin is confounded with weakness or disease or ignorance.²⁶⁸ Christ is the soul's true life, physically and naturally, as well as spiritually, but sin is not a manifestation of Christ, but of the individual will.²⁶⁹

As against externalism, Strong emphasized "Christ, the Life of the Church."²⁷⁰ In developing this phase of his address, he spoke against both the realistic view of substance,²⁷¹ and against the prevailing evangelical view of the Scripture.²⁷² Current evangelical theory faultily treats Scripture "as the original source of truth, instead of regarding it as the mere expression of Christ, who alone is the truth."²⁷³ This results in a double standard, whereby Christ and the Scripture are played against each other. But the appeal must always be to Christ, whether from creed, or from conscience, or from Scripture.²⁷⁴ Christ is not shut up to Scripture for self-expression; philosophy and science also disclose him, although sin "has curtailed and

---

²⁶¹CCEM, 142.
²⁶²CCEM, 143.
²⁶³CCEM, 143.
²⁶⁴CCEM, 148.
²⁶⁵CCEM, 150. Theology narrates the *why*, science the *how*, affirmed Strong. But evolution as the common method of Christ "does not fetter him, because his immanence in nature is qualified by his transcendence above nature" (CCEM, 150).
²⁶⁶CCEM, 151. Strong viewed the creationist theory of the soul's origin as a sign of this view.
²⁶⁷CCEM, 152.
²⁶⁸CCEM, 155.
²⁶⁹CCEM, 155.
²⁷⁰CCEM, 158.
²⁷¹"I would have you notice," Strong urged, "that I have not used the word substance, but the word life. It is a mark of progress in philosophy that it has outgrown the old scholastic terminology of substance and qualities, essence and accidents, and has gone back to the far simpler and more scriptural category of life and its powers. It is good to get back to Christ, for he is the Life" (CCEM, 158).
²⁷²CCEM, 159-161
²⁷³CCEM, 159.

perverted these sources of truth, and therefore Scripture furnishes a rectifying principle,"[275] so that our conclusions are tested by comparing them with the Scripture. But that does not make Scripture "the only and the perfect source of doctrine" for it is an incomplete manifestation of Christ who alone is divine wisdom and truth.[276] The truth is a personal Being.[277]

The significant emphasis found in this address then, which may be taken as supplementary of that in the articles of *The Examiner*, is that (1) Scripture is corrective of the truths of philosophy and science, which are distorted because of the noetic effects of sin; (2) Scripture is not "the only and the perfect source of doctrine," but the living Christ alone is the original source of truth.

2. Address on "The Fall and the Redemption of Man in the Light of Evolution"

Strong read a paper before the Baptist Congress in Buffalo, New York, on November 15, 1898, on the theme, "The Fall and the Redemption of Man in the Light of Evolution."

In this, Strong reiterated the conviction that evolution is the method of the immanent God, yet in view of divine transcendence, the evolutionary method imposes no ultimate limitation. Lotze had underwritten just such a view, Strong emphasized.[278] Absolute continuity is inconsistent with progress, which presupposes new force or new combinations of force, or intelligent will. Miracle is not precluded, but may serve the divine purpose in a moral universe.[279]

The biological view of man does not exclude the theological, Strong affirmed, for the resident forces which produced man are only the manifestation of divine mind and will.[280] Simultaneously, Strong invoked ethical monism in behalf of theistic evolution, in such a way as to oppose fiat creation. The fault of many advocates of the development theory, he complained, is their assumption "that matter is something impersonal and dead, and out of it they try to get a personal and living being called man,"[281]

---

[274]CCEM, 160.
[275]CCEM, 160.
[276]CCEM, 160.
[277]CCEM, 160. Strong added: "Not first doctrine and then Christ; nor first creed and then Christ; not first inspiration and then Christ; not first Scripture and then Christ; but first Christ and then Scripture, inspiration, doctrine, creed; this is both the order of logic and the order of experience. Only Christ in us, a principle of life, makes Scripture, inspiration, doctrine, creed, intelligible; only the Truth within enables us to understand the truth without" (CCEM, 161).
[278]"This conception of evolution is that of Lotze," wrote Strong. "That great philosopher, whose influence is more potent than any other in present thought, does not regard the universe as a *plenum* to which nothing can be added in the way of force" (CCEM, 163).
[279]"Regeneration and answers to prayer are possible for the very reason that these are the objects for which the universe was built. . . . Since we believe in a dynamical universe, of which the personal and living God is the inner source of energy, evolution is but the basis, foundation, and background of Christianity, the silent and regular working of him, who, in the fullness of time, utters his voice in Christ and the cross" (CCEM, 165).
[280]CCEM, 167-168. Here Strong made one of his strongest statements on nature as a part of God: "To all intents and purposes, these (resident) forces are God; for the will of God is the only real force in nature" (CCEM, 168).
[281]CCEM, 168.

whereas matter is conceivable "only as the energizing of an intelligent and personal will."[282] That the evolutionary process manifests the upward struggle of an intelligence and will through lower forms toward rationality and freedom is another way of remarking that "the preincarnate Logos was exhibiting the divine wisdom and power in successive approximations toward humanity" until psychical man was the result.[283]

Strong's doubts about man's animal ancestry were now a thing of the past:

The dust from which the body of Adam was made was animate dust; lower forms of life were taken as the foundation upon which to build man's physical frame and man's rational powers; into some animal germ came the breath of a new intellectual and moral life.[284]

But an evolutionary origin is compatible with a proper doctrine of man's fall, he held.[285] The degradation witnessed in human history necessitates the empirical judgment of a primal, voluntary fall of humanity from God and his law.[286] Sin must be explained in terms of free personality, or it loses its signficance; to refer sin to lower animal impulses, rather than to the will, is to deny its existence.[287] The tendency of man to transmit acquired characters sheds light on inherited corruption.[288]

The moral self-centeredness of man, however, could not destroy his natural connection with the indwelling Christ, who is the ground of all being.[289] Since Christ is the source of the life of the spiritually impenitent, Christ has been afflicted, as the natural life of the race, in the affliction of humanity, and has suffered for human sin.[290] Calvary was the historical manifestation and concrete proclamation of "the age-long *suffering* of the Son of God."[291] This natural suffering of Christ is at the same time an atoning suffering:

This suffering has been an atoning suffering, since it has been due to righteousness. If God had not been holy, if God had not made all nature express the holiness of his being, if God had not made pain and loss the necessary consequences of sin, then Christ would not have suffered. But since these things are sin's penalty and Christ is the life of the sinful race, it must needs be that Christ should suffer. There is nothing arbitrary in the laying upon him of the iniquities of us all. There is an original grace as well as an original sin. The fact that Christ is our life makes it inevitable that we should derive from him many an impulse and influence that does not belong to our sinful nature.[292]

Thus Strong here repeated the thesis that Christ's natural union with the race involved him inevitably in both suffering and gracious atonement.

---

[282] CCEM, 168.
[283] CCEM, 175-176.
[284] CCEM, 169.
[285] CCEM, 169.
[286] CCEM, 170.
[287] CCEM, 170.
[288] CCEM, 171.
[289] CCEM, 172.
[290] CCEM, 173.
[291] CCEM, 177. Strong added: "Not late in human history did he vicariously take our sins upon him, but from the very instant of the fall. The imputation of our sins to him is the result of his natural union with us" (CCEM, 178).
[292] CCEM, 173.

Strong emphasized that all suffering is penal, and not that of Christ alone,[293] but that because Christ was personally pure, he was made a curse for us.[294]

Strong's tendency, in this address, was to refer as much of experience as possible to the operation of the immanent Logos. Not only did he affirm that Christ emerged from a prepared nation as Adam had emerged out of the highest forms of pre-existing life, but the virgin birth is viewed as no more unique than the bringing of man out of a race of apelike progenitors. The new science, Strong declared,

> recognizes more than one method of propagation even in one and the same species, and it is no wonder that in the introduction of him who was the crown and summit of the whole system we should see a return to the original method of parthenogenesis.[295]

The emphases found in this address, and not noted previously, are: (1) Since monism views matter as intrinsically mental and volitional, it is not difficult for this view to derive human life by evolutionary development; (2) man had an animal ancestry, endowed in his case with intellectual and moral life; (3) the empirical observation of human degradation requires the view of a primal, voluntary fall of humanity from a proper, moral and spiritual relation with God: (4) Christ's natural, age-long suffering is at the same time atoning suffering; (5) All suffering is penal, but Christ's is substitutionary because he is personally pure; (6) Christ's suffering is not arbitrary but, since it flows from his natural union with the race, is of the nature of original grace; (7) The virgin birth of Christ constitutes a return of the parthenogenetic method of producing life.

3. Address on "Fifty Years of Theology"

On June 7, 1899, Strong delivered an address on the subject "Fifty Years of Theology" at the fiftieth anniversary of Dr. Alvah Hovey's connection with Newton Theological Institution as professor. In it, Strong stressed some of the elements which composed the reaction against deism which he labeled as the "innermost substance and meaning" of the previous half-century of theology.[296]

The recovery of divine immanence, Strong declared, displaced the mechanical with a dynamical interpretation of nature.[297] Nature's laws are but God's generic, regular, and automatic volitions, but no less free on that account.[298] God's immanence in the soul, as well as in nature, was now being recognized, so that humanity is seen to have its being in God.

---

[293]"This suffering for sin which Christ endured is the suffering of penal inflictions in our stead, for all suffering is penal in the sense that its existence is due to sin, and that it is the expression of God's moral revulsion from iniquity, the revelation of his self-vindicating holiness" (CCEM, 179).

[294]CCEM, 180.

[295]CCEM, 177.

[296]Strong's visit to Newton on this occasion has a double interest, in view of Hovey's sharp disagreement with ethical monism. These differences will be treated in the subsequent chapter.

[297]The symbol of nature is now Darwin's flower, not Paley's watch, Strong pointed out. "God does not create a universe which goes of itself without his presence or control, but the universe is full of his life and is the constant expression of his mind and will" (CCEM, 187).

[298]CCEM, 188.

The rediscovery of the immanent God has involved also the discovery that this immanent God is Christ.[299] Modern theology sees Christ both as Redeemer and as "the one and only principle of divine expression, the one outgoing and revealing agency in the nature of God."[300] This omnipresent living Christ is the answer to Ritschl's exclusively historical Christ and Pfleiderer's exclusively ideal Christ, the two rallying points of German Christology.[301]

Modern theology has rescued from neglect, Strong affirmed, the view that the immanent Christ's method is evolutionary. This view does not impinge upon divine freedom. If every natural operation is due to supernatural will, the power to work miracles is not lacking.[302] The events and sequences of nature are viewed spiritually by faith.

That evolution is predominantly ethical is a fourth characteristic of modern theology. "The world is not simply a lost world given over to the evil one," Strong asserted, but moral forces are at work in it, and "the immanent Christ is progressively transforming it."[303] There is an evolutionary preparation for both righteousness and love. Humanity discloses a conjugal, paternal and filial affection which is underivable from fallen man, and which must be attributed to the Christ of God

whose original grace is counteracting the effects of original sin, and who is thus preparing the way for the publication and reception of his finished redemption.[304]

A fifth, all-inclusive truth attained by the previous half-century of theology, Strong affirmed, is that the ethical meaning of the universe is summed up in the historical Jesus. Christ is not merely the crown of evolution, but its animating spirit, whose mind and heart and will are expressed in all its processes.[305]

Recent theology also had come to see the cross as the revelation of God's eternal suffering for sin, Strong said.[306] By its new discovery of Christ's world-relations, it had reached a profounder view of "that redeeming work of which the whole universe is but the theatre and illustration."[307] Theology has been gravitating toward "the supremacy of righteousness in the nature of God."[308] God's self-love is righteousness, which

---

[299]"Our later theology has, as never before since the times of the apostles," Strong remarked, "identified the Christ of the incarnation with the Logos of God, through whom and unto whom all things were made and in whom all things consist" (CCEM, 190).
[300]CCEM, 190. Strong reaffirmed that "while the transcendent and unknowable God is the Father, the immanent and revealed God is Christ" (CCEM, 190).
[301]CCEM, 191.
[302]CCEM, 193-194.
[303]CCEM, 195.
[304]CCEM, 195-196.
[305]"The historical Jesus is not only God manifest in the flesh, in whom is all the fullness of the Godhead—in bodily form and manifestation, but he is also the gathering up and disclosure of all the ethical meaning of the creation. In other words, Jesus is the immanent Christ of evolution, coming out like a painter from behind his own picture and interpreting to us his work" (CCEM, 197).
[306]Strong criticized the governmental and moral influence theories, the former for conceiving law externally and arbitrarily, and the latter for regarding happiness instead of righteousness as the end of creation (CCEM, 198).
[307]CCEM, 199.
[308]CCEM, 199.

conditions all other love, and He cannot make the universe happy without first making it holy.[309] God's suffering is not a matter of choice, but discloses His nature.[310] The reproaches of those who resist God fall upon Christ, whose life is the inmost principle of their being.[311]

The final step of progress in recent theology, Strong noted, was "its application of the principle of development to Holy Scripture."[312] The communication of revelation to the Biblical writers was not as disjunctive with other noetic activity as once thought:

> The Spirit of Christ which was in them was the Spirit of the immanent Christ working after his common evolutionary fashion. It was not the sudden impact of a power from without but the movement of a power from within, which only in thought was distinguishable from the activity of their own minds and hearts and wills. And inspiration was like grace; it was not infallible nor impeccable.[313]

Christianity requires no particular theory of inspiration, for it had a vigorous existence before the composition of any New Testament book.[314] Nor is the concession to higher criticism of a different form of the manuscripts destructive.[315] The application of evolutionary principles to Scripture serves not to disprove inspiration, but to make it more evident:

> the more composite the authorship of Scripture, the more apparent is the proof of one superintending Mind that combines the scattered *biblia* into one *Bible*.[316]

The modern view sees in Scripture an inspiration

> which, while it does not guarantee the inerrancy of Scripture in every historical and scientific detail, does yet make it, when taken together and when rightly interpreted, infallible for its purpose of communicating moral and religious truth, and able to make us wise unto salvation.[317]

It is clear from these quotations that Strong combined immanentism, evolution, and higher criticism in such a way as to restrict the message of Scripture to moral and redemptive truth. At the same time, the merger of these elements could not help but diminish the view of the essential uniqueness, in qualitative terms, of the Biblical view. This is clear, both from the readiness to sacrifice infallible inspiration, and the affirmation that

> we have no need to doubt the supernatural element either in the world or in the Bible, so long as he (Christ) is recognized as the animating and controlling force in both.[318]

Strong did not intend hereby to lessen the exclusive claim for the Biblical message on the sinfulness of man and the divine provision of atonement,

---

[309] CCEM, 200.
[310] CCEM, 200.
[311] CCEM, 200.
[312] CCEM, 203.
[313] CCEM, 203.
[314] CCEM, 204.
[315] "A book may go by the name of its chief writer, and Isaiah or Zechariah may have a double authorship. The Pentateuch may be Mosaic only for substance; the laws of Leviticus may be later additions in the spirit of what Moses wrote; the speeches in Deuteronomy may be representations by one of Moses' successors on the west of Jordan of instructions by the great lawgiver on the east of Jordan which had been traditionally handed down" (CCEM, 204).
[316] CCEM, 205.
[317] CCEM, 205.
[318] CCEM, 206.

but, without working out its implications, he had in principle lessened the gap between Christianity and the non-Christian religions.

The emphases found in this address, not previously noted are: (1) Directed by the immanent Christ, the ethical evolutionary process results in the progressive victory of moral forces; (2) Christ's natural union with humanity issues in an original grace, whereby holy impulses are imparted even to sinful humanity; (3) Holiness is the fundamental divine attribute; (4) Biblical inspiration is not infallible, but (a) admits of error in historical and scientific detail, (b) is organically infallible for moral and religious truth necessary to salvation; (5) Biblical inspiration is to be referred not to a transcendent, but to an immanent divine activity, and (a) does not preclude a higher critical view of authorship and composition, (b) is not supernaturally disjunctive with universal divine activity.

4. Essay on "The Authority of Scripture"

Of the essays which appear to be included for the first time in *Christ in Creation and Ethical Monism* is one on "The Authority of Scripture."[319] Because the human conscience is "warped and perverted by sin," Strong declared, it is bound to submit to divine authority above individual reason and conscience.[320] The question is not one of authority versus truth, for "authority is as much God's appointed way to truth as reason is."[321] Mankind inevitably chooses an authority, and the individual's choice of the particular authority reveals his character, whether he prefers the authority of self or of God.[322]

Although conscience has its original source in God, it modifies the divine voice.[323] Yet it is a subordinate and limited echo of an infinite righteousness "and in the sphere and for the purposes for which it was given it is sufficient to guide our moral action."[324]

The church represents the collective conscience of redeemed humanity, but its authority is likewise delegated, subordinate and limited, contrary to Roman Catholicism.[325]

It is Christ who is the revelation of God, and who sums up all that is meant by God and by revelation.[326] Christ alone is the Truth, and "all the

---

[319]The circumstance which suggests that even this essay may have appeared previously in some journal, although there is no indication of this in CCEM, is the fact that Strong's article on "Ethical Monism" quotes a paragraph credited to an "Essay on the Authority of Scripture," which is not further identified, yet which consists of 200 words which appear also in the essay now in view (cf. CCEM, 36). In either event since the essay previously considered deals in part with Strong's attitude toward the Scripture, this essay is appropriately considered here.

[320]"It is not only rational for us in our present intellectual and moral state to recognize an authority above that of individual reason and conscience, but this is the only reasonable and conscientious thing for us to do" (CCEM, 114).

[321]CCEM, 115.

[322]CCEM, 115-116.

[323]CCEM, 119.

[324]CCEM, 119.

[325]CCEM, 120.

[326]CCEM, 121. "Christ is nothing less than Deity revealed, God brought down to our human comprehension and engaged in the work of our salvation. Christ is the Word of God, the divine reason in expression. All outgoing, communication, manifestation of the Godhead, is the work of Christ. God never thought anything, said anything, did anything, except through Christ" (CCEM, 121).

lights of conscience, as well as of science, all the truths hid amid the chaff of paganism, as well as all the discoveries made to the chosen people"[327] were His communications. Christ and revelation are one and the same thing and the other the truth of God communicated and made an objective possession of mankind.[328]

Christ is the ultimate source of all religious authority, but in the Scripture His works and words are "most perfectly set forth."[329] The Bible has an authority which is divine, but its authority is delegated, subordinate and "limited to the sphere in which it was meant to move and to the purpose for which it was designed."[330] This purpose was to teach not mathematics and astronomy, but "all religious truth . . . as it is in Jesus."[331] The divine revelation in Christ may have been given without any written record.[332] Though the facts of Christianity had never been recorded, tradition might still be authoritative, without the safety of the church or the authority of the truth depending upon Scripture.[333] Even a written record might be authoritative without special inspiration. Consequently,

> if Christianity could conceivably be authenticated to the world without inspiration, and even without a written record, it is much more true that Christianity does not stand or fall with any particular theory of inspiration.[334]

Inspiration is the qualifying of man to put revealed truth into permanent and written form, and its denial does not imperil the reality of divine revelation.[335] Nevertheless, Strong affirmed his belief "in the inspiration of the Scriptures and of every part of the Scriptures. The Bible not only contains, but it is, the word of God."[336] Yet the Scripture is not the original, but rather the witness to Christ, and is to be reverenced as an organic and progressive account of Christ's historical work and teaching under both old and new dispensations.[337]

To the truly scientific mind, with active conscience and affection as well as merely logical understanding, the Scripture will be "self-evidencing."[338] The Bible, taken organically, is "a complete and sufficient guide

---

[327] CCEM, 122. The word "discoveries" is curious.
[328] CCEM, 122.
[329] CCEM, 123.
[330] CCEM, 123.
[331] CCEM, 123.
[332] Strong pointed out that tradition served in the days of the patriarchs no less than in the primitive church before the writing of the first gospel narrative (CCEM, 123-124).
[333] CCEM, 124.
[334] CCEM, 124. "The facts of Christ's life and teaching are greater than any written record of them, and . . . the substantial truth of the Scripture history may be vindicated just as the truth of many secular narratives has been" (CCEM, 125).
[335] CCEM, 125.
[336] CCEM, 125.
[337] CCEM, 132-133. "The supremacy of Christ, and not any theory of inspiration, is the citadel of our faith. We refuse to confound the citadel with any of those temporary outworks which past ages have constructed to defend it, and with which our modern artillery enables us in some cases to dispense" (CCEM, 126).
[338] When these conditions are met, Strong suggested, "the law and the prophets and the Psalms will speak of Christ; minor obscurities and difficulties will be forgotten in the overpowering impression that this revelation is from God" (CCEM, 126).

to Christ and salvation."[339] But infallible historical, literary, and scientific perfection are beside the purpose of revelation, and "the very humanity of the Bible is the best proof of its divinity."[340] Yet Strong denied the presence of errors of historical detail, translation, exegesis or logic in the original autographs.[341] He refused, however, "to impose on students for the ministry the dogma of absolute inerrancy" in matters which affect neither the substance of Bible history nor Bible doctrine.[342] The question of inerrant original autographs is not sufficiently important to exclude anyone from Christian fellowship who professes to find such error.[343] The fallibility of Scripture in historical and scientific detail would not necessarily involve its fallibility in matters of faith and doctrine.[344] The Scripture is "an absolute authority in matters pertaining to salvation."[345] It is necessary both to be cautious in identifying seeming discrepancies with real errors, and in affirming an *a priori* theory of what the Bible must be.[346] While it may be necessary to concede "literary, historical, and scientific imperfections to some small extent," Strong affirmed, "we can never admit that there are imperfections in Christ."[347]

Strong's emphases in this essay, not yet recorded in other summaries, are: (1) Mankind, as finite and sinful, requires authority; (2) The authority preferred by an individual discloses his attitude toward God; (3) Conscience, while not wholly trustworthy in view of man's sinfulness, is a limited echo of the righteous God; (4) The church has but subordinate and limited authority; (5) The Scripture has subordinate authority, limited to matters of faith and morals, which (a) is self-evidencing when approached by the meeting of specific moral and spiritual conditions for knowledge; (b) is not to be identified with a view of infallible inspiration; (6) Christ is the original and infallible revelation, of whom no imperfection is to be predicted.

5. Essay on "God's Self-Limitations"

The implications of ethical monism for Christology are most clearly foreshadowed in Strong's essay on "God's Self-Limitations."

---

[339]CCEM, 126.
[340]CCEM, 127.
[341]"I do not myself feel compelled to recognize such errors as existing in the original autographs. I have carefully examined one after another of the so-called contradictions between different historical books of the Bible, and I have yet to find one where some reasonable hypothesis will not furnish a reconciliation. The so-called errors of translation, exegesis, logic, seem to me, in almost every case, to be the figments of a shallow criticism or an unbelieving spirit" (CCEM, 127).
[342]CCEM, 127.
[343]CCEM, 129.
[344]CCEM, 129. "If any one says that the most natural explanation of certain apparent discrepancies is that each of the differing authors used the material ready to his hand, and that the Spirit of inspiration did not regard it as worth the while to correct the unimportant variation, I cannot prove that his view is incorrect. It would only enlarge a little my conception of the amount of human imperfection which the Holy Spirit may leave in inspired Scripture. It would only make the Scripture histories a little more like secular histories, two of which may vary in slight details, while both of them in all essentials are perfectly harmonious" (CCEM, 130-131).
[345]CCEM, 130.
[346]CCEM, 131.
[347]CCEM, 134.

After emphasizing that God exists in no necessary relations with the universe, although furnishing in himself the cause and ground of the finite, Strong treated the divine attributes, showing how God is limited by his intrinsic perfections.[348]

But Christ's humiliation discloses a divine self-limitation to stagger human wonder.[349] Christ's person involved a self-limitation affecting God's natural attributes, and his work involved a self-limitation affecting God's moral attributes.[350] The humiliation involved a surrender by Christ of the "independent exercise of his divine attributes."[351]

As a babe He was not omniscient.[352] What is most "like God," Strong asserted, is "this self-limitation of deity to the narrow bounds of humanity, that our humanity might be addressed on its own level and in its own language."[353] But this cloaks the incarnation with mystery.

> How can there be divine attributes that are not used? Fortunately we are not without analogies which help us to comprehend the possibility of it. There is more of resource in *us* than we use; we know more than we can tell; there is more in the memory of every man than he can at this moment recall; every one of us has more power than he now knows of—only the exigency calls it forth.[354]

Strong did not further develop this suggestion, that the latent divine in humanity may furnish a key to the veiled deity involved in the incarnation.

Turning from the divine self-limitation involved in the person of Christ to that involved in the work of Christ, Strong emphasized the moral self-limitation involved in Christ's assumption of human guilt.[355] The development is similar to that set forth in Strong's other essays dealing with this subject.

Strong's emphases of which special note should be taken in this essay are: (1) Mankind, as finite and sinful, requires authority; (2) The authority preferred by an individual discloses his attitude toward God; (3) Conscience, while not wholly trustworthy in view of man's sinfulness, is a limited echo of the righteous God; (4) The church has but subordinate and limited authority; (5) The Scripture has subordinate authority, limited to matters of faith and morals, which (a) is self-evidencing when approached by the meeting of specific moral and spiritual conditions for knowledge; (b) is not to be identified with a view of infallible inspiration; (6) Christ is the original and infallible revelation, of whom no imperfection is to be predicted.

---

[348]CCEM, 88-95.

[349]CCEM, 95-96.

[350]"During his earthly life the God in him was veiled and subject. He voluntarily put his deity under control. God by himself could never be born or suffer or die—but God united to humanity could do all these" (CCEM, 96).

[351]CCEM, 96.

[352]"The Godhead in Christ commonly manifested itself in proportion to the capacity of Christ's humanity—only a little when the humanity was infantile and weak, more and more fully as the humanity became older and more developed. Jesus when a babe was not omniscient; indeed, even in his later years there were some things hid from him" (CCEM, 96-97).

[353]CCEM, 97.

[354]CCEM, 97.

[355]"Calvary was the actual paying of the debt which not he personally, but the human nature of which he had become a part, owed to the law and the holiness of God" (CCEM, 99).

VI. THE 1901 CLASS NOTES IN THEOLOGY

Before proceeding to the final revision of Strong's theology, which appeared in 1907, it may be well, for the sake of completeness, to refer to a few relevant lecture notes made by a student, in 1901, in an inter-leaved copy of the 1896 theology.

In those lectures, Strong set his view of imputation over against the Princeton theology, according to which the imputation of Adam's sin to humanity *precedes* an actual union, as also with the imputation of human guilt to Christ. Strong stressed that imputation is based upon a previous vital union, and considered the outworking of this thesis, in relationship to Christ's atonement, to be his significant theological contribution. His class remarks were summarized:

> Previous to Dr. Strong's work at Rochester there had been no attempt to explain the imputation of the sin of the race to Christ. Dr. Strong says if he has contributed anything to theology it is the teaching of a vital union of Christ with the race. From this union we have the imputation of the sin of the race to Christ.[356]

At the same time, Strong defended his view that the race existed seminally in Adam against the objection that it was simply an extension of medieval realism,[357] although he conceded that the Augustinian theory of Adam's natural headship is an inference from, rather than the specific teaching of, Scripture.

Dr. Strong also told his class that he had arrived at his view of the atonement by a long and gradual process.[358] Strong dictated to his classes a statement of the atonement, the essence of which has already been summarized in connection with various essays which appeared in *Christ in Creation and Ethical Monism*, which more nearly represented his views than the brief changes made in the 1896 revision. This contained the statement that

> while Christ's love explains his willingness to endure suffering for us, only His holiness furnishes his reason for that constitution of the universe and of human nature which makes that suffering necessary. As respects us, his sufferings are substitutionary since his divinity and his sinlessness enabled Him to do for us what we could never do for ourselves. Yet this substitution is also a sharing—not the work of one external to us, but of one who is the life of humanity—the soul of our soul and the life of our life, and so responsible with us for the sins of our race.[359]

At the same time, Strong emphasized that "the historical work of the Incarnate Christ is not itself the atonement, and spoke both of an "eternal suffering" and of an "age long suffering" of God.[360] Strong emphasized

---

[356] ST(1896),CN(1901), 309.

[357] "We do not hold the idea that there is a human nature above and apart from the individual. We do not hold that the individual existed in Adam. We simply hold that the individual is closely related and bound up in the fact" (ST[1896],CN [1901], 409).

[358] "Dr. Strong says it is amazing how his view of the atonement has grown, little by little, by piece-meal. (We cannot hurry ourselves in the gaining of our views—they come slowly.) Ten or twenty years ago he had no such views as he now has of atonement" (ST[1896],CN[1901], 409).

[359] ST(1896),CN(1901), 410.

[360] The historical work, Strong stated, "is rather the revelation of the atonement. This suffering of the Incarnate Christ is a manifestation in space and time of the eternal

further that the penalty borne by Christ does not reflect on divine justice:

Is it necessary to conceive of God as being unjust in punishing one wholly innocent—when that one voluntarily offers himself; when God sees that the one thus offering himself is able to bear the penalty of sin, as the sinner himself is not, and especially when the result of this transfer will be the salvation through the faith and new life of the one who could not have been saved in any other way?[361]

The other emphasis in the 1901 notes refers to eternal punishment, which Strong pressed vigorously against the view of a "second chance." He declared in this connection that, since all light comes from the cosmic Christ, all moral disobedience is essentially a rejection of Him,[362] whereas faithful fulfillment of moral obligation is virtually an acceptance of Him.

VII. THE 1907 FINAL THEOLOGY REVISION

Strong considered his 1907 theology, which appeared in one and three volume editions running 1166 pages, including 107 index pages, as a revision and enlargement of his 1886 work, of which seven previous editions had appeared, each embodying "successive corrections and supposed improvements."[363]

In his final revision, Strong pointed out in a preface written on his seventieth birthday, his perspective disclosed modifications made in the intervening twenty years:

My philosophical and critical point of view meantime has . . . somewhat changed. While I still hold to the old doctrines, I interpret them differently and expound them more clearly, because I seem to have reached a fundamental truth which throws new light upon them all. This truth I have tried to set forth in my book entitled "Christ in Creation," and to that book I refer the reader for further information.[364]

But, while affirming ethical monism, Strong also expressed distress over some "common theological tendencies" of the day which implied a movement away from the deity of Christ, his substitutionary atonement, and a miraculous view of the universe:

How men who have ever felt themselves to be lost sinners and who have once received pardon from their crucified Lord and Saviour can thereafter seek to pare down his attributes, deny his deity and atonement, tear from his brow the crown of miracle and sovereignty, relegate him to the place of a merely moral teacher who influences us as

---

suffering of God on account of human sin. Yet without the historical work which was finished on Calvary, the age long suffering of God could never have been made comprehensible to man" (ST[1896],CN[1901], 411).

[361] ST(1896),CN(1901), 413.

[362] "This question of second probation is not so prominently in the front as it was even 10 years ago. The reason . . . is the fuller grasp of the Cosmic Christ. . . . Even those who have never heard the name of Christ, come in touch with Christ. . . . Every man—those in heathen darkness, in the slums of great cities—has a moral chance. His faithful acceptance of his moral obligation is virtually accepting Christ. His failure to be true to his moral obligation is rejection of Christ" (ST[1896],CN[1901], 590).

[363] ST(1907), vii.

[364] Strong summarized his view as implying "a monistic and idealistic conception of the world, together with an evolutionary idea as to its origin and progress. But it is the very antidote to pantheism" (ST[1907], vii).

does Socrates by words spoken across a stretch of ages, passes my comprehension. Here is my test of orthodoxy: Do we pray to Jesus? . . . What think ye of the Christ? is still the critical question, and none are entitled to the name of Christian who, in the face of the evidence he has furnished us, cannot answer the question aright.[365]

Strong warned of a "second Unitarian defection" worse in its divisive consequences for the churches than that of Channing and Ware a century earlier, from which American Christianity had recovered "only by vigorously asserting the authority of Christ and the inspiration of the Scriptures."[366]

A half century of Christian experience and reflection had confirmed his belief, Strong stated, in the doctrines of holiness as the fundamental divine attribute, of a divine preparation in Hebrew history for man's redemption, of the deity, pre-existence, virgin birth, vicarious atonement and bodily resurrection of Christ, and of his future return in judgment.[367] Strong offered his treatment of ethical monism, inspiration, the divine attributes, and the trinity, as "an antidote to most of the false doctrine which now threatens the safety of the church."[368] He protested that "the recent merging of Holiness in Love, and the practical denial that Righteousness is fundamental in God's nature" were responsible for utilitarian views of law and superficial views of sin, and precluded proper doctrines of atonement and retribution.[369] Aware that contemporary attacks on Christianity assaulted its central beliefs, Strong urged upon his readers the uniqueness and finality of Biblical theism:

Not only the outworks are assaulted, but the very citadel itself. We are asked to give up all belief in special revelation. Jesus Christ, it is said, has come in the flesh precisely as each one of us has come, and he was before Abraham only in the same sense that we were. Christian experience knows how to characterize such doctrine so soon as it is clearly stated.[370]

It is clear, therefore, that in the final statement of what he conceived to be a Biblical ethical monism, Strong refused to move to personalistic idealism as, for example, Borden P. Bowne, whom Strong quoted in the 1907 revision, was fashioning it at Boston University. His sympathies were clearly with evangelical Christianity in such way that, were he convinced that a consistent application of his fundamental stress on ethical monism would require an abandonment of traditional doctrines—as the trinity, creation, special revelation in the Hebrew-Christian movement, an exclusive divine incarnation in Jesus Christ, His vicarious atonement, His bodily resurrection, His personal return and future judgment of the race, the eternal bliss of the redeemed and the eternal punishment of the lost—he would doubtless have sacrificed ethical monism to Biblical theology. But Strong rather viewed ethical monism and special revelation not only as congruous, but as supporting each other, so that the view of Christ as "the one and only

---

[365] ST(1907), viii-ix.

[366] ST(1907), ix

[367] "I believe that these are truths of science, as well as truths of revelation; that the supernatural will yet be seen to be most truly natural; and that not the open-minded theologian but the narrow-minded scientist will be obliged to hide his head at Christ's coming" (ST[1906]), x).

[368] ST(1907), x.

[369] ST(1907), x.

[370] ST(1907), xi.

Revealer of God, in nature, in humanity, in history, in science, in Scripture," interpreted by a context of ethical monism, was in his judgment "the key to theology."[371]

But the influence of personalistic idealism upon aspects of Strong's thought in the 1907 revision is clearly discernible by an alert glance at the forty-one columns of references in the extensive index to persons. The largest number of references are to I. A. Dorner, 127, and William G. T. Shedd, 127; James Martineau, 102; and E. G. Robinson, 101. Dorner, the eminent German theologian, was appealed to both for representative Lutheran doctrinal formulations, and for his appreciation of the new immanentism. The influence of Robinson, Strong's teacher, and of Shedd, neither of whom was interested in qualitative monism, has already been mentioned; Martineau, the Unitarian, was significant for Strong because of his ethical theism. It is significant that, although about eighteen hundred persons were quoted or referred to by Strong in the 1907 revision, Mme. Guyon is mentioned twice; Hegel gets 14 references; Lotze receives 28; John Caird and G. T. Ladd are mentioned 35 times; and Bowne is mentioned 59 times. The only writers not already indicated, who are referred to more frequently than Bowne, and that quite understandably in a reference work on systematic theology, were Julius Miller, 62 times; Charles Hodge, 63 times; Alvah Hovey, 67 times; and Jonathan Edwards, 79 times. In Strong's references, Bowne appeared more frequently than Augustine and Calvin.

The number of references to Bowne, however, is not necessarily important in itself; what is of greater concern is the interaction of these references with Strong's theological views and the revisions undertaken by him. The great majority of references, again, are of such a nature that they might equally well have come from a non-personalist holding evangelical views.

Thus Strong endorsed Bowne's insistence that the noumenal is known in our knowledge of phenomena (6^{372} referring to Bowne's RHS, 47, 207ff.);[373] his complaint that Spencer's view that God is already involves a knowledge of God (8, referring to RHS, 30ff.); his contention that the infinite is not the all (10, to POT, 135); his protest against Kant's limitation of knowledge to phenomena (11, to RHS, 76); his definition of philosophy as involving a study of both epistemology and metaphysics (43, to TTK, 3ff.); his anti-sensationalist emphasis that thinking involves a system of mental principles (52f., to TTK, 60) and that sensation discloses immanent laws of thought (54, to POE, 5); his insistence that sub-normal instances do not jeopardize the case for the universality of rationality and morality (56, to POE, 154) and that human intercourse is possible only because of a common rationality (60, to TTK, 276); his declaration that those who invoke evolution to dispute the positive deliverances of mature consciousness ought to apply the principle to evolution as well (64, to RHS, 163f.); his support for the reality of rational intuition (68, to SIT, 79); his contention, in connection with the cosmological argument, that a cause is demanded only for changing phenomena (73, to MSFP, 107); his assertion of the illogicality of eternal process (74, to RHS, 36); his view of the disciplinary

---
[371] ST(1907), vii.
[372] All such references will be understood to be to ST(1907).
[373] The page references to Bowne's works are as given by Strong.

value of imperfections in the universe (78, to RHS, 364f.); his criticisms of Hamilton's epistemology (96, to IPT, 257f.); his contention that pure sensationalism cannot attain to knowledge of a real world (97, to MSFP, 432); his disagreement with the nominalistic view of divine simplicity (244, to POT, 141); his assertion that the true ethical aim is not happiness but the realization of the good (300, to POE, 96); his affirmation that God's pure self-activity creates objects without dependence on anything beyond itself (381, to TTK, 36); his assertion of the compatibility of imperfection in the universe with God's perfection (402, to POT, 224ff.); his contention that choice does not involve the absence of all causal connection (428, to TTK, 197); his claim that there exists a universal feeling of moral obligation and a very general agreement on formal principles of action and virtues (499, to POE, 156, 188); his warning of the inexplicability of man's moral nature on an appeal to determinism (507, to POE, 135); his contention that freedom is the power of acting in view of ends, rather than apart from motives (507, to MSFP, 169); his view that the prime object of punishment is not deterrent nor preventative (655, to POE, 186, 274); his claim that God's dealings with man involve a complex interaction of the whole universe (MSFP, 794).

Strong's references to Bowne included, at the same time, points of difference, but on elements which did not centrally concern the issue of personalistic idealism. Thus Strong took exception in the interest of traducianism to Bowne's view that the similarity of children to parents is to be explained solely by the inner consistency of the divine nature, and not by heredity (493, to MSFP, 500);[374] to Bowne's view that sin is a relic of animal sensuousness (559, to A, 69) and to Bowne's contention, as against the view of racial guilt in Adam, that general notions are non-existent except as revealed in individuals (625, to TTK, 134); to Bowne's rejection of the forensic imputation of divine righteousness to repentant sinners (722, to A, 74);[375] to Bowne's assertion of the possibility of brute immortality (985, IPT, 315ff.).

But when such agreements and differences, which do not turn specifically upon personalistic idealism, are waved aside, there remain at least two dozen references in which, by way of concurrence or exception, the issue involves more distinctly a personalistic view.

Thus Strong referred favorably to Bowne's statement that objective knowledge of the finite rests on ethical trust in the infinite (61, to MSFP, 472) and that theism is the absolute postulate of all knowledge (61, to MSFP, 480); to Bowne's assertion that belief is pragmatically more rewarding than doubt (71f., to POT, 11ff.) and that life is broader than the certainties of logic (72, to POT, 31f,); to the view that law is not cause, but simply divine method (76, to RHS, 231ff.), that both laws and effects

---

[374]Bowne did not deny the importance of heredity, but insisted that it is but a divinely chosen method. It is curious that Strong, with his emphasis upon God's present creative activity, was not drawn by personalistic considerations to the view of the creationist rather than traducianist theory of the origin of the human soul.

[375]Strong complained that Bowne made righteousness a mere form of benevolence and the atonement but a means to the utilitarian end of the creature's restoration and happiness.

are exercises of the divine will (125, to POT, 210), that preservation is God's continuous volition (413, to IPT, 305),[376] that all force is will (416, to POT, 202),[377] that the cosmic uniformities are but "God's methods in freedom" (536, to TTK), that no single cosmic law is ultimately necessary (536, to POT, 536) and that law is mere method, rather than agent (539, to POT, 161). Equally as significant was Strong's invocation of Bowne against pantheism (103, to POT, 245) and to make the point that a heightened divine immanence does not cancel moral distinctions nor minimize retribution (108, to IG, 130ff.); his references to Bowne along with Josiah Royce, Edward Caird and James Ward for the relation of monism and Christian doctrine (110, to TTK, 297-301, 311-317, and to IG, 5-32, 116-153); his view that authority is not in Scripture alone, but is internal (219, IG, 109f.); his view that grace is somewhat of a moral necessity for God in view of creation (267, 756, to A, 101);[378] his belief that immortality is the demand of our intellectual, moral and religious nature (987, to POT, 254).

But the most significant references remain to be mentioned. Strong accepted Bowne's view that space is a form of intuition and not a mode of existence (279, to MSFP, 127, 137, 143) but, although he referred to Bowne's contention that the ideality of time solves the problem of divine foreknowledge (285, to POT, 159), he did not commit himself to this view. He stressed also Bowne's emphasis on the necessity of regarding the world ground as conscious and intelligent spirit, and not merely as will (405, to POT, 124). The remaining references deal with the crucial issue of the nature of substance, and the relationship of things and persons to God.

The first of the passages to be studied deals with Bowne's view that personality alone is real. The summary of Bowne's view makes it clear that Strong at this time not only understood personalistic idealism to involve qualitative monism and quantitative pluralism, but that his own sympathies lay in this precise direction. Bowne, he wrote,

regards only personality as real. Matter is phenomenal, although it is an activity of the divine will outside of us. Bowne's phenomenalism is therefore an objective idealism, greatly preferable to that of Berkeley who held to God's energizing indeed, but only within the soul. This idealism of Bowne is not pantheism, for it holds that, while there are no second causes in nature, man is a second cause, with a personality distinct from that of God, and lifted above nature by his powers of free will.[379]

---

[376] Strong liked Bowne's reference to "a kind of wholesale willing."

[377] Strong mentioned Bowne's comparison of force to a musical note, which must be incessantly reproduced to exist.

[378] Bowne wrote: "The work of Christ, so far as it was a historical event, must be viewed not merely as a piece of history, but also as a manifestation of that cross which was hidden in the divine love from the foundation of the world, and which is involved in the existence of the human world at all."

[379] ST(1907), 99. Strong proceeded to contrast Bowne's view with that of Royce, as follows: "Royce . . . makes man's consciousness a part or aspect of a universal consciousness, and so, instead of making God come to consciousness in man, makes man come to consciousness in God. While this scheme seems, in one view, to save God's personality, it may be doubted whether it equally guarantees man's personality or leaves room for man's freedom, responsibility, sin and guilt." This should leave no doubt that the tendencies toward qualitative monism in Strong were intended by him as subordinate to the prior claims of qualitative pluralism.

At the same time, Strong called attention to the apparent retention by Bowne, in contrast with his view of the physical universe, of a substance view of the self:

> Bowne claims that the impersonal finite has only such otherness as thought or act has to its subject. There is no substantial existence except in persons.[380]

In the immediate context, Strong relentlessly opposed both Hegel and Spinoza, and the pantheistic idealism contemporary with his own day. To Hegel's doctrine, designated as the view that "there is thought without a thinker," Strong opposed Lotze's remarks:

> We cannot make mind the equivalent of the infinitive *to think*,—we feel that it must be that which thinks; the essence of things cannot be either existence or activity,—it must be that which exists and that which acts. Thinking means nothing, if it is not the thinking of a thinker; acting and working mean nothing, if we leave out the conception of a subject distinguishable from them and from which they proceed.[381]

Strong's own formula, in which he set forth the distinction between being and activity, in contrast with the pantheistic schools, was expressed as follows:

> To Hegel, Being *is* Thought; to Spinoza, Being has Thought + Extension; the truth seems to be that Being *has* Thought + Will, and *may* reveal itself in Extension and Evolution (Creation).[382]

The appeal to Lotze, rather than Bowne, in order to maintain a sharp distinction between the self and its thoughts and activity, is curious.[383] It has already been mentioned that Bowne attacked the soul-substance idea as a myth, and held that activity is the essential element, so that the unity of consciousness is the essence of the self, although in other passages he did not consistently apply this principle that there is no substance behind the subject and outside of knowledge. But Lotze, too, as Strong was aware, had refused to make a sharp distinction between being and activity. For, in his contention that "the passive logically precedes the active; being comes before willing; God *is* pure before he *wills* purity," so that "holy being logically precedes holy willing," Strong consciously took exception to Lotze's view.[384] Against Lotze and Bowne, Strong maintained that "as truth of being logically precedes truth of knowing, and as a loving nature precedes loving emotions, so purity of substance precedes purity of will."[385] Elsewhere in this theology, Strong referred to Bowne in support of the view that immutability is the constancy and continuity of divine nature as the law and source of divine acts (257, to POT, 146).

---

[380] ST(1907), 99.
[381] ST(1907), 100.
[382] ST(1907), 100-101. Strong conceded that Hegel was otherwise interpreted by many philosophers, who hold that thinking, not thought, was Hegel's fundamental idea.
[383] The question raised by later personalistic idealism was, if this sharp distinction is maintained, how can the self be coherent?
[384] ST(1907), 273, referring to the statement of Lotze that "such will of God no more follows from his nature as secondary to it, or precedes it as primary to it than, in motion, direction can be antecedent or subsequent to velocity" (POR, 139) and of Bowne that God's nature is a fixed law of activity or mode of manifestation (POT, 16).
[385] ST(1907), 273.

Before proceeding to the reflection of the new immanentism in the specific areas of the theological inquiry, it will be well to note an additional reference made by Strong to Bowne. In treating the divine omnipresence, Strong quoted Bowne's view that "the infinite must be present in its unity and completeness in every finite thing, just as the entire soul is present in all its acts" (280, to MSFP, 136), and commented that "this idealistic conception of the entire mind as present in all its thoughts must be regarded as the best analogue to God's omnipresence in the universe." In Bowne, this emphasis was safeguarded against any pantheistic inclusion of selves in God, although it will be recalled that Strong viewed selves as well as the physical universe as finite, graded manifestations of God, despite his insistence that they are relatively independent.[386]

Whether ethical monism was indeed as harmonious with Biblical theology as Strong thought, is a subject reserved for study in the next chapter of this dissertation. What comes now into view in Strong's final theology is the influence of ethical monism, whether large or small, in the reformulation of Christian tenets. In what way did ethical monism color Strong's formulation, within a determination not to sacrifice Biblical, redemptive theism, of such aspects of his theology as religious epistemology, and the doctrines of God, both as to his nature and works, and man, as regards his origin, predicament, salvation, and future state?

1. Religious Epistemology

Strong insisted throughout his life that the religious and scientific world-views must not be opposed or divorced in thought, although he strenuously disputed the limitation of the word "science" to non-spiritual, non-noumenal data.[387] The possibility of theology he found now, as thirty years earlier, in a God who has relations with the universe, in the capacity of the human mind for knowing God and certain of his relations, and in the provision of a revelation linking God and man.

Faith is knowledge conditioned upon holy affection. But revelation must not be limited to the Scriptures.[388] External revelation in nature and history precedes and conditions internal revelation.[389] Since Christ is the eternal Word and universal Logos, all theology is Christian theology.[390] Christ is the organ of external, the Holy Spirit of internal revelation.[391]

---

[386]There is a monistic passage in Lotze in which, although stressing the separateness of minds, he emphasized that "nothing is fully actual but the one reality which is in eternal motion" (MET, 293).

[387]As against Kant, Strong protested that "when our primitive beliefs are found to be simply regulative, they will cease to regulate" (ST[1907], 10). Strong's emphasis on transcendental knowledge came in opposition also to the metaphysical reserve of Robinson, his former teacher.

[388]ST(1907), 13.

[389]ST(1907), 13.

[390]ST(1907), 14. "Christianity is absolutely exclusive, because it is absolutely inclusive. It is not an amalgamation of other religions, but it has in it all that is best and truest in other religions . . . God may have made disclosures of truth outside Judaism, and did so in Balaam and Melchisedek, in Confucius and Socrates. But while other religions have a relative excellence, Christianity is the absolute religion that contains all excellencies" (ST[1907], 23).

[391]ST(1907), 13.

Wherever the marks of true religion appear, whether in Unitarians, Romanists, Jews or Buddhists, a demand for religious (though not specifically for Christian) fellowship must be recognized.[392]

God is disclosed in nature, but supremely in the Scriptures.[393] The statement of the 1886 lectures, that the Scriptures are the ultimate standard of appeal, Strong not only retained, but expanded:

> Because of our finiteness and sin, the total record in Scripture of God's past communications is a more trustworthy source of theology than are our conclusions from nature or our private impressions of the teaching of the Spirit. Theology therefore looks to the Scripture itself as its chief source of material and its final standard of appeal.[394]

Christian experience is not an original source of religious truth.

But Biblical truth supplements, rather than contradicts or corrects, natural theology, which prepares the way for Biblical theology.[395] Man's intellectual and moral nature, however, furnishes by its needs an *a priori* reason for expecting a special, authoritative revelation,[396] but one can rise only to hope, and not to assurance, of its provision.[397] But the natural revelation affords certain presumptions with regard to a revelation of grace, such as (1) continuous historical development, (2) original delivery to a single nation by which communication is to be made to all mankind, and (3) preservation in written, accessible, and transmissible documents.[398]

Strong appealed still to miracle and to prophecy as attesting special revelation, but his restatement of miracle issued now in an "alternative and preferable definition" which he considered alongside of that contained in the earlier editions:

> A miracle is an event in nature, so extraordinary in itself and so coinciding with the prophecy or command of a religious teacher or leader, as fully to warrant the conviction, on the part of those who witness it, that God has wrought it with the design of certifying that this teacher or leader has been commissioned by him.[399]

Strong singled out, as marked advantages of this later definition, the following features: (1) recognition of divine immanence and immediate divine agency in nature, as against the assumption of an antithesis between natural law and the divine will; (2) recognition of miracle as simply an extraordinary act of that same God already present in all natural operations; (3) recognition that natural law, as the method of regular divine activity, does not preclude unique exertions of purposive divine power; (4) room for the possibility that " all miracles may have their natural explanations, and may

---

[392] These marks of true religion, attributed to "the inworking of the omnipresent Christ," Strong listed as a rudimentary knowledge of the God of righteousness, some sense of sin and dependence upon divine mercy and a divine way of salvation, and some positive practical moral effort.
[393] ST(1907), 25.
[394] ST(1907), 27.
[395] ST(1907), 28-29.
[396] ST(1907), 112-113. Strong urged such factors as man's necessary conviction of God's wisdom, the actual though complete revelation in nature, the general connection which prevails between our needs and their supply, and the analogies in nature and history of a reparative goodness.
[397] ST(1907), 113.
[398] ST(1907), 114-116.
[399] ST(1907), 118.

hereafter be traced to natural causes," while both miracles and their natural causes may be only names for the one and self-same will of God; (5) reconciliation of the claims of both science and religion, by permitting any possible or probably physical antecedents of miracle, and by maintaining that these antecedents together with the miracle are to be interpreted as divine signs of a special commission.[400]

Since all natural processes, as well as miracles, are also immediate divine operations, it is unnecessary to deny the use of natural processes, as far as they reach, in miracle.[401] If all miracle should have its natural side, the Christian argument would remain unweakened, for miracle would evidence still "the extraordinary working of the immanent God and the impartation of his knowledge to the prophet or apostle who was his instrument."[402] The possibility of miracle, in fact, becomes "doubly sure" to those who see in Christ the immanent God manifested to creatures, for since Christ is the only source of energy and life, the whole history of creation witnesses to the possibility of miracle.[403] The continuity of events, Strong emphasized, is a continuity "not of forces, but of plan."[404] Yet Strong designated as "breaks in the uniformity of nature" the coming of Christ and the regeneration of a human soul.[405]

Strong referred to Lotze's position for support for a view which makes the possibility of miracle depend upon the closest intimacy between the world and the personal Absolute, so that natural movements are carried on only through the Absolute, with the possibility of variation in view of divine transcendence.[406]

From the treatment thus far, the question naturally arises when a monistic theism is necessary to underwrite miracle, or whether miracle underwrites theism. Before handling this question directly, Strong stressed that miracles do not occur uniformly in Biblical history, but only at the great epochs of revelation, when they draw attention to new truth.[407] Miracles do not certify to the truth of doctrine directly, but only indirectly; directly, they certify to the divine commission and authority of a religious

---

[400]ST(1907), 118-119.
[401]"Such wonders of the Old Testament as the overthrow of Sodom and Gomorrah, the partings of the Red Sea and of the Jordan, the calling down of fire from heaven by Elijah and the destruction of the army of Sennacherib, are none the less works of God when regarded as wrought by the use of natural means. In the New Testament Christ took water to make wine, and took the five loaves to make bread, just as in ten thousand vineyards today He is turning the moisture of the earth into the juice of the grape, and in ten thousand fields is turning carbon into corn. The virgin-birth of Christ may be an extreme instance of parthenogenesis" (ST[1907], 119).
[402]ST(1907), 120.
[403]ST(1907), 123. "From the point of view of ethical monism the probability of miracle becomes even greater. Since God is not merely the intellectual but the moral Reason of the world, the disturbances of the world-order which are due to sin are the matters which most deeply affect him. Christ, the life of the whole system and of humanity as well, must suffer; and, since we have evidence that he is merciful as well as just, it is probably that he will rectify the evil by extraordinary means, when merely ordinary means do not avail" (ST(1907), 126).
[404]ST(1907), 123.
[405]ST(1907), 125. Curiously, Strong elsewhere affirmed that a miracle "is not a matter of internal experience, like regeneration or illumination; but is an event palpable to the senses" (ST[1907], 117).
[406]The reference is to Lotze's *Microcosmos*, 2:479ff.
[407]ST(1907), 128.

teacher.[408] But purity of life and doctrine must accompany the miracle, in order to prove a divine commission; miracle and doctrine mutually support each other, forming parts of a single whole.[409] While internal evidence may be more influential with certain minds and ages than external, yet Christian miracles retain their value as evidence.[410] Christ's authority as a teacher of supernatural truth rests upon his miracles, especially that of his bodily resurrection.[411]

As with miracle, so with prophecy, Strong affirmed that

> our faith in an immanent God, who is none other than the Logos or larger Christ, gives us a point of view from which we may reconcile the contentions of the naturalists and supernaturalists. Prophecy is an immediate act of God; but, since all natural genius is also due to God's energizing, we do not need to deny the employment of man's natural gifts in prophecy. The instances of telepathy, presentiment, and second sight which the Society for Psychical Research has demonstrated to be facts show that prediction, in the history of divine revelation, may be only an intensification, under the extraordinary impulse of the divine Spirit, of a power that is in some degree latent in all men.[412]

The human mind "even in its ordinary and secular working gives occasional signs of transcending the limitations of the present," Strong urged.[413] Belief in the continual activity of the divine Reason in human reason encourages the possibility of an extraordinary insight into the future such as is needed at great epochs of spiritual history.[414] Yet, Strong urged, to be genuine prophecy, nothing must exist to suggest the event to merely natural prescience.[415]

Revelation thus has a twofold attestation, that of miracle, which proceeds from divine power, and that of prophecy, which proceeds from divine knowledge.[416] The testimony of the Holy Spirit terminates upon the evidence, for conviction is in terms of truth, the discernment of which has its moral and spiritual conditions.[417] The evidence need not be demonstrative, in matters of morals and religion, for "even a slight balance of probability, when nothing more certain is attainable, may suffice to constitute rational proof and to bind our moral action."[418]

In developing his treatment of the origin of man's idea of God, Strong argued that upon occasion of our cognizing our finiteness, dependence, and responsibility, the mind "directly cognizes the existence of an Infinite and Absolute to whom we are responsible."[419] But this very intui-

---

[408]ST(1907), 129.
[409]ST(1907), 129.
[410]ST(1907), 129-130.
[411]ST(1907), 130.
[412]ST(1907), 134.
[413]ST(1907), 135.
[414]ST(1907), 135. There are many indications of Strong's increasing tendency to explain Biblical revelation as a heightened manifestation of general revelation, e.g., "As the life of God the Logos lies at the basis of universal humanity and interpenetrates it in every part, so out of this universal humanity grows Israel in general; out of Israel as a nation springs the spiritual Israel, and out of spiritual Israel, Christ according to the flesh" (ST[1907], 137).
[415]ST(1907), 135.
[416]ST(1907), 142.
[417]ST(1907), 142.
[418]ST(1907), 142.
[419]ST(1907), 52. Experience inevitably suggests an infinite and unconditioned Being as its correlative, Strong urged (ST[1907], 58).

tive knowledge of God, while logically prior, may be expected, in view of human depravity, to be developed last of all.[420] The conflicting ideas of God are misinterpretations and perversions of a common intuitive conviction.[421] It is not possible to prove that God exists, but it can be shown that he is the presupposition of the existence of knowledge, thought, reason and conscience.[422] This rational intuition of God enables men to receive and to interpret their presentative intuitions of God.[423] Thus man's knowledge of God is more basic than reasoning can demonstrate.[424] The *a priori* argument proves only an abstract and ideal proposition, but not a real Being, yet that Being is presupposed in all reasoning.[425] The *a posteriori* arguments cannot lead from finite premises to the infinite.[426] But the Scripture assumes that God has inlaid the knowledge of him in every man.[427] The arguments from the universe and from abstract ideas of the human mind, however, explicate and confirm the intuitive knowledge of God.[428]

Strong retained his earlier evaluation of the theistic proofs as yielding probability rather than demonstration, and as possessing cumulative worth.[429] The empirical arguments may explicate an intuition which is obscure for lack of reflection.[430] But the teleological argument was now stated in such a way as to regard evolution as a new and higher illustration of purpose and design, with an appropriation by Strong of the views of Bowne and others.[431] Design must be sought in the system as a whole, which justifies imperfection and suffering in the initial stages of development,[432] and which must be viewed as a concomitant of sin.[433] The moral argument is treated as leading to the ideas of divine personality and

---

[420]ST(1907), 55.
[421]ST(1907), 57.
[422]ST(1907), 61. Against Spencer's view that the intuition is really derived from accumulated sensations and contemporary teaching, Strong pointed out that man's earliest experience as well as his latest presupposes this intuition, but he added that Spencer's theory cannot set aside the contention that "if the evolution of ideas is toward truth instead of falsehood, it is the part of wisdom to act upon the hypothesis that our primitive belief is veracious" (ST[1907], 64).
[423]ST(1907), 65.
[424]ST(1907), 66.
[425]ST(1907), 66.
[426]ST(1907), 66.
[427]ST(1907), 68. Strong closed the section on the intuitive knowledge of God with a brief account of George John Romanes' defection from and return to faith: "His later thought recognized that God and nature are not mutually exclusive. So he came to find no difficulty even in miracles and inspiration; for the God who is in man and of whose mind and will nature is only the expression, can reveal himself, if need be, in special ways. So George John Romanes came back to prayer, to Christ, to the church (ST[1907], 70). This is significant, since Romanes' return to faith came in the pattern of a heightened divine immanence.
[428]ST(1907), 71.
[429]ST(1907), 71.
[430]ST(1907), 72.
[431]ST(1907), 76-77.
[432]ST(1907), 78.
[433]"So long as we cannot with John Stuart Mill explain the imperfections of the universe by any limitations in the Intelligence which contrived it, we are shut up to regarding them as intended to correspond with the moral state and probation of sinners which God foresaw and provided for at the creation. Evil things in the universe are the symbols of sin, and helps to its overthrow" (ST[1907], 78).

righteous lordship, and hence must be assigned chief place,[434] and yet Strong granted that the argument has weight "only upon the supposition that a wise, truthful, holy and benevolent God exists, who has so constituted our minds that their thinking and their affections correspond to truth and to himself,"[435] so that the argument is really a development and expression of the intuitive idea of God.[436] The ontological argument Strong dismissed still as of little value, because it "confounds ideal existence with real existence."[437] To the first three arguments, Strong applied, as in previous editions, the law of parsimony in the interest of one Being, possessing infinity and perfection, "not because they are demonstrably his, but because our mental constitution will not allow us to think otherwise."[438]

Scripture records a special revelation of God, which serves as a corrective of man's other ideas, and is necessary in view of man's finiteness and sin. It must not be forgotten, Strong urged, that "all real knowledge has in it a divine element, and that we are possessed of complete consciousness only as we live, move and have our being in God."[439] Inspiration is the result of a special influence of the Logos who lights all men.[440] But for sin, all men would experience moral and spiritual inspiration.[441]

It is a reasonable supposition that God, in giving a revelation, will secure a permanent record of it essentially trustworthy and sufficient for its religious purpose.[442] The facts are accounted for best on the view that inspiration is "characteristically neither natural, partial, nor mechanical, but supernatural, plenary, and dynamical."[443] But no one theory of inspiration is necessary to the Christian faith, although whatever theory is framed "should be the result of a strict induction of the Scripture facts, and not an *a priori* scheme to which Scripture must be conformed.[444]

The divine-human character of Scripture has analogies in the "interpenetration of human powers by the divine efficiency in regeneration and sanctification, and in the union of the divine and human natures in the person of Jesus Christ."[445] Divine action in inspiration is "in general a work within a man's soul rather than a communication to him from

---

[434]ST(1907), 84.
[435]ST(1907), 84.
[436]ST(1907), 84.
[437]ST(1907), 86. Strong remarked that Dorner had given "the best statement of the Ontological Argument: 'Reason thinks of God as existing. Reason would not be reason, if it did not think of God as existing. Reason only is, upon the assumption that God is.' But this is evidently not an argument, but only vivid statement of the necessary assumption of the existence of an absolute Reason which conditions and gives validity to ours" (ST[1907], 87).
[438]ST(1907), 87.
[439]ST(1907), 197.
[440]ST(1907), 197.
[441]ST(1907), 198.
[442]ST(1907), 198.
[443]ST(1907), 211.
[444]ST(1907), 211. "Perhaps the best theory is to have no theory," Strong added.
[445]ST(1907), 212.

without.[446] The divine-human union in inspiration is not to be conceived "as one of external impartation and reception."[447] The divine agents "spoke and wrote the words of God . . . not as from without, but as from within, and that not passively, but in the most conscious possession and the most exalted exercise" of their personal powers.[448] While inspiration uses man's natural powers, those powers do not explain inspiration.[449]

Inspiration may retain every imperfection consistent with truth in a human composition, for it presents divine truth in human forms.[450] All literary methods, even myth and legend, may be used for the divine communication of truth, and we are left to determine in each case the nature of the form of composition.[451] The early sections of Genesis "may be of the nature of myth" in which the historical germ, though not denied, cannot be distinguished by us.[452]

Inspiration guarantees inerrancy only in things essential to the main purpose of the Scripture, and can accomplish its purpose through writings in some respects imperfect.[453] It did not generally involve "a direct communication . . . of the words."[454] The writers appear to have been

so influenced by the Holy Spirit that they perceived and felt even the new truths they were to publish, as discoveries of their own minds, and were left to the action of their own minds in the expression of these truths, with the single exception that they were supernaturally held back from the selection of wrong words, and when needful were provided with right ones.[455]

Inspiration therefore was not verbal except when "the mere communication of ideas or the direction to proper material would not suffice to secure a correct utterance."[456]

As an organic whole, the Scriptures exhibit the work of one divine mind, notwithstanding the ever-present human element.[457] Despite imper-

---

[446]ST(1907), 211. Strong commented: "Even when inspiration is but the exaltation and intensification of man's natural powers, it must be considered the work of God as well as of man. God can work from within as well as from without. As creation and regeneration are works of the immanent rather than of the transcendent God, so inspiration is in general a work within man's soul. . . . Prophecy may be natural to perfect humanity . . . The insight of the Scripture writers into truth so far beyond their mental and moral powers is inexplicable except by a supernatural influence upon their minds; in other words, except as they were lifted up into the divine Reason and endowed with the wisdom of God" (ST[1907], 211).
[447]ST(1907), 212.
[448]ST(1907), 212. Strong illustrated the experience of the Scripture writers by that of the preacher who "under the influence of God's spirit is carried beyond himself, and is conscious of a clearer apprehension of truth and of a greater ability to utter it than belong to his unaided nature, yet knows himself to be no passive vehicle of a divine communication, but to be as never before in possession and exercise of his own powers" (ST[1907], 212). But he added: "The inspiration of the Scripture writers, however, goes far beyond the illumination granted to the preacher, in that it qualifies them to put the truth, without error, into permanent and written form" (ST[1907], 212-213).
[449]ST(1907), 213.
[450]ST(1907), 213.
[451]ST(1907), 214.
[452]ST(1907), 214.
[453]ST(1907), 215.
[454]ST(1907), 216.
[455]ST(1907), 216.
[456]ST(1907), 216.
[457]ST(1907), 217.

fections in non-essential matters, the Bible furnishes "a safe and sufficient guide to truth and to salvation."[458] The presence of historical and scientific errors does not involve the necessity of error in morality and religion.[459] For "as in creation and in Christ, so in Scripture, God humbles himself to adopt human and imperfect methods of self-revelation."[460] The unity and authority of the Bible are "entirely consistent with its gradual evolution and with great imperfection in its non-essential parts."[461]

In considering objections to the doctrine of inspiration, Strong curiously argued two ways on the matter of historical and scientific errors in the Bible. On the one hand, in view of his recent concessions, he contended that the undermining of the scientific trustworthiness of the Bible is not destructive of Christianity, because the Biblical religion, contrary to that of the Indian Vedas, is not dependent upon its physical science, for the Scriptures "aim only to declare the creatorship and lordship of the personal God."[462] On the other, he retained the statements of his earlier edition, that "science has not yet shown any fairly interpreted passage of Scripture to be untrue."[463] Similarly, while he sought to defend the Bible against the charge of historical errors, he insisted that inspiration is "consistent with much imperfection in historical detail and its narratives 'do not seem to be exempted from possibilities of error.' "[464] Even if the apostles wrongly employed Rabbinical methods of argument, inspiration would not be disproved, for truth may be made known in such a manner as to leave its expression to human dialectic and rhetoric.[465] Nor does the composite character of Biblical books thought to have been written by other authors invalidate inspiration.[466] Job could not have been written in patriarchal times, Jonah and Daniel may be dramatic compositions of later date, Isaiah is the work of an exilic as well as a pre-exilic author, but such concessions do not invalidate inspiration.[467]

Scripture has but a mediate and relative authority, "though human and imperfect records, and needing a supplementary and divine teaching to interpret them,"[468] and the living Christ alone is the ultimate authority.[469]

2. The Nature and Decrees of God

In discussing the divine attributes, Strong retained the distinction between substance and attributes, although he insisted that they "are correlates,—neither one is possible without the other."[470] The divine essence is revealed only through the attributes, however, and is unknowable apart

---

[458]ST(1907), 218.
[459]ST(1907), 218.
[460]ST(1907), 219. This is significant for its anticipation of Strong's later Christology.
[461]ST(1907), 220.
[462]ST(1907), 222.
[463]ST(1907), 224.
[464]ST(1907), 228.
[465]ST(1907), 233.
[466]ST(1907), 238.
[467]ST(1907), 238-241.
[468]ST(1907), 220.
[469]ST(1907), 219.
[470]ST(1907), 243. The application to God of the categories of substance and attributes he said, a necessity of rational thought (ST[1907], 243).

from the attributes.[471] At the same time, Strong opposed both nominalistic and realistic views of the attributes, holding that the attributes inhere in the divine essence.[472]

Strong continued to subordinate the rational to the Biblical method of knowing the attributes.[473] He retained the classification of attributes presented in the 1886 edition of his theology. The treatment of the attributes likewise is largely unchanged, except in details.

There is a tendency to quote extensively from philosophical theists, and to employ their material on divine attributes in such a way as to minimize the necessity for special revelation in arriving at a specifically Christian concept of God. The treatment of divine personality is developed not by an exclusive appeal to special redemptive disclosure, but rather the integral elements of personality, self-consciousness and self-determination, are championed alternately by Biblical and philosophical appeals.[474] The treatment of divine infinity is developed in opposition to pantheism; God exists in no necessary relation to the finite.[475] But at the same time, God's infinity is viewed as infinite energy of spiritual life, so that the transcendent element in God is not exhausted either in creation or redemption.[476] The immutability of God is established by an appeal both to Scripture and reason.[477] The unity of God likewise is referred to special revelation and to philosophy.[478]

Strong's treatment of divine love and holiness was expanded, in accordance with the preface, to emphasize that love is not the all-inclusive ethical attribute of God,[479] and that holiness is the fundamental divine attribute and therefore God requires propitiation.[480] If the concept of God which Strong defended was in almost all points orthodox, including the divine infinity, triunity and transcendence, he did modify the statement of divine love to stress that it "involves also the possibility of divine suffering, and the suffering of sin which holiness necessitates on the part of God is itself the atonement."[481] At the same time, Strong resisted the view that holiness is a form of love as involving the denial of the existence of holiness, and with this the denial that any atonement is necessary for man's salvation.[482] He emphasized that mercy is optional with God, whereas holiness is invariable.[483] As against Lotze and Bowne, moreover, Strong

---

[471] ST(1907), 246.
[472] ST(1907), 245.
[473] ST(1907), 247. The Biblical method he defined as the inductive study of the facts revealed about God in the Scripture.
[474] ST(1907), 252-253.
[475] ST(1907), 255.
[476] "Transcendence is not mere outsidedness,—it is rather boundless supply within . . . The former conception of infinity is simply supra-cosmic, the latter alone is properly transcendent" (ST[1907], 255).
[477] ST(1907), 257.
[478] ST(1907), 259.
[479] ST(1907), 263.
[480] ST(1907), 295.
[481] ST(1907), 266. Strong supported this with appeals to the writings of Bowne and Royce, among others.
[482] ST(1907), 272.
[483] ST(1907), 272.

urged that holy being logically precedes holy willing. "To make holiness a matter of mere will," Strong protested, "instead of regarding it as a characteristic of God's being, is to deny that anything is holy in itself."[484] But he emphasized that God's holiness is not passive purity, but "purity willing."[485]

Strong's vindication of the doctrine of the trinity is discussed in this, as in previous volumes, after the section on divine attributes is concluded,[486] as if the Biblical redemptive disclosure of divine triunity is not important for establishing the divine nature with regard to attributes.

The case for divine triunity is established in terms of Biblical revelation. The Scriptures teach that the Father, the Son and the Spirit are divine,[487] are personal, and are one in essence.[488] Strong maintained that "Scripture reveals to us a social Trinity and an intercourse of love apart from and before the existence of the universe." But simultaneously he argued philosophically that

Love before time implies distinctions of personality before time. There are three eternal consciousnesses and three eternal wills within the divine nature . . . The two varying systems (i. e., Sabellianism and Arianism) which ignore this tripersonality are unscriptural and at the same time exposed to philosophical objection.[489]

Curiously, however, Strong replied to Arianism in part on the ground that "Arius appealed chiefly to logic, not to Scripture."[490] But he also found in the modern organic views of society an encouragement to trinitarian thought.[491] The psychic phenomenon of dual personality in a single human consciousness should give hesitancy to a denial that three consciousnesses may exist in one God.[492]

Christ is the only revealer of God, the "only outgoing principle in the Godhead," Strong affirmed.[493] The whole creation and its forces and laws are the work and manifestation of the immanent Christ, who is the life of nature, of humanity, and of the church, and the principle of progress and improvement in history.[494] Evolution is his method, and the laws of nature his habits, for nature is but the steady and constant will

---

[484]Strong's objection to Lotze and Bowne appears to derive from a failure to grasp that, for those thinkers, an activistic view of substance as *being willing* replaces that of the older view of substance. Strong maintained that "as truth of being logically precedes truth of knowing, and as a living nature precedes loving emotions, so purity of substance precedes purity of will" (ST[1907], 273).
[485]ST(1907), 268-275.
[486]ST(1907), 304-352.
[487]ST(1907), 305-326.
[488]ST(1907), 313.
[489]ST(1907), 326.
[490]ST(1907), 329.
[491]"Humanity at large is also an organism, and this fact lends new confirmation to the Pauline statement of organic interdependence. Modern sociology is the doctrine of one life constituted by the union of man . . . No man can have a conscience to himself. All men moreover live, move and have their being in God. Within the bounds of the one universal and divine consciousness there are multitudinous *finite* consciousnesses. Why then should it be thought incredible that in the nature of this one God there should be three *infinite* consciousnesses?" (ST[1907], 322).
[492]ST(1907), 332, 346.
[493]ST(1907), 332.
[494]ST(1907), 332. Strong added that "the intellectual and moral impulses of man, so far as they are normal and uplifting, are due to Christ" (ST[1907], 332).

of Christ.[495] He is the principle of induction and the medium of intercommunication between minds, as well as the medium of interaction between things.[496]

Although Strong reserved Christology for special treatment, this section on divine triunity affords some advance indications of concessions made to higher criticism and bearing upon this subject. The deity of Christ is clearly affirmed on Scriptural ground, and it is said that the constant recognition of his divinity in Christian experience is not an independent witness to his claims "since it only tests the truth already made known in the Bible."[497] Strong conceded occasions of ignorance during the humiliation of Christ, but denied that he was involved in error or false teaching, even in the assignment of writings to Moses and David in contradiction to higher critical assumptions, for "it is possible that he intended only to *locate* the passages referred to, and if so, his words cannot be used to exclude critical conclusions as to their authorship."[498] But the main discussion is specifically referred to the later treatment of Christology.

The statement of the doctrine of divine decrees[499] remained substantially unchanged. Strong re-emphasized that the divine thoughts are not automatically creative.[500] He re-affirmed his conviction that the decrees render events certain, but not necessary, and that God's foreknowledge is based on this foreordination.[501] He stressed also that this certainty of man's actions is consistent with human freedom.[502]

3. The Works of God

Strong's treatment of creation reflects the same disturbing presence of his older and newer views, side by side and unreconciled, because his method of revision often included the addition of supplementary notes, in small type, to the earlier material. Consequently, the newly added notes must be taken as reflective of his latest position.

Creation, he defined, as previously, as "designed origination, by a transcendent and personal God, of that which itself is not God."[503] But this was not to be taken as implying duality of substance. Just as man creates ideas and volitions without the use of pre-existing material, and these volitions "are not ourselves, and we are greater than they," so the universe is related to God.[504] Creation is

not simply the idea of God, or even the plan of God, but it is the idea externalized, the plan executed; in other words, it implies an exercise, not only of intellect, but also

---

[495]ST(1907), 311. In his prior treatment of the divine attributes, Strong wrote: "The uniformity of nature and the reign of law are nothing but the steady will of the omnipresent God. Gravitation is God's omnipresence in space, as evolution is God's omnipresence in time" (ST[1907], 282).
[496]ST(1907), 311.
[497]ST(1907), 313.
[498]ST(1907), 314.
[499]ST(1907), 353-370.
[500]ST(1907), 354.
[501]ST(1907), 356.
[502]ST(1907), 360.
[503]ST(1907), 371.
[504]ST(1907), 371.

of will, and this will is not an instinctive and unconscious will, but a will that is personal and free. Such exercise of will seems to involve, not self-development, but self-limitation, on the part of God; the transformation of energy into force, and so a beginning of time, with its finite successions.[505]

This view of creation, Strong acknowledged, "is so nearly that of Lotze"—for whom the only real creation was that of finite personalities, matter being only a mode of the divine activity—that Strong included a condensation of Ten Broeke's statement of the Lotzean view.[506] This summary, although Strong did not comment upon these specific points, included the statement that space is merely a form of dynamic appearance, and that physical phenomena are activities of the Infinite to which man gives a substantive character because he thinks under the form of substance and attribute.

Strong denied that the doctrine of creation is bound to the phrase "creation out of nothing," and contended that "the phrase is a philosophical one, for which we have no Scriptural warrant."[507] Its intention can be expressed better, he insisted, in the phrase "without use of pre-existing materials."[508] Creation is not "an emanation from the substance of Deity, but is a making of that to exist which once did not exist, either in form or substance."[509] But Strong hastened to explain that "substance is not necessarily material," but is to be conceived rather after the analogy of our ideas and volitions, as a manifestation of spirit.[510] But "nature is not God nor a part of God, any more than our ideas and volitions are ourselves or a part of ourselves," Strong urged.[511] Although a "partial manifestation" of God, nature does not exhaust him.[512]

All persons of the Trinity have a part in the work of creation, the Father being the originating, the Son the mediating, and the Holy Spirit the realizing cause.[513] All creative activity is exercised through Christ.[514] The Spirit is "the principle of our natural self-consciousness, uniting subject and object in a subject-object" and "may be regarded as the perfecting and realizing agent in the externalization of the divine ideas."[515]

Proof of the doctrine of creation rests upon Scripture.[516] But our own

---

[505] ST(1907), 371.
[506] ST(1907), 372. Strong commented: "Bowne, in his Metaphysics and his Philosophy of Theism, is the best expositor of Lotze's system" (ST[1907], 372). This statement, more than the frequent quotations from Bowne and other idealists, suggests how influential Bowne may have been in bringing the personalistic view to Strong's attention.
[507] ST(1907), 372.
[508] ST(1907), 372.
[509] ST(1907), 372. "There is nothing divine in creation but the origination of substance," Strong added (ST[1907], 373).
[510] ST(1907), 373.
[511] ST(1907), 373. Creation differs in kind from the eternal process of the divine nature in virtue of which theologians speak of generation and procession, Strong added, for it is not an instinctive or necessary process of the divine nature, but the free act of a rational will. But elsewhere he stated that "Christ's creation of man may be like his own begetting by the Father" (ST[1907], 381).
[512] ST(1907), 373.
[513] ST(1907), 373.
[514] ST(1907), 373.
[515] ST(1907), 373.
[516] ST(1907), 374.

creation of ideas and volitions furnishes a remote analogy for divine creation without pre-existing materials.[517] Creation is not simply God's thought, but also God's will. It is

thought in expression, reason externalized. Will is creation out of nothing, in the sense that there is no use of pre-existing material. In man's exercise of the creative imagination there is will, as well as intellect.[518]

The new conception of "nature as the expression of the divine mind and will" should make creation more comprehendable, Strong urged, than the old conception of the "world as substance capable of existing apart from God."[519]

The Biblical doctrine is to be distinguished from that of emanation, which holds that "the universe is of the same substance with God, and is the product of successive evolutions from his being."[520] Such a view contradicts the divine holiness, since "man, who by the theory is of the substance of God, is nevertheless morally evil," and logically leads to pantheism.[521] The doctrine of emanation is "distinctly materialistic," Strong protested, whereas he viewed the universe as "an expression of God, but not an emanation from God."[522] Emanation holds that "some stuff has proceeded from the nature of God, and that God has formed this stuff into the universe," he continued, whereas matter is "not composed of stuff at all" but is "merely an activity of God."[523] Creation involves an act of divine will, whereas emanation views the world as necessary or inevitable.[524] The true view is not the materialistic emanation imagined by Swedenborg, but rather

divine energizing in space and time. The universe is God's system of graded self-limitation, from matter up to mind. It has had a beginning, and God has instituted it. It is a finite and partial manifestation of the infinite Spirit. Matter is an expression of spirit, but not an emanation from spirit, any more than our thoughts and volitions are. Finite spirits, on the other hand, are differentiations within the being of God himself, and so are not emanations from him.[525]

This energy of divine will, required for creation, is not eternally active; a distinction must be made between the plan and its execution.[526] "A God existing in necessary relations to the universe, if different in substance from the universe, must be the God of dualism," Strong affirmed, and

---

[517]ST(1907), 380.
[518]ST(1907), 380.
[519]ST(1907), 381.
[520]ST(1907), 383.
[521]ST(1907), 383.
[522]ST(1907), 384.
[523]ST(1907), 385.
[524]Strong appealed to Lotze for the distinction: "Lotze, Philos. Religion, xlviii, li, distinguishes creation from emanation by saying that creation necessitates a divine will, while emanation flows by natural consequence from the being of God. God's motive in creation is love, which urges him to communicate his holiness to other beings. God creates individual finite spirits, and then permits the thought, which at first was only his, to become the thought of these other spirits. This transference of his thought by will is the creation of the world" (ST[1907], 385).
[525]ST(1907), 386. The reference to finite spirits here is ambiguous on the question, whether they are parts of God or not. The subject is postponed to Strong's subsequent treatment, which leaves this beyond doubt.
[526]ST(1907), 388.

if he is "of the same substance with the universe, must be the God of pantheism."[527]

As against the theory of creation from eternity, Scripture requires the view that the universe had a beginning, and "reason itself is better satisfied" with this view.[528] Eternity is not merely a prolongation of time into the endless past, but rater, is superiority to the law of time.[529]

Strong introduced his appraisal of the Mosaic account of creation by affirming that evolutionary schemes which ignore the freedom of God "are pantheistic in their tendencies, for they practically deny both God's transcendence and his personality."[530] The error of many statements of the doctrine is that evolution is regarded as an eternal or self-originated process.[531] The Mosaic account recognizes original creation, unlike the heathen cosmoganies,[532] and also subsequent development.[533] Strong granted the "probability that the great majority of what we call species were produced" by natural descent from a "few original germs," and held that if all present species of living creatures were derived thus, and the original germs were themselves evolved from inorganic forces and materials, it would not follow that the Mosaic account has been proved untrue.[534] The interpretation of the word *bara* need only be revised to give it the meaning of mediate creation, or creation by law, he affirmed.[535]

The influence of the new immanentism upon Strong's statement of beginnings is reflected in the suggestion that "we may even speak of an immanent transcendence of God—an unexhausted vitality which at times makes great movements forward,"[536] since both higher and lower forms of energy are constantly dependent upon God.

Strong declared again for the pictorial-summary interpretation of Genesis, remarking that the narrative's general correspondence with scientific teaching and "its power to adapt itself to every advance in human knowledge" differentiate it from all other cosmoganies.[537] Strong retained his scheme of geologic ages, which assumed for its background the substantial truth of the nebular hypothesis and the scientific conclusions of Dana and Guyot, although he acknowledged that "any such scheme of reconciliation may be speedily outgrown.[538]

---

[527] ST(1907), 389.
[528] ST(1907), 387.
[529] ST(1907), 387.
[530] ST(1907), 390. "God is not bound by law or to law," Strong emphasized. "Wisdom does not imply monotony or uniformity. God can do a thing once that is never done again. Circumstances are never twice alike. Here is the basis not only of creation but of new creation, including miracle, incarnation, resurrection, regeneration, redemption. . . . Law is only a method; it presupposes a lawgiver and requires an agent. Gravitation and evolution are but the habitual operations of God. If spontaneous generation should be proved true, it would be only God's way of originating life" (ST[1907], 390).
[531] ST(1907), 391.
[532] ST(1907), 391.
[533] ST(1907), 392.
[534] ST(1907), 392.
[535] ST(1907) 392. The meaning of mediate creation, Strong added, "might almost seem to be favored" by the mode of statement in Genesis 1:11, 20; 2:7, 9.
[536] ST(1907), 393.
[537] ST(1907), 394.
[538] ST(1907), 395.

Physical pain and imperfection are embraced in the universe as foreseen consequences of sin and constitute, in part, a means of future discipline and redemption, Strong held.[539] Bushnell's idea of "anticipative consequences" was accepted.[540] At the same time Strong rejected the view that evil is the indispensable condition of the good, and that sin is a direct product of God's will; rather, in spite of itself, sin is made by an overruling providence to contribute to the highest good.[541] The present universe, viewed as a partial realization of a developing divine plan, is the best possible for this specific moment.[542]

Strong's treatment of the doctrine of preservation emphasized that preservation is a positive divine agency, not a mere refraining to destroy, and that it implies a natural concurrence of God in all operations of matter and mind.[543] Although personal wills not reducible to God's will exist, yet no person or force could exist without divine concurrence.

Force implies a will which it expresses directly or indirectly.[544] We know of force only through our own volitions. "Since will is the only cause of which we have direct knowledge," Strong repeated from his earlier essays, "second causes in nature may be regarded as only secondary, regular, and automatic workings of the great first Cause."[545] Strong therefore adopted "the view of Maine de Biran, that causation pertains only to spirit."[546]

Preservation is therefore God's "continuous willing," which leaves room for human freedom, responsibility, sin and guilt.[547] The physical universe is in no sense independent of God, for its forces are only his constant willing and its laws are the divine habits.[548] Finite personal beings have "a real existence and a relative independence" but "retain their being and their powers only as they are upheld by God."[549]

Even on the monistic approach, Strong held,

we may speak of second causes in nature, since God's regular and habitual action is a second and subsequential thing, while his act of initiation and organization is the first. Neither the universe nor any part of it is to be identified with God, any more than my thoughts and acts are to be identified with me.[550]

---

[539] ST(1907), 402.
[540] ST(1907), 403.
[541] ST(1907), 404.
[542] ST(1907), 404.
[543] ST(1907), 411.
[544] ST(1907), 412.
[545] ST(1907), 412. "It is often objected that we cannot thus identify force with will, because in many causes the effort of our will is fruitless for the reason that nervous and muscular force is lacking. But this proves only that force cannot be identified with human will, not that it cannot be identified with the divine will. To the divine will no force is lacking; in God will and force are one" (ST[1907], 412).
[546] ST(1907), 412. Strong criticized Hodge's theology on this ground, as well as the objection of his former teacher at Yale, Noah Porter, who had written that "because we derive our notion of cause from will, it does not follow that the causal relation always involves will; it would follow that the universe, so far as it is not intelligent, is impossible" (*Human Intellect*, 588). Strong replied that "no dead thing can act" (ST[1907], 412, 413).
[547] ST(1907), 413.
[548] ST(1907), 413-414.
[549] ST(1907), 414.
[550] ST(1907), 416-417.

The doctrine of continuous creation maintains a true insistence that all force is will, but erroneously maintains that "all force is *divine* will, and divine will in *direct* exercise," whereas the forces of nature are "secondary and automatic, not primary and immediate, workings of God."[551] Preservation takes a mean position between the denial of first cause and the denial of second causes.[552]

Since Christ sustains all creation, preservation involves his suffering, and "this suffering is his atonement, of which the culmination and demonstration are seen in the cross of Calvary."[553]

Providence explains the evolution and progress of the universe, as preservation explains its continuance, and creation its existence, Strong pointed out.[554] As the only revealer of God, Christ is the medium of providence, as well as of every other divine activity.[555] The Hebrew writers "saw in second causes the operation of the great first Cause"[556] and, because even the acts of wicked men entered into the divine plan, they sometimes represented God as doing what finite spirits were permitted to do.[557]

Special providence is not to be distinguished from general providence in terms of miracle, Strong added, but only in terms of the impression produced upon men.[558]

Miracles and works of grace like regeneration are not to be regarded as belonging to a different order of things from God's special providences. They too, like special providences, may have their natural connections and antecedents, although they more readily suggest their divine authorship. Nature and God are not mutually exclusive,—nature is rather God's method of working. Since nature is only the manifestation of God, special providence, miracle, and regeneration are simply different degrees of extraordinary nature. Certain of the wonders of Scripture, such as the destruction of Sennacherib's army and the dividing of the Red Sea, the plagues of Egypt, the flight of quails, and the draught of fishes, can be counted as exaggerations of natural forces, while at the same time they are operations of the wonder-working God.[559]

Strong declared the "line between the natural and the supernatural, between special providence and miracle" to be arbitrary, and insisted that "the same event may often be regarded either as special providence or as miracle" accordingly as one adopts the viewpoint of its relation to other events or that of its relation to God.[560]

Divine answer to prayer may come, even when a change of the sequences of nature is involved, by new combinations of natural forces but without suspension or violation of law, or by the operation of divinely

---
[551] ST(1907), 416.
[552] ST(1907), 418.
[553] ST(1907), 419.
[554] ST(1907), 419.
[555] ST(1907), 419.
[556] ST(1907), 424. Strong illustrated with the words of Psalm 29:3, "the God of glory thundereth."
[557] ST(1907), 424.
[558] ST(1907), 432.
[559] ST(1907), 432.
[560] ST(1907), 432. Jesus' healings likewise "may be susceptible of natural explanation, while yet they show that Christ is absolute Lord of nature" (ST[1907], 432-433).

prearranged natural agencies.[561] In view of God's immanence, an answer to prayer by natural means is as much a revelation of personal divine care as a suspension of the laws of nature.[562]

Strong's treatment of the doctrine of angels, including Satanology, was substantially unchanged.[563] He emphasized, however, that "good angels are not to be considered as the meditating agents of God's regular and common providence, but as the ministers of his special revelation in the affairs of the church."[564] Their power is dependent and derived, and is exercised "in accordance with the laws of the spiritual and natural world" and hence is non-miraculous."[565]

Strong defended the doctrine of heaven against the objection that it is precluded by modern belief in an infinite space peopled with worlds, on the ground that the notion of an infinite universe is unwarranted. But simultaneously he affirmed that the notions of "heaven as a definite place" and of "spirits as confined to fixed locality" are likewise without certain warrant in Scripture and in philosophy.[566] "We know nothing," he wrote, "of the modes of existence of pure spirits."[567] Heaven and hell, therefore, he viewed as essentially conditions corresponding to spiritual character. Angels may be free from the laws of time and space. The existence and working of good and evil angels Strong accepted "as a matter of faith, without professing to understand their relations to space."[568]

Angels, like men, were created in Christ and are sustained by him, so that he "must suffer in their sin."[569] God, if he consistently could, would save them.[570] One reason no redemption may be provided for fallen angels is that their incorporeal being afforded "no opportunity for Christ to objectify his grace and visibly to join himself to them."[571] But the silence of Scripture does not prove that no salvation is provided for them, for their present judgment is temporary, and their final state remains to be revealed.[572]

4. Anthropology

The origin of man, even more than the evolution of lower creatures, requires a reference to a divine originating agency, Strong insisted.[573] But the Scriptures do not disclose the method of his creation, so that mediate creation, whereby man's physical system is derived by natural descent from the lower animals, is not precluded.[574] Since evolution is

---

[561]ST(1907), 434, 435.
[562]ST(1907), 436.
[563]ST(1907), 443-464.
[564]ST(1907), 452. Their intervention is occasional and exceptional, Strong added, by divine permission or command.
[565]ST(1907), 453.
[566]ST(1907), 459.
[567]ST(1907), 459.
[568]ST(1907), 460.
[569]ST(1907), 464.
[570]ST(1907), 464.
[571]ST(1907), 464.
[572]ST(1907), 464.
[573]ST(1907), 465.
[574]ST(1907), 465. God may have breathed into "animated dust," using natural means "as far as they would go," Strong urged. Thus "man sustained to the

but the divine method, it does not make a Creator superfluous.⁵⁷⁵ But a doctrine of man's emergence "at the proper time, governed by different laws from the brute creation yet growing out of the brute" is perfectly consistent with the Scriptures.⁵⁷⁶ Theistic evolution recognizes the whole process of human creation as "equally the work of nature and the work of God."⁵⁷⁷

But what chiefly constitutes man as essentially distinct from the brute "could not have been derived, by any natural process of development, from the inferior creatures."⁵⁷⁸ Psychology attests this radical difference between human and animal intelligence, "especially man's possession of self-consciousness, general ideas, the moral sense, and the power of self-determination."⁵⁷⁹ While the divine inbreathing was a mediate creation in what it presupposed "existing material in the shape of animal forms," it was nonetheless an immediate creation in that "only a divine reinforcement of the process of life turned the animal into man."⁵⁸⁰ Man came not from, but through, the brute, by an activity of the immanent God who created both.⁵⁸¹ Comparative physiology has adduced no single instance of the transformation of one animal species into another, nor has it demonstrated the development of an animal body into that of a man.⁵⁸² All evolution is unintelligible apart from new impulses to the process by the direct activity of the immanent God.⁵⁸³ The soul was an immediate creation of God, but the body, too, was "in this sense an immediate creation also."⁵⁸⁴ Darwin was right, that man has evolved by gradual change and improvement of lower into higher forms of life, but his theory is only partially true.⁵⁸⁵ For the laws of man's organic development are but divine methods and proofs of divine creatorship, and man appeared on the scene as no longer brute, but as a self-conscious, self-determining image of the Creator, capable of free moral decision.⁵⁸⁶

---

highest preceding brute the same relation which the multiplied bread and fish sustained to the five loaves and two fishes . . . or which the wine sustained to the water which was transformed at Cana" (ST[1907], 465).

[575] ST(1907), 466.
[576] ST(1907), 466.
[577] ST(1907), 466.
[578] ST(1907), 466.
[579] ST(1907), 466.
[580] ST(1907), 466.
[581] ST(1907), 467. "While we grant, then, that man is the last stage in the development of life and that he has a brute ancestry, we regard him also as the offspring of God. The same God who was the author of the brute became in due time the creator of man. Though man came *through* the brute, he did not come *from* the brute, but from God, the Father of spirits and the author of all life" (ST[1907], 469).
[582] ST(1907), 470.
[583] ST(1907), 470.
[584] ST(1907), 470.
[585] ST(1907), 470. "It was not Darwin, but disciples like Haeckel, who put forward the theory as making the hypothesis of a Creator superfluous. We grant the principle of evolution, but we regard it as only the method of divine intelligence, and must moreover consider it is preceded by an original creative act, introducing vegetable and animal life, and as supplemented by other creative acts, at the introduction of man and at the incarnation of Christ" (ST[1907], 473).
[586] ST(1907), 472.

In the same discussion, Strong applied the new immanence by anticipation to the doctrine of regeneration. "Both man's original creation and his new creation in regeneration," Strong wrote, "are creations from within, rather than from without. In both cases, God builds the new upon the basis of the old."[587]

Since man is a personal being in the divine image, divinely originated and sustained, he is related naturally to God as Father.[588] This natural sonship "underlies the history of the fall, and qualifies the doctrine of sin," and also prepares the way "for the spiritual sonship of those who join themselves in him by faith."[589] God is physically and naturally the Father of all mankind, but morally and spiritually the Father only of those renewed by his Spirit.[590] The descent of humanity from a single pair underlies the organic unity of mankind in the fall, the provision of salvation for the race in Christ, and "constitutes the ground of man's obligation of natural brotherhood to every member of the race."[591]

Strong retained his dichotomous view of man, emphasizing that man's spiritual nature possesses duality of powers,[592] but unity of substance. He supported his earlier traducian view of the origin of the soul with the insistence that the Biblical passages cited by creationists "may with equal propriety be regarded as expressing God's mediate agency."[593] Strong oposed creationism as involving "endless miracle," whereas "God works in nature through second causes."[594] The individuality of a law of variation impressed upon the human species by the immanent God.[595] Traducianism "admits a divine concurrence throughout the whole development of the human species" whereby a superintending Providence supervises "special improvements in type at the birth of marked men,

---

[587]ST(1907), 472.
[588]ST(1907), 474.
[589]ST(1907), 474.
[590]ST(1907), 475.
[591]ST(1907), 476.
[592]ST(1907), 486. Strong added this curious comment to the discussion of dichotomy: "Man is different in kind, though possessed of certain powers which the brute has. . . . The animal is different in kind from the vegetable, though he has some of the same powers which the vegetable has. God's powers include man's; but man is not of the same substance with God, nor could man be enlarged or developed into God. So man's powers include those of the brute, but the brute is not of the same substance with man, nor could he be enlarged or developed into man" (ST[1907], 486).
[593]ST(1907), 491. "We do not hesitate to interpret these . . . passages as expressive of mediate, not immediate, creatorship,—God works through natural laws of generation and development so ar as the production of man's body is concerned. None of the passages . . . forbid us to suppose that he works through these same natural laws in the production of the soul. The truth in creationism is the presence and operation of God in all natural processes. A transcendent God manifests himself in all physical begetting" (ST[1907], 492).
[594]ST (1907), 495. God does not "create a new vital principle at the beginning of each separate apple, and of each separate dog. Each of these is the result of a self-multiplying force, implanted once for all in the first of the race. To say . . . that God is the immediate author of each new individual, is to deny second causes, and to merge nature in God. The whole tendency of modern science is in the opposite direction. Nor is there any good reason for making the origin of the individual human soul an exception to the general rule" (ST[1907], 495).
[595]Genius is "often another name for Providence," Strong wrote (ST[1907], 492).

similar to those which we may suppose to have occurred in the introduction of new varieties in the animal creation."[596]

The striking thing about Strong's treatment of the soul is the almost complete absence of any reference to the self-psychology, as against the traditional soul-substance view. Man's nature, as noted, he viewed as twofold, material[597] and immaterial, and he supported dichotomy as against trichotomy. There occurs, however, an incidental comment of Strong's, to the effect that *"substance* does not necessarily imply either *extension* or *figure. Substantia* is simply that which stands under, underlies, supports," he wrote, "or in other words that which is the ground of phenomena."[598] Therefore the mind, while created, did not come into being, Strong urged, by any "dividing up, or splitting off, as if the mind were a material mass."[599] In this connection, Strong referred to Ladd, and to Lotze whom Ladd quoted, as repudiating the idea that the mind is susceptible of division. In the quotation from Ladd[600] occurs the statement: "The child's mind does not exist before it acts. Its activities *are* its existence." Strong's only comment on the quotation was:

So we might say that a flame has no existence before it acts. Yet it may owe its existence to a preceding flame. The Indian proverb is: "No lotus without a stem."[601]

That appears to be the sum-total of Strong's interaction with the newer self-psychology. Elsewhere, it should be recalled, he insisted on the distinction between being and activity.[602]

Strong retained the insistence that the moral reason is depraved by sin, so that conscience "has only a perverse standard by which to judge."[603] Conscience is the echo of God's voice, but only the echo.

The soul has will-power to choose between motives,[604] Strong claimed, consistently with his essays taking exception to Edwards' view of the will. But, as against Arminianism, Strong contended that the soul always acts in view of motives. Motives are internal as well as external, but they are not causal, as natural law is.[605] Man has a conditional and limited freedom.[606] Man has the power of contrary choice, limited by his permanent moral state, although the latter can be overruled in divine regeneration.[607] Man is totally depraved, so that the sinful bent of his affections is constant and inveterate, but he is not as bad as he might be.[608]

Man's present state contrasts with that of his origin, which was holy and childlike.[609] But man possessed a likeness to God in terms both of

---

[596]ST(1907), 496.
[597]Strong nowhere discussed the relationship of the human body to the physical universe in idealistic terms.
[598]ST(1907), 495.
[599]ST(1907), 495.
[600]Ladd, *Philosophy of Mind*, 206, 259-366.
[601]ST(1907), 495.
[602]*Supra*, 158.
[603]ST(1907), 501.
[604]ST(1907), 504.
[605]ST(1907), 506.
[606]ST(1907), 507.
[607]ST(1907), 507.
[608]ST(1907), 510.
[609]ST(1907), 514.

personality and holiness. The Logos so indwells and constitutes the principle of humanity's being that mankind "shares with Christ in the image of God."[610] This divine element in man takes away all right "to use a human being merely for our own pleasure or profit."[611] This leads also to "kind and reverent treatment" of the lower animals in which "so many human characteristics are foreshadowed."[612] In view of the fall, however, the dignity of human nature consists not so much in man's actual state, as in the divine intention for him, looking to the restoration of the lost image by the soul's union with Christ.[613]

Strong's statement of divine law did not differ essentially from the earlier development. The phrasing is not reconciled, at times, with a one-substance theory of reality, as when, having defined God's law as "a general expression of the divine will enforced by power" and existing under the two forms of elemental law and positive enactment, Strong described the former as "law inwrought into the elements, substances, and forces of the rational and irrational creation."[614] Moral law is a revelation of eternal reality, not simply a test of obedience.[615] By positive enactment Strong intended published expressions of the divine will.[616] Such are general moral precepts, as written summaries of elemental law or authorized applications of it to human conditions, and ceremonial or special injunctions.[617]

The treatment of sin remained quite solidly on the orthodox side.[618] But there are significant changes looking to immanentism. Strong retained the emphasis, against the New School tendency to limit sin to mere act, that sin is coextensive with activity rather than state; sin is "not passive impurity but is impurity willing."[619] But alongside the evil bent of human will a perpetual immanent divine power operates so as to counteract greatly the force of evil "and if not resisted leads the individual soul— even when resisted leads the race at large—toward truth and salvation."[620] This divine principle in man strives against the selfish will, furnishing an

---

[610] ST(1907), 515.
[611] ST(1907), 516. In receiving man, Strong added, "we receive Christ, and in receiving Christ we receive him who sent Christ. . . . Christ is the vine, and all men are his natural branches, cutting themselves off only when they refuse to bear fruit, and condemning themselves to the burning only beoause they destroy, so far as they can destroy, God's image in them, all that makes them worth preserving" (ST[1907], 516).
[612] ST(1907), 517.
[613] "Because of his future possibilities, the meanest of mankind is sacred" (ST[1907], 517).
[614] ST(1907), 536.
[615] "God's nature is reflected in the laws of our nature. Since law is inwrought into man's nature, man is a law unto himself. To conform to his own nature, in which conscience is supreme, is to conform to the nature of God. The law is only the revelation of the constitutive principles of being, the declaration of what must be, so long as man is man and God is God" (ST[1907], 539).
[616] ST(1907), 544.
[617] ST(1907), 545.
[618] ST(1907), 549-582.
[619] ST(1907), 550. The same tendency to an activistic view, found in the insistence that divine holiness is "purity willing" rather than passive purity, is seen in this formulation of sin. But in both cases, Strong retained the motion of an underlying state, along with the activity.
[620] ST(1907), 551.

original grace even more powerful than original sin.[621] The essential principle of sin is selfishness.[622] Although man is derived from a brute ancestry, he is under no necessity to violate the law of his being, and retains power to recognize and realize moral ideals.[623] While the Augustinian estimate of heathen virtues as "splendid vices" must be rejected, for they "were relatively good and useful,—they still, except in possible instances where God's Spirit wrought upon the heart, were illustrations of a morality divorced from love to God" and consequently lacked the main element demanded by the law, and as such were infected with sin.[624] The law "judges all action by the heart from which it springs," and therefore "no action of the unregenerate can be other than sin."[625] Biblical passages which seem on the surface to ascribe a goodness to certain men which renders them divinely acceptable actually involve "a merely imperfect and fancied goodness, a goodness of mere aspiration and impulse due to preliminary working of God's Spirit," or a goodness resulting from conscious faith in divine salvation.[626] The noble impulses of unregenerate men must be attributed to Christ, not to unaided human nature, and these influences of grace, "if resisted, leave the soul in more than its original darkness."[627]

The origin of human sin is traced to the personal act of Adam.[628] The general character of the story of the fall is historical, and its particular features are "incidents suitable to man's condition of innocent but untried childhood."[629] Man fell by "wilful resistance to the inworking God," Strong held. "Christ is in all men as he was in Adam, and all good impulses are due to him."[630]

Adam's sin is "the cause and ground of the depravity, guilt, and condemnation of all his posterity" because "in virtue of their organic unity, the sin of Adam is the sin of the race."[631] Strong defended his view of imputation against "the arbitrary and mechanical charging to a man of that for which he is not naturally responsible."[632] Rather, it is "the reckoning to a man of a guilt which is properly his own, whether by virtue of his individual acts, or by virtue of his connection with the race."[633] It is clear from this latter statement how Strong had shaped a principle of imputation which would involve Christ in guilt, on ethical monist assumptions.[634]

Strong affirmed the doctrine of original sin to be "only the ethical interpretation of biological facts—the facts of heredity and of universal congenital ills, which demand an ethical ground and explanation."[635] He therefore viewed the doctrine rather as an inference from Scripture, than as a matter of direct Biblical teaching.[636] But the "final test of every theory . . . is its conformity to Scripture," Strong affirmed.[637]

---

[621]ST(1907), 552.
[622]ST(1907), 559.
[623]ST(1907), 560.
[624]ST(1907), 570.
[625]ST(1907), 570
[626]ST(1907), 574.
[627]ST(1907), 574.
[628]ST(1907), 582.
[629]ST(1907), 583.
[630]ST(1907), 587.
[631]ST(1907), 593.
[632]ST(1907), 594.
[633]ST(1907), 594.
[634]Strong asserted that a real union furnishes the realistic basis for imputation between Adam and his descendants, Christ and the race, and believers and Christ.
[635]ST(1907), 596.
[636]The Augustinian theory of Adam's natural headship, that Adam and his descendants are naturally and organically one, "explains the largest number of facts, is least open to objection, and is most accordant with Scripture," Strong wrote (ST[1907], 597).
[637]The lower views, Strong complained, have "no proper idea of the union of the

The doctrine of original sin "has for its correlate," Strong held,

the idea of original grace, or the abiding presence and operation of Christ, the immanent God, in every member of the race, in spite of his sin, to counteract the evil and to prepare the way, so far as man will permit, for individual and collective salvation.[638]

But this activity of the Holy Spirit does not of itself remove the depravity or condemnation derived from the fall of Adam.[639]

Strong continued to oppose his view of Adam's natural headship to the representative view involved in the theory of federal headship.[640] "Imputation of sin cannot precede and account for corruption," he protested; rather, "corruption must precede and account for imputation."[641] Adam's sin is imputed to mankind immediately, not as something foreign, but "because it is ours—we and all other men have existed as one moral person or one moral whole in him."[642] The recent conceptions of the reign of law and of the principle of heredity, Strong held, tended to support such an anthropology. "The doctrine of Adam's Natural Headship," he wrote, "is only a doctrine of the hereditary transmission of character from the first father of the race to his descendants." In view of this, he added, "we use the word 'imputation' in its proper sense—that of reckoning or charging to us of that which is truly and properly ours."[643]

The hypothesis of "a determination of the will of each member of the race prior to his individual consciousness" furnishes the key to "many more difficulties than it suggests," for it throws light on the problem of "our accountability for a sinful nature which we have not personally and consciously originated."[644] The Augustinian view of man's guilt in Adam, therefore, affords the best solution of the facts of inborn depravity and our accountability for it.[645] But the theory of the method of racial union with Adam is, Strong stressed again, "merely a valuable hypothesis" to explain the Scripture teaching "that the sin of Adam is the immediate cause and ground of inborn depravity, guilt and condemnation to the whole human race."[646]

Anticipating the later treatment of the imputation of the sins of humanity to Christ, Strong urged that there is "a *physical and natural* union with Christ which antedates the fall and which is incident to man's

---

believer with Christ, and so they have no proper idea of the union of the race with Adam. . . . To make Christ's death the mere *occasion* of the death of the believer, and Adam's sin the mere *occasion* of the sins of men, is to ignore the central truths of Paul's teaching—the *vital union* of the believer with Christ, and the *vital union* of the race with Adam" (ST[1907], 609).

[638]ST(1907), 596.
[639]This influence of the immanent God "mitigates the effects of this Fall and strives to prepare men for salvation" but it does not remove human depravity or condemnation; rather, it "only puts side by side with that depravity and condemnation influences and impulses which counteract the evil and urge the sinner to repentance" (ST[1907], 603).
[640]ST(1907), 612-616.
[641]ST(1907), 616.
[642]ST(1907), 620.
[643]ST(1907), 621.
[644]ST(1907), 624.
[645]ST(1907), 624.
[646]ST(1907), 625.

creation."⁶⁴⁷ Christ's immanence in humanity "guarantees a continuous divine effort to remedy the disaster caused by man's free will," Strong stated, "and to restore the *moral* union with God which the race has lost by the fall."⁶⁴⁸

The Biblical testimony makes plain that "Christ submitted to physical death as the penalty of sin, and by his resurrection from the grave gave proof that the penalty of sin was exhausted and that humanity in him was justified."⁶⁴⁹ Human guilt is removed only for those "who come into vital union with Christ"; the salvation of infants, however, does not require personal faith on their part. ⁶⁵⁰

5. Soteriology

Heathenism afforded a preparation for the coming of Christ "not wholly negative."⁶⁵¹ God had a part in the heathen religions; Confucius, Buddha and Zoroaster were "at least reformers, raised up in God's providence."⁶⁵² This "positive preparation" in non-Biblical religion "receives greater attention when we conceive of Christ as the immanent God, revealing himself in conscience and history."⁶⁵³ Christ as "the great educator of the race" exerted as preincarnate Word an influence upon heathen conscience.⁶⁵⁴ But this positive element in paganism was slight, contrasted with Biblical revelation.⁶⁵⁵

Biblical revelation promises redemption of mankind through a Mediator, who united both a divine and a human nature to reconcile God to man and man to God.⁶⁵⁶ The Trinitarian "sometimes declares himself as believing that Christ is God *and* man," Strong protested, "thus implying the existence of two substances. Better say that Christ is the "God-man," he added, "who manifests all the divine powers and qualities of which all men and all nature are partial embodiments."⁶⁵⁷ But on the very next page of his theology, Strong proposed to defend "the reality and integrity of the two natures" and the "union of the two natures in one person."⁶⁵⁸

---

⁶⁴⁷ST(1907), 635.
⁶⁴⁸ST(1907), 635.
⁶⁴⁹ST(1907), 657.
⁶⁵⁰The reference to vital union with Christ is here not clearly reconciled to Strong's monism.
⁶⁵¹ST(1907), 665.
⁶⁵²ST(1907), 665.
⁶⁵³ST(1907), 665.
⁶⁵⁴ST(1907), 666.
⁶⁵⁵"Heathenism's altars and sacrifices, her philosophy and art, roused cravings which she was powerless to satisfy. Her religious systems became sources of deeper corruption. There was no hope and no progress. . . . Classical nations became more despairing, as they became more cultivated. . . . The convictions of heathen reformers with regard to divine inspiration were dim and intangible, compared with the consciousness of prophets and apostles that God was speaking through them to his people (ST[1907], 666).
⁶⁵⁶ST(1907), 669.
⁶⁵⁷ST(1907), 672. Strong shrank, he admitted, from views which seem to imply a "partition of the divine nature" by the suggestion that all finite existence is a part of God, yet he recognized the truth "of the essential oneness of all life, and of God in Christ as the source and giver of it," (ST[1907], 700) and also affirmed that "we know of but one underlying substance and ground of being (ST[1907], 699).
⁶⁵⁸ST(1907), 673.

The supernatural birth of Jesus may receive light from the scientific possibility of parthenogenesis in the highest orders of life.⁶⁵⁹ The creation of a new humanity in Christ is scientifically quite as possible as its first creation in Adam; and in both cases there may have been "no violation of natural law, but only a unique revelation of its possibilities."⁶⁶⁰ A new impulse from the Creator could save the Redeemer from the "long accruing fatalities of human generation."⁶⁶¹

Strong committed himself to a modified *kenosis* Christology. He contended that Jesus appeared "first to become fully conscious that he is the Sent of God" at his twelfth year.⁶⁶² He was ignorant in certain respects not only as a babe, and as a child, but also as a man.⁶⁶³ His activity must be referred to the one person in whom both natures were united.⁶⁶⁴ "To say that, although in his capacity as man he was ignorant, yet at the same moment in his capacity as God he was omniscient," Strong urged, "is to accuse Christ of unveracity."⁶⁶⁵ The state of humiliation meant that

Omniscience gives up all knowledge but that of the child, the infant, the embryo, the infinitesimal germ of humanity. Omnipotence gives up all power but that of the impregnated ovum in the womb of the Virgin. The Godhead narrows itself down to a point that is next to absolute extinction.⁶⁶⁶

"The divine in Christ, during most of his earthly life," Strong added, "is latent, or only now and then present to his consciousness or manifested to others."⁶⁶⁷

The moderate kenosis view on which Strong insisted took middle ground between an insistence on the extinction of the Logos and Docetism—but which insisted on "no limit to his descent, except that arising from his sinlessness."⁶⁶⁸ The union of deity and humanity was complete in him from the moment of conception, but the human nature, as it developed, appropriated increasingly to its conscious use the latent fulness of the divine.⁶⁶⁹

Strong defended the view that Christ's human nature found its personality only in union with the divine nature, so that his humanity was *inpersonalized* by the deity.⁶⁷⁰ The two natures are bound together by a unique and inscrutable bond which constitutes them "one person with a single consciousness and will—this consciousness and will including within their possible range both the human nature and the divine."⁶⁷¹

---

⁶⁵⁹ST(1907), 676. ⁶⁶²ST(1907), 675. ⁶⁶⁵ST(1907), 695. ⁶⁶⁸ST(1907), 705.
⁶⁶⁰ST(1907), 676. ⁶⁶³ST(1907), 675. ⁶⁶⁶ST(1907), 703. ⁶⁶⁹ST(1907), 705.
⁶⁶¹ST(1907), 676. ⁶⁶⁴ST(1907), 695. ⁶⁶⁷ST(1907), 705. ⁶⁷⁰ST(1907), 679.
⁶⁷¹ST(1907), 684. Whereas John Henry Newman, the Baptist church historian, held with most orthodox theology to the view that will belongs to nature rather than to person, Strong held that will belongs to personality. On Strong's approach, the view of dual consciousness and will became a subtle form of Nestorianism (ST[1907], 689, 690). "Self-consciousness and self-determination do not belong to nature as such," Strong wrote, "but only to personality. For this reason, Christ has not two consciousnesses and two wills, but a single consciousness and a single will. This consciousness and will, moreover, is never simply human, but is always theanthropic—an activity of the one personality which unites in itself the human and the divine" (ST[1907], 695). Strong did not deny, he made clear, that Christ's human nature has a will, but only that it had a will before its union with the divine nature, and separately from "the one will which was made up of the human and the divine **united**" (ST[1907], 695).

The two natures are "organically and indissolubly united in a single person" so that attributes and powers of both natures are described to the one Christ.[672]

Strong took momentary note of the Lutheran view, that the attributes of the one person are imparted to each of the constituent natures—which position might have been serviceable in the application of a monistic position—but he did not commit himself definitely to it.[673] In a passage curiously unreconciled with the monistic approach, however, Strong urged against the view that the divine Logos in the incarnation reduced himself to the condition and limits of human nature, the contention that "since attributes and substance are correlative terms, it is impossible to hold that the substance of God is in Christ, so long as he does not possess divine attributes."[674] Strong held, to the contrary, that Christ possessed divine attributes, but surrendered their independent exercise during his humiliation.[675]

Elsewhere, however, Strong contended that Christ's union of divine and human natures "makes the latter possessed of powers belonging to the former."[676] But "the attributes of the divine nature," Strong insisted, "are imparted to the human without passing over into its essence."[677] The humiliation of the God-man, however, involved but rare manifestation of this divine power. The communication of the contents of the divine nature to the human nature of Christ was mediated by the Holy Spirit, so that the God-man knew, taught and performed "only what the Spirit permitted and directed."[678] But when thus permitted, he taught not by an externally communicated power, as in the case of the prophets, but "by virtue of his own inner energy."[679]

Similarly, the union had an effect upon the divine nature.[680] While "the divine nature in itself is incapable of ignorance, weakness, temptation, suffering or death, the one person Jesus Christ was capable of these" as a consequence of the union, so that the divine Saviour suffered, and was ignorant, "not in his divine nature, but derivatively, by virtue of his possession of a human nature."[681] Although in his divine nature he was impassible, the God-man was capable, through union with humanity, of "absolutely infinite suffering."[682] The humiliation involved the "continuous surrender, on the part of the God-man, so far as his human nature was concerned, of the exercise of those divine powers with which it was endowed by virtue of its union with the divine."[683]

Strong appealed to the New Testament as justifying the view of a consubstantiality of mankind and Christ, the manifested God.[684] The ground of possibility of the union of deity and humanity in a single person is grounded, Strong explained, in man's original creation in the divine image. Brutes are incapable of union with God, Strong urged, but

---

[672]ST(1907), 684.
[673]ST(1907), 686.
[674]ST(1907), 687.
[675]ST(1907), 687, 703.
[676]ST(1907), 696. [678]ST(1907), 696. [680]ST(1907), 697. [682]ST(1907), 697.
[677]ST(1907), 696. [679]ST(1907), 696. [681]ST(1907), 697. [683]ST(1907), 703.
[684]ST(1907), 692. Strong cited Hebrews 2:11 and Acts 17:26.

human nature is capable of the divine, in the sense not only that it lives, moves, and has its being in God, but that God may unite himself indissolubly to it and endue it with divine powers, while yet it remains all the more truly human. Since the moral image of God in human nature has been lost by sin, Christ, the perfect image of God after which man was originally made, restores that lost image by uniting himself to humanity and filling it with his divine life and love.[685]

But Strong maintained "not merely an indwelling of God in Christ, but an organic and essential union" so that Christ is "not the God-man by virtue of his possessing a larger measure of the divine than we, but rather by being the original source of all life, both human and divine."[686] Christ is qualitatively different from all men, in that "he is himself God, self-revealing and self-communicating, as men are not."[687]

Christ's exaltation consisted in the resumption by the Logos of the independent exercise of divine atributes, the withdrawal by the Logos of all limitation in the communication of the divine fulness to the human nature, and the corresponding exercise by the human nature of those powers belonging to it by virtue of union with the divine.[688] The ascension proclaimed him as "the reinstated God, the possessor of universal dominion."[689] The Christ present with us today, when we pray, Strong held, "is not simply the Logos, or the divine nature of Christ," as if his humanity were separated from his divinity and localized in heaven.[690] For deity and humanity are inseparably united; the manhood is ubiquitous by virtue of union with the Godhead.[691] But Christ's human body is not omnipresent, for it exists in spatial relations; his human soul, however, is ubiquitous.[692] Almost by way of afterthought, Strong added his conviction that

> the modern conception of the merely relative nature of space, and the idealistic view of matter as only the expression of mind and will, have relieved this subject of many of its former difficulties. If Christ is omnipresent and if his body is simply the manifestation of his soul, then every soul may feel the presence of his humanity even now and "every eye" may "see him" at his second coming, even though believers may be separated as far as is Boston from Pekin. The body from which his glory flashes forth may be visible in ten thousand places at the same time.[693]

Strong did not apply the monistic principle more directly however.

Christ's work has prophetic, priestly and kingly aspects. All preliminary religious knowledge, outside as well as within the Biblical movement, must be traced to the preparatory work of the Logos.[694]

---

[685] ST(1907), 693. The last limit of divine indwelling is not furnished by creation and providence, Strong pointed out, for beyond these "there is the spiritual union between the believer and Christ, and even beyond this, there is the unity of God and man in the person of Jesus Christ" (ST[1907], 693).

[686] ST(1907), 694. Christ's humanity differs from his deity "not merely in degree, but also in kind" and this difference is that "between the infinite original and the finite derivative, so that Christ is the source of life, both physical and spiritual, for all men" (ST[1907], 699).

[687] ST(1907), 699.
[688] ST(1907), 706.
[689] ST(1907), 708.
[690] ST(1907), 709.
[691] ST(1907), 709.
[692] ST(1907), 709.
[693] ST(1907), 709-710.
[694] ST(1907), 711. "All the natural light of conscience, science, philosophy, art, civilization, is the light of Christ, the Revealer of God," Strong wrote (ST[1907], 711).

Christ's priestly office involves his sacrifice and intercession, Strong outlined, in the traditional manner.

The vicarious sacrifice, Strong insisted, now as at the outset of his teaching, satisfied "an immanent demand of the divine holiness" by removing "an obstacle in the divine mind to the pardon and restoration of the guilty."[695] God sent his Son "to expiate sin by his sacrificial death."[696]

Yet "whatever God did in condemning sin," Strong added, "he did through Christ," so that "Christ was the condemner, as well as the condemned."[697] Human personality is not self-contained, having its being and completeness only in Christ the Logos; he is "generic humanity, of which we are the off-shoots."[698] Christ's righteousness must condemn sin by visiting it with penalty.[699]

In Strong's statement of Christ's assumption of penalty, one finds revisions of his earlier theology which intensify the stress upon the necessity for atonement in virtue of his pre-incarnate union with humanity. The emphasis falls upon Christ's voluntary endurance of the suffering which is the penalty of sin, along with the emphasis that "as the Life of humanity, he must endure the reaction of God's holiness against sin which constitutes that penalty."[700] At the same time, Strong emphasized that Christ's holiness alone "furnishes the reason for that constitution of the universe and of human nature which makes this suffering necessary."[701] Christ is therefore obligated to make atonement not because of some external standard of holiness to which he is answerable, but is himself the source of that standard which implicates him in the guilt of humanity.[702]

Developing his view of atonement on monistic premises, Strong now tended to place the emphasis on substitution alongside that of sharing. Christ's sufferings are substitutionary, Strong urged, "since his divinity and his sinlessness enable him to do for us what we could never do for ourselves," but at the same time

> this substitution is also a sharing—not the work of one external to us, but of one who is the life of humanity, the soul of our soul and the life of our life, and so responsible with us for the sins of the race.[703]

Strong frankly acknowledged that his conception of the atonement had "suffered some change" from the older view of the atonement as a "mere historical fact" accomplished in "a few hours upon the Cross" and involving

---

[695] ST(1907), 713.
[696] ST(1907), 714.
[697] "Conscience in us, which unites the accuser and the accused," Strong wrote, "shows us how Christ could be both the Judge and the Sin-bearer" (ST[1907], 714).
[698] ST(1907), 714.
[699] ST(1907), 714.
[700] ST(1907), 714.
[701] ST(1907), 714. Strong added: "Scripture declares the ultimate aim of the Atonement to be that God 'might himself be just' . . . and no theory of the atonement will meet the demands of reason or conscience that does not ground its necessity in God's righteousness, rather than in his love" (ST[1907], 715).
[702] The reason for Christ's suffering "is to be found only in that holiness of God which expresses itself in the very constitution of the universe. Not love but holiness has made suffering invariably to follow sin, so that penalty falls not only upon the transgressor but upon him who is the life and sponsor of the transgressor" (ST[1907], 736).
[703] ST(1907), 715.

"a literal substitution of Christ's suffering for ours, the payment of our debt by another," so that "upon the ground of that payment we are to go free."[704] Strong insisted that his new theory retained this element of substitution, but that it made room for an equally true aspect, providing a permanent as well as a once-for-all application of the atonement. Of a finished redemption he declared:

> All this is true. But it is only a part of the truth. The atonement, like every other doctrine of Christianity, is a fact of life; and such facts of life cannot be crowded into our definitions, because they are greater than any definitions that we can frame. We must add to the idea of *substitution* the idea of *sharing*. Christ's doing and suffering is not that of one external and foreign to us. He is bone of our bone, and flesh of our flesh; the bearer of our humanity; yes, the very life of the race.[705]

This historical work of Christ "is not itself the atonement," Strong contended, "but rather is "the revelation of the atonement."[706] It is a time-space manifestation by the incarnate Christ "of the eternal suffering of God on account of human sin."[707] But the age-long divine suffering "could never have been made comprehensible to men" were it not for the historical suffering on Calvary.[708] Christ's historical sacrifice is both "the final revelation of the heart of God" and "the manifestation of the law of universal life . . . that sin brings suffering . . . and that we can overcome sin in ourselves and in the world . . . only by union with him through faith."[709] But Christ's sufferings do not terminate with the cross.[710]

Strong developed the summary of Biblical representations of the atonement essentially in harmony with his earlier theology, in which the main stress fell on the view of a vicarious, expiatory sacrifice. He granted that "the idea of substitution needs to be supplemented by the idea of sharing, and so relieved of its external and mechanical implications," but insisted that "to abandon the conception itself is to abandon faith in the evangelists and in Jesus himself."[711] The doctrine of satisfaction, Strong emphasized, means "simply that there is a principle in God's being which not simply refuses sin passively, but also opposes it actively."[712] The almost universal prevalence of sacrifice, together with its bloody nature which apparently precludes man's institution of it, supports the Biblical view of

---

[704] ST(1907), 715.
[705] ST(1907), 715.
[706] ST(1907), 715.
[707] ST(1907), 715. The incarnation revealed "a union with mankind which antedated the Fall. Being thus joined to us from the beginning, he has suffered in all human sin . . . The Cross was the concrete exhibition of the holiness that required, and of the love that provided, man's redemption . . . The imputation of our sins to him is the result of his natural union with us. He has been our substitute from the beginning. We cannot quarrel with the doctrine of substitution when we see that this substitution is but the sharing of our griefs and sorrows by him whose very life pulsates in our veins" (ST[1907], 716).
[708] ST(1907), 715. Christ became incarnate "in order to reveal the Atonement" (ST[1907], 719). "The eternal love of God suffering the necessary reaction of his own Holiness against the sin of his creatures and with a view to their salvation—this is the essence of the Atonement" (ST[1907], 762).
[709] ST(1907), 716.
[710] ST(1907), 768.
[711] ST(1907), 721.
[712] ST(1907), 724.

divine establishment.[713] Against the Bushnellian or moral influence theory of atonement, Strong protested that

> while it embraces a valuable element of truth, namely, the moral influence upon men of the sufferings of the God-man, it is false by defect, in that it substitutes a subordinate effect of the atonement for its chief aim, and yet unfairly appropriates the name of "vicarious," which belongs only to the latter.[714]

Against the Irvingian theory of a gradually extirpated depravity by Christ's progressive purification of a corrupted human nature which he presumably assumed, Strong protested that on this view "men are saved, not by any objective propitiation, but only by becoming through faith partakers of Christ's new humanity."[715]

While insisting that the atonement satisfies a principle of the divine nature, Strong voiced dissatisfaction over views, such as the Anselmic "commercial theory" and the Princeton theology of federal headship, which conceive the principle in too formal and external a manner, as he put it.[716] The external merit of the transfer of Christ's work requires an internal ground, to be found in the believer's union with Christ.[717] "Salvation is by substitution," Strong declared, and "the substitution is by incorporation."[718] Consequently, "substitution, representation, reconciliation, propitiation, satisfaction, are only different aspects of the work which Christ does for us," he commented, "by virtue of the fact that he is the immanent God, the Life of humanity, priest and victim, condemning and condemned, atoning and atoned."[719]

The atonement "is a satisfaction of the ethical demand of the divine nature, by the substitution of Christ's penal sufferings for the punishment of the guilty."[720] While this substitution is a matter of grace, it does not as such "violate or suspend law, but takes it up into itself and fulfills it."[721] What maintains the righteousness of the law is that

> the source of all law, the judge and punisher, himself voluntarily submits to bear the penalty, and bears it in the human nature that has sinned.[722]

The atonement is not made by a third party, but God himself provides it.[723] Yet Christ stands in such relation to humanity

---

[713] ST(1907), 726.
[714] ST(1907), 735. Strong added: "If Christ is a 'vicarious sacrifice,' then he makes atonement to God *in the place and stead* of sinners. Christ's suffering *in and with* sinners, though it is a most important and affecting fact, is not the suffering in their stead in which the atonement consists. Though suffering in and with sinners may be in part the *medium* through which Christ was enabled to endure God's wrath against sin, it is not to be confounded with the *reason* why God lays this suffering upon him; nor should it blind us to the fact that this reason is his standing in the sinner's place to answer for sin to the retributive holiness of God" (ST[1907], 735).
[715] ST(1907), 744. [717] ST(1907), 750. [719] ST(1907), 755. [721] ST(1907), 752.
[716] ST(1907), 748. [718] ST(1907), 750. [720] ST(1907), 752. [722] ST(1907), 752.
[723] The atonement has its ground on God's part in (1) divine holiness which must condemn sin and (2) divine love "which itself provides the sacrifice, by suffering in and with (the) Son for the sons of men" and "through that suffering opening a way and means of salvation" (ST[1907], 761).

that what God's holiness demands Christ is under obligation to pay, inevitably does pay, and pays so fully, in virtue of his twofold nature, that every claim of justice is satisfied, and the sinner who accepts what Christ has done in his behalf is saved.[724]

Christ, as the immanent God, as "the Life of humanity" is

laden with responsibility for human sin, while yet he personally knows no sin. Of this race-responsibility and race-guilt which Christ assumed, and for which he suffered so soon as man had sinned, Christ's obedience and suffering in the flesh were the visible reflection and revelation. Only in Christ's organic union with the race can we find the vital relation which will make his vicarious atonement either possible or just. Only when we regard Calvary as revealing eternal principles of the divine nature, can we see how the sufferings of those few hours upon the Cross could suffice to save the millions of mankind.[725]

Being "one with the race," Christ's union with humanity was such that he "had a share in the responsibility of the race to the law and the justice of God."[726] He so shared man's life as the immanent God that he was "justly and inevitably subjected . . . to man's exposures and liabilities, and especially to God's condemnation on account of sin."[727]

Christ's "share in the responsibility of the race" to divine law and justice "was not destroyed by his incarnation, nor by his purification in the womb of the virgin,"[728] Strong wrote. But, whereas all men born by ordinary generation inherit depravity, guilt and penalty, in consequence of Adamic sin, the human nature which Christ assumed was supernaturally purged of its depravity, but neither guilt nor penalty was taken away. Strong added:

There was still left the just exposure to the penalty of violated law. Although Christ's nature was purified, his obligation to suffer yet remained. He might have declined to join himself to humanity, and then he need not have suffered. He might have sundered his connection with the race, and then he need not have suffered. But once born of the Virgin, once possessed of the human nature that was under the curse, he was bound to suffer. The whole mass and weight of God's displeasure against the race fell on him, when once he became a member of the race.[729]

Strong appears to have taught that Christ's obligation to suffer, in view of his immanent, organic relation to the race as its creator and sustainer, was transmuted into an inevitablility of suffering by his incarnation.[730] For he affirmed:

---

[724] ST(1907), 754.
[725] ST(1907), 754.
[726] ST(1907), 755. "Christ's union with the race in his incarnation is only the outward and visible expression of a prior union with the race which began when he created the race. . . . He who is the life of humanity must, though personally pure, be involved in responsibility for all human sin" (ST[1907], 758).
[727] ST(1907), 755.
[728] ST(1907), 756.
[729] ST(1907), 757. Such a passage appears obviously unreconciled with other statements, which do not condition the divine suffering upon incarnation, but regard it as unavoidable, in view of Christ's organic connection with the race. Even in this passage, indeed, Strong wrote of Christ's "obligation to suffer" as *remaining*, after his supernatural birth. Since Christ is "essentially humanity, the universal man, the life of the race," Strong added, "he must bear in his own person all the burdens of humanity, and must be" the redemptive agent (ST[1907], 757).
[730] ST(1907), 759.

With Christ's obligation to suffer, there were connected two other, though minor, results of his assumption of humanity: first, the longing to suffer; and secondly, the inevitableness of his suffering.[731]

Christ as the life of humanity is "its representative and surety" and "justly yet voluntarily" bears its guilt and shame and condemnation as his own.[732] Had the Son borne the penalty of our sins "not voluntarily, but compulsorily," the suffering of the innocent for the guilty would have been "an act of manifest injustice."[733]

The guilt which Christ "took upon himself" by his union with humanity, Strong pointed out, was not the guilt of personal sin, nor that of inherited depravity (which was removed by supernatural purification of the human nature he assumed), but "solely the guilt of Adam's sin, which belongs, prior to personal transgression, and apart from inherited depravity, to every member of the race."[734] Christ assumed this "original sin and inherited guilt, but without the depravity that ordinarily accompanies them."[735]

The emphasis in Strong's thought which gives the key to these statements is that Christ's guilt was, in virtue of his organic union with humanity, "not only an imputed, but also an imparted guilt."[736] Strong was troubled by the objection that the doctrine of atonement involves God in injustice by the punishing of the innocent,[737] and sought to show how "a sharing of our guilt on the part of Christ was possible."[738] Christ was "conscious of innocence in his personal relations," Strong wrote, in formulating his position, "but not in his race relations."[739] Regarding Christ's suffering:

if it be asked whether this is not simply a suffering for his own sin, or rather for his own share of the sin of the race, we reply that his own share in the sin of the race is not the sole reason why he suffers; it furnishes only the subjective reason and ground for the proper laying upon him of the sin of all. . . . He who is the life of humanity must, though personally pure, be involved in responsibility for all human sin . . . This suffering was an enduring of the reaction of the divine holiness against sin and so was a bearing of penalty . . ., but it was also the voluntary execution of a plan that antedated creation . . ., and Christ's sacrifice in time showed what had been in the heart of God from eternity.[740]

Since Christ's humanity was derived from Adam, he was in Adam so far as his humanity was concerned "just as we were, and had the same race-responsibility with ourselves."[741] Christ was not only punished for sinful

---

[731]Strong added: "He felt the longing to suffer which perfect love to God must feel, in view of the demands upon the race, of that holiness of God which he loved more than he loved the race itself; which perfect love to man must feel, in view of the fact that bearing the penalty of man's sin was the only way to save him. . . . The second minor consequence of Christ's assumption of humanity, was, that being such as he was, he could not help suffering; in other words, the obligatory and the desired were also the inevitable. Since he was a being of perfect purity, contact with the sin of the race, of which he was a member, necessarily involved an actual suffering, of an intenser kind than we can imagine. . . . Because Christ was pure, yet had united himself to a sinful and guilty race, therefore 'it must needs be that Christ should suffer' " (ST[1907], 759-760).

[732]ST(1907), 761. [734]ST(1907), 757. [736]ST(1907), 759. [738]ST(1907), 759.
[733]ST(1907), 768. [735]ST(1907), 757. [737]ST(1907), 758. [739]ST(1907), 758.
[740]ST(1907), 758.
[741]"As Adam's descendant, he was responsible for Adam's sin," Strong affirmed, "like every other member of the race; the chief difference being, that while we

humanity, but was "under *obligation* to suffer punishment;—in other words, Christ is 'made sin,' not only in the sense of being put under *penalty*, but also in the sense of being put under *guilt*."[742] The guilt which Christ bore is not simply his by imputation; guilt was imparted, no less than imputed, to him.[743] By his natural union with the race he was made "a sinful person; a condemned person; (and) put under guilt, or obligation to suffer."[744]

The penalty which rested upon Christ was not borne only on Calvary, for "his whole life of suffering was propitiatory, so (that) penalty rested upon him from the very beginning of his life."[745] But penalty and guilt cannot be separated, Strong maintained. Therefore "if Christ inherited penalty, it must have been because he inherited guilt."[746] Consistently with this, Christ's human nature itself required atonement because of his participation in race guilt:

> If it be asked whether Jesus, then, before his death, was an unjustified person, we answer that, while personally pure and well-pleasing to God . . ., he himself was conscious of a race-responsibility and a race-guilt which must be atoned for . . .; and that guilty human nature in him endured at last the separation from God which constitutes the essence of death, sin's penalty.[747]

To the view that Christ assumed a human nature proleptically redeemed, Strong replied:

> If it be asked whether he, who from the moment of the conception "sanctified himself" . . ., did not from that moment also justify himself, we reply that although, through the retroactive efficacy of his atonement and upon the ground of it, human nature in him was purged of its depravity from the moment that he took that nature; and although, upon the ground of that atonement, believers before his advent were both sanctified and justified; yet his own justification could not have proceeded upon the ground of his atonement, and also his atonement have proceeded upon the ground of his justification. This would be a vicious circle; somewhere we must have a beginning. That beginning was in the cross, where guilt was first purged.[748]

As against the insistence that depravity is the correlative of guilt, Strong urged that the two are distinguished in civil life.[749]

---

inherit from Adam both guilt and depravity he whom the Holy Spirit purified, inherited not the depravity, but only the guilt. Christ took to himself, not sin (depravity), but the consequences of sin. In him there was abolition of sin, without abolition or obligation to suffer for sin; while in the believer, there is abolition of obligation to suffer, without abolition of sin itself" (ST[1907], 759).

[742]ST(1907), 761.
[743]ST(1907), 761.
[744]ST(1907), 761.
[745]"This penalty was inherited," Strong held, "and was the consequence of Christ's taking human nature" (ST[1907], 761).
[746]Strong found imitations of Jesus' "subjection to the common guilt of the race" in his circumcision, ritual purification, and baptism (ST[1907], 761). These afforded "a recognition and confession of his implication in that guilt of the race for which death was the appointed and inevitable penalty" (ST[1907], 762).
[747]ST(1907), 762.
[748]ST(1907), 762.
[749]"If it be said that guilt and depravity are practically inseparable, and that, if Christ had guilt, he must have had depravity also, we reply that in civil law we distinguish between them,—the conversion of a murderer would not remove his obligation to suffer upon the gallows; and we reply further, that in justification we distinguish between them,—depravity still remaining, though guilt is removed. So we may say that Christ takes guilt without depravity, in order that we may have depravity without guilt" (ST[1907], 762).

Strong contended that his "ethical theory" of the atonement, as he denominated it, "most fully meets the requirement of Scripture," especially in holding that the necessity of the atonement is absolute, being demanded by the immanent holiness of God.[750] At the same time, it showed "most satisfactorily" how the demand of the divine holiness was met, by "the propitiatory offering of one who is personally pure, but who by union with the human race has inherited its guilt and penalty."[751] If one who is personally innocent "can in no way become involved in the guilt and penalty of others," then innocent suffering for the guilty is an act of injustice, but this hypothesis is contrary to both Scripture and fact.[752]

Strong asserted that patriarchs and heathen who had never heard the name of Christ, but who had cast themselves as helpless sinners upon the divine mercy, had "doubtless been saved through Christ's atonement."[753]

The treatment of the intercessory aspect of Christ's priestly office, and also of his kingly office, were not substantially changed. In fact, Strong seems to have concluded any extended revision of his theology, in terms of ethical monism, with the detailed changes and additions to the doctrine of atonement, which comes almost at the end of the second of the three volumes which comprise the 1907 theology.[754]

The doctrine of election is stated in the same spirit as in earlier editions, with apparently but one comment in the interest of monism. It is an important one, however, although part of a paragraph unimpressively inserted into a fifteen-page discussion. Divine election, Strong observed,

is only the ethical side and interpretation of natural selection. In the latter God chooses certain forms of the vegetable and animal kingdom without merit of theirs. They are preserved while others die. In the matter of individual health, talent, property, one is taken and the other left. If we call all this the result of system, the reply is that God chose the system, knowing precisely what would come of it.[755]

In this statement the doctrine of election appears to be reduced to the foreordination of the specific created order which God elected to create. Strong did not, however, develop the statement in such a way as to set aside the prevailing emphasis of the section, on a divine election of certain sinful men to be made voluntary partakers of Christ's salvation.[756]

The section on the believer's union with Christ was expanded, but in such a way as to preclude the mystical doctrine of absorption which involves a suspension of individual personality. Strong emphasized, however, that

---

[750] ST(1907), 764.
[751] ST(1907), 765.
[752] ST(1907), 768.
[753] ST(1907), 772.
[754] The records of The American Baptist Publication Society indicate that volumes one and two were published in 1907, volume three in 1909, and the three volumes later produced as a single volume in 1912, but for convenience and elimination of unnecessary confusion the reference ST(1907) is retained. C. W. Hodge commented on "the apparent absence" of ethical monism in the third volume, in which, he remarked, "there appears to be little, if any, of this monistic philosophy" (C. W. Hodge, Rev.[1910], 335).
[755] ST(1907), 786.
[756] ST(1907), 779.

it is easier today than at any other previous period of history to believe in the union of the believer with Christ. That God is immanent in the universe, and that there is a divine element in man, is familiar to our generation. All men are naturally one with Christ, the immanent God, and this natural union prepares the way for that spiritual union in which Christ joins himself to our faith.[757]

He protested against the misconstruction of this doctrine as "a union of essence, which destroys the distinct personality and subsistence of either Christ or the human spirit,—as held by many of the mystics."[758] The union is a vital one, Strong declared, but "Christ's life is not corrupted by the corruption of his members."[759] Christ's satisfaction to divine justice removed all external obstacles to man's return to God, but evil affections and will, and consequent guilt, remain as internal obstacles which he removes by uniting himself to believers "in a closer and more perfect manner than that in which he is united to humanity at large."[760]

The logical consequences of this union—regeneration, conversion, justification, sanctification and perseverance, as Strong enumerated them— are treated with little reference to the monistic principle. In expanding regeneration, Strong urged that the experience does not add anything to the soul, as though its substance were changed.[761] The change effected in regeneration is exclusively moral, he affirmed. "There is indeed a new entrance of Christ into the soul, or a new exercise of his spiritual power within a soul," he commented, "but the effect of Christ's working is not to add any new faculty or substance, but only to give new direction to already existing powers."[762] Strong retained the earlier emphasis that regeneration is an instantaneous change "in a region of the soul below consciousness" and consequently is known only in its results.[763]

The new immanentism is applied in the development of the section on conversion. The operations of grace, Strong declared, are not to be restricted "to the preaching of the incarnate Christ."[764] Heathen who have no knowledge of a personal Christ may be saved "by casting themselves as helpless sinners upon God's plan of mercy, dimly shadowed forth in nature and providence."[765] For Christ is everywhere present, guiding the operations of the material world and in the minds of men as the Spirit of truth and goodness.

---

[757] ST(1907), 798.
[758] ST(1907), 799.
[759] ST(1907), 801.
[760] ST(1907), 802. "As Christ's union with the race secures the objective reconciliation of the race to God, so Christ's union with believers secures the subjective reconciliation of believers to God" (ST[1907], 802).
[761] "We have given over talking of vitality, as if it were a substance or faculty. We regard it merely a mode of action. Evolution, moreover, uses what already exists, so far as it will go, instead of creating new; as in the miracle of the loaves, and as in the original creation of man, so in his recreation or regeneration" (ST[1907], 825).
[762] ST(1907), 825.
[763] ST(1907), 826.
[764] ST(1907), 843.
[765] ST(1907), 842. Although they know nothing of the cross, such faith is implicitly a faith in Christ, Strong affirmed, and in consequence of this they may receive salvation from the Crucified One (ST[1907], 842, 843).

In formulating the doctrine of justification, Strong conceded that a statement of justification which emphasizes its vital side is necessary, but that "the forensic conception of justification furnishes its complement and has its rights also."[766]

Union with Christ is indissoluble, Strong urged: "Regeneration is the beginning of a work of new creation, which is declared in justification, and completed in sanctification," so that the believer's experience is part of one whole which would be negated if the union could be severed.[767] This emphasis, although lending itself to explication in terms of Christ's natural as well as spiritual union of the race, Strong did not develop further in that setting; the statement of perseverance proceeds along the line of Strong's earlier editions.

6. Ecclesiology

Strong developed the Baptist view of the nature, organization, government and ordinances of the church without any clear allusion to his monistic presuppositions.[768] The discussion of baptism made reference to the baptism of Jesus in such a way as to recall Strong's view, already stated, that Christ's assumption of human nature involved him in hereditary guilt apart from hereditary corruption, which he presumably acknowledged by submitting to baptism,[769] but no other revision in the interest of later views was discovered.

7. Eschatology

The changes which Strong made in the section devoted to eschatology supplemented, in the main, his emphasis in previous statements of his theology, without significant change of viewpoint. The ethical argument, that the divine moral administration required a vindication in a future life, he held as probably having had more power over humanity than any other. But while the argument "proves life and punishment for the wicked after death," he affirmed, "it leaves us dependent on revelation for our knowledge how long that life and punishment will be."[770] Later, however, he acknowledged that the rational proofs themselves rest upon the presupposition of a rational, moral God who had made man in his image, so that they yield "not an absolute demonstration, but only a balance of probability, in favor of man's immortality."[771] The final appeal, as in his previous volumes, was to Scripture, which furnishes "clear revelation" of a fact for which reason provides "little more than a presumption."[772] The most impressive and conclusive proof is Christ's resurrection.[773]

Although rejecting any doctrine of a second probation, on the ground that Scripture regards the decisions of this life as final and character

---

[766] ST(1907), 851.
[767] ST(1907), 882, 883.
[768] ST(1907), 887-980.
[769] ST(1907), 943.
[770] ST(1907), 988.
[771] ST(1907), 990.
[772] ST(1907), 990.
[773] ST(1907), 997.

as fixed for eternity, Strong held that the reaction against the notion of purgatory should not obliterate a proper doctrine of the intermediate state. "In that state there is a gradual purification, and must be," he insisted, "since not all impurity and sinfulness are removed at death."[774]

The main features of Strong's previous eschatology are elsewhere retained, including his post-millennial view that the kingdom of Christ steadily enlarges its boundaries through the proclamation of the Gospel until the millennium shall be introduced with Christianity's general prevalence throughout the earth.[775] As against the view of his former teacher, Robinson, that a finite act cannot have infinite qualities,[776] Strong replied that "sin as a finite act demands finite punishment, but as endlessly persisted in demands an endless, and in that sense, an infinite punishment."[777] But the section on eschatology appears not to have been changed in the specific interest of ethical monism.

VIII. THE 1922 PRIMER, *What Shall I Believe?*

It is apparent from this study how extensively Strong revised his evangelical theology in the interest of ethical monism, while at the same time retaining a basic insistence on the necessity of special revelation, the authority of Scripture for faith and morals, and such historic doctrines as the Trinity, the deity of Christ, his propitiatory atonement, his bodily resurrection, his personal and visible return, a future judgment of all men turning upon their relationship to Christ, and the eternal bliss of the righteous and eternal punishment of the wicked. Whether the appeals to ethical monism and to Biblical authority were thus compatible, or whether the dual appeal meant that neither was efficaciously invoked, remains as an inquiry to be pursued in the subsequent chapter.

The publication of Strong's transition to the new immanentism apparently began in 1894. The application of the principle to the various doctrines was not made, in the measure to which Strong applied it most fully, until the final 1907 revision of his theology. Since that revision, like previous revisions of Strong's earlier theologies, frequently involved supplementary inserts into the running exposition, rather than complete rewriting, one often finds the earlier and later views side by side, with the suggestion that the earlier view must not be set aside, but that it also must be supplemented by the monistic approach. It is a matter of pure speculation, whether the monistic principle would have come to greater expression, had Strong's theology gone through the process of a disciplined rewriting, rather than extended supplementation. It is clear that the essays and addresses which were devoted to specific subjects to which the principle of monism was applied frequently disclose a more organized

---

[774] ST(1907), 1002. Strong added: "The purging of the will requires time" (ST [1907], 1002).
[775] ST(1907), 1008. Strong objected to premillennialism that it supposes "that for the principle of development under the dispensation of the Holy Spirit, God will substitute a reign of mere power and violence" (ST[1907], 1012).
[776] Robinson, ST, 292.
[777] ST(1907), 1051.

and thorough application of the new immanence than the somewhat spotty revisions to the systematic theology. One circumstance, however, precludes the view that only a failure completely to rewrite his theology prevented a more thorough monistic statement. That is the valedictory volume which came from Strong's pen, titled *What Shall I Believe?* written just before, published a year after, his death in 1921.[778]

The main thrust of that volume made it clear that Strong had no interest in a monism that would require the setting aside of special revelation, the noetic significance of the Bible, redemption through Jesus Christ alone, and other articles of the Christian faith which he had championed in the final revision of his theology.[779] At the same time, he held that truth was to be found in evolutionary and higher critical views.[780] Methods of composition which are unhistorical are yet well fitted to convey essential truth, and may have been used in the composition of the Old Testament, he added.

But Strong did not, in these convictions, waver about the truth of monism. Indeed, he held it possible for both higher critics and fundamentalists, between whom he claimed middle ground,

to reconcile their differences by a larger view of the deity and omnipresence of Christ.... It is with the hope of doing something to bring about such a reconciliation, that I print this new statement of doctrine.[781]

And, as in earlier statements of his position Strong affirmed the priority of special revelation and yet frequently formulated his position as though Biblical conclusions could be reached on independent philosophical grounds, so in this final volume the two approaches are often to be found.

Contemporary philosophy, as well as science, "now sees the world to be psychic," Strong affirmed. "But a *psychic* world demands a Psyche," he added, "for 'psychic' means 'possessed by, or manifesting a *psyche* or a soul.'"[782] The Psyche which accounts for the universe must be

a mighty will, creating, upholding, energizing all material things; material things indeed are only the forms of his volition, while he, as spirit, is the invisible cause of all.[783]

Human beings are capable of relatively independent action, since they are created wills, although human bodies are products of God's constant volition.[784]

---

[778] In the introduction John Henry Strong, a son, wrote: "This little 'Primer' is his valedictory. Its last words were dictated the day before the horses and chariots of fire descended. It is a charge also to all believers that remain" (WSIB, 6).

[779] In the preface, the author stated: "I wish, however, to say at the very start that the truth which I present is not derived from either philosophy or literature, although I use these to throw light on it. Before I knew much of philosophy or literature I had learned that truth, from Scripture and from my own experience" (WSIB, 7).

[780] Strong insisted that "there is a downward as well as an upward evolution, and that the higher criticism is not the supreme arbiter in the interpretation of Scripture, but that it must be the Spirit of God" (WSIB, 8).

[781] WSIB, 9.
[782] WSIB, 16.
[783] WSIB, 17.
[784] WSIB, 18.

Strong developed the doctrine of God in the interest of divine triunity by an appeal to non-revelational factors. Consciousness implies duality, or an object known as well as a subject knowing.[785] Human experience affords instances of triple consciousness within the same human personality. But no analogy suffices, for

> three persons in one Personality constitute a union so unique that earthly analogies are only imperfect pointers toward its absolute perfection,—they simply suggest that there is nothing irrational, but rather the highest reason, in the conception that an eternal Spirit completes the self-knowledge and voluntary activity of Deity.[786]

Trinitarian theology, Strong asserted, is necessary to belief in a living, loving and self-sufficient God.[787]

Strong stressed the natural activity of the Word in all human consciousness and morality. Christ is the universal principal of science, law, benevolence, progress, and the Holy Spirit the principle of unity and fellowship.[788]

Christ is the agent in the creation both of "what we call matter" and of intelligent beings.[789] This is "not a creation out of nothing" but rather "the differentiation of his one infinite Will into myriads of finite wills."[790] Christ's mighty Will discloses its power "in myriads of finite wills, some intelligent, some unintelligent, some spiritual, some material."[791] The whole physical universe is alive, and its life is Christ.[792] To explain it, a "correlating Intelligence and Will must be assumed."[793] The creation of matter is but the beginning of Christ's volitions in time and space, under the law of cause and effect; the creation of mind is his addition to bodies of a freedom of intelligent control which gives them a relative independence and makes them "capable of virtue, and therefore responsible."[794]

---

[785]WSIB, 18.
[786]WSIB, 19.
[787]WSIB, 20. "The Father is God unexpressed, and independent of space and time. The Son is his one and only medium of expression, his only word of communication to creatures. The Holy Spirit is the organ of fellowship; making the Trinity an infinite society of communion and love, even without the existence of creation" (WSIB, 19). Strong reiterated that "God never thinks, speaks, or acts, except through Christ" (WSIB, 20).
[788]WSIB, 26. The Spirit is "the persuader of social, national, and universal peace, and real author of all unity, organization and law" (WSIB, 27).
[789]WSIB, 23.
[790]WSIB, 23. The emphasis of this section is clearly much more reflective of personalistic absolutism, than of personalistic pluralism. The monistic element in Lotze, with which thinkers like F. H. Bradley, B. Bosanquet, Rudolf Eucken, R. B. Haldane, Henry Jones, Josiah Royce, and Mary Whiton Calkins aligned themselves, seems here to predominate. But it should not be forgotten that Strong, at any rate, apparently intended this emphasis to be understood as correlative to and harmonious with the insistence that neither nature nor man is a part of God.
[791]WSIB, 23.
[792]Modern science is concluding, Strong held, "that what we call matter is only centres of *force;* and that force is simply *will* in action" (WSIB, 24).
[793]WSIB, 24. "The atom . . . is the expression of the mind and will of an *immanent* God," Strong stressed (WSIB, 25).
[794]WSIB, 25.

Christ is "the ground of all individual existence."[795] All natural life is derived from and shared by him except the will to do evil.[796] The subliminal consciousness may be "the peculiar element of Christ's activity and control."[797] Since Jesus was the only-begotten Son of God, subliminal and conscious activity "become practically one in him."[798] His life is the source of all other lives, and in him alone is the divine fulness.[799] This possession of the divine fulness in the subliminal consciousness of Christ may be used in explanation both of his absolute authority and of his earthly limitations, if a pantheistic implication is avoided by stressing that Christ is transcendent as well as immanent, and if it be recalled that humanity at large has "so infected this subliminal source of good that it has become instead a constant source of evil, to be counteracted by providence and to be overcome by regeneration."[800]

Strong emphasized anew that God's fundamental attribute is holiness, and that this is self-affirming purity, rather than self-communicating love.[801] Christ was the Redeemer because "even from the beginning he suffered for human sin."[802] God hates sin not mainly for its dreadful consequences, but because "it is the *opposite of his nature*."[803] The one object of the divine self-revelation in creation is the restoration of man to sonship in union with Christ.[804] God's plan from eternity included the permission of sin and the provision of grace.[805]

The first man was not a savage, but he was a child.[806] The first chapter of Romans tells the story of primitive man and his declension.[807] But human history is "God's evolution of his plan for man's redemption through the work of Christ and of the Holy Spirit, which culminated in the suffering of the cross and the founding of the church."[808] Special revelation came to a chosen people, but God had witnesses in every land; Confucius, Buddha and Zoroaster "were his partial agents" but their teachings were "mixed with error."[809] Christ incarnate summed up all partial revelations, adding his personal testimony and example.[810] Human

---

[795] WSIB, 29.
[796] WSIB, 29. "All appearances of God in the Old Testament from Abraham to Isaiah were appearances of Christ". . . . "Every voice of conscience that was ever spoken to us was his voice" (WSIB, 28).
[797] WSIB, 29.
[798] WSIB, 29.
[799] WSIB, 30. "Common men are only *sparks* from the divine flame," Strong declared, by way of contrast (WSIB, 30).
[800] WSIB, 30, 31.
[801] WSIB, 34.
[802] WSIB, 39.
[803] WSIB, 39.
[804] WSIB, 41.
[805] WSIB, 43.
[806] "He was undeveloped, but he had right intuitions and inclinations, and he was free to choose between good and evil," Strong wrote (WSIB, 43).
[807] WSIB, 45.
[808] WSIB, 45.
[809] WSIB, 46. Strong added significantly: "The coin they furnished had more of lead in it than silver; and the washing of silver that gave it currency did not prevent it from being a counterfeit of the true, nor from making its authors 'thieves and robbers,' when their doctrine stole the hearts of men away from Christ" (WSIB, 46).
[810] WSIB, 46.

history therefore exhibits a downward evolution in view of sin, and an upward evolution due to the presence of Christ as the life of humanity.[811]

The written word expresses the eternal Word, but it came through "weak and halting methods of human composition."[812] Evolution is the ordinary method of Christ's working, but this does not exclude absolute creation, incarnation, miracle and resurrection as preceding, explaining or supplementing the evolutionary process.[813] The composition of Scripture may include an evolutionary element, involving any method of literary composition consistent with truth.[814] Christ may work from within as well as from without. Inspiration may be "only the reinforcement of a faculty normal to sinless man, but which he has lost by transgression."[815] Christ's revelation may be progressive, requiring his final and personal appearing to disclose its organic connection and meaning.[816] But because the whole process issues from the one mighty Spirit of Christ, Christian experience recognizes the written word, received organically and rightly interpreted, as the supreme rule of faith and practice.[817]

Higher criticism has thrown valuable light on methods of Scripture composition, but cannot set aside the fact, attested by confessions of faith, that the great majority of believers have found the Bible to teach Christ's deity, pre-existence, incarnation, virgin birth, miracles, vicarious atonement, physical resurrection, omnipresence, and final coming as judge of all.[818] But the Bible is not all divine dictation, but rather, is mostly human utterance. The divine word made human is limited by many imperfections.[819] Scripture must be taken as a whole.[820] Christ is the sufficient guarantor of Scripture.[821] His superintendence makes the written word, "with all its literary and human short-comings, an expression of the eternal Word, and gives it unity, sufficiency, and authority, as a rule of faith and practice."[822]

The Scripture may be properly interpreted only by one in union with Christ.[823] For he is the key to the understanding of the Bible.[824] The written word is so pervaded by the divine Spirit that it is superior to merely human teachings.[825] The Bible provides its own demonstration of genuineness and authority.[826] But Christ is the sole ultimate authority.[827]

---

[811] WSIB, 47.
[812] WSIB, 48.
[813] WSIB, 49.
[814] WSIB, 49-50.
[815] WSIB, 46.
[816] WSIB, 50.
[817] WSIB, 50.
[818] WSIB, 51.
[819] WSIB, 52.
[820] "Shall we doubt the death of Christ," Strong asked, "because the evangelists do not precisely agree as to the superscription on his cross?" (WSIB, 53).
[821] WSIB, 54.
[822] WSIB, 55.
[823] WSIB, 56.
[824] WSIB, 57.
[825] WSIB, 58.
[826] WSIB, 59.
[827] WSIB, 62. The precise relationship of the authority of the Bible to Christ's ultimate authority was not more carefully worked out.

Strong appealed for a new surrender to a larger view of Christ, as the only means of reconciling literalists and higher critics, with both of whom he found complaint.[828] Christ's natural union with humanity prepared the way for his spiritual union with believers; he is the life of the universe and of humanity.[829] In Christ, God fully gives himself to us, when our life is interpenetrated with his.[830] He not only gives himself to us, but "so identifies himself with us in love as to share all our burdens and sins."[831] In this final statement of "the Christian doctrine of the Atonement," the emphasis on expiatory substitution and on forensic justification seem in the introductory treatment almost to have dissapeared, in the interest of justification by incorporation. "If critics had only seen the Atonement as a fact of life, all their objections to its vicarious element, as a matter of book-keeping, would have vanished," Strong declared. He added:

If Christ is our life, if all we have and are is derived from him, and if he is God manifest in the flesh, but essentially independent of space and time, then the Atonement is a *biological necessity*.[832]

But Christ's atonement also provided satisfaction to the divine holiness, Strong urged. The atonement has a necessity related to the fundamental holiness of God.[833] As self-affirming righteousness, God attaches suffering to sin as its penalty.[834] Christ's earthly suffering disclosed the age-long suffering of God and "rather *revealed* the Atonement, than made it."[835] For it exhibited the atonement made both before and after the incarnation by the extra-mundane Logos.

That Strong found it difficult to reconcile this insistence on propitiation, however, within the broader emphasis on incorporation, is seen in his affirmation that the placing of humanity's sin and guilt upon Christ "is no external transfer of guilt and penalty, but the voluntary suffering of God himself in the person of his Son."[836] Strong, while seeking to retain the emphasis on imputation, sought for an inner principle which would make it a natural consequence of Christ's relation to humanity. God's eternal suffering for sin makes objective atonement for mankind.[837] Christ's atonement is accomplished through his solidarity with the race "of which he is the life, and so is its representative and surety, justly yet voluntarily bearing its guilt and shame and condemnation as his own."[838]

Strong reserved for special treatment a discussion of imputation, holding that it is "the point in theology which most needs explanation, and which I conceive that I have been the first to explain."[839] The three imputations

---
[828]WSIB, 63.
[829]WSIB, 64-65.
[830]WSIB, 65.
[831]WSIB, 66.
[832]WSIB, 67.
[833]WSIB, 69.
[834]WSIB, 69.
[835]WSIB, 70.
[836]WSIB, 70.
[837]WSIB, 71.
[838]WSIB, 70.
[839]WSIB, 85.

which are set forth in Scripture as essential to evangelical doctrine—that of Adam's sin, to humanity; that of all human sin, to Christ; and that of Christ's merits and righteousness, to the believer—seem "at first sight to involve a sort of legal friction," he affirmed.[840] Apparently the imputations involve "the crediting to one part of what belongs exclusively to another; an arbitrary treatment of wholly moral issues; an external transfer, either of guilt or of righteousness."[841] But the reason and necessity of the atonement are grounded in the fact that Christ is the one and only manifestation of God in nature and humanity:

> He who gives himself to a sinful humanity, if he be holy, must suffer; and the suffering of the holy God on account of sin is the essence of the Atonement.[842]

But while this removes the Atonement from criticisms of an external and legal statement, there is no reason for rejecting the truth of "blood-atonement." But the blood of the cross is "the symbol of Christ's *life*—the life with which he had endowed us at our creation,—but which by regeneration and sanctification he has changed into moral life and power."[843]

Christian redemption is delivered from the charge of "an unmoral reliance upon the work of another" by insisting that it is the surrender of our life to one who is the only source of moral life, in order to be conformed to his image.[844] Faith is primarily an act of will, in which one commits himself to Christ as Lord and Saviour.[845] Man's first duty is to merge himself in Christ.[846] Thus he receives peace, purity and power.[847] The continuously transforming and assimilating power of Christ's life is secured to the believer, for both soul and body, looking ultimately to glorification.[848]

The doctrine of sanctification is not only consistent with belief in evolution but, Strong contended, "is the *only logical conclusion from the theory of theistic evolution.*"[849] It is as consistent that the moral and spiritual life of the race should be derived from a single source, as that its physical and natural life should be so derived. Evolution has required but one Adam, so that it is useless to protest that "evolution should give us many Christs."[850]

---

[840] WSIB, 85.
[841] WSIB, 85.
[842] WSIB, 95.
[843] WSIB, 95-96.
[844] WSIB, 68.
[845] Strong's treatment of union with Christ placed less emphasis on the cognitive aspect of faith than his earlier studies. He did not rule out the intellectual aspect, but he used such strong language as that "Faith in Christ is . . . a leap in the dark" (WSIB, 78). Yet he defended it as "the most rational act of one's life" (WSIB, 78). Elsewhere he stated that the believer's mystical union with Christ is inscrutable "not in the sense of being unintelligible to the Christian or beyond the reach of his experience, but only in the sense of *surpassing in its intimacy and value any other union of souls that we know*" (WSIB, 83).
[846] WSIB, 79.
[847] WSIB, 80.
[848] WSIB, 81.
[849] WSIB, 82.
[850] WSIB, 82.

Rejection of Christ results in progressive deterioration of the whole man, Strong stressed.[851] Scripture warrants neither annihilation nor "external and positive inflictions" upon the lost, but the principle of evolution as applied to the wicked suggests an endless reversion to animal type.[852] The essence of hell is the sinner's own memory, conscience and character, and not necessarily any positive inflictions.[853] This furnishes a cue to the nature of heaven, for acceptance of Christ gives promise of upward evolution.[854] The prospect of "an eternal growth in the wisdom, favor and lordship of the infinite God" is held out.[855]

As to the consummation of history, Strong claimed to find elements of truth in both premillennial and post-millennial views.[856] The spiritual triumph of Christ in history may well be followed by a physically impressive manifestation.[857] The return of Christ will be literal and visible.[858] Redeemed humanity looks forward to a future glorification which will involve also a resurrection body.[859]

Strong supplemented his primer with what presumes to be a brief statement of ethical implications of evangelical Christianity. Actually, however, it is more of the nature of Strong's personal appeal to his readers for a living commitment to Christ. In the spirit of monism, he asked:

Will you say that you have never seen God? The answer will be that you have never seen anything else, for every atom in the universe has been a manifestation of him.[860]

These words were part of the conclusion, dictated, as Strong's son commented in the introduction, the day before Strong's death.

---

[851] WSIB, 97.
[852] WSIB, 98. "Refusing Christ, the sinner may himself become the refuse of the universe, scrapped and cast off forever," Strong commented (WSIB, 99).
[853] WSIB, 99.
[854] WSIB, 100.
[855] WSIB, 100.
[856] WSIB, 102.
[857] WSIB, 103.
[858] WSIB, 107.
[859] WSIB, 104.
[860] WSIB, 116.

Chapter IV

THE EVALUATION OF STRONG'S FINAL POSITION

The outworking of Strong's ethical monism resulted in dissatisfactions at home and afield.

"In correcting the proofs of my father's work on theology," wrote C. A. Strong, "I was so repelled by the unnaturalness of the suppositions which theologians made in order to reconcile the conflicting stories in the Gospels, that the foundations of my belief in Christianity began to crumble and I could not become a minister myself as I had intended."[1]

The tensions which the elder Strong's final theology set in motion were not alone a family affair. C. A. Strong became an ardent panpsychist,[2] but ethical monism had repercussions throughout the American theological world. From the side of evangelicalism and from the side of liberalism came vigorous attack.

Curiously enough, the complaints from both the conservative and the liberal forces often struck a common note. The concessions which Strong had made to the new philosophy, it was held, would involve him, if consistently applied, in far greater compromise of his evangelical convications than he stood ready to concede. Ethical monism as Strong formulated it, the critics suggested, was an half-way house. Either a consistent appeal to special revelation, grounded scripturally, and authoritatively and objectively given to man, or a consistent development of the new immanentism, with its insistence upon a doctrinal development which would in no way set aside the essentially creative function of human reason. To profess belief, as Strong did, both in a unique, once-for-all divine revelation necessitated because of the noetic effect of human sin, with a simultaneous commitment to such doctrines as the trinity, the primal perfection and fall of man, the divine institution of sacrifice, the incarnation, virgin birth, substitutionary atonement, bodily resurrection and future return of Jesus Christ viewed as essentially divine, and also in an inward, spiritual view of God's relationship to humanity as implied by the new immanence indicated, it was declared, a failure to apply either principle whole-heartedly.

---

[1] C. A. Strong, Art.(1930), 313.
[2] "I had the good fortune to study under William James," C. A. Strong wrote. "The question debated in his classes, beginning with that of the infinity of time and space, interested me so much that, free at last from a false position and able to follow my natural bent, I chose philosophy as a calling" (Art.[1930], 313). George Santayana tells of young Strong's year of study at Harvard, in transition from the ministry to the teaching of philosophy: "He had lost his faith in revelation. Modernist compromises and ambiguities were abhorrent to his strict honesty and love of precision" (Santayana, *Persons and Places*, 249). The central philosophic difficulty to which he dedicated himself was bequeathed by ethical monism: "The relation of mind and body became my especial problem" (Art.[1930], 314). Note the titles of some of his books: *Why the Mind Has a Body*, *The Origin of Consciousness*, *A Theology of Knowledge*, and *Essays on the Natural Origin of the Mind*. Another son, John Henry Strong, resisted his father's philosophical views and re-

I. DISSATISFACTIONS FROM THE SIDE OF EVANGELICALISM

The idealistic philosophies, at the beginning of the twentieth century, were in almost all the alert academic centers vigorous competitors with historic Christianity in offering a supernaturalistic answer to the threat of the rising naturalism. In almost every denomination, theologians were called upon, in their studies and lectures, to decide whether in the last analysis philosophical theism was to be regarded as the friend or foe of Biblical theism. Strong's answer, as an outstanding Baptist theologian, was not without parallels in other communions, and especially the Methodists, whose theology was being conditioned by the influence of personalistic idealists like Borden P. Bowne, and then Albert C. Knudson.

The conservative Presbyterian theology of the day was uncompromisingly hostile to the idealisms, and Strong's final revision was quick to draw fire from Princeton's Caspar Wistar Hodge, whose father had penned the standard Presbyterian theology of that day, approached only by Shedd's theology for its influence in Presbyterian circles. The younger Hodge reviewed Strong's final 1907 revision and also the 1922 primer, and the fifteen year interval disclosed no development on Hodge's part to view with favor an idealistic statement of Christianity. "What Dr. Strong has done," Hodge wrote, "is simply to superimpose his monism upon his previous and more adequate view, without ever really having effected a reconciliation between them."[3] Those words were written of the first two of the three 1907 volumes. In reviewing the last volume, Hodge complained again that Strong's ethical monism and Christian supernaturalism "stood often side by side, unharmonized, and incapable of being harmonized."[4] And in his review of Strong's parting work, *What Shall I Believe?* Hodge wrote:

It is Augustinianism combined with idealistic monism. It is our opinion . . . that monism and Augustinianism do not combine very well. We think that Dr. Strong maintained his firm evangelicalism because of his deep religious and Christian experience and his endeavour to be loyal to the Scriptures, and in spite of rather than because of his philosophy.[5]

Hodge did concede that nobody, in his opinion, had excelled Strong "in the attempt to work out and state clearly a theistic monism and to combine it with evangelical Christian truth," and added the wish that "all idealistic monists were like Dr. Strong," but the words were not intended to modify a fundamental conviction on the part of the Princeton Presbyterian that Biblical theism and philosophical theism were not as harmonious as Strong would make them out to be.[6]

The Princeton theologians, in fact, had observed in Strong's writings the increasing concession to monism in a theology which, when the 1886 edition appeared, had been heartily recommended to Presbyterian divinity

---

maintained in the evangelical tradition. His books include *Jesus: The Man of Power* and *A Man Can Know God*.
[3] C. W. Hodge, Rev.(1908), 338.
[4] C. W. Hodge, Rev.(1910), 335.
[5] C. W. Hodge, Rev.(1922), 681. "We can agree with Dr. Strong that monism may be either theistic or pantheistic," Hodge wrote, "but we find it easier to conceive on a pantheistic rather than on a theistic basis" (Rev.[1922], 681).
[6] C. W. Hodge, Rev.(1922), 681.

students, especially for its high views of inspiration and imputation. B. B. Warfield commented on the 1896 revision:

> The reader will naturally wish to know what effect this radical change of view has had on the fabric and expositions of his *Systematic Theology*. The answer must be, much less as yet than could have been expected. . . . Dr. Strong's "ethical monism" is pantheizing idealism saved from its worst extremes by the force of old habits of thought; and, of course, it must eat deeper into the system or again recede from it.[7]

When *Christ in Creation and Ethical Monism* appeared, an anonymous reviewer *The Presbyterian and Reformed Review*, the Princeton journal, added that

> fortunately the new (and as we think mistaken) views have not as yet eaten very deeply into the substance of Dr. Strong's thought.[8]

But the appearance of the 1907 revision, with its extensive concessions, was the signal for sterner reactions. By that time it had become clear that Strong's monistic affinities promised to be permanent, and that evangelical convictions, whatever loyalty Strong professed to them, had to fight for survival within the monistic context.

In Methodist fundamentalist circles too the opposition to Strong's newer outlook was evident. Strong's articles contributed to *The Examiner* on ethical monism provoked a prompt reply from A. J. Behrends in *The Methodist Review*. Behrends wrote:

> Baptists have not, thus far in their religious history, disclosed any disposition to court the alliance of philosophical pantheism; but if these articles represent or secure any considerable following a theological revolution among the Baptists is impending. It is not likely that such will be their effect; and they are more apt to find sympathetic readers in other denominations than in the one to which their author belongs.[9]

The incompatibility of monism and evangelicalism was also urged by Behrends. Strong's monistic "language does not fit his thoughts," he affirmed, and "his *irenicon* is the disintegration and the death of all Christian faith."[10] Strong was charged with making "unguarded and fatal concessions" in his desire for theological harmony.[11] The Rochester theologian would "disclose the deeper unity of the creeds," complained Behrends, "by destroying every one of them."[12]

Behrends wrote as a Methodist pastor who had earlier been a Baptist, but evangelical scholars in the latter denomination were not hesitant to speak for themselves. For Alvah Hovey contributed to the December, 1894, issues of *The Watchman* a series of three articles titled "Dr. Strong's Ethical Monism" in which the Newton Theological Institution president

---

[7] Warfield, Rev.(1897), 357, 358.
[8] Anonymous, Rev.(1901, 326.
[9] Behrends, Art.(1895), 357. "The articles are startling in their significance," Behrends commented, "as coming from one who is not a novice, who is not given to careless and hasty composition, who weighs his words, and whose judgment commands wide respect among his brethren. That they have been read with incredulous amazement is very plain; and that their influence is regarded with alarm, as likely to be injurious, is evident from the criticism which they have already received" (Art.[1895], 357).
[10] Behrends, Art.(1895), 361.
[11] Behrends, Art.(1895), 369.
[12] Behrends, Art.(1895), 369.

found himself unable to share Strong's "expectation of success" in finding a monistic philosophy useful as an ultimate framework for Christianity. The third of these articles was devoted to an examination of the Biblical evidence for monism, and concluded with the judgment that "no single passage of the Bible appears to us really favorable to monism, while there are hundreds that discountenance it."[13] Hovey especially disputed the appeal to Bible verses like John 1:3-4 and Colossians 1:16-17 in the interest of the monistic hypothesis.[14]

II. DISSATISFACTIONS FROM THE SIDE OF LIBERALISM

If evangelical theologians were thankful for Strong's retention[15] of fundamental Biblical doctrines despite his commitment to ethical monism, those who had made the transition to a liberal theology or philosophy of religion were quite disappointed with what seemed to them to involve an irreconcilable merger. Strong's views won only a partial acceptance;[16] on the whole, they were received with equal caution by conservative and liberal alike. Although Strong's announced intention had been the reconciliation of the two Protestant viewpoints, neither appeared to be placated by his statement, and liberals whose sympathies were both for and against an idealistic interpretation of reality aligned against him, on the ground that he retained still an authoritarian view of revelation which did violence to the emphasis on human creativity involved in a theology loyal to the heightened emphasis on divine immanence.

The reaction of William Adams Brown may be taken as illustrative of those who, from the liberal side, shared the evangelical protests, that the traditional doctrines and a thorough application of a heightened divine immanence could not be maintained simultaneously. Concerning the revisions made by Strong, Brown wrote:

These changes . . . are far-reaching in importance, involving the entire shifting of the basis of authority from an external and dogmatic basis to one which is spiritual

---

[13]Hovey, Art.(1894), 3, 12.

[14]He protested also against the interpretation of John 15:5-6 in monistic terms, contending that the passage is but a strong warning against apostasy. Hovey referred to Acts 27:22-24 and 27:31 as somewhat parallel. Monism is unnecessary for understanding such verses, Hovey affirmed, and serves only to introduce new dogma" (Thomas, Art. [1900], 12).

[15]Prof. Jesse B. Thomas, in an article on Strong's CCEM titled "Dr. Strong's Last Work," wrote: "It is noticeable that Dr. Strong has not allowed his new views to obliterate or dislocate the older and fundamental theological doctrines, of which he has been so long a representative and champion. He is still a dualist and an Augustinian. He has, apparently, added monism as a hypothetical periphery, within which his theology may dwell peaceably with current physical and metaphysical dogma" (Thomas, Art. [1900], 12).

[16]The central point of reserve varied from circle to circle. Sometimes it was Strong's metaphysical monism, again his view of the Scriptures or of the atonement. As often as not, it was his commitment to theistic evolution. The December 27, 1900, issue of *The Watchman* commented that "the battle between evolution and the older type of orthodoxy is still on. No American thinker of established repute has done more than our own President Strong, of Rochester, to reconcile the two tendencies, but his views have only won a partial recognition" (*The Watchman*, Vol. 81, No. 52 [Dec. 27, 1900], 8).

and inherent. It is the more to be regretted that the insight so clearly expressed . . . should not have been allowed to determine the treatment in other parts of the volume. Had this been done we cannot help believing that structural changes would have taken place more radical than any which we have discovered in our survey.[17]

III. Dissatisfactions Over Basic Assumptions

The basic issue involved in Strong's change of view was, as his liberal critics frequently were more quick to see than his evangelical disputants, his subscription to a post-Kantian theory of knowledge which, when consistently applied, meant that prophets and apostles did not, any more than other human instruments, passively receive and transmit their divine messages unchanged, but were creative mediators, who conveyed their views, however advanced, through fallible and errant human personalities. For the liberal school, the emphasis on a heightened divine immanence involved also, among idealists, a special approach to the problem of epistemology, whereby divine and human consciousness were brought into such close intimacy that the authoritarian emphasis on a divinely imparted revelation could not be retained without a companion emphasis on man's creative contribution to its reception. The question was not whether man was totally passive in the reception of revelation, nor whether personality or stylistic peculiarities in any way colored or modified its expression—for evangelical and liberal theologians frequently agreed on such issues—but whether the new approach to divine-human relationships did not require an intensified inwardness according to which the notion of an objectively imparted disclosure, the definitive content of which man could not in any way attain because of the noetic effect of sin, and which was thus conveyed to chosen instruments in such a way as to safeguard them from error, had to be abandoned in the interest of a formula according to which revelation was viewed as more continuous with the ordinary creative activities of human reason. If the physical universe is the divine thought objectified, by an act of will, and if the all-embracing divine consciousness integrates human consciousness in such a manner that prophecy and special revelation are viewed as intensified expressions of universal noetic experiences, a principle is introduced which, while removing on one side the objective, authoritarian nature of revelation, eliminates at the same time any consistent appeal for infallibility of Biblical doctrine.

The reaction of evangelicals to Strong's modified viewpoint discerned this compromise of Biblical authority more clearly at the level of specific doctrines, which Strong reformulated to their dislike in the application of the monistic theory. Their customary protests were that the reformulations were not Biblical, and that they involved further compromise despite Strong's determination to avoid that course. The liberal reaction, essentially, did not disagree with these complaints. Liberalism had broken with an

---

[17]Brown added: "It is one of the misfortunes of theology as of all philosophical disciplines, that one cannot make a change at any point of his system without being logically committed to corresponding changes in all. We cannot but feel that more is involved in Dr. Strong's principle of the immanent Christ than has yet received full expression even in his revised system" (Brown, Art. [1897], 154, 155).

authoritarian, inscripturated revelation, and consequently was not particularly concerned with the first protest; and, with reference to the second, it concurred vigorously, and traced Strong's reserve and hesitancy about further modification to the lingering influence of traditional ways of thought, at the expense of maturing to the transfer from an outer, authoritarian to an inner, so-called spiritual view of revelation. Where Strong hesitated, liberal theologians, whether of monistic metaphysical leanings or not, proceeded to complete the transition in the modernistic seminaries of the Northern Convention; in time, Strong's own seminary, known today as the Colgate-Rochester Divinity School, made the transition also. In personalistic idealistic circles, the theological implications of what was considered a self-consistent personalistic idealism were carried out far to the left of Strong's position by the writings of Borden P. Bowne, and later by Albert C. Knudson in theology and by Edgar S. Brightman in philosophy of religion.[18]

Strong had been influenced by a reference to ethical monism in his statements of revelation, of inspiration, of Christology, of imputation and of atonement; why should he hesitate there, rather than to apply the princple to his whole system, and that in a more coherent and less reserved manner? That was a question which, in different rhetorical dress, was being asked both in conservative and liberal schools, the former in the interest of Biblical authority, and the latter in the interest of a consistent compromise of that principle.

The Princeton theologians most clearly discerned the shift in Strong's principle of authority, however haltingly applied by him. When Strong's 1886 edition was commended to Princeton students, F. L. Patton had declared its defense of inspiration and the exhibition of the various theories of it to be "the best that we have seen in a work of this kind."[19] The later judgment pronounced on Strong's writings, however, found the younger Hodge and Warfield assigning a large share of credit for Strong's remaining evangelical convictions respectively to "his deep religious and Christian experience,"[20] and to "the force of old habits of thought."[21]

There was a reason, however, for the failure of evangelical thinkers to criticize Strong's views basically in terms of the compromise of an objective principle of authority. For another basic criticism seemed equally obvious, and appeared not as difficult to define, in view of Strong's continued insistence, along with a new concept of authority, on the great evangelical doctrines. This other charge was the countenancing of pantheism. The

---

[18]Two comments are necessary here, however. In a sense, Bowne, Knudson and Brightman, by their radical pluralism, which escapes all suggestion of quantitative monism, may be considered—in this regard, at least—a movement to the right, although in terms of application, they mark more of a rupture with evangelical Christianity than Strong's overt development did, as will be seen. Again, it should be mentioned that, within personalistic pluralism, the thinkers indicated here are not without their serious differences: Bowne, with his incomplete and Knudson and Brightman with their complete break with a soul-psychology for a self-psychology; Bowne and Knudson with their absolute and Brightman with his finite God.
[19]Patton, Rev.(1887), 365.
[20]C. W. Hodge, Rev.(1922), 681.
[21]Warfield, Rev. (1897), 358.

suspicion was widely shared, rightly or wrongly, that Strong's ethical monism was reducible to an essential variety of pantheism, with its elimination of moral distinctions by regarding all of reality as a self-manifestation of God. It was from this vantage point that Behrends declared that Strong's evangelical doctrinal affirmations

> appear as qualifications in a monistic theory of being, with which they cannot be made to agree. Consistency demands either the repudiation of the theory or the surrender of the qualifications. The logical outcome of the theory is pantheism.[22]

In the same mood, Warfield complained of Strong's new view that

> it is serious enough, however, that it has already led him to identify all things with "self-limitations of God," and to involve Christ from and by virtue of creation itself in human life and human sin, and to make His sufferings the inevitable effect of this: a construction that cannot but work injuriously upon the doctrines of the Incarnation and Substitutive Expiation.[23]

In fact, the tendency to identify Strong's ethical monism with pantheism was so widespread that he prepared an article devoted in the main to differentiating the two views.[24]

Strong's demurrer emphasized that in his view, as in that of Lotze, God must be conceived as transcendent to creation, rather than as exhaustively revealed in it; that the physical universe and man are to be regarded as creations rather than as emanations; and that human spirits are not parts of God, but are dependent free agents. These emphases, which became central elements in the metaphysics of personalistic idealism developed from Lotze by the Boston personalists, especially by Bowne, Knudson and Brightman, had not yet, at the turn of the century, won a sufficient following in America so that personalism and pantheism were immediately distinguished.[25]

But apart from this circumstance, Strong's language had encouraged, at times the suspicion of pantheism, despite his repudiation of that view. For the charge of pantheistic leanings came not only where the identification was hastily made,[26] but also where Lotze's writings were known. The younger Hodge, for example, disputed Strong's right to the Lotzean tradition. Strong's exposition of monism was held to preclude the psychological dualism or qualitative pluralism which he affirmed:

---

[22]Behrends, Art.(1895), 360.
[23]Warfield, Rev.(1897), 358.
[24]See the earlier summary of his article, "Ethical Monism Once More" (CCEM, 51-86).
[25]J. Oliver Buswell, Jr., has reported that while during his seminary studies he was not conscious of Strong's compromises of the evangelical view, when in the pastorate he became more and more dissatisfied with Strong's formulation. "I was confirmed in my opinion by remarks made to me by Professor A. T. Robertson of Louisville Seminary just a year or two before his death," Buswell writes. "Robertson had openly accused Strong of pantheism. I asked him personally about the matter. His reply was characteristically sharp. 'Yes,' he said, 'according to Strong, the end of my little finger is a piece of God!' " (*The Bible Today*, Vol. 42, No. 5 [Feb., 1949], 157). It is clear from this that Strong was suspected of teaching both qualitative and quantitative monism.
[26]As by Behrends, who rejected the claim that Strong's viewpoint was new, and held that this could be said only of its "rhetorical garment." Behrends contended: "The leading philosophical concepts, and even much of the phraseology, may be

The question is whether, when God created the world, He created a something which was not part of Himself and which has some principle of relative persistence. By affirming that the whole of finite existence is a "self-limitation" of God, Dr. Strong really leaves no room for asserting the creation of finite persons, so that his view cannot consistently be made to harmonize with that of Lotze, which latter view Dr. Strong affirms to be very like his own.[27]

The difficulty, therefore, derived from Strong's insistence that all reality is a manifestation of God, humanity being designated specifically as "God's self-limitation under the law of freedom."[28] Such a view, Hodge contended, precluded psychological dualism:

If, as Dr. Strong seems to hold, the whole external world is force and that force the divine will energizing, and if humanity is also a "self-limitation" of God, it would seem to follow that there is no place left for any real distinction between either the body and soul or humanity and God. . . . If the universe and humanity are each God's "self-limitations," it is difficult to see how any doctrine of Creation can be maintained or how idealistic pantheism, with its destruction of Christian doctrine, can be avoided.[29]

The hesitancy to grant that Strong viewed finite personalities as outside of God, therefore, derived from his overall insistence that every aspect of the created universe, humanity included, is a self-limited manifestation of God.

It is not sufficient, at this point, to think it an adequate defense of Strong that he thought the quantitatively monistic and pluralistic passages to be reconcilable, for the two create, at times, an insuperable tension. On the one hand, Strong insisted that the physical universe and selves are not parts of God; on the other hand, that all reality is a finite, graded differentiation of one underlying substance and ground of being. If the attempt is made to relieve this surface tension by affirming that the monistic element is to be understood against the background of the prior claim of the pluralistic element, passages are not wanting in Strong to make it clear that the monistic emphasis is treated no less centrally than the pluralistic. If then, one is ready on this ground to classify Strong as a personalistic absolutist rather than as a personalistic pluralist, and thus to assign to him the view of quantitative as well as qualitative monism, passages are abundant in which Strong insisted that pantheism is destructive of any worthwhile religion, and that human freedom and responsibility are sacrificed if selves are viewed as parts of God. It appears necessary, therefore, to hold that the pluralistic intention of Strong's ethical monism was not clearly nor satisfactorily worked out and that, while anti-pantheistic in spirit, it did not demonstrate how the freedom of finite individuals could be maintained without serious compromise.[30]

---

found in the writings of Descartes, Leibnitz, Spinoza, and Malebranche; and the theological representative of the system is Schleiermacher, who, to say the least, is fearlessly consistent in accepting the results of his pantheistic scheme" (Behrends, Art. [1895], 362).

[27] C. W. Hodge, Rev.(1908), 338.
[28] Strong, ST(1907), 90.
[29] C. W. Hodge, Rev.(1908), 336.
[30] The struggle to keep the self metaphysically independent failed in all post-Hegelian personalistic absolutism, whether in the efforts of Bosanquet, Bradley, Pringle-Pattison, Hocking, Royce, Calkins, and others. It was successfully carried through by the personalistic pluralists (Bowne, Brightman, Howison, Schiller, Ward, and others), but in radical competition with Biblical anthropology at many points.

Side by side, therefore, and without that detailed out-working of the relationship of the two emphases, one finds in Strong two insistences. There is the mood of qualitative monism: Christ is the soul and life of humanity,[31] Christ's will is differentiated into myriads of finite wills,[32] finite spirits are differentiations within the being of God himself,[33] God is the one underlying substance and ground of all being.[34] There is another mood, in which all varieties of pantheism are indicted,[35] in which Lotze is championed against pantheism and Bowne heralded as the best exponent of Lotze's views,[36] in which man's free will is insisted upon so that humanity can resist as well as obey Christ,[37] in which it is affirmed that nature is no more a part of God than our ideas and volitions are a part of ourselves.[38]

But of Strong's intentions, and of the possibility of affirming coordinately a metaphysical monism and a psychological dualism, there can be no doubt. The vindication, by Bowne, Knudson, Brightman and others, of the claim of personalistic idealism to represent a viewpoint competitive with pantheistic idealism, has been firmly established during the past generation. And it is clear, from Strong's own writings, that he would have been among the first to abandon the newer immanentism, were he not satisfied that he could retain a relatively independent existence for finite personalities, so that the reality of moral distinctions could be preserved, and the holiness of God and the freedom of man's will sustained.[39]

It was therefore along the line of the other basic criticism, of the substitution for an outer principle of revelational authority, that the issues of Strong's new position were to be determined ultimately.[40] Thus William Adams Brown, speaking for the liberal wing, called attention to a change in Strong's attitude toward "the place of the religious experience itself as

---

[31]CCEM, 228.
[32]WSIB, 23.
[33]ST(1907), 386.
[34]ST(1907), 700. It is not difficult to see how, given such terminology, Charles Hodge might have applied his criticisms against quantitative monism to Strong's view, i.e., that such a theory "supposes that the substance of God admits of partition or division; that the attributes of God can be separated from his substance; and that the divine substance can become degraded and polluted" (Hodge, ST, 1, 555).
[35]CCEM, 3.
[36]ST(1907), 372.
[37]CCEM, 288-289.
[38]ST(1907), 373. The distinction here depends for its significance upon a substance theory of reality. If being is equated with activity, as contemporary personalism maintains, then man's ideas and volitions are not only parts of himself, but are the self, for there is then no self beyond conscious experience. Strong broke with a realistic view of substance, but hesitated to appropriate a self-psychology.
[39]The recognition of a theistic rather than pantheistic monism is found in Hodge's review of Strong's parting work, WSIB: "We do not think that the Scripture teaches that 'matter is Christ's self-limitation under the law of necessity,' or that 'humanity is Christ's self-limitation under the law of freedom'. . . . We can agree with Dr. Strong that monism may be either theistic or pantheistic, but we find it easier to conceive on a pantheistic, rather than on a theistic basis" (C. W. Hodge, Rev.[1922], 681.
[40]It is curious that the younger Hodge, in his review of ST(1907) declared only that "Dr. Strong upholds the authority of the Scripture, and bases his theology upon the Bible" and then proceeded to criticism in terms of pantheism and the modification by Strong of individual doctrines (C. W. Hodge, Rev. [1908], 335).

a source of theology."[41] Strong had revised his definition of inspiration, from 1896 to 1907, so as to remove the emphasis on a divine influence which secured the inerrant production of a permanent and written form of divine truth, in the interest of conceding scientific and historical inaccuracy while insisting on spiritual efficaciousness when the writings are "taken together and interpreted by that same Spirit who inspired them."[42] The principles which Strong set forth, which tended to replace an objective by an internal authority, despite his affirmation of the supreme authority of the living Christ, were as follows:

> The human mind can be inhabited and energized by God while yet attaining and retaining its own highest intelligence and freedom. The Scriptures being the work of the one God, as well as of the men in whom God moved and dwelt, constitute an articulated and organic unity. The unity and authority of Scripture as a whole are entirely consistent with its gradual evolution and with great imperfection in its non-essential parts.[43]

That God accomplishes his purpose through imperfect writings by virtue of inner enlightenment by the Holy Spirit,[44] involved a transfer of external for internal authority. For the principle of a scripture-based divine revelation, authoritative and infallible, to provide a permanent, written disclosure of supernatural truth, had now been discarded.

Doubtless the significance of the transition involved in this change was obscured for many evangelical critics of Strong's position, even as it was for Strong himself. For, under the pressure of higher criticism, and an evolutionary view of origins and of primitive and comparative religions, numerous evangelicals, both in the British Isles and in America, made the transition both to theistic evolution and a higher critical view of the Bible, limiting the infallibility of the latter to its moral and spiritual teaching, without any deep-seated awareness that a genuinely objective authority had actually been sacrificed in the process. The fact that so many mediating conservatives, at the turn of the century, combined their higher critical and evolutionary views of the Bible with an uncompromised insistence on traditional doctrinal affirmations served to conceal, in evangelical circles, the far-reaching result involved in a consistent break with an infallible, Bible-grounded revelation, discerned more clearly by liberal thinkers. The reconstruction of Christian doctrine by a consistent appeal to an inner

---

[41] Brown, Art.(1908), 154. It will be recalled that Bowne, too, in his youth, held the traditional view of the Scriptures (McConnell, BPB, 153), but later rejected Biblical inerrancy and infallibility for practical certainty, and insisted that revelation must be tested by human moral and spiritual insight (McConnell, BPB, 186).

[42] ST(1907), 196.

[43] ST(1907), 220. Bowne, too, refused to separate the authority of the Bible from that of the church and of the Christian consciousness, when in 1904 he was tried for heresy by the New York East Conference of the Methodist Episcopal church (McConnell, BPB, 196). But Bowne's rupture with traditional doctrine was far greater, as will be indicated, than Strong's. Revelation, for Bowne, was not objectively given, but came through the moral life of the community through the insight of godly men; therefore he refused to conceive of revelation in terms of once-for-all Biblical disclosure (McConnell, BPB, 195-197).

[44] Strong wrote that "we know what parts are of most value and what is the teaching of the whole" because "the same Spirit who inspired the Bible is promised to take of the things of Christ, and, by showing them to us, to lead us progressively into all the truth" (ST[1907], 221).

principle of inspiration alone did not lead, for liberal spokesmen, beyond a unipersonal God, a special revelation distinguishable only in terms of a higher degree of general revelation and not as qualitatively different in kind, the superiority of Christ conceived in ethical rather than in metaphysical terms, a rejection of the miraculous, and the discard of any doctrine of expiatory atonement.[45] Strong made it clear in the preface of his 1907 theology, and in his valedictory volume written in 1921, that the sacrifice of these doctrines involved also the sacrifice of the total Christian view of things. But he did not think that his modification of the traditional Protestant view of revelation and inspiration endangered the central doctrines. Had he thought so, he would have preferred the received tradition to any of the reconstructions in the interest of ethical monism—for this much he said repeatedly. But the fact is that he revised the traditional view in such a way as to vitiate, in the eyes of liberal critics like William Adams Brown, a genuinely objective authority in the Reformation sense.

Whereas the liberal attack concentrated rather on the broad epistemological issue, along with a concern to show that the greater stress on divine immanence than affirmed in traditional theology required a further modification of inherited theology than Strong had been willing to make,[46] the evangelical criticism of Strong included an evaluation of changes involved in the statement of the specific doctrines, and an endeavor to show that Strong's views now were inconsistent with the Scriptures, or involved him in inner contradiction, or both.

IV. DISSATISFACTIONS WITH SPECIFIC DOCTRINES

The difficulties which Strong's newer conception of revelation and inspiration involved have already been discussed in their main issues. Before proceeding to a survey of the effect of ethical monism upon other doctrines, however, it is well to observe additional elements of tension in the religious epistemology at which Strong finally arrived.

Strong held that God's use of human nature involved a compromise of Christ's omniscience in the incarnation, as well as the fallibility of the written word.[47] This raised the question not only of the objectivity of revelation, but also of the significance of the historical element in revelation, especially the relationship of the immanent Christ to Jesus of Nazareth. It is clear that at this point a more radical criticism, under the impulse of the new immanentism, would have lessened the exclusive nature of the revelation in Jesus Christ. Strong had conceded, in his later revision, that

---

[45]Bowne had submitted for the traditional view of inspiration "the conception of a historical and gradual unfolding in accordance with God's general laws in life and history and humanity" (Bowne, IG, 104), and had affirmed that "we need no infallible authority, whether of book or church. . . . What we need, and what we have, is a truth that carries practical conviction with it" (IG, 112).

[46]A. C. Knudson, in response to the writer's inquiry, recalled having spoken once to Bowne concerning Strong, and having received a response which may be noted appropriately here. "The impression Bowne's response left with me," Knudson wrote, "was that he did not think that he had thought his way through the personalistic system and seen its full theological implications. The impression, however, is general and I do not recall any specific statement that he made."

a more positive preparation for Christianity than he had thought earlier must be granted to the non-Biblical religions.[48] Furthermore, he had granted that no theory of inspiration is necessary to Christianity, in view of the spiritual authority of the living Christ and of the "self-evidencing" nature of Scripture.[49] The monistic view of the universe enabled one to establish the supremacy of Christ without any necessary reference to inspiration, he contended.[50] But the question remained whether monistic theology, if it involved a divine immanence which precluded a superintendence of human consciousness such as to safeguard it from error in the recording of divine teaching, did not at the same time involve a compromise, on the same ground, of the traditional view of an imported revelation, even if only the infallibility of spiritual and moral, as distinguished from scientific and historical, factors, is in view.[51]

One of the disturbing features of this question is that Strong, not in intent but in method, depreciated the principle of special revelation at numerous points in the development of his final system. While uncompromisingly professing the priority of revelation, he nonetheless appealed to philosophy, side by side with the Scriptures, as if to imply what he elsewhere denied, that philosophy would independently lead to revelational conclusions.[52] An example of this fluctuating appeal, which involves in practice a minimizing of the significance of special revelation in the interest of general revelation, is found in the affirmation that "the system of things cannot be conceived as a universe without postulating an omnipresent reason and will" which the Christian believer "instinctively identifies with him from whom he receives the forgiveness of sins, who dwells as a living presence in his soul, and before whom he bows in unlimited worship and adoration." Strong added: "In all this he only follows the lead of Scripture, for the Scripture too identifies the omnipresent, living, and upholding God with Jesus Christ."[53]

---

[47]"Our modern theology has immensely gained in candor and insight," he wrote, "by acknowledging that the same method of human growth which was adopted by the incarnate Word was also adopted in the production of the written word, and that both these manifestations of the immanent Christ consist with and throw light upon one another" (CCEM, 206).

[48]ST(1907), 665. In his earlier editions Strong had, of course, insisted upon a general revelation elsewhere, but gave the vitiating effect of sin a heightened role.

[49]CCEM, 126.

[50]"The supremacy of Christ, and not any theory of inspiration, is the citadel of our faith," Strong wrote. "We refuse to confound the citadel with any of those temporary outworks which past ages have constructed to defend it, and with our modern artillery enables us in some cases to dispense" (CCEM, 126).

[51]The movement of personalistic idealism to an autonomous morality is here significant.

[52]While Strong affirmed that "the new philosophy must approve itself to reason, conscience, Scripture, before it has earned a right to supplant the old," he declared also that "the test of truth in a theory . . . is . . . that it is capable of explaining other things" (CCEM, 29, 30). The appeal to coherence and to revelation are carried on side by side in such a way as to suggest at times that an adequate coherence is to be found only in a revelational setting, and again, that philosophical coherence pursued independently of a revelational appeal leads to the revelational setting.

[53]CCEM, 149.

Since Strong had weakened the objective authority of Scripture in the interest of the supreme authority of the living Christ, and since by a kenosis Christology he had raised the question of the relationship of the immanent Logos and the historical Jesus, it is not surprising that William Adams Brown should have expressed disappointment that, in view of the concessions to an inner, spiritual principle of revelation, Strong nonetheless retained the conventional order of approach to the study of revelation, discussing first the inspiration of the Scriptures and then the doctrine of the trinity, rather than consistently invoking the significance of religious experience in view of the universal activity of the divine Spirit.[54] On such an approach, the appeal to special, objective revelation would be displaced entirely by an appeal to philosophical coherence of a type which begins with a far greater confidence in the competence of human reason to attain metaphysical knowledge, apart from supernatural regeneration, than did the Protestant tradition.[55]

1. *The Nature of God*

The application of Strong's religious epistemology to the doctrine of God involved him in some curious tensions.

It was protested that the monistic merging of nature in God compromised the divine unity, for it allegedly involved "the notion of a being infinitely complex and internally discordant."[56] Those who lodged this complaint, however, had to acknowledge that the world of nature was understood on the traditional approach by reference to a divine plan. Consequently, to explain the real world as "made of various combinations of the divine volitions" did not necessarily involve a compromise of divine unity. That all movement in nature is "God's direction of himself" need not have been destructive of "the simplicity of the essential life of God" and "its infinite and holy harmony," Behrends' protest to the contrary.[57] But the traditional view also made sin, usually with a reference to anticipative consequences, a factor in the explanation of the interpretation of the behavior of nature. And that there is deep insight in the complaint that the "inclusion of the whole universe in the idea of God, robs that idea of clearness, simplicity and self-consistency,"[58] is evident from the movement of one wing of recent personalistic idealistic thought in the direction of a finite God, in whom the principle of evil is regarded as a given, in order to account for that aspect of the behavior of nature, such

---

[54] Brown, Art.(1908), 155.

[55] Bowne had suggested, in his spirit, that special revelation is admissible only as absorbed to general revelation: "Assuming that God was revealing himself in Jewish history and in the lives and thoughts of holy men, it is still permitted to inquire whether this revelation breaks with all known historical and psychological laws, or whether we can trace even in revelation laws with which we are elsewhere familiar" (IG, 89).

[56] Hovey, Art.(1894), 1, 10.

[57] Behrends, Art.(1895), 365.

[58] Hovey, Art.(1894), 1, 10. In the same article Hovey added: "Strong's view throws back into the very nature of God the multiple conflicts that can be observed in the universe" (11). Behrends took the same attitude: Strong's view "may seem to bring unity and order into the cosmos, but it carries eternal chaos into the being of God" (Behrends, Art. [1895], 365).

as destructive physical calamities and diseases, the presence of which is held to be irreconcilable with the purpose of a sovereign God in a normal world.

Strong's argument to an objectively real God on philosophical grounds, and the subsequent appeal to revelation for the affirmation of divine tripersonality, had in it all the difficulties of a Thomistic epistemology, which affirms the partial competency of the human reason in such a way as to raise the possibility of its total competency.[59] From the argument that we know matter only as force, and that force is a product of will, Strong reasoned that matter—since physical force is not an exertion of human will—must be an exertion of divine will.[60] He granted the possibility of developing this by reference to a unipersonal God.[61] But he protested, against such a view, that "the only God whom the New Testament knows as active and manifested is Jesus Christ," and that the Biblical revelation therefore involves an identification of the triune God with the deity required by ethical monism.[62]

It has already been noted that, in developing the doctrine of divine tripersonality, Strong fluctuated between revelational and philosophical appeals, despite his clear proclamation of revelational priority. The type of

---

[59] Since man is assumed to be able to get philosophical certainty in metaphysical truth up to a certain point, can that competency consistently be denied mid-way? Cf. A. E. Burtt, *Types of Religious Philosophy*, 461-472.

[60] CCEM, 69. "Instead of being agnostics, we are bound to see God in everything; instead of finding no design in the universe, it is more true to say that there is nothing but design" (CCEM, 32).

[61] It may be recalled that, in his earliest treatments of the theistic evidences, Strong argued along idealistic lines that God is the presupposition of all reasoning, without making clear just how much of a natural theology he intended thereby to imply. To that pre-monistic type of argument, Patton had already replied that Strong's "defence of the intuitive nature of belief in God is at least questionable, especially when the author affirms that 'he who denies God's existence must tacitly assume that existence in his own argument by employing logical processes whose validity rests upon the fact of God's existence.' This would be a strong position if it could be maintained, and perhaps it can be maintained to the extent of saying that we must choose between Theism and Agnosticism" (Patton, Rev.[1887], 365). The issue that might have been raised is whether it is obvious that reason is given *in* rather than *to* God apart from a revelation appeal.

[62] CCEM, 32, 69. Bowne went beyond Lotze in the affirmation of transcendental empiricism, which also marks an important distinction from Strong's view. Lotze and Bowne both emphasized the constitutive activity of the self, the necessary unit of the mental subject, in Kantian fashion, but without Kant's *ding-an-sich* (MSFP, 375). They assigned more importance to the self than to the process of thought (i. e., the operation of the categories); the thinking self now displaced the former significance of the *ding-an-sich* as well. The conscious nature of experience involved for Bowne a transcendental self, or a unitary intelligence, through whom the categories alone can be understood. Strong referred this to the Logos, and at this point merged Biblical revelation and personalistic philosophy; for Strong, an ontological trinity was a central article for Christian faith, and special revelation an integral element in arriving at a satisfactory world view. Whereas Bowne moved to theism via transcendental empiricism, Strong moved there with the assurance of special revelation. Bowne's decisive argument for theism was the intelligibility of the universe coupled with the demand of our aesthetic and moral natures. Bowne avoided the word "personality" in M, possibly because it gave offense to trinitarians; later he used it more and more, and in 1905 he decided to call his system "personalism" (McConnell, BPB, 131). Bowne preferred this term to personal idealism because of its emphasis on the will as well as the idea factor in reality.

argument varied from such psychological abnormalities as dual personality, and the usual idealistic arguments that consciousness, knowledge and love each require an object—the consistent development of which can hardly issue in more than a binitarianism. But two further difficulties ensued for trinitarianism, on Strong's approach. For one thing, the argument that since "within the bounds of the one universal and divine consciousness there are multitudinous finite consciousnesses" and consequently there may be "in the nature of this one God three infinite consciousnesses"[63] was actually double-edged, for, given a kenotic Christology, what was to prevent the the explanation of the historical Jesus in terms only of another finite consciousness within one infinite consciousness?[64] The very monistic impulse which had encouraged Strong's sympathy toward the new metaphysics, it might be argued, would press vigorously against the notion of three ultimate, infinite, self-consciousnesses. For another thing, Strong may have cut himself off from a revelational appeal which would have precluded this development of his argument. For he emphasized repeatedly that "God never thought anything, said anything, did anything except through Christ."[65] This conviction he carried so far as to stress that "the transcendent and unknowable God is the Father, the immanent and revealed God is the Christ."[66] He added that "all outgoing, communication, manifestation of the Godhead is the work of Christ."[67] "Christ and revelation," he affirmed, "are one and the same thing from different points of view."[68] Now it is clear that such passages would preclude a merely human Jesus. But at the same time they appear to commit one definitely to a Sabellian view of an economic trinity or an agnosticism concerning the Father which has all the atmosphere of the Spencerian "unknowable."[69] In his affirmation that all reality and revelation are the work of the immanent or transcendent Christ, Strong had lost the evangelical emphasis that the redemptive and creative centrality of Christ is not such as to preclude a genuinely objective disclosure of the transcendent and immanent triune God. He had moved more and more to a philosophical, and away from a revelational, justification for trinitarianism, despite the overt affirmation that priority must be assigned to revelation.[70] In coming by this route to identify the universal divine mani-

---

[63]ST(1907), 332.
[64]Behrends replied to Strong that the view "that finite personalities share in the substance of God, as do Father, Son and Holy Ghost in the one divine essence . . . is a two-edged sword. . . . It reduces the Trinity to the category of speculations and assumptions for which not a particle of solid evidence can be offered" (Behrends, Art.[1895], 368).
[65]CCEM, 121.
[66]CCEM, 190.
[67]CCEM, 121.
[68]Christ is "the divine Word, God revealing himself, and, since we can never known as the unrevealed God, the only God with whom we have to do or with whom we shall ever have to do" (CCEM, 122).
[69]"We can know God only so far as he has revealed himself," Strong commented. "The immanent God is known, but the transcendent God we do not know any more than we know the side of the moon that is turned away from us" (ST[1907], 25). "Christ is practically, and so far as we are concerned, all there is of God and of the universe" (CCEM, 41).
[70]Patton had already complained, in reviewing ST(1886), prior to Strong's commitment to ethical monism, of the tendency in this direction. The defence of the Trinity should rest squarely on the vindication of the deity of Christ, not upon

festation with the Christ of Biblical revelation, he seriously jeopardized his argument for divine triunity.[71]

2. The Works of God

Strong's theological revision in the interest of ethical monism had important consequences for his view of God's relationship to nature. The points of controversy concern especially the doctrines of creation and of miracle, in view of an intensified stress on divine immanence.

Strong had indicated Biblical theism, as championed by those who denied metaphysical monism, as yielding too much ground to deism, and as involving a now-antiquated view of matter.

Curiously enough, in his pre-monistic statements, Strong had carefully differentiated Biblical theism from deism. In his 1888 essay stating his objections to philosophical idealism, Strong emphasized that the Biblical teaching that "in Him we live and move and have our being" maintains a proper immanence, with a wholesome protest against both deism and monistic idealism.[72] But after his espousal of ethical monism, Strong created a constant sympathy for his new view by identifying the older representation of divine immanence as a species of deism. "A universe that manifests God is more intelligible than a universe that is forsaken by God," he urged.[73] Strong designated the new immanentism as "a practical re-discovery of God in the universe and in the soul."[74]

But supporters of the traditional theism replied to followers of Lotze that the issue was between two types of immanence, and not between a forsaken and manifested God. Alvah Hovey opposed the new immanentism, but insisted on "an intimate and perpetual union between God and nature" delineated by the Scriptures in terms of universal divine presence, universal

---

a priori reasons, he complained. The doctrine may be "essential to any proper theism" but Strong "does not make it clear that it is, and we do not believe that the man who gives up the Trinity is logically bound to give up Theism" (Patton, Rev.[1887], 366). It is curious how revelational trinitarians and philosophical unitarians often stood side by side against philosophical trinitarians.

[71]Bowne's 1904 heresy trial marked not so much an affirmation on his part of trinitarianism, as a denial that the quotations attributed to him involved unitarianism; his 1909 *Studies in Christianity* quite cautiously treat the issue. But the movement of personalistic idealism away from trinitarianism is seen in Knudson's readiness to find the central significance of the doctrine in its affirmation of the Christlikeness of God (Knudson, DOG, 426-428).

[72]PAR, 58-74. In that essay Strong had lumped together "Caird, Green and Seth in Great Britain" and "Harris, Bowne and Royce in America" as able advocates of "the system of Hegel" and of the evolutionary hypothesis in opposition to agnostic materialism (PAR, 61).

[73]CCEM, 78. The Christian church has been "far too greatly influenced" by deism, Strong held (CCEM, 148). Bowne, too, at times opposed the "instructed theist," who holds that "nature is but the form and product" of God's ceaseless activity, with "the self-running nature and the absentee God," as if there were no middle ground (Bowne, IG, 24). But he also wrote, in contrasting deism and perpetual creation, of "two extreme views and an indefinite number of intermediate ones" (T. 226-227).

[74]CCEM, 187. "The theology of fifty years ago," Strong conceded, "did not so much deny God's immanence as it forgot God's immanence" (CCEM, 189). But the fact remained that the standard evangelical theologies of Strong's day, and Strong's earlier writings also, stressed both divine immanence and transcendence, clearly repudiating deism, and idealism also.

dependence on God, and the existence of all things in Him.⁷⁵ All things are bound to God by the threefold tie of origin, control and destination, he insisted.⁷⁶ In stressing an intimate relationship with God, necessary to the preservation of nature, he used words which one might expect rather in the newer views:

> The regularity and force of nature are signs of his steadfast will. We ought to think of Him as revealed by gravitation, by cohesion, by crystallization, by the color of every cloud and shell, by the symmetry of every plant and animal, by the miracle of growth in every living thing, by the orderly sweep of the planets, the faithful return of the seasons, and the onward march of the human race."⁷⁷

But at the same time, there was no sympathy for any conception of nature as immediate divine activity and being, whereby reciprocal individual activities are included in God as the universal life by virtue of substantial unity.⁷⁸ For "the Scriptures also teach," wrote Hovey, "the existence of a world of things, animate and inanimate, in distinction from God."⁷⁹

Strong also stated this issue, at times, in terms of a dynamical as against a mechanical view of nature. The traditional formulation of divine immanence protested against the view of nature as a self-sustained mechanism, but it refused to identify matter in terms of metaphysical monism. The resistance to the new view did not come, however, from traditional realists alone. It is true that some evangelicals, like Behrends, took that line of attack.⁸⁰ But opposition came also from those who affirmed, like the younger Hodge, "no desire to maintain an 'atomic' rather than a 'dynamic' conception of matter" as long as the finite created and non-divine character of matter was preserved.⁸¹

It appeared, indeed, that Strong had stopped mid-way in his rupture with a substance philosophy.⁸² He insisted firmly upon metaphysical monism;

---

⁷⁵Hovey, SER, 61.
⁷⁶Hovey, SER, 62.
⁷⁷Hovey, SER, 62.
⁷⁸Alvah Hovey struck back at the new immanentism: "The view which we defend rejects deism on the one hand and pantheism on the other; but asserts a constant relation of God to every part of nature, and of every part of nature to God. In particular, it asserts the dependence of nature upon God for the continuance as well as for the origin of its powers" (SER, 53).
⁷⁹Hovey, SER, 57.
⁸⁰Against the monistic view that there is an original and essential identity of matter and mind, Behrends held that consciousness refuses to identify the two, and that a true view finds their unity in the creative and causative energy of the Primal Will, without obliterating an essential difference between matter and mind (Behrends, Art.[1895], 358-359).
⁸¹The issue of dynamic as against atomic matter is, Hodge commented, "a question for physical science" (C. W. Hodge, Rev.[1908], 336).
⁸²It will be recalled that Bowne, although revolting against a substantial view, frequently retained the vocabulary of substance in his writings. But the passages in which Strong insists upon one substance, of which all reality is a graded manifestation, and in which there are three infinite and a multitude of finite persons, appear to the modern personalist as somewhat Spinozistic. Strong's refusal to equate being and activity, and his insistence that being has activity, is quite congruous with Spinoza's view of substance manifested under the attributes of thought and extension. But, in fairness to Strong, it must be mentioned that he had no affection for Spinozism; that he regarded pantheism as the enemy of true religion; that he opposed his insistence on divine transcendence and human freedom and responsibility to Spinoza. Strong's treatment of essence and attribute has more affini-

the physical universe is a finite, graded manifestation of deity, the divine thought being externalized thus by an act of will. Yet he wrote that the regular forces of nature are "not divine will in *direct* exercise." The forces of nature, Strong stated, are "secondary and automatic, not primary and immediate workings of God."[83] In the same mood, Strong held that second causes are admissible in nature, since the universe is no more identifiable with God than an individual's thoughts and will with the individual.[84]

This distinction, between the activity of the self and the self itself, was one which personalistic idealism did not sustain. The insistence by Brightman, that the soul or agent is not to be distinguished from states of consciousness, but rather consists of the total unity of consciousness, is the prime motivation in his contention that nature is a part of God.

Strong's admission of second causes, and his suggestion that the habitual workings of God do not represent the divine will in direct exercise, no less than his insistence that the divine attributes inhere in a divine substance which is known in knowing the attributes, and his retention of a soul-psychology,[85] were concessions to a substantialist view which later exponents and developers of Lotze's personalism, such as Brightman,[86] were reluctant to make. The "ghost" of the older substance theory must be banished, they declared unhesitatingly, in the interest of the ultimate and exclusive activity of mind and will.

It is true that not all personalistic idealists have followed Brightman in the identification of nature as a part of God.[87] The determining factor,

---

ties with the Scholastic than the Spinozistic tradition. But whereas Strong refused to equate being and personality or self, treating personality as an attribute of God, even after his espousal of ethical monism, the Lotze-Bowne tradition has placed a central emphasis on personality as the divine essence.

[83] ST(1907), 416.

[84] ST(1907), 416, 417.

[85] Bowne fluctuated, it will be recalled, between a soul-psychology and a self-psychology, and in some passages regarded the soul as transcendent to consciousness. But Bowne's emphasis that being is activity required a far closer relationship of thinker and thought than Strong's distinction between being and activity. If nature is God's thought volitionally externalized, then it would appear for Bowne to be a part of God, except as the creative activity of human thought contributes to its phenomenal appearance. Bowne, in insisting that a fundamental monism underlies the plurality of spontaneous thought, affirmed that "the interaction of the many is possible only through the unity of an all-embracing One, which either coordinates and mediates their interaction, or of which they are in some sense phases or modifications" (Bowne, T, 59). But he opposed speaking of the world as a "mode of God" (T, 201). He did not object, however, to calling the world a mode of the divine activity (T, 203). At the same time he insisted that the world is not a part of God, contending that thought is mental activity, and not a mode of mind (T, 207).

[86] Brightman, POR, 216-218.

[87] Three more or less representative personalistic viewpoints appear to have emerged: (1) Charles Hartshorne, from the pan-psychistic perspective, distinguishes nature from God more than other personalists. For him, nature is the activity of myriads of cells, yet all the monads belong on the psychic side, to God, although nature as a whole is not a part of God. (2) For Bowne, Knudson and L. Harold DeWolf, the distinction between phenomenal nature and God is maintained because of the creative activity of the human mind. (3) Brightman's identification of nature as a part of God derives from his insistence that the self consists of the unity of consciousness, and that the divine activity manifested in nature is therefore part of the divine person. Whereas the second view refuses to identify nature is a part

in the refusal of numerous personalists to identify nature in this manner, to a large extent is the important value assigned by thinkers like Knudson[88] to the Kantian critique. Nature as known by man, it is emphasized, is a joint product both of God's activity and of the creative activity of the knowing human mind as it operates at the levels of perception, understanding and reason.[89] It is significant, however, that this distinction between nature and God, on this approach, grows out of epistemological considerations and not, as in the case of Strong, out of concessions apparently made to a semi-substantialist view of the physical universe. That nature is not a part of God does not imply, for these thinkers, that it involves any reality other than the divine activity and the human knower.

But the identification of nature as part of God, which conservative thinkers regarded as the consistent implication of ethical monism despite Strong's repudiation of the view, encouraged the hostility of evangelical thinkers.[90] They condemned it both as unbiblical and as justifying idolatry.[91] The theory's lack of Biblical support, Hovey wrote, "would not be altogether deadly since some truths are not found in Scripture, but at least true teaching must be consistent with Scripture." To the sacred writers, he contended, "the difference between God and nature is the difference between the Infinite and the finite, the original and the originated, the Creator and the created."[92] Hovey might have strengthened his case by contending that while the Scripture frequently assigns directly to God the activity which has customarily been referred to second causes,[93] nowhere is it affirmed that nature is God, or that any natural elements are a part of God. Yet all this, Strong doubtless would have conceded, despite a terminology which at times would seem to imply a pantheistic view of the physical

---

of God largely because the importance of human creativity in the knowledge situation, Brightman attributes human experience of color, etc., to the elements of the non-rational Given in God.

[88]The Biblical idea of creation, Knudson declared, "implies that the world is distinct from God. However dependent it may be upon him, it is not identical with him. The world is not itself God, nor is it his body, nor is it in any other sense a part of him. It is the product of his will, of his energizing; and as such it stands apart from him as his work, as his deed. . . . Creation implies the objectivity of the world, its otherness to God. . . . The material world is an effect of the divine activity. . . . It has an existence distinct from that of God so that it cannot in itself or in any of its parts properly be identified with him" (DOR, 27-28).

[89]L. Harold DeWolf follows Knudson in this insistence that nature is the appearance to human experience of a part of the activity of God, or that nature is a part of God's activity as that activity appears to man. DeWolf holds that nature is not to man what it is to God, i. e., what it is in and for itself, not only because of the peculiar forms of human experience (which Kant pointed out), but also because of the meanings derived from the interaction of that activity with our own emotional and volitional psychological "sets." On DeWolf's approach, sin and guilt are contributory factors in making nature as we know it what it is.

[90]That nature is a finite, graded manifestation of God, or a self-limitation of God, seemed flatly to contradict the affirmation that nature is other than God.

[91]Hovey, Art.(1894), 2, 11.

[92]Hovey, Art.(1894), 3, 12.

[93]Strong commended "Bishop Berkeley's noble words, 'God ceaseless conversation with his creatures'" as aptly descriptive of nature. "The Scriptures do not content themselves with past tenses," he pointed out. "The heavens declare the glory of God and the God of glory thundereth,—nature, in other words, is the manifestation of a present God" (CCEM, 187).

universe. And, it might have been asked, if the Biblical expressions assigning second causes to God are to be taken literally, why are not those passages assigning the acts of wicked men to God's foreordination to be explained in terms of efficient divine causation?[94] Hovey proceeded, instead, to emphasize "the excuse" which a monistic view of nature "might furnish for idolatry."[95] The first chapter of Romans sharply indicts the confusing of the creation with the Creator, and pronounces judgment upon the worship of the created universe and its parts as if divine. The effect of a monistic view, Hovey thought, would be to encourage the conclusion "that idolatry is a valid folly."[96]

But for many evangelicals the central issue was, as the younger Hodge put it, "whether, when God created the world, He created a something which was not part of Himself and which has some principle of relative persistence."[97] The doctrine of creation, therefore, served as the touchstone of the controversy. Lotze had already specified that the terminology of creation by God intends "not to designate a deed of his so much as the absolute dependence of the world upon his will in contradistinction to its involuntary emanation from his nature."[98] The main question was, did not the new view involve the retention of creation in a verbal sense only, merely as an accommodation to traditional ways of thought, whereas in fact the relationship of God and nature was now conceived in a quite different fashion?

It was not merely Strong's designation of all reality as "a self-limitation of God," and his suggestion that nature is a finite, graded manifestation of deity, which raised the question of his right to the terminology of creation, although this seemed already to preclude the possibility of any existent characterized by even relative independence.[99] Nor was the difficulty alone the newer emphasis on God as the divine ground of existence, rather than its cause in the sense stressed by the older statements of the cosmological argument, although this emphasis tended already to set aside the notion of a once-for-all divine creative act in the interest of a constant creative process.[100] The main difficulty was with the broad notion of the externaliza-

---

[94] Strong remarked in his treatment of permissive providence that "as the Hebrew writers saw in second causes the operation of the great first Cause . . . so, because even the acts of the wicked entered into God's plan, the Hebrew writers sometimes represented God as doing what he merely permitted finite spirits to do" (ST[1907], 424). Curiously, he added that in some of these instances, God's providence "may be directive as well as permissive," but he did not work out the possible implications of this for the problem of evil (ST[1907], 424).

[95] Hovey, Art.(1894), 1, 10.

[96] Hovey, Art.(1894), 1, 10. Hovey added: "A philosopher may perhaps entertain the opinion that God is the only substance, without peril to his Christian faith, but a common Christian will be in great danger of inferring from it that all finite beings and things are parts of deity or mere illusions. He will probably conclude that the universe is God. . . . It may certainly be doubted whether any monistic philosophy would have suggested to us the Christian idea of God" (10).

[97] C. W. Hodge, Rev.(1908), 338.

[98] Lotze, POR, 74.

[99] C. W. Hodge, Rev.(1908), 338.

[100] This was already to confuse the dependency of nature with creation, Hovey urged, for there is no reference to the origination of real being or substance (Hovey, SER, 24).

tion of the divine thought in such a manner as not to involve the origin of a new substance.[101] Strong wrote, of course, of a substantial character of the physical universe, but in contrast with realism, because he refused to equate being and activity.[102] But the precise reality of this being, involved in the externalization of the divine thought by an act of will, Strong did not elaborate. The distinction of nature as involving the indirect exercise of God's will because of the regularity of the divine activity, hardly shed light on the question, how the professed non-realist substantiality of nature, as involving something more than divine activity, was to fit in with a qualitative monism?

The problem may be best focussed by a brief reference to divine transcendence, the treatment of which it has seemed best to postpone until this point. Strong defined God's transcendence in terms of the incomplete manifestation of his nature which the universe affords. Nature is both dependent on him and not fully disclosive of him, for his habitual actions do not preclude miraculous acts.[103] True, nothing in the universe is not in God; everything in the universe, in its limited form, is a divine self-limitation.[104] But God's thoughts are not creative, for the divine self-manifestation requires an act of volition to secure externalization of the divine thought. God's thought, consequently, is not limited to the regular, nor irregular activities of the created universe. He has, if one may use the terminology of modern personalistic idealism, imaginative no less than creative thoughts, and the difference between the latter and the former is that the externalization of divine thought requires an act of volition. But now, surely God's imaginative thoughts cannot be conceived as being involuntary thoughts, for they too must be in a sense actively willed. Is there any distinction between a purely imaginative universe in the divine volition, and the divine thought volitionally "externalized," since the origination of real being or substance is ruled out on the monistic approach, except in terms of the duration of the divine idea? If all divine ideas are voluntary—the denial of which would seem to require the view of an involuntary[105] divine behavior—what essential difference can there be between voluntary imaginative ideas and other ideas, since both have the element of volition and idea, and reality is defined in terms of these two elements? The critics of Strong, while they appear not to have become explicit about this difficulty, which may have been the factor which drove Strong to halt mid-way in his discard of a substance philosophy, nevertheless insisted that

---

[101] The Biblical teaching regarding creation is more naturally understood of the origin of both substance and form, Hovey wrote, "than of the mere shaping and ordering of things in nature, or of any states in the divine spirit, however conscious and real" (Hovey, SER, 51).

[102] CCEM, 28.

[103] In view of Strong's modified statement of miracle, to be examined shortly, it will be seen that divine transcendence must be understood mainly in terms of the fact that nature is not an exhaustive divine manifestation.

[104] The transcendence of God, in traditional theology, specified that God's personal life exists absolutely independently of the universe, and is independent of space and time. Strong now referred to creation as the work "of the immanent rather than of the transcendent God" (ST[1907], 211).

[105] The word suggests, of course, the essential element in the view of divine emanation, in which the appearance of the universe is not referred to a voluntary divine act.

any view of creation which stopped short of the origination of new substance was artificially truncated.

If the "externalization" of divine thought involves the presence of something more than that same volition present also in divine imaginative activity, then already a world of nature as a relatively independent reality appears as a necessary conception; Strong had suggested that the distinction between God's habitual and miraculous activity permits viewing the former under the category of secondary causation. If the word "externalization" designates anything more than the divine making of the world of nature to appear to finite minds as objectively real,[106] there would seem to be no *a priori* objection to a dynamic concept of matter which involves some sort of creation not reducible to divine substance or activity. And why may not a certain relative independence or reality, it was asked, belong to matter as well as to mind—since Strong insisted on the relative freedom of finite spirits? If God can make an agent, declared Hovey, he can make an instrument.[107]

There were hints in Strong's final theology, in fact, in which the force of the latter type of argument appears to be circumvented by what may be interpreted as a movement on his part, doubtless unguardedly, in the pantheistic direction. For the creation of man is compared with the eternal divine begetting of the three personal distinctions in the Godhead. Although Strong carefully emphasized that the divine begetting is eternal and necessary, whereas creation is temporal and free,[108] he added that "Christ's creation of man may be like his own begetting by the Father,"[109] apparently intending to suggest that there is no division of the divine essence in the production of multitudinous finite personalities within the single divine essence. Consequently, as Strong insisted on finite selves with a relative independence, he opened the door to the possibility of matter which was not simply divine thought externalized, but externalized in such a way as to grant to matter a relative independence; as Strong minimized the outsidedness of finite selves, he veered toward the pantheism for which he professed such deep antipathy.

Since Strong's problems in the area of anthropology are to be treated later, it will be well at this point to concentrate attention on that second center of controversy raised by Strong's new view of the relation of God to nature, i.e., the problem of miracle. It will be recalled that in his final 1907 theology revision Strong retained side by side the older definition of miracle set forth in the earlier fifth edition, and a "preferable definition" reflective of the later monistic assumptions. The newer definition discards the reference to miracle as an event inexplicable in terms of the laws of

---

[106]Hovey led the way for the evangelical realists, affirming that it impeaches the veracity of God to suggest that he compels us by our mental constitution to look upon the unreal as real, for it represents him as producing illusions in the minds of men (Hovey, SER, 33-34).
[107]Hovey, SER, 27, 28.
[108]ST(1907), 373.
[109]ST(1907), 381.

nature[110] and substitutes an emphasis on natural causes,[111] since Christ is the immanent God whose constant will is manifested in nature.[112]

Evangelical theologians were quick to comment on the implications of the newer definition.[113] "Does the distinguishing mark of a miracle, then, lie simply in its purpose, or merely in the subjective conviction that God has wrought it?," inquired the younger Hodge.[114] He appealed to Strong's destruction of the distinction between the natural and the supernatural as "an explicit avowal that there is no warrant for distinguishing a miracle from any other event in the external world, so far as the question of its cause is concerned."[115] Such a view, Hodge affirmed, meant the loss of Christian supernaturalness. He wrote

This view, which is carried out would be fatal to evangelical Christianity, is simply the result of Dr. Strong's "Ethical Monism." It is more consistent with the Christianity of the New Testament writers than any other form of monism which breaks down the essential distinction between the Infinite and the finite.[116]

Others, like Behrends, attacked the assumption that the forces of nature are to be identified with divine will. Granting that nature cannot be identified with human willing, since the universe is given to man rather than willed by him, the fact is, Behrends insisted, that omnipotence of will is not a substitute for energy.[117] Energy of nature, Behrends countered, is either posited by a peculiar act of creative divine power, or is another name for that power itself which the divine will directs.[118] Such a view, it was felt, was not as destructive of the Biblical miraculous as that involved in monistic assumptions.

But liberal thinkers were no more satisfied with Strong's statement of miracle than were evangelicals. Brown protested that, while Strong evidenced by the new definition the effect of monism upon a scheme of doctrine originally forged under quite different presuppositions, he nonetheless retained traces of a discarded position, by retaining the older statement and labelling the new as "preferable."[119] But this was not so

---

[110]ST(1907), 118.
[111]ST(1907), 119. The thesis of "the supernatural natural and the natural supernatural" had found frequent expression in Bowne's writings.
[112]ST(1907), 123.
[113]Strong's " 'preliminary definition' is not so bad," Hodge commented (C. W. Hodge, Rev.[1908], 336-337).
[114]C. W. Hodge, Rev.(1908), 337.
[115]C. W. Hodge, Rev.(1908), 337.
[116]C. W. Hodge, Rev.(1908), 337. This absorption of nature to God, in Strong's thought, clearly encouraged the evangelists to suspect that ethical monism also involved the absorption of humanity to God, and focussed attention, as we shall see, upon passages which seemed to suggest it.
[117]Force and personal will are erroneously assumed to be convertible, Behrends held. Cases of human paralysis demonstrate that willing can be important apart from physical and moral agencies at human command. The will to force is not the same as force (Behrends, Art.[1895], 364).
[118]Behrends, Art.(1895), 364.
[119]"The extent of the distance traversed between this point of view and that which is marked by the earlier definition is apparent to all. The only question which suggests itself is why, since Professor Strong has so firmly planted himself upon the new ground, he should any longer retain in his text evidences of the discarded position" (Brown, Rev.[1908], 152).

serious as the midway position in which Strong seemed to lag, by affirming on the one hand that all nature is to be referred to immediate divine volition, while attempting on the other hand to distinguish between habitual and special volitions in such a way as to distinguish miraculous from other acts. This latter attempt involved curious tensions, for Strong insisted, with regard both to prophecy and miracle, that the two are but heightened expressions of what is everywhere latent, and yet sought to give them some unique reference in terms of supernatural activity. This was doubtless a factor in the suggestion that the terminology of secondary causation could be retained, provided the only distinction intended is that between regular and unusual divine volitions. But if the inconsistency in Strong's thought at this point was not evident to contemporary liberals, it could not escape more recent personalistic idealists. For it has been pointed out that, if the world of nature is but the externalized thought of God, this contrast between the habitual and the irregular can be maintained only at the expense of the divine omniscience, since it involves the divine mind in "after thoughts" not included in the original plan of the universe. If, to the contrary, it be insisted that the one eternal divine plane involved all acts, so that the divine mind embraces at once both habitual and unique acts—an element upon which Strong insisted in his formulation of the divine decrees—then the distinction between the two would seem to be removed in all but a verbal manner.[120] For, on Strong's monistic assumptions, the divine volition is no less[121] involved in the accomplishment of the so-called habitual activities, than in the non-habitual.

3. Anthropology

It has already been noted that the immediate reaction of evangelical theologians to Strong's view was a concern lest, by concessions to pantheism, he had blurred the reality of moral distinctions and made God the author of sin.

The changes which the new view involved for Strong's treatment of human origins are apparent. Wholly apart from the question of an evolutionary view of origins, touching which comment will be made shortly, it is clear that the new immanence had left its mark. One evidence of this is the new emphasis on human moral experience as affording a key to theological constructions, and especially with regard to the doctrine of a primal fall:

The long course of depravity and degradation that has been universal in human history points back to a fall of humanity, and this fall is no natural development, but rather a willful departure of the very first representatives of the race from God and from his law.[122]

The movement from Biblical authority to experience, in the reconstruction of man's initial moral predicament, could not stop with a joint insistence

---

[120] Bowne had insisted that "even when we come to the distinctly miraculous, we cannot suppose it to break with all law" (Bowne, IG, 88).
[121] Strong's distinction between the direct and indirect exercise of the divine will should be recalled, but the difficulty remains nonetheless.
[122] CCEM, 170.

on theistic evolution and man's original holiness, despite Strong's view.[123] For the new immanentism suggested more continuity of divine activity than was involved in such a view. Strong had, in fact, made concessions to this continuity at certain points. He declared that Christ is in all men as he was in Adam,[124] who fell by wilful resistance to the inworking God, in such a way as to suggest that the immanent Logos minimized the noetic effect of sin more than traditional theology would have countenanced. Strong's view that the original grace is more powerful than original sin might well raise the question whether man is after all, as he had contended, "dead in trespasses and sin." It was this emphasis on the immanent Christ as the source of all truth with a somewhat lessened stress on the negating influence of sin upon the thought and volition of man, which made it possible to find, outside the Hebrew-Christian tradition, positive anticipations of the Biblical revelation. But, for all this, Strong had applied the new principle hesitatingly, in the opinion of subsequent personalists.[125] For the acceptance of evolutionary origin meant, for subsequent monistic theology, that man did not fall from an original righteousness; man's moral conformity to God came to be viewed as a gradual acquirement, through a normal process of moral trial and error.[126] Since on this approach man's moral discontinuity with the divine does not involve a defection from original righteousness, so that the notion of the imputation of Adamic guilt to his posterity falls away, the effect of sin is no longer such as to require a special soteriological revelation, and more competence is assigned to human reason than on the traditional approach. It is not merely an accident, but in the interest of theological consistency within modern personalistic assumptions, that the disparity between general and special revelation is eliminated, except in terms of a higher degree of the same divine movement.

The intensified continuity involved in the monistic approach left its impression also on Strong's reformation of the doctrine of regeneration, although again in such a way that others who applied the approach more consistently felt compelled to go beyond his concessions. Strong had affirmed, it will be recalled, that the principles of evolution and immanence should be applied both to man's original creation and to his spiritual re-creation:

Both man's original creation and his new creation are creations from within, rather than from without. In both cases, God builds upon the basis of the old.[127]

Evolution reveals the divine method, he contended elsewhere, in grace as well as in nature.[128] At the same time, Strong retained the emphasis of

---

[123] It is noteworthy that contemporary neo-supernaturalism, as projected by Emil Brunner and Reinhold Niebuhr, rejects the conviction of the primal righteousness of man in the sense in which Strong retained it, and substitutes a symbolical for an historical view of the fall of Adam.
[124] ST(1907), 587.
[125] ST(1907), 552.
[126] The evolutionary view was held to give a better explanation than traditional theology of the development of man's moral nature, both individual and racial, by reference to a gradual growth of ethical ideas and the mutual significance of the inner sense of ought arising from man's social conditions and necessities.
[127] ST(1907), 472.
[128] CCEM, 77. Bowne too had contended, practically from his college days when

traditional theology upon a supernatural regeneration of the elect, by a divine act, whereby the natural tendency of enmity toward God in view of Adamic corruption, is reversed in the interest of a bent towards divine holiness. Now, from the standpoint of monistic theology, it was this emphasis on a divine reversal—upon a "crucifixion" of the natural man and the sudden, radical "birth" of a new man—which had to be set aside in the interest of a theology within which perfection was presumed to be attained by the slow, gradual improvement of the "old nature." And evangelical theologians had seen, what apparently Strong had not, that a consistent appeal to evolution and monism could not escape a rejection of the supernaturalistic interpretation of regeneration to be found in Biblical theology.[129]

But, when all this is said, the prime difficulty which evangelical theologians found with Strong's anthropology was an uneasiness that, for all his insistence on man's moral freedom, the dangers of pantheism where not averted. This problem was not as acutely felt by non-evangelical thinkers, who assumed man's moral continuity with the divine, and did not retain the Biblical view of man as a sinner by nature, although they, no less than the evangelicals, were concerned that the significance of moral freedom not be destroyed.

It will be recalled that, while Strong insisted on man's moral freedom, he yet declared that there might be multitudinous finite consciousnesses, just as there are three infinite consciousnesses, within the bounds of the one universal and divine consciousness.[130] Strong therefore did not appropriate every opportunity, as later personalistic idealists do, to stress that selves are not parts of God, but are outside of God, although this appears to have been his intention. Evangelical scholars like the younger Hodge protested that once humanity, as well as the physical universe, is regarded as "a self-limitation of God," there is no room for a doctrine of creation.[131] Strong had emphasized, of course, that humanity is a divine self-limitation "under the law of freedom," but other factors encouraged evangelicals to fear that pantheism was evaded in word only. Hovey replied that although "the divine life circumscribed and acting as finite spirits is free," yet this at the same time, "brings strife and sin into the life of God."[132] Strong intends to safeguard freedom of the will and human responsibility, Hovey added, but "the logical tendency of monism is to deny human responsibility by referring it to God, the only real being."[133] Behrends sought to show that Strong's view yielded to this tendency, despite his contrary profession. His first argument was that the freedom of finite spirits

---

Darwin's books had already been in circulation for almost a decade, that if we know the Cause behind evolution, the method is harmless (McConnell, BPB, 26, 182).

[129]John Roach Straton, in his article on "Evolution" contributed to *International Standard Bible Encyclopedia* wrote that "it is inconceivable that there should come about in Ev. by 'resident forces' and 'fixed laws' an automatic reversal of process which changes the whole nature of the one in whom it occurs."

[130]ST(1907), 332.

[131]C. W. Hodge, Rev.(1908), 337.

[132]Hovey, Art.(1894), 2, 10. "This may be the coming philosophy," Hovey added, "but we submit that it does not exalt or clarify one's conception of God, nor does it help one to solve the problem of sin" (10).

[133]Hovey, Art.(1894), 2, 10.

is known only in consciousness, but "ethical monism discredits consciousness in its interpretation of nature" on non-realist lines.[134] The monists, of course, replied that no non-mental world is given in experience. Behrends contended, further, that if the all-embracing consciousness of God integrates finite consciousnesses as Strong insisted, human freedom is lost, for self-consciousness is "separateness in consciousness, which refuses to be eliminated or sublimated."[135] The monists here replied that, apart from man's implication in a transcendental rational and moral God, all meaning evaporates from human experience. Behrends pointed out also that, on the monistic approach, the aches and pains of suffering human bodies are converted into the divine habits of thought,[136] and that to regard finite spirits as "circumscriptions of the divine essence" includes Satan no less than mankind among the divine self-limitation.[137] It has already been noted that the problem involved in the former point has encouraged, in part, a modern personalistic movement toward the doctrine of a finite god. The latter point was not distressing to monistic thought in so far as it insisted, along with Strong, upon a psychological dualism or quantitative pluralism; the moral freedom allowable to finite spirits outside of God represented various grades of depravity. It is quite clear, from this discussion, that evangelical theologians feared, rather than demonstrated, a pantheistic anthropology on Strong's part; they were prone to share Behrend's view that, once metaphysical oneness of substance is granted, the resultant monism "can be called ethical only by courtesy."[138] But it was the logic of enthusiasm, rather than of demonstration, which here prevailed.[139] One circumstance, however, is clear. Subsequent personalistic thought, which left no doubt about the separate personality of finite selves as outside of God, at the same time freed humanity theologically from guilt, depravity and penalty of sin which traditional theology had assigned him, and to which Strong's view clung.[140] But if the case against Strong was not clear-cut in the area of anthropology, because the pantheizing statements must be viewed as concessions within a deeper pluralistic intent, the evangelical theologians were confident that, in the areas of Chistology and soteriology, Strong had so compromised traditional doctrine as to leave no doubt of his destruction of the central tenets of Christianity.

---

[134]Behrends, Art.(1894), 366. Behrends added: "There is no better evidence that man is free than that fishes and birds are second causes" (366).
[135]Behrends, Art.(1894), 367.
[136]Behrends, Art.(1894), 366.
[137]Behrends, Art.(1894), 366.
[138]Behrends, Art.(1894), 370.
[139]But Strong had clearly used language which personalistic idealists would resist. When he wrote of Christ "the whole race lives, moves, and has its being in him; for he is the soul of its soul and the life of its life" (CCEM, 288), Strong hardly reflected the emphatic and thorough-going pluralism which Bowne and Brightman combine with qualitative monism. Strong's intentions, however, were clearly in the pluralistic direction, despite the occasional use of language in a manner which suggests absolute idealism.
[140]The nature of the divine-human encounter is one of the central issues of contemporary theology. Strong, despite his firm intention to put selves outside of God, made some serious concessions to the pantheistic mood of Bosanquet, Bradley, Pringle-Pattison, Royce and Hocking, and halted short of the radical pluralism of Bowne, Knudson and Brightman. But the contemporary personalists, in their placing of selves outside of God, at the same time substitute an autonomous ethic

4. Christology

The central problems with reference to Christology, on Strong's later assumptions, may be divided into those concerning the pre-incarnate Logos and the God-man. It may be well to treat these in reverse order.

That Strong sought an explanation for the virgin birth along the lines of parthenogenesis has already been indicated.[141] Since on the monistic approach the distinction between the natural and the supernatural was eliminated, it was necessary that he abandon the view that the virgin birth is significant because the event is an impossibility within nature as constituted, apart from special divine activity; all nature, on the monistic view, involves such immediate activity. Even more significant was the suggestion that Christ fully manifested all the powers and qualities partially embodied in man and nature, which indicates a distinction mainly in terms of a higher degree of a lesser and universal divine manifestation, and is more compatible with a contrast of the whole and the part, than with that of Creator and creature. Christ's veiled deity has analogies, Strong held, in the unappropriate resources of human life generally. But not alone on the side of Christ's humanity, but on that of his deity also, Strong tended to narrow the disparity from ideal mankind. In the incarnation, he affirmed, "the Godhead narrows itself down to a point that is next to absolute extinction."[142] This was developed by the affirmation that Christ was not omniscient, neither as a babe nor later. Yet Strong guarded against the view that Christ erred. Whatever historical and scientific errors are conceded in the Bible, he stressed, "we can never admit that there are imperfections in Christ."[143] At the same time, he conceded that God had adopted human and imperfect methods of self-revelation not only in creation and Scripture, but also in the disclosure in Christ.[144]

While formally accepting the Chalcedonian Christology, Strong leaned actually to a modified kenosis theory.[145] Some evangelical theologians were quick to see that, in this circumstance, the monistic presuppositions were active, especially in Strong's affirmation that Christ had but one will, con-

---

for the traditional theonomous ethic, and take a less serious view of sin. The neo-supernaturalists generally affirm a theonomous morality, but treat the fall of man as symbolic rather than literal history.

[141]Bowne accepted the virgin birth on aesthetic grounds, but not as a fundamental doctrine, in contrast with his attitude toward the person of Christ and the incarnation. But "nothing whatever of importance depends on it," he wrote (Bowne, SIC, 386). The controversy has generally assumed the "undivineness of the natural" now "ruled out by the doctrine of the divine immanence in all natural processess," he explained (SIC, 386-387).

[142]ST(1907), 703. Strong commented that "omniscience gives up all knowledge but that of the child, the infant, the embryo, the infinitesimal germ of humanity. Omnipotence gives up all power but that of the impregnated ovum in the womb of the Virgin."

[143]CCEM, 134.

[144]ST(1907), 219.

[145]Bowne too accepted kenosis Christology and spoke of the "depotentiation" of the Son of God (McConnell, BPB, 183). The Chalcedonian formula, he protested, "goes beyond both Scripture and reason" (Bowne, SIC, 92). But R. T. Flewelling has rightly remarked that the Christological interest remained an important part of Bowne's system (Flewelling, PPP, 157).

sciousness, and knowledge,[146] as against the doctrine of two consciousnesses and of two wills, which Strong designated as an unwarranted addition to the Chalcedonian doctrine. The younger Hodge asked:

What meaning, then, can attach to the bare assertion that there were two natures in Christ? Was the one will omnipotent? If so what becomes of the reality and completeness of the human nature? Or was the one will finite and limited? If so what becomes of the divine nature?[147]

There was no question, Hodge added, that for all Strong's effort to distinguish his view from the kenotic theory, Strong had yielded it to nonetheless.[148] With a kenotic Christology, consistent liberal thinkers were as dissatisfied in their own way as the evangelicals; it seemed to compromise the integrity of Christ's humanity, in which they were interested, no less than that of Christ's deity, on which the evangelicals placed stress. That Strong's position was a temporary[149] expedient has been made plain by subsequent tendencies in Christological thought, in which the abandonment of Chalcedonian Christology has issued in a humanitarian view of Christ. For Strong, that transition did not appear necessary and, indeed, it is evident that, had it appeared to be so, he would have moved in the direction of the traditional, rather than of the modern, theology. For in the preface to his final theology revision, it will be recalled, he singled out as the test of orthodoxy one's reply to the question: "do we pray to Jesus?" For evangelical theologians, the question seemed to take on its traditional significance only if, contrary to Strong's view of a Godhead narrowed in Jesus to a point bordering on absolute extinction, one insisting instead that "in Him dwelleth all the fulness of the Godhead bodily."[150]

If, however, Strong's treatment of the incarnation did not satisfy either evangelicals or liberals, his discussion of the relationship of the pre-incarnate Logos to humanity seemed to the theological conservatives to destroy the very foundations of a Biblical view, whether by implicating the eternal Christ in sin, or by making the atonement a matter of necessity rather than of grace.

It may be remembered that Strong felt the monistic doctrine of Christ's natural union with the race to be the only satisfactory reply to the criticism that Christ's atonement for man's sin is external, arbitrary and mechanical, since it assigned him penalty without guilt of any kind.[151] Imputation

---

[146]In this emphasis, curiously, the kenosis theologians and those who held to a strictly human Jesus linked hands.
[147]C. W. Hodge, Rev.(1908), 338-339.
[148]C. W. Hodge, Rev.(1908), 339.
[149]John Stewart Lawton has singled out Strong's view that Christ's consciousness and will are always theanthropic, and never simply either human or divine, as "a ready stop-gap in the face of the new psychology" (*Conflict in Christology*, 262. London: Society For Promoting Christian Knowledge, 1947).
[150]Colossians 2:9. Curiously, in answering the complaint that Strong's view makes any "true doctrine of atonement impossible by regarding Christ as no more divine than any other of the scores of men," Strong replied by quoting this verse and commenting that "Christ is not distinguished from men in Scripture by being a different substance from humanity, but rather by having that substance in its completeness and perfection" (CCEM, 83).
[151]"The atonement of Christ seems foolishness to the so-called philosopher," Strong wrote, "only because he regards it is an external, arbitrary, mechanical transfer of guilt and penalty. Guilt and penalty, he says, are individual and personal, and can-

involves that which truly and properly belongs to an individual in view of guilt, Strong wrote.[152] This principle is applied to the imputation of racial guilt to Christ, and of Adamic guilt to the race. His adoption of the view of "realism," that the race was in Adam *realiter* and consequently sinned in him, he regarded as more satisfactory than the view of Adam's federal headship, which made Adam's sin that of the race by the representative principle.[153] Since evangelicals have themselves divided over the question of natural or federal headship, and the issues with which this study is concerned are of a broader nature, this controversy need is not detailed.[154] Spokesmen for the representative theory replied that, on their view, Adam was designated the federal head of the race because he was its natural head, and not arbitrarily. But the more central issue was whether Strong's assignment of guilt to Christ did not either involve God in sin or destroy the reality of sin for man.

Strong denied, it is true, that the pre-incarnate Christ was involved in personal impurity; the age-long sufferings which he bore are a curse, in his case, just because he suffered penalty as one personally pure.[155] But Christ is guilty because he so shared man's life that he "justly and inevitably" was exposed to "condemnation on account of human sin."[156] Humanity's rejection of God falls on Christ, who must suffer because his life is the inmost principle of man's being.[157] To this assumption, that Christ must share man's guilt and penalty because he gave life to mankind and sustains humanity in being, the evangelical theologians made prompt reply. On the one hand, to identify the life of humanity so closely with that of Christ would seem to destroy the very independence of finite persons for which Strong had argued, in differentiating his view from pantheism. "It is impossible that he who is the natural life of humanity should not be responsible for the sin committed by his own members," Strong wrote. "It is impossible that he should not suffer, that he should not make reparation, that he should not atone."[158] To these assertions, Jesse B. Thomas responded that if Christ's

---

not be thus transferred. There is no justice, he says, in punishing one for the sins of another, and especially in punishing the innocent for the sins of the guilty" (CCEM, 178).

[152] ST(1907), 596-621.

[153] Evangelicals who held the theory of natural headship dissented from Strong's formulation. Strong's reconstruction of the Augustinian position, Behrends wrote, "is enough to make even the Bishop of Hippo turn over in his grave" (Behrends, Art[1895], 368).

[154] The Princeton theologians replied that "the 'realistic' view, besides resulting in a well-nigh exploded metaphysics and one that would have a destructive influence on other Christian doctrines, seeks a ground for the personal responsibility of each individual, in regard to Adam's sin, in an act that was totally unconscious and involuntary so far as each is concerned. This appears to us far more arbitrary than the principle of representative responsibility" (C. W. Hodge, Rev.[1908], 338).

[155] CCEM, 179.

[156] ST(1907), 752-754.

[157] CCEM, 200.

[158] CCEM, 87.

"members" be a part of himself, this would imply Christ's personal sharing in sin, personal obligation to make reparation, and why not also, personal repentance on behalf of all?[159]

Hovey was even more direct:

> The monistic assumption subordinates all men so completely to Christ, that it is impossible to hold them guilty, if He is holy. This, however, is only a statement of the way it looks to one man.[160]

On the other hand, the union of Christ with humanity as Strong stated it, if it did not destroy the reality of sin on man's part, seemed at the same time to involve Christ personally in sin, whatever effort Strong made to avoid that conclusion. Patton had already warned against the danger of such an implication in Strong's system before the latter's espousal of ethical monism, when reviewing the 1886 theology. There the union of Christ with the race which was in view centered in the incarnation, rather than in a monistic creation, but Strong insisted that guilt was imparted as well as imputed to Christ, although he was supernaturally preserved from corruption. This was, it will be recalled, the earlier effort which Strong made to meet the objection that the innocent mechanically suffers for the guilty. But by holding that guilt was imparted as well as imputed to Christ, although he was personally pure, Strong seemed to raise the same issue which followed from the later monistic union which presumably implicated him in the same way. Patton replied that to make Christ not innocent raises

> a far greater and more serious objection . . . not relieved by saying that Christ was free from depravity by reason of his miraculous conception.[161]

Since Christ was obligated to suffer by becoming a member of Adam's race, Patton added in protest, this view

> makes a sinner the world's Saviour, destroys the voluntary character of Christ's atonement, and puts Christ in the position of the Jewish high-priest, who needed to atone first for his own sin and then for that of his people.[162]

When Strong later grounded Christ's guilt and obligation to suffer in the pre-incarnate creative union with mankind, he did not discard this insistence that in his incarnation Jesus assumed human nature which was in Adam *realiter* and had thus been corrupted, but supernatural purification so removed depravity that he bore only guilt, and that not for any personal sin.[163] For now, by this dual reference, Christ owed the penalty of death twofold on His own account, by virtue of his pre-incarnate relationship to humanity, and of subsequent Adamic guilt. And the reference to monism furnished an undergirding for the insistence that responsibility can attach only to a sin in the origination of which once has participated.[164] But the

---

[159]Thomas, Art.(1900), 11.
[160]Hovey, Art.(1894), 2, 11.
[161]Patton, Rev.(1887), 367.
[162]Patton, Rev.(1887), 367.
[163]Although Strong called this a combination of the ideas of "substitution" and of "sharing," C. W. Hodge noted rightly that "Jesus had, then, by a participation in the 'realistic' sense, the guilt of Adam's sin which attached to humanity. In a word, sin was not imputed to Him, but He had just as much of the race sin as He was not relieved of" (C. W. Hodge, Rev.[1908], 339).

twofold reference seemed to evangelical theologians to intensify, rather than to relieve, the difficulties, for it seemed to involve Christ the more securely in personal guilt. The younger Hodge stated the problem clearly:

> Here, then, is a dilemma, viz.—if Christ can be said to have "had a part" in the origination of our sins, by reason of his connection with humanity, then, He would be responsible, according to the logic of Dr. Strong's view, just in the sense in which He is held by Dr. Strong to be responsible for Adam's sin. Hence, Christ would owe the penalty of death on His own account for our sins, and, hence, could not be our substitute. On the other hand, if Christ had no part in the origination of these sins of ours, then, according to Dr. Strong's theory of responsibility, Christ would have no actual responsibility for our actual sins, in which case it is, to say the least, a fair question whether the representative relationship on the basis of the Covenant is not a more adequate basis for the imputation of our sins to Christ. . . . Indeed, the logic of Dr. Strong's view demands a responsibility of our Lord *on His own account* for all human sin, as Dr. Strong acknowledges. . . . But if this is so, how can Christ be said to bear our sins as our substitute?[165]

Strong had thus, to the mind of many evangelical theologians, replaced the Biblical view of a gracious atonement with that of a necessitated atonement—necessitated indeed not alone because of a more intimate creative union of Christ and humanity which seemed to verge toward pantheism, but because of a supposed guilt on Christ's part which, it seemed to them, could not escape compromising the personal purity of the pre-incarnate Logos.

For later personalistic idealism, which had broken with the notion of a primal fall from righteousness in which all humanity was implicated, and also with any appeal to an *a priori* Biblical authority, the tensions existing in Strong's formulation were to be met by several modifications of the traditional theology. For one thing, the identification of the immanent Logos with the historical Jesus was now maintained on the narrower pattern of Sabellianism, and its exclusiveness was found in a greater intimacy of the union of divine and human, held to be of such degree as to be the practical equivalent of a difference in kind. The whole Biblical scheme of imputation and atonement was abandoned; in view of the emphasis on the dignity and worth of human personality, it was assumed that the transfer of another's penalty or merit is immoral. The historical Jesus was regarded as the supreme divine revelation of spiritual and moral achievement, to whom a relative absoluteness must be assigned in terms of religious example. But any metaphysical sonship, as distinguished from the remainder of humanity, was denied. In him, more than in any other, the universal disclosure of divine ideals appeared in such a way that he may be singled out as the supreme revelation of God but, insisted subsequent personalism, such metaphysical formulations as the doctrine of the Trinity, or of Christ's pre-existence, are to be given only a symbolic significance. In this spirit Knudson proposed that the meaning of incarnation be broadened "so as to make it practically synonymous with the divine immanence," on

---

[164]ST(1907), 510.

[165]C. W. Hodge, Rev.(1908), 340. This was clearly a leading question. If before Christ can properly bear all race sin he must be personally involved in race sin, then must it not be maintained that before he can personally bear all personal sin he must likewise be personally involved?

which interpretation the highest degree of immanence would be designated to Jesus.[166]

5. Soteriology

The treatment of Christological tensions in Strong's final view touched quite inescapably upon certain phases of soteriology also. But central considerations in this sphere remain to be evaluated.

It has already been inquired, in the section on Christology, whether Christ if guilty could provide atonement and whether, if obligated to do so, the atonement can be regarded still as a gracious divine provision. It might here be added that evangelical theologians insisted that the distinction between guilt and corruption, on which Strong insisted, cannot be maintained.[167] Unless the penalty were endured by a person not already indebted to justice, the concept of atonement is inapplicable, it was held.[168] The atonement was, on Christ's part, convenantally and not essentially necessary, in terms of his relationship to humanity. Strong's reformulation seemed to evangelical scholars to jeopardize an atonement, the divine mercy, the sinlessness of Christ, and the seriousness of sin on man's part.

The tensions were complicated by the fact that, on Strong's approach, Christ's atonement was in a sense self-justifying. Through the retroactive efficiency of the atonement, Strong held, Christ's human nature was purged of its depravity from the moment of incarnation, and was delivered also from the race guilt in which he was involved.[169] To evangelical thinkers this seemed to involve an inescapable circularity, for they insisted that if Christ were genuinely guilty in any sense, he could not atone; and if he provided atonement, he could not have been under guilt.

But at another major point, that of the supposed eternal suffering of Christ, the question of the destruction of Biblical theology seemed to be involved. Evangelical thinkers saw in Strong's affirmation that the historical death was but a paedagogical manifestation of a supra-historical suffering, a sacrifice of the doctrine of a once-for-all atonement.[170] They insisted that the divine compassion for lost man antedates the fall, in terms of the eternal plan of God, but that the compassion must not be confused with a vicarious suffering on account of sin. They found in Scripture no evidence of any divine displeasure with Christ, whether at the fall of primal man or at his incarnation, with the lone exception of the historical passion. Whatever sufferings were ascribed to Christ, on Strong's approach, could not be described as vicarious, in the Biblical sense.[171] The evangelicals insisted

---

[166]Knudson, DOR, 331, 332.
[167]Shedd insisted that Christ's relationship to humanity involved him neither in personal guilt nor pollution (*Dogmatic Theology*, II, 59, 82).
[168]Shedd *Dogmatic Theology*, II, 457, 462.
[169]ST(1896), 416.
[170]Cf. Hebrews 9:25-28.
[171]Despite his insistence on substitutionary atonement as primary, Strong had affirmed that all sufferings are penal, because due to sin, but that in Christ's case the sufferings become a substitutionary atonement because he was personally pure (CCEM, 179). Here Strong apparently overlooked the customary insistence, that the substitutionary element results from the fact that Christ's sufferings alone propitiate a divine principle of holiness and justice.

that, while Calvary is a concrete presentation of the eternal fact that holiness must punish sin, the atonement—in any Biblical meaning—can hardly be regarded on that account as eternal. Strong's readiness to speak of the present suffering of Christ for sin, so that while the historical suffering is ended the supra-historical suffering will continue until sin no longer exists,[172] seemed to evangelical theologians to evacuate the historical passion of all final significance.

Two further difficulties would seem to suggest themselves here. If what God does at any one time, as disclosive of his character, must be done always, the question arises whether an eternal rather than temporal creation need not be affirmed, on Strong's approach. Again, if it is of the essence of the Divine Spirit to manifest himself, must not the concept of special, historical revelation give way entirely to the priority of general, universal revelation? A second difficulty concerns also this contrast of temporality and eternity, applied in another way. Strong vacillates in his references to Christ's sufferings, speaking of them at times as eternal, and again as age-long, with the suggestion in the latter case that they date from the creation of or the primal fall of man.[173] But if Christ suffered not eternally, but only from the time of man's fall, is not the tension between the historical and the supra-historical merely retained in another manner—for it his sufferings are not eternal, do not all the tensions remain which Strong had urged, on his approach, against the traditional view of a merely historical suffering on Calvary?

In striving with these inner difficulties of his view, Strong appeared not to sense, what was apparent to later exponents of a monistic theology. "The modern doctrine of the divine immanence," Knudson wrote, "does not furnish a favorable background for the idea of mediation."[174] In that spirit, subsequent personalism cut the ties to the Biblical view of a once-for-all propitiatory atonement. Strong thought that the emphasis on substitution and sharing could be retained mutually, in his newer statement of the doctrine, but in subsequent theology influenced by monistic immanence, the emphasis on redemption by incorporation displaced that on redemption by meditation.

6. *Eschatology*

Especially at one point in Strong's eschatology—and the supremely important one—did ethical monism appear to have implications other than those which he associated with his newer views. That is the doctrine of the future destiny of all mankind.

Strong, it will be recalled, insisted unreservedly on the eternal punishment of the impenitent, and denied the possibility of a second probation. But

---

[172]CCEM, 80-82.
[173]Strong had replied to the charge that this view "makes Christ's atonement compulsory" that it "only puts Christ's original act of free surrender farther back and makes the sacrifice contemporaneous with creation (CCEM, 79) but this distinction seemed again to destroy the moral necessity for atonement on which he also insisted.
[174]Knudson, DOR, 378-379. Bowne had shown the way here also, by coupling his belief in redemption with vigorous criticism of the doctrine of substitutionary atonement or penal satisfaction (McConnell, BPB, 198-199). His detailed treatment appeared in SIC, 115-183.

there was an element in his theology, as shaped by ethical monism, which seemed to demand, instead, a doctrine of universal restoration.

For if Christ, as the life of humanity, was so implicated in human sinfulness that it was necessary for him to provide atonement, does not the necessity for the application of the atonement also follow? If the sinfulness of man is so rooted in Christ, as humanity's life, that he sustains a natural race guilt, is not the obligation on his part, assuming Strong's systematization, not merely that of providing a conditional atonement, but rather one of applying that atonement to all finite creatures, whether angelic or human, whom Christ sustains? It is true that Strong held that no man is finally condemned on account of race guilt, but that Christ's sacrifice atoned for racial sin; it is for their personal rejection of Christ, in which the will consents to Adamic revolt, and the refusal to appropriate the redemption from personal guilt available in Christ, for which men are punished. But is not Christ the life of humanity also, in regard to post-Adamic sin, no less than in regard to Adamic sin? If his union with the race in the one instance is such that he is obligated to provide atonement, does this not require at the same time a universal extension of the principle? Was it possible for Strong, on his own premises, to defend eternal punishment of the wicked against the doctrine of universal restoration? Behrends thought not, and, in expressing his views, furnished at the same time an anticipation of the direction in which liberal personalism was destined to move once the new immanence was applied more thoroughly than in Strong's approach, by the elimination of any necessity for substitutionary atonement at all, because of a prior elimination of any principle in the divine nature which requires propitiation. When this step was taken in subsequent personalistic thought, the new immanence had worked itself around to the denial of what Strong had insisted upon most vigorously in his 1907 preface, that the divine holiness is not merely a form of the divine love. But Strong had introduced tensions unrelievable within a monistic structure into his defense of an alternative view. It was with prophetic insight that Behrends asked, how can

universal restoration be logically evaded, though Dr. Strong declines to push his Christology to this extreme? But others will do it even if he does not.[175]

For subsequent personalism was united in its rejection of the doctrine of eternal punishment, though it divided over the doctrine of a conditional immortality[176] and the notion of universal restoration.[177] The abandonment of eternal punishment derived from the assignment of a greater value to human personality in its present state, assumed to be morally continuous with God, than that assigned by traditional theology, which made divine creation and redemption of man as sinner the joint determinants of value.

---

[175]Behrends, Art.(1895), 369.
[176]Knudson seems open to this alternative (DOR, 469), which Brightman also avows.
[177]Bowne rejected conditional immortality, contending that personal immortality provides a necessary opportunity for the expansion of human life (McConnell, BPB, 221) and, in the same tradition, L. Harold DeWolf rejects conditional immortality, contending, among other arguments, that every human soul is intrinsically valuable (cf. article on "Immortality, conditional" in *An Encyclopedia of Religion* [Vergilius Ferm, editor], 362-363 [New York: The Philosophical Library, 1945]).

CONCLUSIONS

This dissertation is an attempt to determine the influence of personalistic idealism upon the theology of Augustus Hopkins Strong, who became through his teaching, writing and speaking ministries the most influential theologian of the Northern Baptists.

The dissertation seeks to answer three questions: (1) to what extent were Strong's convictions colored by the growing monistic philosophy of intensified divine immanence? (2) what were the interactions and processes, so far as they are discoverable, by which this transition was encouraged and facilitated? (3) was the final formulation of Strong's theology, which took the form of "ethical monism," of such a nature by virtue of organic consistency that it afforded a coherent system secure against the possibility of necessary modification?

The observations which have hitherto been made on these three points have been of the general, somewhat disconnected nature of reviews of Strong's works, or brief articles or series inquiring into his theology; to the author's knowledge, no detailed, systematic study has been made of Strong's views across the years, in an effort to provide a definitive study pertaining to the questions stated above. The more thorough study has been discouraged in some measure, doubtless, by the unsystematic integration of Strong's later personalistic views into his earlier evangelical theology without a thorough revision of the earlier system, but rather by way of absorption, modification, and limited revision. The fact that Strong's final revised theology continued to be used for decades, and is used to this day, in some of the conservative Baptist divinity schools, with an emphasis on his evangelical commitments and the elimination of the "monistic concessions" indicates the absence of an actual maturation to the implications of the new view to which Strong professed loyalties. The originality of this study, then, is to be found in its effort to suggest the rather obscure influences which operated upon him directly; to specify in a thorough manner the precise element of change which entered his theological views under personalistic influences; and to evaluate in an extended manner the internal self-consistency of the final statement of Strong's beliefs. The bibliography will indicate the volumes which were useful in the fulfillment of this endeavor.

The author's conclusions are as follows:

(1) Although Strong tended to state his revisions in the interest of ethical monism as acceptable modifications of a basic evangelical framework, he had in fact subscribed to a new theory of religious knowledge which, by its emphasis on inner rather than external authority, would have involved him, if consistently applied, in theological changes far beyond his expressed intentions.

(2) Strong's partial application of this principle was such that his revised theology was not fully acceptable to either conservatives or liberals; not to the former, because of the concessions to the latter; not to the latter, because of concessions of the former.

(3) The influences which Strong suggests as encouraging his adoption of an intensified divine immanence include Ezekiel G. Robinson, his

former teacher; Hermann Lotze, and his leading American interpreter in Strong's day, Borden P. Bowne. This study casts doubt on any substantial influence from Robinson in this direction. The precise manner in which Strong effectively came in touch with Lotze's views remains undiscerned; even a son of the Rochester theologian, who studied theology in his father's classroom, stated that the father concentrated on the results, rather than on the processes, of his thinking. There is nothing to indicate that Strong's trip to Germany, coming as it did in his earlier years, was an important factor in this connection. The evidence points rather to the American exponents of Lotze who were active in the 1890's, and from Strong's frequent quotation and expressed appreciation of Bowne's writings especially, it would appear that Bowne, if not the central influence, was at least one of the major contributors, directly or indirectly, to Strong's adoption of the philosophy of immanence.

(4) Strong's "ethical monism" had a vital element of discontinuity, as well as of continuity, with the Lotze-Bowne tradition. Although Strong's expressed intentions mark him as an exponent of qualitative monism and quantitative pluralism, the pluralistic element in his system is compromised by expressions which the radical pluralism of contemporary personalistic idealists, and Bowne before them, would not have tolerated. Strong's intentions, however, are clear, both from his express statements, and from the serious view of sin and the need of divine redemption which is a central factor in his system. But, contrasted with the compromise of the pluralistic element in Strong's theology, the tradition of personalistic idealism places a superior emphasis on divine transcendence in God's relationship to human selves. If Strong's qualitative pluralism appears at times to have been obscured, the same may be said of his quantitative monism, in view of his refusal to break entirely with a substance philosophy.

(5) Although the Biblical and Christological interest was peculiarly central in Bowne, his system involved a more fundamental shift from revelational theism than did Strong's and the tendency of contemporary personalistic idealism has been to move still further than Strong from the traditional Protestant theology, in the interest of a more consistent application of the emphasis on the heightened divine immanence to which Strong subscribed.

(6) Strong himself, in view of his insistence on the doctrine of the Trinity, the deity of Christ, substitutionary atonement and supernatural regeneration, as involved in the very warp and woof of Biblical Christianity, would probably have chosen evangelical Christianity rather than contemporary personalism, if he had felt the options were thus limited.

(7) Strong's revision of traditional doctrines, in the interest of metaphysical monism, discloses a halfness and hesitancy, because of his conviction that the old and the new could be retained as two phases of a deeper truth, without the necessity for absorbing one in terms of the other. This is illustrated by his appropriation of the notions both of substitution and of sharing with regard to the atonement; again, in his hesitation to break completely with a substance philosophy; further, by the derivation of the necessity of atonement, but not of its application, from his view of Christ's union with the race.

BIBLIOGRAPHY

ADAMS, GEORGE P., and WILLIAM PEPPERELL MONTAGUE.—CAP
Contemporary American Philosophy (2 vols.).
New York: The Macmillan Company, 1930.

ANONYMOUS.—Rev. (1901) of Strong, CCEM
The Presbyterian and Reformed Review, XII (1901), 325-326.

BEHRENDS, A. J.—Art. (1895)
"Ethical Monism."
The Methodist Review, LXXVII (1895), 357-369.

BOWNE, BORDEN PARKER.—PHS
The Philosophy of Herbert Spencer.
New York: The Methodist Book Concern, 1874.

———————SIT
Studies in Theism.
New York: The Methodist Book Concern, 1879.

———————MSFP
Metaphysics: A Study in First Principles.
New York: Harper & Bros., 1882.

———————POT
The Philosophy of Theism.
New York: Harper & Bros., 1887.

———————POE
The Principles of Ethics.
New York: Harper & Bros., 1892.

———————TTK
The Theory of Thought and Knowledge.
New York: Harper & Bros:. 1897.

———————M
Metaphysics.
New York: Harper & Bros., 1898.

———————T
Theism.
New York: The American Book Company, 1902.

———————IG
The Immanence of God.
New York: Houghton, Mifflin Company, 1905.

———————SIC
Studies in Christianity.
New York: Houghton, Mifflin Company, 1909.

BRIGHTMAN, EDGAR SHEFFIELD.—POR
A Philosophy of Religion.
New York: Prentice-Hall, Inc., 1940.

BROWN, WILLIAM ADAMS.—Art. (1897)
"Recent Tendencies in Theological Thought."
The American Journal of Theology, I (1897), 118-136.

———————Art. (1908)
"Recent Treatises on Systematic Theology."
The American Journal of Theology, XII (1908), 150-155.

CALKINS, MARY WHITON.—PPP
The Persistent Problems of Philosophy.
New York: The Macmillan Company, 1936.

FLEWELLING, RALPH TYLER.—PPP
Personalism and the Problems of Philosophy.
New York: The Methodist Book Concern, 1915.

HODGE, CASPAR WISTAR.—Rev. (1908) of Strong, ST(1907), I, II
The Princeton Theological Review, VI (1908), 335-341.

———————Rev. (1910) of Strong, ST(1907),III
The Princeton Theological Review, VIII (1910), 335.

———————Rev. (1922) of Strong, WSIB
The Princeton Theological Review, XX (1922), 681-682.

HODGE, CHARLES.—ST
Systematic Theology (3 vols.).
New York: Charles Scribner and Company, 1872.

HOVEY, ALVAH.—SER
Studies in Ethics and Religion.
Boston: Silver, Burdett & Co., 1896.

———————Art. (1894)1
"Dr. Strong's Ethical Monism."
The Watchman, LXXV (1894) No. 50, 10-11.

———————Art. (1894)2
"Dr. Strong's Ethical Monism."
The Watchman, LXXV (1894) No. 51, 10-11.

———————Art. (1894)3
"Dr. Strong's Ethical Monism."
The Watchman, LXXV (1894) No. 52, 10-11.

JOHNSON, E. H. (ed.).—EGR
Ezekiel Gilman Robinson: An Autobiography.
Boston: Silver, Burdett & Co., 1896.

KNUDSON, ALBERT C.—POP
The Philosophy of Personalism.
New York: The Abingdon Press, 1927.

———————DOG
The Doctrine of God.
New York: The Abingdon Press, 1930.

———————DOR
The Doctrine of Redemption.
New York: The Abingdon Press, 1933.

LOTZE, HERMANN.—MIC
Microcosmus (4th ed.) (2 vols.).
Edinburgh: T. & T. Clark, n.d.

———————MET
Metaphysic (2 vols.).
Oxford: Clarenden Press, 1874.

———————OOM
Outlines of Metaphysic.
Boston: Ginn, Heath & Co., 1884.

———————OOP
Outlines of Psychology.
Boston: Ginn, Heath & Co., 1884.

———————POR
Outlines of the Philosophy of Religion.
Boston: Ginn, Heath & Co. 1885.

———————OPP
Outlines of Practical Philosophy.
Boston: Ginn & Company, 1895.

MALONE, DUMAS (ed.).—DOAB
Dictionary of American Biography.
New York: Charles Scribner's Sons, 1936.

McCONNELL, FRANCIS JOHN.—BPB
Borden Parker Bowne.
New York: The Abingdon Press, 1929.

PATTON, F. L.—Rev. (1887) of Strong, ST(1886)
The Presbyterian Review, VIII (1887), 365.

ROBINSON, EZEKIEL GILMAN.—CT
Christian Theology.
Rochester: Press of E. R. Andrews, 1894.

STRONG, AUGUSTUS HOPKINS.—LOT
Lectures on Theology.
Rochester: Press of E. R. Andrews, 1876.

———————LOT(CN)
Student's class notes in long hand, written in interleavings of copy of Strong, LOT, by a student at Rochester Theological Seminary from 1882-1885.

———————ST(1886)
Systematic Theology.
New York: A. C. Armstrong and Son, 1886.

www.ingramcontent.com/pod-product-compliance
Lightning Source LLC
Chambersburg PA
CBHW070736160426
43192CB00009B/1457

—————PAR
Philosophy and Religion.
    New York: A. C. Armstrong and Son, 1888.
—————ST(1889)
Systematic Theology. 2nd ed. (Rev.).
    New York: A. C. Armstrong and Son, 1889.
—————ST(1890)
Systematic Theology. 3rd ed. (Rev.).
    New York: A. C. Armstrong and Son, 1890.
—————ST(1892)
Systematic Theology. 4th ed. (Rev.).
    New York: A. C. Armstrong and Son, 1892.
—————Art. (1896)
"Dr. Robinson As A Theologian."
    EGR. Boston: Silver, Burdett & Co.
—————ST(1896)
Systematic Theology. 5th ed. (Rev.).
    New York: A. C. Armstrong and Son, 1896.
—————ST(1896)CN
Student's class notes in long hand, written in interleavings of copy of Strong, ST(1896), by a student at Rochester Theological Seminary about that time.
—————CCEM
Christ in Creation and Ethical Monism.
    Philadelphia: The Griffith and Roland Press, 1899.
—————ST(1896)CN(1901)
Student's class notes in long hand, written in interleavings of copy of Strong, ST(1896)CN, by a student at Rochester Theological Seminary in 1901.
—————ST(1907)
Systematic Theology. 1 vol. and 3 vols.
    Philadelphia: The Griffith and Roland Press, 1907.
—————OHCT
One Hundred Chapel-Talks to Theological Students.
    Philadelphia: The Griffith and Howland Press, 1913.
—————WSIB
What Shall I Believe?
    New York: Fleming H. Revell Company, 1922.

STRONG, CHARLES AUGUSTUS.—Art. (1930)
    "Nature and Mind," in Adams and Montague, CAP, 313.

THOMAS, JESSE B.—Art. (1900)
    "Dr. Strong's Last Work"
        The Watchman, LXXXI (1900), 11

WARFIELD, BENJAMIN B.—Rev. (1897) of Strong, ST(1896)
    The Presbyterian and Reformed Review, VII (1897), 357-358.